BASICS of ANCIENT ETHIOPIC

BASICS *of* ANCIENT ETHIOPIC

A COMPLETE GRAMMAR, WORKBOOK, AND LEXICON

ARCHIE T. WRIGHT

ZONDERVAN ACADEMIC

Basics of Ancient Ethiopic
Copyright © 2022 by Archie T. Wright

Requests for information should be addressed to:
Zondervan, *3900 Sparks Dr. SE, Grand Rapids, Michigan 49546*

Zondervan titles may be purchased in bulk for educational, business, fundraising, or sales promotional use. For information, please email SpecialMarkets@Zondervan.com.

Library of Congress Cataloging-in-Publication Data

Names: Wright, Archie T., author.
Title: Basics of ancient Ethiopic : a complete grammar, workbook, and lexicon / Archie T. Wright.
Description: Grand Rapids : Zondervan, 2022. | Series: Zondervan language basics series | Includes index.
Identifiers: LCCN 2022009723 | ISBN 9780310539049 (paperback)
Subjects: LCSH: Ethiopic language x Grammar. | Ethiopian languages.
Classification: LCC PJ9021 .W75 2022 | DDC 492/.8182421--dc23/eng/20220413
LC record available at https://lccn.loc.gov/2022009723

Some exercises adapted from Thomas O. Lambdin, *Introduction to Classical Ethiopic (Ge'ez)* (Missoula, MT: Scholars Press, 1978), and used with permission.

The six images of Ethiopic manuscripts are courtesy of the Ethiopic Manuscript Imaging Project, Steve Delamarter, director. Used with permission.

Any internet addresses (websites, blogs, etc.) and telephone numbers in this book are offered as a resource. They are not intended in any way to be or imply an endorsement by Zondervan, nor does Zondervan vouch for the content of these sites and numbers for the life of this book.

All rights reserved. No part of this publication may be reproduced, stored in a retrieval system, or transmitted in any form or by any means—electronic, mechanical, photocopy, recording, or any other—except for brief quotations in printed reviews, without the prior permission of the publisher.

Cover design: LUCAS Art & Design
Interior design: Kait Lamphere

To Bella and Zach,
my loving, amazing, encouraging kids.

CONTENTS

Foreword xvii
Acknowledgments xix
Abbreviations xxi

Chapter 1: Introduction 1
    1.1   Learning Gəʿəz 2
    1.2   Goal 2
    1.3   Memorization 2
    1.4   Vocabulary 3
    1.5   Exercises 3
    1.6   Discipline and Time 3

Chapter 2: The Gəʿəz Alphabet 4
    2.1   Introduction to the Alphabet 4
    2.2   Diacritical Signs 6
    2.3   Labialized Consonants 7
    2.4   The Gəʿəz Article (or Lack Thereof) 8
    2.5   Numerals 8
    2.6   Amharic Symbols 8
    2.7   Rules of Contraction and Assimilation 9
            2.7.1   Patterns and Roots of Verbs, Nouns, and Adjectives 9
    2.8   Rules for Gutturals 9
            2.8.1   Gutturals and Preceding Short Vowels 9
            2.8.2   Rules of Long Vowels 10
            2.8.3   Rules for III-ወ and III-ይ Verbs and the *u* and *i* Vowels 10
            2.8.4   Assimilation of Consonants 11
    2.9   The Negated Causative Prefix አ and the Imperfect and Subjunctive First Singular 11
    2.10 Manuscript Inconsistencies in Spelling 11
    2.11 Exercises 12

Chapter 3: Pronunciation and Syllabification 13
    3.1   Vowels 13
    3.2   Consonants 14
    3.3   Accents 14
    3.4   Consonantal Root System, Vowel Patterns, and Syllables 15
    3.5   Vocabulary 16
    3.6   Exercises 16

Chapter 4: Gəʿəz Nouns 19
    4.1   Noun Gender 19
    4.2   Noun Number 19
    4.3   Nouns and the "Article" 19
    4.4   Nouns in the Plural 20
    4.5   Nouns and the Possessive Pronominal Suffix 22
    4.6   Vocabulary 25
    4.7   Exercises 25

Chapter 5: Construct Nouns 27
    5.1   The Noun Construct State 27
    5.2   Vocabulary 28
    5.3   Exercises 28

Chapter 6: Prepositions 31
    6.1   Role of Prepositions 31
    6.2   Identifying Prepositions 31
    6.3   Prepositions with Pronominal Suffixes 32
    6.4   Indicator of Possession 34
    6.5   Indicator of Existence 34
    6.6   Vocabulary 35
    6.7   Exercises 35

Chapter 7: Introduction to Ethiopic Verbs 39
    7.1   Introduction 39
    7.2   Quadriliteral Root Forms 40
    7.3   G Verbs 40
    7.4   Inflection of the Perfect Verb 40
    7.5   The D Stem 41
    7.6   Special Considerations 41
    7.7   Vocabulary 41
    7.8   Exercises 42

Chapter 8: Adjectives (Part 1) 45
    8.1   Introduction 45
    8.2   Attributive Adjectives 45
    8.3   Demonstrative Adjectives 46
    8.4   Adjectives in the *Qətul* Pattern 46
    8.5   Adjectives as Predicates 47
    8.6   Vocabulary 48
    8.7   Exercises 48

Chapter 9: Adjectives (Part 2) 53
    9.1   Introduction 53
    9.2   The Adjective in the Comparative Position 53
    9.3   The Adjective Pattern *Qăttāl* 53
    9.4   Adjectives Ending in -ā+ዊ and -ā+ይ 54
    9.5   Miscellaneous Adjective Patterns 54
    9.6   Vocabulary 55
    9.7   Exercises 55

Chapter 10: Perfect Guttural Roots 61
    10.1   Perfect II Guttural Roots 61
    10.2   Perfect III Guttural Roots 61
    10.3   Perfect III-ወ/ የ Roots 62
    10.4   Perfect G-Stem with II Guttural and III-የ 63
    10.5   Vocabulary 64
    10.6   Exercises 64

Chapter 11: The Perfect Verb with Object Suffixes 67
    11.1   Perfect Verbs with Object Suffixes 67
    11.2   Perfect Verbs with Third-Person Object Suffixes 68
        11.2.1   Alterations to the Verb Endings 68
        11.2.2   Altered Patterns 69
        11.2.3   Complicated Rules 69
    11.3   Partitive Apposition 70
    11.4   Vocabulary 70
    11.5   Exercises 71

Chapter 12: Special Constructions 74
    12.1   The ወልዱ፡ ለንጉሥ፡ Construction 74
    12.2   The Quantifier ኵል- 74
    12.3   The ቀተሎ፡ ለንጉሥ፡ Construction 75
    12.4   The Preposition እልበ . . . ዘእንበለ፡ 75
    12.5   Vocabulary 76
    12.6   Exercises 76

Chapter 13: Pronouns (Part 1) 80
- 13.1 Personal Pronouns 80
- 13.2 Pronouns in Non-Verbal Predicate 80
- 13.3 The "Neutralized Copula" ወአቱ፡ 81
- 13.4 The Demonstrative Pronouns 81
- 13.5 Interrogative Pronouns 82
- 13.6 Interrogative Adverbs 83
- 13.7 Interrogatives with ዘ- 83
- 13.8 Interrogatives with አከ፡ 83
- 13.9 Vocabulary 84
- 13.10 Exercises 85

Chapter 14: Pronouns (Part 2) 89
- 14.1 Relative Pronouns and Relative Clauses 89
- 14.2 Indefinite Pronouns 91
- 14.3 Independent Personal Pronouns 91
- 14.4 The Phrase በ፡ ዘ- as an Indefinite Pronoun 93
- 14.5 Vocabulary 93
- 14.6 Exercises 93

Chapter 15: Medio-Passive Verbs 97
- 15.1 Medio-Passive Verbs 97
- 15.2 Gt Medio-Passive Verbs 97
- 15.3 Usage of the Gt Passive Verbs 98
- 15.4 Vocabulary 100
- 15.5 Exercises 100

Chapter 16: Glt Reciprocal Verbs 103
- 16.1 Gəʿəz Verbs of Reciprocity 103
- 16.2 Glt Verbs of Repeated Action 104
- 16.3 Vocabulary 104
- 16.4 Exercises 105

Chapter 17: Numbers and Cardinal Adverbs 109
- 17.1 Cardinal Numbers 109
- 17.2 Ordinal Numbers 110
- 17.3 Numbers above Ten 112
- 17.4 The Tens Numbers 20–90 112
- 17.5 Cardinal Adverbs 112
- 17.6 Names of Months in Ethiopic Calendar 113
- 17.7 Vocabulary 113
- 17.8 Exercises 114

Chapter 18: Causative Verbs 117
    18.1   Causative Verbs CG, CD, CL, CQ 117
    18.2   The Meaning of Causative CG Verbs 118
    18.3   Causative CG Verbs Derived from Transitive G Verbs 119
    18.4   Causative CD, CL, and CQ Verbs 120
    18.5   Notes on the Gəʿəz Verbal System 120
    18.6   Vocabulary 121
    18.7   Exercises 121

Chapter 19: The Infinitive 125
    19.1   Base Forms of Gəʿəz Infinitive Verbs 125
    19.2   The G Verb Infinitive Base 125
    19.3   Use of the Infinitives 126
    19.4   Vocabulary 127
    19.5   Exercises 128

Chapter 20: Participles 131
    20.1   Perfect Active Participles 131
    20.2   Perfect Active Participle Inflection 131
    20.3   Perfect Passive Participle Inflection 132
    20.4   Vocabulary 133
    20.5   Exercises 133

Chapter 21: The Imperfect 137
    21.1   Imperfect Strong G Verbs 137
    21.2   Pattern for the Imperfect G Verb 137
    21.3   Negating the Imperfect Verb Forms 138
    21.4   Other Oddities of the Imperfect Verb Form 138
    21.5   The Imperfect and Object Suffixes 138
    21.6   Independent Uses of the Imperfect 139
    21.7   Dependent Uses of the Imperfect 139
    21.8   Vocabulary 140
    21.9   Exercises 140

Chapter 22: The Subjunctive 144
    22.1   The Subjunctive G Strong Verbs 144
    22.2   Inflection of the Subjunctive 145
    22.3   Subjunctive with the Object Suffixes 145
    22.4   Function of the Subjunctive Verb 146
    22.5   Vocabulary 147
    22.6   Exercises 147

Chapter 23: The Imperative ... 152
- 23.1 Imperative Strong G Verbs ... 152
- 23.2 The Agent Noun ቀታሊ፡ ... 152
- 23.3 Frequent Agent Nouns ... 153
- 23.4 Vocabulary ... 154
- 23.5 Exercises ... 154

Chapter 24: Verbal Adjective ቅቱል፡ ... 159
- 24.1 The Verbal Adjective ቅቱል፡ ... 159
- 24.2 ቅቱል፡ Adjectives as Adverbs ... 161
- 24.3 Additional Notes on Adjectival Complements ... 161
- 24.4 Vocabulary ... 161
- 24.5 Exercises ... 162

Chapter 25: Verbal Nouns ... 166
- 25.1 The Verbal Noun or Participle ... 166
- 25.2 The ቅትለት፡ Pattern ... 166
- 25.3 The ቅትል፡ Pattern ... 167
- 25.4 The ቅተል፡ Pattern ... 167
- 25.5 The ቅታል፡ Pattern ... 167
- 25.6 The ቀተል፡ Pattern ... 168
- 25.7 The ቀታል፡ Pattern ... 168
- 25.8 The ቀትል፡ Pattern ... 168
- 25.9 The Cognate Accusative ... 168
- 25.10 Vocabulary ... 169
- 25.11 Exercises ... 169

Chapter 26: Special Nouns ... 173
- 26.1 Nouns of Place in the $məC_1C_2āC_3$ Pattern ... 173
- 26.2 Nouns in the $măC_1C_2ăC_3$ Pattern ... 173
- 26.3 Nouns in the $măC_1C_2əC_3$ Pattern ... 174
- 26.4 Vocabulary ... 174
- 26.5 Exercises ... 174

Chapter 27: I Guttural G Verbs (Remaining Forms) ... 180
- 27.1 Remaining Forms of I Guttural G Verbs ... 180
- 27.2 I Guttural Causative Verb (አምነ፡) ... 182
- 27.3 I Guttural Reflexive Verbs ... 183
- 27.4 I Guttural Causative Reflexive Verbs ... 183
- 27.5 I Guttural Verbal Adjectives in the ቅቱል፡ (Qətul) Pattern ... 183
- 27.6 I Guttural ቀታሊ፡ Agent Nouns ... 184
- 27.7 I Guttural Verbal Nouns ... 184

27.8   I Guttural Nouns from the Pattern መቅተል(ት)፡ 184
27.9   I Guttural Nouns from the Pattern ምቅታል፡ 185
27.10 Vocabulary 185
27.11 Exercises 185

Chapter 28: G Verbs with II Guttural Roots 190
28.1   G Verbs with II Guttural Roots 190
28.2   II Guttural Causative Verbs (ሰአከ፡) 191
28.3   II Guttural Reflexive Verbs 192
28.4   Irregular Forms 192
28.5   II Guttural Verbal Adjectives in the ቅቱል፡ Pattern 193
28.6   II Guttural ቀታሊ፡ Agent Nouns 193
28.7   II Guttural Verbal Nouns 193
28.8   Nouns with a Prefixed መ- 194
28.9   The Verb ብህለ፡ – "Say" 194
28.10 Vocabulary 194
28.11 Exercises 195

Chapter 29: G Verbs with III Guttural Roots 201
29.1   III Guttural Root Verbs 201
29.2   III Guttural Causative Verbs (በጽሐ፡) 203
29.3   III Guttural Reflexive Verbs (ተበጽሐ፡ – "Arrive") 203
29.4   III Guttural and Subject or Object Suffix 204
29.5   III Guttural Verbs Previously Introduced 204
29.6   III Guttural Verbal Adjectives 205
29.7   III Guttural Agent Nouns 205
29.8   III Guttural Verbal Nouns 205
29.9   Nouns with a Prefixed ም 205
29.10 Vocabulary 206
29.11 Exercises 206

Chapter 30: G I-ወ Root Verbs: The Remaining Moods 212
30.1   I-ወ Root Verbs 212
30.2   Causative I-ወ Root Verb (ወፈረ፡ – "Go into the country") 214
30.3   Reflexive I-ወ Root Verb 214
30.4   Causative-Reflexive I-ወ Root Verb 215
30.5   I-ወ Root Verbal Adjectives in the ቅቱል፡ Pattern 215
30.6   I-ወ Root Verbal Nouns 215
30.7   I-ወ Root Agent Nouns from ቀታሊ፡ 216
30.8   I-ወ Root Nouns with Prefixed ም (with Various Vowels) 216
30.9   Vocabulary 216
30.10 Exercises 216

Chapter 31: G II-ወ/የ Root Verbs: The Remaining Moods 220
- 31.1 II-ወ/የ Root Verbs 220
- 31.2 Alternate Forms for II-ወ 221
- 31.3 II-ወ/የ Root Verbal Adjectives in ቅቱል፡ 222
- 31.4 II-ወ/የ Root Verbal Nouns 222
- 31.5 II-ወ/የ Root Agent Nouns from ቀታሊ፡ 222
- 31.6 Other Nouns of Note 223
- 31.7 II-ወ/የ Root Nouns in the Pattern of ምቅታል፡ 223
- 31.8 Vocabulary 223
- 31.9 Exercises 224

Chapter 32: G Verbs from III-ወ/የ Roots: The Remaining Moods 227
- 32.1 III-ወ/የ Root Verbs 227
- 32.2 III-ወ/የ Root Verbal Adjectives in ቅቱል፡ Pattern 229
- 32.3 III-ወ/የ Root Agent Nouns from ቀታሊ፡ 230
- 32.4 III-ወ/የ Root Verbal Nouns 230
- 32.5 III-ወ/የ Nouns with Prefixed ም 230
- 32.6 Vocabulary 231
- 32.7 Exercises 231

Chapter 33: Gt and Glt Verbs: The Remaining Moods 237
- 33.1 Gt Imperfect, Subjunctive, and Imperative Forms 237
- 33.2 Glt Reciprocal Verbs in the Imperfect, Subjunctive, and Imperative Forms 238
- 33.3 The Verb ሀለወ፡ – "Exist, Be" with the Subjunctive and Imperfect 239
- 33.4 Vocabulary 240
- 33.5 Exercises 240

Chapter 34: CG Verbs: The Remaining Moods 245
- 34.1 CG Imperfect, Subjunctive, and Imperative Forms 245
- 34.2 CG Verbal Nouns 247
- 34.3 CG Agent Nouns 247
- 34.4 Vocabulary 248
- 34.5 Exercises 248

Chapter 35: D, Dt, CD Verbs: The Remaining Moods 255
- 35.1 D Verbs: Imperfect, Subjunctive, and Imperative 255
- 35.2 Dt Verbs: Imperfect, Subjunctive, and Imperative Forms 256
- 35.3 D Verbal Adjectives 258
- 35.4 D Agent Nouns 258
- 35.5 D Verbal Nouns 259
- 35.6 Dt Verbal Nouns 260
- 35.7 D Verb Nouns with Prefixed ም- 260

35.8	CD Verbs.	260
35.9	Vocabulary	261
35.10	Exercises	262

Chapter 36: L, CL, Lt, CGt, CDt, CLt, CGlt Verbs: The Remaining Moods . . . 267

36.1	The L, CL, Lt Verbs: Imperfect, Subjunctive, and Imperative Forms.	267
36.2	The L, CL, Lt Verbal Adjective, Agent Noun, and Verbal Noun	268
36.3	CGt, CDt, CLt, CGlt Imperfect, Subjunctive, and Imperative Forms.	269
36.4	Vocabulary	271
36.5	Exercises	271

Chapter 37: Multiliteral Verb Roots. 274

37.1	Quadriliteral Verb Roots.	274
37.2	Quadriliteral Verbs with II-ወ/የ	276
37.3	Quadriliteral Verbs of Special Note	278
37.4	Nouns and Adjectives	278
37.5	Quinquiliteral Verb Roots	279
37.6	The N Quinquiliteral Verb	279
37.7	Vocabulary	280
37.8	Exercises	280

Chapter 38: Syntax . 283

38.1	Sentence Structure	283
38.2	Other Components of Syntax and Interpretation.	283
	38.2.1 Conditional Parts of a Sentence	283
	38.2.2 Definiteness of the Noun	284
	38.2.3 Indefiniteness of the Noun	284
	38.2.4 Relationship between Nouns.	284
	38.2.5 Verbs Governing the Noun in the Accusative	285
	38.2.6 Verbs Subordinated to Other Verbs	285
	38.2.7 Simple Sentences	285
	38.2.8 Interrogative Sentences	286
	38.2.9 Copulative Clauses	286
	38.2.10 Attributive Relative Clauses	286
	38.2.11 Optative Expressions.	287
	38.2.12 Adjective Issues	287
	38.2.13 Adverb Issues	287
	38.2.14 Contrary-to-Fact Conditions	287
	38.2.15 The "If . . . How Much More . . ." Construction	287
	38.2.16 Repeated Prepositions በበ፡ ለለ፡ ዘዘ፡	287
	38.2.17 Third-Person Singular Pronominal Suffixes: Special Purpose – -ሁ, -u, -ሃ, -ā	287
	38.2.18 Other Issues of Special Note.	288

Lexicon 289
Manuscript Images 313
Appendix: An Advanced Reading: The Confession of Faith of Emperor Gelawdewos 326
Bibliography 330

FOREWORD

In the present book, Archie T. Wright provides a valuable introduction to Geʿez. It shall be especially useful for students of two kinds: (1) those who come to it with prior knowledge in one or more Semitic languages (e.g., Hebrew, Aramaic, Syriac, Arabic) or in one of the related languages (e.g., Amharic, Tigrinya, Gurage) and (2) those with special interest in biblical and related studies. The chapters as a whole convey a basic orientation to the morphology, grammar, and syntax needed to negotiate foundational texts within the vast corpus of sacred literature transmitted in the Horn of Africa since the fourth century CE. Many of the "biblical" writings and other religiously influential texts preserved in Geʿez can be traced back to translations from other languages such as Greek or Arabic; in addition, Geʿez literature reflects an interwovenness with other carriers of sacred tradition in the Levant such as Syriac, Armenian, and Hebrew. However, Geʿez is also a carrier of an abundance of regionally and locally produced texts (chronicles, foundational narratives, commentary, poetry, hagiographies, liturgies, calendrical computations, "magical" scrolls). As such, it warrants attention in its own right. The existence of manuscripts in many parts of the globe, though especially in churches, monasteries, museums, and institutions of contemporary Ethiopia today, testifies to a unique scribal culture and living liturgical tradition that thrives within the Ethiopian and Eritrean Tewahedo Orthodox traditions into the twenty-first century. The stage is set for a flourishing discipline that is attracting increasing attention around the world, while in communities, schools, and institutions Geʿez is celebrated and can be studied as a unique bearer of ancient cultural heritage.

Helpful grammars to Geʿez have been published by specialists since the nineteenth century (August Dillmann,[1] Franz Praetorius,[2] Samuel Mercer,[3] Thomas Lambdin,[4] Stefan Weninger,[5] Stephan Procházka,[6] Amsalu Aklilu,[7] Josef Tropper,[8] and Maija Priess[9]), and such will no doubt be published in the future, as the study of Geʿez literature is a fast-evolving discipline. In this book, users will find especially helpful the

---

1. See August Dillmann, *Ethiopic Grammar*, enlarged, improved, and edited by Carl Bezold (1899) and translated into English by J. A. Crichton (London: Williams & Norgate, 1907). The original was written in 1857.

2. *Äthiopische Grammatik mit Paradigmen, Litteratur, Chrestomatie und Glossar* (Karlsruhe: H. Reuther, 1886).

3. *Ethiopic Grammar: With Chrestomathy and Glossary* (Oxford: Clarendon, 1920).

4. *Introduction to Classical Ethiopic (Geʿez)*, Harvard Semitic Studies 24 (Cambridge: Harvard University Press, 1978), which provided the basis for Osvaldo Raineri, *Introduzione alla lingua ge'ez (etiopico classico)* (Rome: Edizioni Orientalia Christiana, 2002).

5. *Geʿez (Classical Ethiopic)* (München: Lincom Europa, 1993).

6. *Altäthiopische Studiengrammatik*, Orbis Biblicus et Orientalis Subsidia linguistica 2 (Fribourg: Academic Press; Göttingen: Vandenhoeck & Ruprecht, 2004).

7. *Yä-Gəʿəz mämmariya mäṣḥaf—Gəʿəz Textbook* (Addis Ababa: Shama Books, 2010).

8. See the revised and expanded publication of Tropper's German grammar (2002) in English by Josef Tropper and Rebecca Hasselbach-Andee, *Classical Ethiopic: A Grammar of Gəʿəz* (Winona Lake, IN: Eisenbrauns, 2021).

9. *Lexicon of Gəʿəz: Verbs for Students*, Moran Etho 37 (Kerala, India: St. Ephrem Ecumenical Research Institute, 2015), xii–xxxvi. See also Aaron Butts, *Ethiopic Paradigms: A Summary of Classical Ethiopic Geʿez Morphology* (Leuven: Peeters, 2022).

use of the Ge'ez script throughout, not only in the presentation of the material itself but also in the many carefully prepared workbook-style exercises attached to each chapter, as well as in the lexicon. The short reading selections at the end offer readers transcriptions for several texts based on manuscripts for which photographs are provided. The discursive style of the chapters lends a conversational feel to the chapters, inviting readers into a participatory process of learning. Those who work through Wright's *Basics of Ancient Ethiopic* will find themselves well served. Indeed, the foundation on offer here furnishes an initial link into a manuscript culture that goes a long way to whet the appetite for further study.

Loren T. Stuckenbruck
Ludwig Maximilian University of Munich

ACKNOWLEDGMENTS

The origins of this textbook began in the city of Durham, England, where I took up my doctoral studies at Durham University with Professor Loren Stuckenbruck, my *Doktorvater*, and now good friend and colleague. Loren invited me, and my now close friend Ron Herms, to study Ethiopic Gəʿəz with him in his office in the Abbey House on Palace Green. It was there that we took up the task of working through Thomas Lambdin's *Introduction to Classical Ethiopic (Geʿez)*. It was then that we quickly learned the major drawback to Lambdin's text was his use of transliteration in all the lessons and exercises. This proved to be a major deterrent when it came to reading the primary sources in the "original" Gəʿəz script. The three of us often talked of the need for a textbook that would use the Gəʿəz script once past the opening chapters in order to prepare the student to read the Ethiopic manuscripts of the many texts from the Enochic and Jubilees corpuses, among others, found in the Ethiopic manuscript traditions. I owe a deep debt of gratitude to Loren and Ron for their encouragement to write this grammar and see it come to fruition.

In addition, I owe many thanks to Dr. Chris Beetham at HarperCollins for having the vision to place this volume in the Zondervan Language Series. I hope it does him and the series justice by its inclusion in such a significant suite of products for language learning in the field of biblical studies. I also want to give special recognition to Dr. Ralph Lee and Dr. Logan Williams for their close readings of what proved to be a very complex volume. Dr. Lee's expertise in Gəʿəz, his knowledge of the Ethiopian culture, and teaching of the language has added immensely to the quality of this work. In the end though, I take full responsibility for the content found within and any errors it may contain. I want to acknowledge and thank Dr. Steve Delamarter for his contribution of the beautiful manuscript images that are included in the volume. The images certainly add to the volume by revealing the various manuscript traditions in which we find Ethiopic Gəʿəz. Finally, I want to thank Kaitlynn Merckling for her ongoing encouragement while trying to complete this volume and two other volumes (*Satan and the Problem of Evil* and *The Spirit Says*) at the same time.

I do hope this volume will accomplish my intention to make accessible the Gəʿəz language in its "original" script and that many more students will be able to read and understand the very important manuscripts that are written in Ethiopic Gəʿəz.

Archie T. Wright
Norfolk, Virginia, March 2022

ABBREVIATIONS

acc.	accusative	Gk.	Greek
act.	active	HB	Hebrew Bible
adj.	adjective	I	first consonant of root
adv.	adverb	II	second consonant of root
c	common gender	III	third consonant of root
C_1	consonant, first	i.e.	that is
C_2	consonant, second	impv.	imperative
C_3	consonant, third	inf.	infinitive
CD	causative D stem	L	root with lengthened first stem vowel
CE	Common Era	m. or masc.	masculine
CG	causative G stem	mp	masculine plural
CL	causative L stem	ms	masculine singular
CQ	causative Q stem	n.	number
cp	common plural	nom.	nominative
cs	common singular	obj.	object
conj.	conjunction	p.	page
D	root with doubled second consonant	part.	participle
dat.	dative	perf.	perfect
def.	definite	pl.	plural
dir.	direct	pred.	predicate
e.g.	for example	prep.	preposition
esp.	especially	prn.	pronoun
etc.	similar range of meaning(s)	Q	verb with four root consonants
f. or fem.	feminine	rel.	relative
fig.	figure	sing.	singular
fp	feminine plural	subj.	subjunctive, subject
fs	feminine singular	suff.	suffix
G	simple root verbs		

Chapter 1

INTRODUCTION

The ancient culture of Ethiopia is reflected in the history of her languages. In approximately 1000 BCE, the people of northern Ethiopia began establishing commerce and political contacts with the peoples of southwest Arabia on the other side of the Red Sea. It is believed that the language of Gəʿəz (pronounced *Geh-ehz*) emerged from this interaction between the various people groups. Gəʿəz,[1] also called Classical or Ancient Ethiopic, is a South Semitic language. However, Gəʿəz is no longer one of the primary spoken languages in Ethiopia, but it does survive in some isolated monastic communities, and thus the pronunciation of some consonants is not completely certain. Gəʿəz remains the main language used in the liturgy of the Ethiopian and Eritrean Orthodox Churches, and the Ethiopian Catholic Church. Its primary purpose is a language of theologizing and philosophizing in monastic communities. The poetic tradition of qənē employs the language to fashion complex theological compositions, which are then used during each liturgy, and remains significant within the context of the Ethiopian Orthodox Church. The Fidel, the alphabet of modern Amharic, which is one of the languages of the citizens of Ethiopia, has been adapted from the alphabet of Gəʿəz. There are approximately eighty-six indigenous languages in Ethiopia.[2]

Gəʿəz began as the spoken language during the rule of the Aksum Empire (the commercial and political capital of the day) for the first six centuries of the Common Era. It is thought that during this period, early Christian missionaries used Gəʿəz to translate Scripture for the native people beginning in the fourth century CE. At present, the oldest surviving Gəʿəz manuscript is the Garima Gospels thought to be dated from the fifth or sixth century CE.[3] Monastic tradition ascribes the gospels to the fifth century monk Saint Abba Garima. Abba Garima is one of the "Nine Saints" instrumental in evangelizing the ancient empire of Aksum. Almost all texts from this period are Christian in nature, many of them translations from Greek, Syriac, and Coptic. Tradition holds that the translation of the Christian Bible was undertaken by Syrian monks known as the "Nine Saints." This translation contains eighty-one books, forty-six of the Old Testament and thirty-five of the New Testament. A number of translations are "deuterocanonical" such as the Ascension of Isaiah, Jubilees, and 1 Enoch. First Enoch is notable since its complete text has survived in no other language. However, as a result of the decline of the empire, the popularity of Gəʿəz decreased, and beginning in the tenth-century CE Amharic (the principal language of modern Ethiopia) became more widespread.

---

1. The reader will find the spelling of Gəʿəz in this manner throughout the textbook. The inverted "ə" is used to indicate the short "e" vowel.

2. Many thanks for this information from personal correspondence with Ralph Lee, August 2021.

3. There are likely older fragments among these manuscripts, but the dates are yet to be verified (personal correspondence with Loren T. Stuckenbruck, March 22, 2021).

The script of the Gəʿəz alphabet is fully vocalized, quite different from the consonant vowel system that is typical of Hebrew, Aramaic, or Syriac script. Like other Semitic languages, the grammatical features of the language can be easily deciphered from the Ethiopic Gəʿəz texts. However, readings of various texts by European scholars have been heavily influenced by their own language resulting in various contradictions in translation and interpretation. In addition, the reading of Gəʿəz has been influenced by modern Amharic language, which may offer quite a different vocal reading than the ancient texts. Pronunciations in this grammar will follow that of Thomas O. Lambdin, *Introduction to Classical Ethiopic (Geʿez)* (Missoula, MT: Scholars Press, 1978; repr., Leiden: Brill, 2006), unless otherwise noted (see, e.g., Lambdin's short "e" [p. 8] and the short "ə" used in this work).[4]

1.1 Learning Gəʿəz

As with any foreign language, learning Gəʿəz takes time and commitment. Unfortunately, we cannot do the plug-in made famous on the movie *Matrix* in which we could just attach a cable to a port in the back of our head and – presto! – we know Gəʿəz. No, it takes good study habits and a willingness to spend the time in the textbook and with the vocabulary to learn a language.

1.2 Goal

The main purpose of this book is to help you read and understand and communicate the ancient texts that have been passed down to us in Gəʿəz; these include biblical and extra-biblical texts, including the very important books of 1 Enoch and Jubilees, among others. As an important set of documents that help us better understand the biblical tradition and the passing on of these traditions, it is becoming increasingly more imperative for scholars and students to be able to work with these texts in their original language to help us better understand the traditions of biblical and extra-biblical texts that are extant in other languages.

1.3 Memorization

In order to properly learn Gəʿəz, one must memorize various components of the language including vocabulary, word forms, points of grammar, and several additional details. It cannot be avoided when one chooses to learn a language. Although for most of you this will not be your first ancient language that you are undertaking to learn, I include below a list of helpful keys that may provide steps for new students to ancient languages to memorize the vocabulary and grammar of the language more easily:

1. Make or buy flashcards of each word you come across in the textbook and those that are new to you in the exercises. 3×5 index cards cut into thirds are often the best option if you do not buy a

---

4. Ron Herms and I had the opportunity to study Gəʿəz with Loren Stuckenbruck while undertaking my PhD in Durham, UK from 2000 to 2005. This time of study was instrumental in stirring my interest in Second Temple Jewish literature and Christian origins. We used Lambdin's textbook, which uses the transliteration of the Gəʿəz, and thus was the reason I undertook this work in order to offer a textbook from which students would learn the Gəʿəz script from the beginning rather than leaning on the crutch of transliteration. I hope it serves its purpose well for those who are interested in the texts and traditions that are extant in Gəʿəz.

premade set. Writing out the words often helps a great deal with memorization. Another option is to use ANKI software to develop flashcards (see https://www.ankiapp.com/).

2. You should use as many mnemonic devices as possible when memorizing. The Gəʿəz word for house is *bēt*, "he <u>bet</u> the house." You can also include pictures on the flashcards for vocabulary words. The more points of contact you can associate with a word the easier it will be to memorize.

3. When reading through your cards pronounce the word aloud; this too will help with memorization. It also helps to pronounce it as you are writing out the word. Studies have shown that auditory memorization increases retention by about 20% over those who do not pronounce the words during the learning process.

1.4   Vocabulary

In each chapter you will find a list of relevant vocabulary words related to the material that was covered in that particular chapter. These words are those that will appear quite frequently in the extant text in Gəʿəz. It is important that you commit these words to memory to assist you in becoming a more proficient reader of ancient Gəʿəz.

1.5   Exercises

Within each chapter you will find accompanying exercises related to the material being discussed in the chapter plus previous material. It is important that you complete these exercises if you wish to be successful in learning Gəʿəz. The exercises are constructed to help you learn the grammar of the various chapters in the textbook and see the vocabulary in context. The exercises will include passages from Scripture and passages from some of the key extra-biblical texts that are extant in Gəʿəz. Working through these translations and exercises will be key to understanding and retaining the grammar of each chapter.

1.6   Discipline and Time

For most individuals, it takes a great deal of time and discipline to learn a new language. You must be willing to spend the time to memorize vocabulary and patterns and read the textbook. This time must be spent daily in order to be successful in this task; you cannot cram a language into your head and remember it; it will not work. Discipline is the bottom line in learning Gəʿəz, but it comes at a cost, one that must be paid daily. I wish you all the best as you enter the ancient world of Gəʿəz and the very important texts that are extant in the language.

Chapter 2

THE GƎʿƎZ ALPHABET

2.1 Introduction to the Alphabet[1]

The Gəʿəz alphabet as we know it today was likely borrowed from the Old South Arabic monumental script as early as the eighth century BCE. Early inscriptions in Gəʿəz and Gəʿəz manuscripts have been dated as early as the fifth century BCE. Gəʿəz literature properly begins with the Christianization of Ethiopia in the fourth century CE. Manuscripts from this period consistently use what appears as a hand printed form with each letter written separately and an identifying mark between each word (:). According to some scholars, those who began using the alphabet demonstrated an orthographic acumen rare in the Semitic world. The original South Arabic Script of the consonantal alphabet was altered into a fully vocalized syllabary (consonant/vowel cluster) with the addition of various strokes and modifications to the individual consonants (see table 2.1).[2]

The Gəʿəz alphabet consists of twenty-six base forms of the consonants and an additional six syllabary forms of each base form. The originators of the alphabet maintained the traditional order of the letters and included no labialized consonants (see table 2.2). In some grammars the syllabary columns are numbered–first, second order . . . , but this may prove to be more confusing for students and therefore is not facilitated here. As you will see, table 2.1 consonants in the first column have the short vowel "ă" as in "bat."[3] It is extremely important that you master this column before going on to memorize the others. Make sure you analyze each column closely, since there are patterns that will help you memorize and recognize each syllabary. Gəʿəz has its own distinct set of signs for numbers; these are displayed in table 2.3. As with the syllabaries, there are consistent elements in their written forms that will help you recognize each form.

---

1. It should be noted that there are some comparisons made between Gəʿəz and Hebrew in this grammar; however, many students who will use this book come with the knowledge of Semitic languages other than Hebrew, such as Syriac or Arabic. For Ethiopian students, Amharic or Tigrinya will be a helpful comparative language for learning Gəʿəz. Unfortunately drawing all these comparisons is beyond the scope of this volume.

2. Author's note: In writing this volume I have consulted multiple sources and draw from their expertise of Ethiopic Gəʿəz. These sources include Thomas Lambdin, *Introduction to Classical Ethiopic (Geʿez)* (Missoula, MT: Scholars Press, 1978); August Dillmann and Carl Bezold, *Ethiopic Grammar*, 2nd ed. (Eugene, OR: Wipf & Stock, 2005 [1899]); Stephan Procházka, *Altäthiopische Studiengrammatik* (Göttingen: Vandenhoek & Ruprecht, 2004); and Amsalu Aklilu, *Geʿez Textbook* (unpublished). I have attempted to present the grammatical concepts found in the Lambdin textbook but with significant variations, in particular the presentation of the material in Gəʿəz script. I am indebted to all these authors, but especially to Lambdin, from whose book I first began to learn Ethiopic Gəʿəz.

3. Students should be aware that there is no singular transliteration system for Gəʿəz; you will encounter several in other grammatical aides or lexicons. This volume will follow a transliteration system that is a mix of *The SBL Handbook of Style* (Atlanta: SBL Press, 2014), 64, Lambdin's *Introduction to Ethiopic (Gəʿəz)*, and my own system: short "a" = "ă"; "u" = u; "i" = i; long "e" = ē; short "e" = ə; and "o" = o. Students should be aware of other transliteration systems such as that in Wolf Leslau's *Comparative Dictionary of Geʿez* (Leipzig: Harrassowitz, 1987) or the Hamburg University Project, which can be found at https://betamasaheft.eu/Guidelines/?q=transliteration&id=transliteration-principles.

In addition, you will discover there are special punctuation markings for the colon (፡), semicolon (፤), comma (፥) and the period (።) (table 2.4). In addition to these punctuation markers, each word in Gəʿəz ends with a marker that shows separation of words (፡) except where the punctuation marks listed above appear in the text. Gəʿəz manuscripts may include some additional Amharic letters in particular referring to personal or place names (table 3.5).

TABLE 2.1: Gəʿəz Alphabet

Name	English Equivalent	hă	hu	hi (ee)	hā	hē	hə	ho	hua
Hōi	h (hi)	ሀ	ሁ	ሂ	ሃ	ሄ	ህ	ሆ	ሇ
Lāw	l (lap)	ለ	ሉ	ሊ	ላ	ሌ	ል	ሎ	ሏ
Ḥaut	ḥ (has)	ሐ	ሑ	ሒ	ሓ	ሔ	ሕ	ሖ	ሗ
Māy	m (map)	መ	ሙ	ሚ	ማ	ሜ	ም	ሞ	ሟ
Šaut	š (saw)	ሠ	ሡ	ሢ	ሣ	ሤ	ሥ	ሦ	ሧ
Reʼes	r (red)	ረ	ሩ	ሪ	ራ	ሬ	ር	ሮ	ሯ
Sāt	s (sat)	ሰ	ሱ	ሲ	ሳ	ሴ	ስ	ሶ	ሷ
Qāf	q (kick)	ቀ	ቁ	ቂ	ቃ	ቄ	ቅ	ቆ	ቋ
Bēt	b (bat)	በ	ቡ	ቢ	ባ	ቤ	ብ	ቦ	ቧ
Tāw	t (toe)	ተ	ቱ	ቲ	ታ	ቴ	ት	ቶ	ቷ
Ḥarm	x (loch)	ኀ	ኁ	ኂ	ኃ	ኄ	ኅ	ኆ	ኋ
Nahās	n (nat)	ነ	ኑ	ኒ	ና	ኔ	ን	ኖ	ኗ
ʼAlef	ʼ vowel	አ	ኡ	ኢ	ኣ	ኤ	እ	ኦ	
Kāf	k (kill)	ከ	ኩ	ኪ	ካ	ኬ	ክ	ኮ	ኳ
Wawē	w (will)	ወ	ዉ	ዊ	ዋ	ዌ	ው	ዎ	
ʿAin	ʿ vowel	ዐ	ዑ	ዒ	ዓ	ዔ	ዕ	ዖ	
Zay	z (zoo)	ዘ	ዙ	ዚ	ዛ	ዜ	ዝ	ዞ	ዟ
Yaman	y (yap)	የ	ዩ	ዪ	ያ	ዬ	ይ	ዮ	
Dant	d (dad)	ደ	ዱ	ዲ	ዳ	ዴ	ድ	ዶ	ዷ
Gamel	g (goal)	ገ	ጉ	ጊ	ጋ	ጌ	ግ	ጎ	ጓ
Ṭay	ṭ (tap)	ጠ	ጡ	ጢ	ጣ	ጤ	ጥ	ጦ	ጧ
Pāy	p (pat)	ጰ	ጱ	ጲ	ጳ	ጴ	ጵ	ጶ	ጷ
Ṣadāy	ṣ (cats)	ጸ	ጹ	ጺ	ጻ	ጼ	ጽ	ጾ	ጿ
Ṣappā	ḍ (cats)	ፀ	ፁ	ፂ	ፃ	ፄ	ፅ	ፆ	
ʼAf	f (far)	ፈ	ፉ	ፊ	ፋ	ፌ	ፍ	ፎ	ፏ
Piesā	ṗ (pat)	ፐ	ፑ	ፒ	ፓ	ፔ	ፕ	ፖ	ፗ

One should keep in mind these pronunciations are approximations. They may be different from Ethiopian Amharic or other languages used within the various people groups in the same way Koine Greek is pronounced differently than Modern Greek. The Alef ʾ(አ) and the Ain ʿ(ዐ) follow the pattern of the Hebrew א and the ע in that they have no consonantal sound of their own and are pronounced as the vowel sound that is part of the syllabary.

The guttural symbols in Gəʿəz can present the student with some difficulty in distinguishing between sounds of what seem to be very different letters. While there is a technical distinction between the letters ʿ(ዐ), ʾ(አ), which proves to be important when it comes to identifying and understanding verbal roots and connections with other Semitic languages, in practice this distinction is not made; apart from a few words these letters may be used interchangeably. Similarly, the *h* (ሀ), *ḥ* (ሐ), *x* (ኀ), like some consonants in other Semitic languages, had their own distinct pronunciation in the original Gəʿəz language, but in contemporary practice of reading Gəʿəz, there is no distinction made over their use or pronunciation except for a few unique words.

In addition to the difficulties in distinguishing the sound of some consonants, the variety of spellings of some words can often cause significant confusion for the student when trying to locate words in lexicons. Multiple forms of spellings of certain words can be found in manuscripts as well as in critical editions of Ethiopic texts. For example, the word ሐሠመ፡ may be spelled ሐሠመ፡ ሐሰመ፡ ሀሠመ፡ ሀሰመ፡ ኀሠመ፡ ኀሰመ፡. Perhaps more importantly, words such as ሐለየ፡ and ኀለየ፡, which have two different meanings, may not be spelled as expected when encountered in a text (whether in a printed edition or a manuscript). It is important for the student to be aware of these variations, otherwise consulting lexicons can become quite confusing and discouraging.

Memorization of a new language can be difficult, especially one with non-Latin consonants. It may help with memorization or recognition of the consonantal forms if you group them according to their shapes:

TABLE 2.2: Consonantal Groups

Single Stem	Two Stems	Three Stems	Round or U	Hooked
ቀ ተ ጎ ኀ የ ገ ፐ	ለ ሰ በ አ ከ ዘ ደ ጸ ፀ	ሐ ጠ	ሀ መ ሠ ወ ዐ ፈ	ረ ፈ

2.2 Diacritical Signs

The diacritical signs (vowels) are added to each of these base forms (the *hă* column in table 2.1 above) which gives you the $C_1 ă$[4] configuration: ሀ *hă*; ሁ *hu*; ሂ *hee*; ሃ *hā*; ሄ *hē*; ህ *hə*; ሆ *ho*.

---

4. C1ă indicates the first consonant of the word, C1, followed by the vowel "ă."

Many of the vowels attach to the base form of the consonant the same way (see 2.1 above). The *u* vowel attaches to all the consonants as a small arm of the right side of the letter, e.g., the ለ with the *u* vowel appears as ሉ and is pronounced *lu*. The *i* vowel is a small arm attached to the bottom right side of the base letter, e.g., ሊ is pronounced *lee* (with some minor variations, the base form ረ, with the *i* vowel appears as ሪ and the የ appears as ዪ). The long *ā* appears in several variations depending on the base form of the letter. The consonants with two or three stems shorten the left or two left legs for this vowel (or one could say it lengthens the right leg, which may make it easier to remember it is a long *ā*). The other consonantal forms are not quite so simple. The single stem consonants have a line that comes off the bottom, primarily from the right side, and tends to slant to the left. The ተ has a leg extend down and to the left, ታ, forming the *tā*. The ገ has a leg extension that slants to the left also, ጋ, forming the *gā*. The ነ which appears as ና, *nā*, a 180° reversal of the consonant, is one of the exceptions, along with the ረ, which becomes ራ *rā* with a short leg jutting out of the front and the ፈ, ፋ, *fā* has a leg drop straight down from the circle portion of the letter.

The long *ē* vowel appears consistently as a circle added to the bottom right side of the base form of the consonant. The ለ appears as ሌ *lē*; በ appears as ቤ *bē*, etc. The tendency will be for you to pronounce these two letters as *lo* and *bo*, so you need to be particularly careful in the memorization of the alphabet table. Unfortunately, the short *ə* vowel has no set pattern for change and thus will be the most difficult to memorize and to recognize. The key will be to know all the other clues and when you come across these forms you will realize this is the short *ə* option. Similarly, the *o* vowel does not have a set pattern for all the consonants, but there are some helpful clues. The consonants with two stems generally shorten the right-side leg: for example, ሰ becomes ሶ, *so*; the ደ appears to lengthen the left leg while shortening the right leg, ዶ, *do*. Most of the single stem consonants add a circle at the top of the base form, e.g., ቀ becomes ቆ, *qo*, but there are many exceptions to this group (see 2.1 above).

2.3 Labialized Consonants

There are four special consonant sounds in Gəʿəz that are identified as labialized consonants. Each has the addition of a "w" sound attached to the plain consonant. Notice there is no *u* vowel included in this set of syllabaries.

TABLE 2.3: Labialized Consonants

English Equivalent	Base Consonant	$q^wă$	q^wi	$q^wā$	$q^wē$	$q^wə$
q^w	ቀ	ቇ	ቊ	ቋ	ቌ	ቍ
x^w	ኀ	ኈ	ኊ	ኋ	ኌ	ኍ
k^w	ከ	ኰ	ኲ	ኳ	ኴ	ኵ
g^w	ገ	ጐ	ጒ	ጓ	ጔ	ጕ

TABLE 2.4: Punctuation Markings

Approximate English Equivalent	Gəʿəz
Word space	፡
Full stop	።
Comma	፣
Colon	፥
Semi-colon	፤
Preface Colon	፦
Question Mark	፧
End of Paragraph	፨

2.4   The Gəʿəz Article (or Lack Thereof)

Gəʿəz has no definite or indefinite article which can make for some interesting interpretations of certain terms (see further discussion in ch. 38 on syntax). The definiteness or indefiniteness of a word can be determined by its context in the sentence: ፍኖት፡ *fənot* can be read as "a road" or "the road."

2.5   Numerals

Like the consonant/vowel syllabaries, the Gəʿəz Numerals each have their own particular symbol that matches the English equivalent.

TABLE 2.5: Numerals

English Equivalent	Gəʿəz	English Equivalent	Gəʿəz	English Equivalent	Gəʿəz	English Equivalent	Gəʿəz
1	፩	7	፯	40	፵	100	፻
2	፪	8	፰	50	፶	1000	፲፻
3	፫	9	፱	60	፷	10000	፼
4	፬	10	፲	70	፸		
5	፭	20	፳	80	፹		
6	፮	30	፴	90	፺		

Note: The Number 6 in some older manuscripts the loop is not closed and so is very similar to the number 7.

2.6   Amharic Symbols

The following table provides some Amharic syllabaries that will appear at times in Gəʿəz documents. As noted, these appear primarily in proper names and places. You can see the similarities between some of the Amharic symbols and the Gəʿəz symbols—though note the added straight hat on six of the letters and the circles on the last letter at the bottom of the table.

TABLE 2.6: Amharic Symbols in Gəʿəz Documents

English Equivalent	Hă	Hu	Hi	Hā	Hē	Hə	Ho	Hua
ś	ሸ	ሹ	ሺ	ሻ	ሼ	ሽ	ሾ	ሿ
v	ቨ	ቩ	ቪ	ቫ	ቬ	ቭ	ቮ	ቯ
č	ቸ	ቹ	ቺ	ቻ	ቼ	ች	ቾ	ቿ
ñ	ኘ	ኙ	ኚ	ኛ	ኜ	ኝ	ኞ	ኟ
ḫ	ኸ	ኹ	ኺ	ኻ	ኼ	ኽ	ኾ	
ž	ዠ	ዡ	ዢ	ዣ	ዤ	ዥ	ዦ	ዧ
j	ጀ	ጁ	ጂ	ጃ	ጄ	ጅ	ጆ	ጇ
č̣	ጨ	ጩ	ጪ	ጫ	ጬ	ጭ	ጮ	ጯ

2.7 Rules of Contraction and Assimilation

You will discover throughout this grammar occasions in which various grammatical rules result in the assimilation of personal endings or the contraction of verb tense prefixes. Rather than attempt to explain each of these cases throughout the grammar, the following section will set out rules that will govern most of these special cases in which it appears a verb or noun may lose a prefix or an ending when it meets a particular consonant or set of consonants, gutturals being the most problematic.

2.7.1 Patterns and Roots of Verbs, Nouns, and Adjectives

Like most Semitic languages, the verbs, nouns, and adjectives in Gəʿəz are constructed from a three-consonant root system, although there are words that have four or more root consonants. These three consonants have distinct vowel patterns that are added to the consonant pattern of C1C2C3 that at times will have a prefix or a suffix added to the consonant-vowel pattern. As you will see throughout the grammar, there are a variety of patterns. Some of the more common patterns include the *qătl*, *yəqtăl*, *qătil*, *qətăl*, *qətul*. Further explanation of how these patterns vary are explained below and in the chapters to follow.

2.8 Rules for Gutturals

The consonants አ, ዐ, ሀ, ሐ, and ኀ can create changes in the expected declension patterns (like the Hebrew gutturals א, ע, ה, ח). The good thing about these changes is they generally follow a fixed set of rules. In what follows, "G" refers to a guttural letter.

2.8.1 Gutturals and Preceding Short Vowels

When a guttural consonant closes a syllable, the preceding short *ă*, as in -*ă* + G, the short vowel lengthens to an -*ā* as in -*ā* + G. The verbal pattern of *yəqtăl* in its normal form will appear as ይግብር፡ (*yəgbăr*), while the III Guttural jussive form, as in ይስማዕ፡ (*yəsmāʿ*), shows the lengthening of the short *ă* *መ* to the long *ā* *ማ* preceding the III Guttural.

In the pattern *qătl* and the nouns that form from it, e.g., ገብር፡ (*găbr*), shifts to ባሕር፡ (*bāḥr*) with the long *ā* preceding the guttural. However, the causative verbs with the አ prefix do not follow this rule; thus, the initial *ă* vowel in the strong verb አንበረ፡ (*ănbără*) does not change with the I Guttural in አዕበየ፡ (*ăʿbăyă*) to a long *ā* as in አዕበየ፡ (*āʿbăyă*).

The transition from *ă* to *ā* is not the only change before gutturals. With the *qătil* forms such as ጠቢብ፡ (*ṭăbib*) the *ă* vowel shifts to *ə* as in the word ልሒቅ፡ (*ləhiq*). In the imperfect *yəqăt(t)əl* form,[5] as in ይነብር፡ (*yənăb[b]ər*), the short *ă* vowel shifts to *ə* as in the word ይልህቅ፡ (*yəlăh[h]əq*). However, if the term has a prefix with an *ă* vowel preceding a guttural as in ተአኀዛ፡ (*tăʾxză*), the *ă* vowel *does not* shift to the short *ə* vowel (*təʾxză*). Similarly, if a word is preceded by an attached preposition that has the short *ă* vowel, such as በአገራ፡ (*băʾăgără*), the *ă* vowel *does not* shift to the short *ə* vowel (*bəʾăgără*). However, this vowel shift can also go in the opposite direction. For example, the imperfect *yəqăt(t)əl* form, as in ይነብር፡ (*yənăb[b]ər*),

---

5. It should be noted that in several word forms the middle root letter doubles in transliteration, but this does not appear in the Gəʿəz script. This "doubling" of the middle root letter simple means holding the sound longer than the non-doubled letter. A modern reading of Gəʿəz does not maintain the doubling sound of guttural consonants or labialized consonants—these appear as two double consonants *kk* plus the labialization on the second of the two *kkʷ*.

appears as የሐውር፡ (yăhăwər), not ይሐውር፡ (yəhăwər). In addition, qətăl forms such as ነበር፡ (nəbăr), when the initial consonant precedes a guttural the short ə vowel shifts to the short ă vowel as in ለአከ፡ (lăăk).

Some III Guttural verbs will drop the short ə vowel if the preceding syllable also includes a short vowel. One common example is the verb ሰምዐ፡, pronounced săm'a, without the short ə pronounced on the II consonant. However, when a suffix is added to this verb that begins with a consonant, the vowel on the II consonant becomes a long ā vowel as in ሰማዕኩ፡ (sămāʿku). If the suffix begins with a vowel, then the vowel on the II consonant regularly appears as a short ə vowel ይስምዐኒ, yəsmaʾəni.

2.8.2 Rules of Long Vowels

Syllables containing long vowels can also have their vowel shortened to an ə vowel when the feminine ት (t) ending is added. The vowel u is frequently affected by this feature while the i vowel is less affected. For example, the feminine form of the word ክቡር፡ (kəbur), ክብርት፡ (kəbərt), has shortened the u to the ə vowel due to the addition of the feminine ት (-t) ending. For the less affected i verb form, as in the term ልሂቅ፡ (ləhiq) when the feminine ት ending is added as in ልህቅት፡ (ləhəqt), the i vowel shortens to the ə vowel. The long ā vowel when attached to a consonant in a similar position will at times remain long as in ሠናይ፡ (šăn[n]āy) plus the feminine ending ት = ሠናይት፡ (šăn[n]āyt), or at times the ና in ሠናይት፡ will shorten to ነ as in ሠነይት፡ (šăn[n]ăyt).

2.8.3 Rules for III-ው and III-ይ Verbs and the u and i Vowels

When a III-ው or III-ይ verb appears with no verb ending or an object suffix, the ው or ይ will appear as vowels u or i respectively as in the case of the imperfect verb form for ተለው፡ (tălăwă) as ይተሉ፡ (yətălu) and in the case of a III-ይ, ሰተየ፡ (sătăyă), the ይ shifts to the i vowel in the imperfect, ይሰተይ፡ (yəsătăyi).

If the verb ending or an object suffix begins with a vowel the III-ው and III-ይ will remain with the addition of the vowel as in the case of ይተልዉ፡ (yətălwu) and ይሰትዩ፡ (yəsătyu) (3mp forms). In the case of the third-person singular verb with an object suffix, e.g., 1cs suffix ኒ (ni), the III-ው remains as in the case of the imperfect verb plus suffix ትተልወኒ፡ (tətălwăni) – "she will follow me." In the case of the III-ይ with the addition of an object suffix, e.g., 3cs suffix, the III-ይ remains and the "o" suffix ("it") attaches to the III-ይ as in this example: ይሰትዮ፡ (yəsătyo), "he will drink it."

The final syllable of the noun or adjective forms of these III-ው and III-ይ roots will end in the consonant form as in መኃትው፡ (măxātəw), "lamps," and ላሕይ፡ (lāhəy), "beautiful." When the feminine ending ት is added to the noun or adjective, the combination of the short ə vowel followed by the III-ው generally results in the ə vowel and the ው (ዕለውት፡ [ʿələwt]) changing to the u vowel as in ዕሉት፡ (ʿəlut). The III-ይ form can have some variation in how it forms. At times the ə vowel and the III-ይ is retained, ላሕይት፡ (lāhəyt), "beautiful," while generally it will shift to i vowel from ብልይት፡ (bələyt) to ብሊት፡ (bəlit). In addition, there are other variations that occur with nouns and adjectives such as those that end in ă vowel plus ዊ (wi), which can appear as ă vowel plus ዊይ (wiy) or ă vowel plus ወይ (wəy). These variants occur with the plural endings ā vowel plus ን or ā vowel plus ት. Another such variant is words ending in the ē vowel with the plural ending ā vowel plus ት can vary between ፍሬያት፡ (fərēyāt) or ፍርያት፡ (fərəyāt). Another variation involves the ă vowel plus ው which may result in the presence of a vowel or consonant as in "it will open" – ይትረነው፡ (yətrăx[x]ăw) or ይትረኖ፡ (yətrăx[x]o); in the second form the ነ has combined with the ው to form ኖ (xo). When III-ይ nouns end in the ē vowel (e.g., ፍሬ፡ [fərē], "fruit") have the plural ending -āt, the result can vary as to the final form of the word, ፍሬያት፡ (fərēyāt) or ፍርያት፡ (fərəyāt). The final III-ው is that which is combined with the long ā vowel. The student will discover that the *ā+ው* can remain, as in the word ሕያው፡ (*ḥăyāw*), "living," while at the same time the *ው* can disappear, as in the word ተስፋ፡ (*tăsfā*) rather than the expected ተስፋው፡ (*tăsfāw*).

II-*ው* adjectives in the *qətul* pattern can offer some variation when the vowel-consonant-vowel pattern appears as in ሙዉት፡ (*məwut*) or as ሙውት፡ (*məw[w]ət*), "dead."

2.8.4 Assimilation of Consonants

The assimilation of consonants is uncommon in Gəʿəz but will occur when connected to consonants with similar sounds. The two most common assimilations occur with the feminine ending ት when it occurs next to a dental consonant (d or t sound). For example, with the masculine word ከቡድ፡ (*kəbud*), "heavy," the expected feminine form would be ከቡድት፡ (*kəbədt*), but the ት assimilates because of the dental consonants, and the correct form is ከብድ፡ (*kəbəd[d]*; note the vowel change in the second radical from *u* in the masculine to a short *ə* in the feminine). When the feminine ending ት comes up against another *t* sound as in ሥጡጥ፡ (*šəṭuṭ*), the expected form would be ሥጥጥት፡ (*šəṭəṭt*), but again the ት assimilates and the correct from is ሥጥጥ፡ (*šəṭəṭ[ṭ]*).

The ት of the passive prefix ይት (*yət*) for some imperfect and subjunctive forms (Gt, Dt, Lt, Qt, Glt) will assimilate when it comes in contact with the dental stops or sibilants such as ጠ ደ ጸ ሰ ሠ ፀ ዘ. For example, the expected form of the verb ይትሰሚይ፡ (*yətsăm[m]ăy*) – "he will be named" with assimilation becomes ይሰሚይ፡ (*yəs[s]ăm[m]ăy*), distinguished from the active form ይሰሚ፡ (*yəs[s]ămi*).

In addition to the assimilation of ት, the ክ (*k*) of the verbal subject endings (ኩ, ኪ, ከ, ከሙ, ከን [*ku, ki, kă, kəmu, kən*]) can assimilate when they come in contact with a ቀ (*qă*) or ገ (*gă*). The verb "you stole" would appear as ሰረቅሙ፡ (*sărăq[q]mu*) but not as ሰረቅከሙ፡ (*sărăqkmu*), and the verb "I fell" would appear as ወደቁ፡ (*wădăq[q]u*), but not as ወደቅኩ፡ (*wădăqku*).

2.9 The Negated Causative Prefix አ and the Imperfect and Subjunctive First Singular

When the causative prefix አ of the first-person singular imperfect and subjunctive verb is negated with the ኢ, the አ shifts to a ያ. For example, the verb "I caused to kill," አቅትል፡, appears as ኢያቅትል፡, "I did not cause to kill." It is important to pick up this shift in order to recognize the first-person form of these verbs.

2.10 Manuscript Inconsistencies in Spelling

Like other Semitic languages, Gəʿəz has some letters that can be confused with others by both the reader and the copier of ancient manuscripts. There are several letters in Gəʿəz that create inconsistencies in spelling in manuscripts. These letters include the following ጸ ፀ አ ኣ ሀ ሐ ኀ ሠ ሰ. Much of this can be attributed to the evolution of the language, while others, of course, are a result of scribal error.

For various reasons, such as scribal copying or dictation, two of the initial problematic letters were the ፀ and the ጸ. The ጸ began to conflate with the ፀ and resulted in variations in the spelling of some root words. As a result, the student may find both spellings in Dillmann's or Leslau's lexicons or at least a note pointing to the other spelling. One of the more understandable inconsistencies is the confusion between the short አ and the long ኣ; the difference being the short left leg, which could be easily miswritten by a scribe. This confusion can at times lead to a misreading of particular verbal forms, e.g., ሰብሐት፡ (*səbəḥāt*) or

ሰብሓት፡ (səbəḥāt), the difference being the short left leg on the ሕ. According to Lambdin, the latter could be read as a D verbal noun (see ch. 35).⁶

The most pronounced inconsistencies occur with ሀ, ሕ, and ኅ. There are several misspellings of certain roots within manuscripts, but generally the misspelling is consistent throughout a singular manuscript. A similar confusion is seen in the possible merging of the ሠ and the ስ in later Amharic and resulted in the copyist misspelling certain roots. All these inconsistencies must be closely watched by the reader of the ancient manuscripts.

Students should also be aware that like other Semitic languages, there are letters that look quite similar, and it can be confusing when trying to read original manuscripts that are subject to faded ink or other damage. Some of these letters include ኀ, xă, with ኅ, xə, and ጎ, go; ሰ, să, with ለ, lă; የ, yə, with ዶ, do; ደ, dă, with ጸ, ṣă; ነ, nə, with ገ, gă; and ወ, wə, with ዉ, wu.

2.11 Exercises

Practice writing out the consonants in order to memorize them for recognition.

1. ሀ ____
2. ለ ____
3. ሐ ____
4. መ ____
5. ሠ ____
6. ረ ____
7. ሰ ____
8. ቀ ____
9. በ ____
10. ተ ____
11. ኀ ____
12. ነ ____
13. አ ____
14. ከ ____
15. ወ ____
16. ዐ ____
17. ዘ ____
18. የ ____
19. ደ ____
20. ገ ____
21. ጠ ____
22. ጰ ____
23. ጸ ____
24. ፀ ____
25. ፈ ____
26. ፐ ____

---

6. See Lambdin, *Introduction*, 14.

Chapter 3

PRONUNCIATION AND SYLLABIFICATION

3.1 Vowels

Like the other Semitic languages, the Gəʿəz script was originally consonantal. These consonants have through time generally not shifted in form; rather they remain the unvarying form of the word. However, vowels in the Semitic families are often changing and shifting in the formation of words. In addition, for the most part vowels in the ancient Semitic languages remained without outward sign. Yet over time, this so-called defect in the languages was remedied by the inclusion of a visible vowel system (such as the Masoretic vowels of the Hebrew Bible). The vowel system of Gəʿəz evolved quite unlike the system found in Masoretic biblical Hebrew. Unlike the separate vowel markers we find in Hebrew (the *kamatz*, *patach*, *seghol*, etc.), the vowels in Gəʿəz are attached to the consonant, thus creating what is called a syllabary—a consonant vowel cluster.

It is generally understood, although not completely accepted, that there are seven primary vowels in Gəʿəz—two short vowels and five long vowels (see table 3.1).

TABLE 3.1: Primary Gəʿəz Vowels

English Equivalent	Short hă	Long hu	Long hi (ee)	Long hā	Long hē	Short hə	Long ho
h	ሀ	ሁ	ሂ	ሃ	ሄ	ህ	ሆ
	ă as in "hat"	u as in "boot"	i as in "machine"	ā as in "cave"	e as in "eight"	ə as in "get"	o as in "coat"

Note that the short *ă* is the base form of the consonant, in this case the *h* is pronounced as *hă* as in "hat." In the case of every base consonant, the short *ă* is to be pronounced unless another vowel form is present. The long *ē* and *o* are often preceded by a labial or palatal consonant sound. The short *ə* vowel (*ə*, or at times *ĕ* in other transliteration formats) when appearing with a consonant can often have no vowel sound and the symbol simply represents the letter (at the end of a syllable or word); in the case of table 3.1, ህ represents the *h* consonant. In the case where it is acting as a vowel sound, it relates to the Hebrew *shewa*. It should be noted that unlike the *dagesh forte* in Hebrew, Gəʿəz has no indicator of a doubled consonant, only when separated by a vowel will two similar consonants appear. However, when transliteration is used to write out Gəʿəz, the doubling of a consonant is present in the transliteration but is not present in Gəʿəz.

3.2 Consonants

Generally, Gəʿəz consonants have an English equivalent that should be familiar to English speakers. You will note the English equivalents in table 3.1; however, a few may offer some difficulty in pronunciation for the native English speaker.

There are five guttural consonants in Gəʿəz ʿ (ዐ), ʾ (አ), h (ሀ), ḥ (ሐ), x (ኀ). The h (ሀ) is pronounced as an ordinary English "h" as in "hope" (Hebrew ה). Originally, ḥ was an "h" sound spoken from the back of the throat (Hebrew ח); and x was spoken as the "ch" as in "Bach" (Hebrew כ), but in practice they are often pronounced the same. The other two gutturals ʿ (Hebrew ע) and ʾ (Hebrew א) are considered vowel markers; they only have the sound of the vowel identified in the syllabary form—e.g., ዑ, u and ኡ, u.

The following four consonants are considered glottal stops[1] in Gəʿəz: ṭ (ጠ); ṣ (ጸ), ḍ (ፀ), and q (ቀ). As can be seen in table 3.1 there are two "p" sounds in Gəʿəz. Both only occur in loanwords from other languages. The plain ṗ (ጰ) is also a glottal stop consonant and occurs in such words as παῦλος, Paul. The second p (ፐ) is pronounced as a normal English "p" but is rare.

Four other consonantal sounds need to be identified in Gəʿəz; these are labialized sounds (made by the rounding of the lips to varying degree). Their pronunciation is very straightforward. They are the kw (ኰ) as in ኵሎ፡ kwəllo – "every, all"; xw (ኈ) as in ኈላቍ፡ xwəlāqu – "number"; gw (ጐ) as in ጕንድ፡ gwēnd – "tree trunk"; and qw (ቈ) as in ቈረራ፡ qwērărā – "cold."

All Gəʿəz consonants can occur as single or doubled letters. The doubled consonant is pronounced or held longer when spoken or read, however, it will generally not appear as a doubled consonant and only in the transliteration.

3.3 Accents

There are two primary rules that govern the accent of Gəʿəz vocabulary:

A. The accent of all finite verbal forms without object suffixes falls on the penultimate syllable, e.g.,
   a. ነበረ፡ năbără
   b. ቀተለት፡ qătălăt
   c. ይቀትሉ፡ yēkătēlu
   d. The exception to the rule is the second-person feminine plural perfect form (ክን፡, kēn)–e.g., ነበርክን፡ năbărkēn
B. The accent falls on the last syllable on most nouns, adjectives, and adverbs unless it ends in a final ă. If so, then it is on the penultimate syllable.

---

1. A glottal stop is defined as a sound made when the flow of air is cut off completely at the glottis (top of larynx) while forcibly ejecting the air in the mouth.

There are exceptions to these two simple rules (words in construct, the proclitic negative, prepositions before nouns), which we will discuss with the relevant sections of grammar throughout the book.

3.4 Consonantal Root System, Vowel Patterns, and Syllables

In Gəʿəz neither a lone consonant nor lone vowel constitutes a word, only the combination of the two begins the process of forming a syllable. Like biblical Hebrew, every syllable must have one consonant and one vowel–whether short or long–a syllable cannot contain more than one vowel (unless it is a single sound *dipthong*). A syllable can contain one or two consonants—ዝ, *zə*, ቃል፡, *qāl*; consonant–vowel–consonant is considered a closed syllable. Every Gəʿəz syllable must begin with a consonant sound. Some words may appear to end in two consonants—usually with compound words, e.g., አንትኩ፡, *ənt-kū* not *əntəkū*.

Similar to other Semitic languages, Gəʿəz builds on a three consonant root and vowel pattern, often adding a prefix or suffix to the root and vowels. The pattern reads as $C_1vC_2vC_3$–the small "v" being the vowel attached to the consonant. Gəʿəz follows the three consonant root system with patterns that include "noun," "adjectival," and "verbal."

TABLE 3.2: Consonantal Groups

Noun	Translation	Consonant root	Vowel Pattern	Prefix/suffix
ደቂቅ፡ *dāqiq*	offspring	ደቀቀ፡	$C_1\breve{a}C_2iC_3$	
ነቢያት፡ *nābiyāt*	prophets	ነበየ፡	$C_1\breve{a}C_2iC_3\bar{a}t$	ት
መሠጌር፡ *māšāggēr*	fisherman	ሠገረ፡	$^{m\partial}C_1\breve{a}C_2\bar{e}C_3$	መ
ገዳማት፡ *gādāmāt*	wildernesses	ገደመ፡	$C_1\breve{a}C_2\bar{a}C_3\bar{a}t$	ት

Consonantal roots are the building blocks by which any language creates words. In Gəʿəz there are three classes of roots. The first and lowest class of root (consonant + vowel) appears in "interjections" that emerge out of the utterance of human feeling or emotion. The most common root in this category is "O!" (አ). It is most used in addressing someone in the vocative case – "O man!": አገብር፡. Another frequently used interjection in Gəʿəz is "woe": ወይ፡ always followed by the dative ለ፡ "woe to me" ወይ፡ ለተ፡.

The second class of consonantal root is the pronominal root. These roots belong to words that will serve to point to other words, i.e., modifiers—they contain the determinative additions to words and the greater part of particles that express the relationship of clauses in a sentence. Demonstratives are the most common of the pronominal roots—ት, ደ, ስ, ዝ (in their syllabary forms—particularly the ት in the feminine ending and personal suffixes). The ደ (common in Aramaic) is only used with the preposition በ, ዲበ፡ "upon." The pronominal ዝ is used as the demonstrative pronoun ዝ *zə* – "this," and the relative pronoun ዝ *zā* – "who," and the particles ዝየ፡ *zəya* – "here," ማእዜ፡ *māʾəzē* – "when?," ይእዜ፡ *yəʾəzē* – "now," and ጊዜ፡ *gizē* – "point of time."

The two liquid consonants ን and ለ also serve as demonstrative pronouns with the addition of a preceding or succeeding vowel. አን፡ *ʾənā* (also serves as "not") serves to help form the personal አንቲ፡ *ʾəntī*, demonstrative እንትኩ፡ *əntəku*, and relative እንታክቲ፡ *əntākti* pronouns. The second liquid, ለ, appears often as part of the demonstrative እሉ፡ *əlu* and እላ፡ *əlā* and relative እለ፡ *əlă* pronouns. Similar to the እን፡, a negative is formed from the አል፡ *ăla* – "not", አልቦ፡ *ălbo* – "there is not," and አላ፡ *ălā* – "but."

The third class of consonantal roots contains those that carry an idea, conception or notion. Several of these triliteral words, like Hebrew, have a weak middle radical, as in መዊት፡, *măwit*; here the *wi* proves to be a weak vowel consonant. However, most roots are strictly consonantal. There are also quadrilateral and multiliteral roots in Ethiopic. Like Hebrew, the third-person, masculine, singular, perfect form of the word is used for referring to the three-consonant root, e.g., for ንግር፡ ngr we pronounce the root ነገረ፡ *năgără*. We will discover other root forms as we examine the various verbal and noun forms of the Gəʿəz language and will discuss in detail the significance of the weak consonant/vowel of the root.

3.5 Vocabulary

*__Note:__ the vocabulary list from here forward will no longer have the transliteration.

1. ምድር፡ – land, earth, ground
2. እግዚአብሔር፡ – Lord, God
3. አብ፡ – father
4. ዕለት፡ – day
5. ሰብአዊ፡ – man, humankind
6. ወለት፡ (f.); ወልድ፡ (m.) – child
7. እዝን፡ – ear
8. ዐይን፡ – eye
9. እሳት፡ – fire
10. ልብ፡ – heart
11. ዝ፡ ዛቲ፡ ዝንቲ፡ – this
12. እድ፡ – hand
13. ደም፡ – blood
14. መንፈስ፡ – spirit, breath
15. ሌሊት፡ – night
16. ዓመት፡ – year
17. ስም፡ – name
18. መጽአ፡ – come
19. ወፅአ፡ – go, come forth, emerge
20. ቦአ፡ – enter
21. ወድቀ፡ – fall down
22. ህየ፡ – there
23. በህየ፡ – in that place
24. እምህየ፡ – from there, from that place
25. ዝየ፡ – here
26. በዝየ፡ – in this place
27. እምዝየ፡ – from here, from this place
28. ወረደ፡ – descend, come down
29. ነበረ፡ – sit, remain, dwell
30. ወ – and, but

3.6 Exercises

A. Translate the following:

1. ነበ፡ ገብር፡

2. ዲበ፡ ሐመር፡

3. ቡኁበ፡ ብእሲት።
___

4. እምነ፡ ብእሲ።
___

5. ዳበ፡ ምድር።
___

6. በዲበ፡ ሐመር።
___

7. ቡኁበ፡ ብእሲት።
___

8. እምነ፡ ገዳም።
___

9. ወረዱ፡ እምዲበ፡ ደብር።
___

10. ነበረት፡ በውስተ፡ ቤት።
___

B. Translate the following:

1. ወፅአ፡ አርዌ፡ እምታሕተ፡ ቤት።
___

2. ገብኡ፡ አግብርተ፡ ንጉሥ።
___

3. ነበረ፡ ታሕተ፡ ዕፅ።
___

4. ወረደ፡ ዝናም፡ እምውስተ፡ ሰማይ።
___

5. ገብአ፡ እንተ፡ ፍኖተ፡ ደብር።
___

6. ጐየ፡ እምነ፡ አራዊተ፡ ገዳም።
   _____

7. ሐረ፡ ነቢይ፡ እምዝየ፡ ወዐርገ፡ ውስተ፡ ሰማይ።
   _____

8. ሐረ፡ እንተ፡ ፍኖተ፡ ጊደም።
   _____

9. ወድቀ፡ ዕፅ፡ ዲበ፡ ቤተ፡ ነቢይ።
   _____

10. መጽአ፡ እምውስተ፡ ሰማይ።
    _____

11. ጐየ፡ አንስተ፡ መሠግራን።
    _____

12. ወድቀ እምውስተ ዕፅ።
    _____

13. ወረደ፡ በረድ፡ ወዝናም።
    _____

14. ወድቁ፡ አቋጽለ፡ ዕፀው፡ ውስተ፡ ፍኖት።
    _____

15. በጽሐ፡ አንስተ፡ ሀገር።
    _____

C. Genesis 1:1–3: Translate the following:

¹ በቀደሚ፡ ገብረ፡ እግዚአብሔር፡ ሰማየ፡ ወምድረ።

² ወምድርሰ፡ ህለወት፡ እምትካት፡ ዕራቃ፡ ወኢታስተርኢ፡ ወኢኮነት፡ ድሉተ፡ ወጽልመት፡ መልዕልተ፡ ቀላይ፡ ወመንፈሰ፡ እግዚአብሔር፡ ይጼልል፡ መልዕልተ፡ ማይ።

³ ወይቤ፡ እግዚአብሔር፡ ለይኩን፡ ብርሃን፡ ወኮነ፡ ብርሃን።

Chapter 4

GƎʿƎZ NOUNS

4.1 Noun Gender

There is no specific criterion offered for identifying the gender of a noun in Gǝʿǝz. There are no particular endings that assist in identifying feminine nouns; for example, in Hebrew, the הָ or the ת endings identify feminine singular nouns, although the ending Gǝʿǝz consonant ት can often denote a feminine noun. Gender of nouns or adjectives can be identified by the relationship they have with a particular noun/adjective or verb. For example, ዝንቱ፡ ብእሲ፡, zǝntu bǝʾsi – "this man," tells us that ዝንቱ፡ is a masculine demonstrative adjective; while ዛቲ፡ ብእሲት፡, zāti bǝʾsit – "this woman" tells us that ዛቲ፡ is a feminine demonstrative adjective. We know this because gender identification is fixed for human beings only; most other nouns appear in either gender although many follow a particular gender predilection.

Two simple rules can be followed although there are often exceptions to the rules. 1) Nouns that name months, stars, rivers, metals, and weapons tend to be treated as masculine; and 2) Nouns denoting towns, cities, districts, and paired parts of the body (much like Hebrew) follow the feminine gender. It is possible that the varied gender identification is due to the gender of the underlying Greek word from which the Ethiopic text was possibly translated. It may also be due to the expressive function of the noun: feminine may indicate a diminutive or familiar use by a particular translator.

4.2 Noun Number

Similar to gender designation, Gǝʿǝz nouns denoting humans have regular verbal and adjectival agreement in the plural. Other plural nouns may have singular or plural verbs and modifiers.

4.3 Nouns and the "Article"

There is no term for the definite article (the word "the") or the indefinite article (the word "a") in Gǝʿǝz. However, a conceptional word that is the single representative of its class is considered determined or definite, such as God, sun, life, West, etc.; these terms may be considered undetermined when an adjective is added that suggests some appositional expression, e.g., "a wicked death," or "a strange life." As in Hebrew, all proper names in Gəʿəz are considered determined. The article may be added to the translation when the noun in question has been previously inferred, such as in Matthew 4:25, "many people followed him," followed by Matthew 5:1, "when he saw *the* people," referring to the people in 4:25. Context generally will determine the translation inclusion of the article "the" in phrases such as ሕዝበ፡ እስራኤል። – "*the* people of Israel" or መንግሥተ፡ ሰማያት። – "*the* kingdom of heaven." As can be seen below, a noun can be determined or undetermined depending on the context:

ሀገር፡ – a city or the city
ንጉሥ፡ – a king or the king
ቤት፡ – a house or the house
ደብር፡ – a mountain or the mountain

4.4 Nouns in the Plural

Gəʿəz nouns form the plural in two ways:

1. Pattern replacement (called broken plurals)—ደብር፡ – mountain, but አድባር፡ – mountains.
    a. Generally, they have a prefix, or a suffix added to the singular form of the noun to form the plural.
    b. On occasion, the broken plurals will appear with the -ā+ት ending.
2. Nouns with added endings or suffixes are referred to as external plurals: ዓmት፡ – year, but ዓmታት፡ – years.
    a. Two endings are used to form the external plurals – (-ā+ን and -ā+ት).
    b. The (-ā+ን) ending is generally restricted to nouns identified as male humans.
        i. መሠግር፡ – fisherman; መሠገራን፡ – fishermen
        ii. ሊቅ፡ – elder, chief; ሊቃን፡ – elders, chiefs
    c. The (-ā+ት) ending forms the plural of most other nouns.
        i. ነቢይ፡ – prophet; ነቢያት፡ – prophets
        ii. ንግሥት፡ – queen; ንግሥታት፡ – queens
        iii. ገዳም፡ – wilderness; ገዳማት፡ – wildernesses

There is no set of rules to follow when trying to form the plural of a noun. Some nouns have two plural forms; however, nouns generally follow a set of syllabary patterns.

TABLE 4.1 NOUN PATTERNS

Syllabary Pattern of Plural Form	Singular Noun	Definition	Plural Noun	Definition
$C_1əC_2ăC_3$	እግር፡	foot	እገር፡	feet
$ăC_1C_2āC_3$	ደብር፡	mountain	አድባር፡	mountains
$ăC_1C_2uC_3$	ሀገር፡	city	አህጉር፡	cities

Syllabary Pattern of Plural Form	Singular Noun	Definition	Plural Noun	Definition
$ăC_1C_2əC_3$	በትር፡	rod, staff	አብትር፡	rods, staffs
$ăC_1C_2əC_3t$	ገብር፡	servant	አግብርት፡	servants
$C_1ăC_2ăC_3t$	ንጉሥ፡	king	ነገሥት፡	kings
$C_1ăC_2āC_3əC_4t$	መልአክ፡	angel, messenger	መላእክት፡	angels, messengers
$C_1ăC_2āC_3əC_4$	አንቀጽ፡	gate	አናቅጽ፡	gates
$ăC_1āC_2əC_3$	በግዕ፡	sheep	አባግዕ፡	sheep

There are several often used bi-consonantal nouns that appear in the plural with an -ăw ending. It would be a good idea to commit these particular nouns to memory.

TABLE 4.2 BI-CONSONANTAL PLURAL NOUN FORMS

Singular Noun	Definition	Plural Form	Definition
እድ፡	hand	እደው፡	Hands
ዕፅ፡	tree	ዕፀው፡	Trees
አፍ፡	mouth	አፈው፡	Mouths
አብ፡	father	አበው፡	Fathers
ዕድ፡	male	ዕደው፡	Males
እኍ፡	brother	አኀው፡	Brothers

Man and woman also create some oddities in Gəʿəz.

1. ብእሲ፡ – "man" becomes ሰብእ፡ in the plural – "men."
   a. This may be a peculiarity similar to the Hebrew איש, *ish*, and אנשים, *anashim*.
   b. ሰብእ፡ may be translated as "men," "people," or "humankind"
2. ብእሲት፡ – "woman" becomes አንስት፡ in the plural – "women."

Several nouns in Gəʿəz can designate a singular item (tree) or a collective (group of trees)

Gəʿəz Singular	Translation	Gəʿəz Plural	Singular Collective
ዕፅ፡	tree	ዕፀው፡	group of trees
ያፍ፡	bird	አዕዋፍ፡	fowl
ሕዝብ፡	people	አሕዛብ፡	people, nation
ደቂቅ፡	offspring		offspring

Context will determine how the noun is to be translated when there is a conflict with form and meaning.

4.5 Nouns and the Possessive Pronominal Suffix

A pronominal suffix, attached directly to a noun, resembles a pronoun, which specifies a person, place, or thing, while functioning primarily as another part of speech. *His* in *his choice* is a pronominal adjective. In Gəʿəz, pronominal suffixes are added to nouns, verbs, and prepositions. There are two basic forms (with some variation based on the ending of the noun), the nominative and the accusative. The following table represents the noun form with consonant endings:

TABLE 4.3: Possessive Suffixes for Nouns Ending in Consonants

Translation	Nominative Form	Nom. Suffix Form	Accusative Form	Acc. Suffix Form
My gospel	ወንጌልየ፡	-የ -yă	ወንጌልየ፡	-የ -yă
Your (m.s.) gospel	ወንጌልከ፡	-ከ -kă	ወንጌለከ፡	-ă+ከ -ăkă
Your (f.s.) gospel	ወንጌልኪ፡	-ኪ -ki	ወንጌለኪ፡	-ă+ኪ -ăki
His gospel	ወንጌሉ፡	-u	ወንጌሎ፡	-o
Her gospel	ወንጌላ፡	-ā	ወንጌላ፡	-ā
Our gospel	ወንጌልነ፡	-ነ -nă	ወንጌለነ፡	-ă+ነ -ănă
Your (m.p) gospel	ወንጌልከሙ፡	-ከሙ -kəmu	ወንጌለከሙ፡	-ă+ከሙ -ăkəmu)
Your (f.p.) gospel	ወንጌልከን፡	-ከን -kən	ወንጌለከን፡	-ă+ከን -ăkən
Their (m.) gospel	ወንጌሎሙ፡	-o+ሙ -omu	ወንጌሎሙ፡	-o+ሙ -omu
Their (f.) gospel	ወንጌሎን፡	-o+ን -on	ወንጌሎን፡	o+ን -on

As can be seen there are contrasts between the nominative and accusative in the 2nd singular m. and f. forms and the 3rd singular m. forms. In addition, the 1st person and 2nd person plural forms also differ between the nominative and accusative. Each of these forms changes the connecting vowel (the vowel that is added to connect the suffix to the noun) from the nominative to the accusative forms: short ə to short ă in the 2nd singular, 1st plural, and 2nd plural forms, and *u* to *o* in the 3rd m. singular form.

The second group of nouns to consider includes those nouns that end with an *i*. As can be seen in the table below, the primary shift is from the *i* ending to the long *ē* ending in the accusative, although this does not happen in every case, but only in the second-person singular and plural forms. However, the suffixes themselves differ from those discussed above; below there is the addition of ሆ (*ho*) in the third singular and plural forms.

TABLE 4.4: Possessive Suffixes for Nouns Ending in *i*

Translation	Nominative Form	Nom. Suffix Form	Accusative Form	Acc. Suffix Form
My scribe	ጸሓፊየ፡	-i+የ	ጸሓፊየ፡	i+የ
Your scribe	ጸሓፊከ፡	-i+ከ	ጸሓፌከ ፡	ē+ከ
Your scribe	ጸሓፊኪ፡	-i+ኪ	ጸሓፌኪ፡	ē+ኪ
His scribe	ጸሓፊሁ፡	-i+ሁ	ጸሓፊሁ፡	i+ሁ

Translation	Nominative Form	Nom. Suffix Form	Accusative Form	Acc. Suffix Form
Her scribe	ጸሐፊሃ፡	-i+ሃ	ጸሐፊሃ፡	-i+ሃ
Our scribe	ጸሐፊነ፡	-i+ነ	ጸሐፊነ፡	-i+ነ
Your scribe	ጸሐፊክሙ፡	-i+ክሙ	ጸሐፌክሙ፡	-ē+ክሙ
Your scribe	ጸሐፊክን፡	i+ክን	ጸሐፌክን፡	ē+ክን
Their scribe	ጸሐፊሆሙ፡	-i+ሆሙ	ጸሐፊሆሙ፡	-i+ሆሙ
Their scribe	ጸሐፊሆን፡	-i+ሆን	ጸሐፊሆን፡	-i+ሆን

The third group of nouns to consider includes those that end in a long vowel other than the *i* vowel noted above. Note the group below uses the same set of endings as do the *i* vowel suffixes above in table 4.2.

TABLE 4.5: Possessive Suffixes for Nouns Ending in Long Vowels Other Than *i*

Translation	Nominative Form	Nom. Suffix Form	Accusative Form	Acc. Suffix Form
My affliction	ምንዳቤየ፡	-ē+የ	ምንዳቤየ፡	-ē+የ
Your affliction	ምንዳቤከ፡	-ē+ከ	ምንዳቤከ፡	-ē+ከ
Your affliction	ምንዳቤኪ፡	-ē+ኪ	ምንዳቤኪ፡	-ē+ኪ
His affliction	ምንዳቤሁ፡	-ē+ሁ	ምንዳቤሁ፡	-ē+ሁ
Her affliction	ምንዳቤሃ፡	-ē+ሃ	ምንዳቤሃ፡	-ē+ሃ
Our affliction	ምንዳቤነ፡	-ē+ነ	ምንዳቤነ፡	-ē+ነ
Your affliction	ምንዳቤክሙ፡	-ē+ክሙ	ምንዳቤክሙ፡	-ē+ክሙ
Your affliction	ምንዳቤክን፡	-ē+ክን	ምንዳቤክን፡	-ē+ክን
Their affliction	ምንዳቤሆሙ፡	-ē+ሆሙ	ምንዳቤሆሙ፡	-ē+ሆሙ
Their affliction	ምንዳቤሆን፡	-ē+ሆን	ምንዳቤሆን፡	-ē+ሆን

All Gəʿəz plural nouns use the connecting vowel *i* prior to adding the pronominal suffix to the noun stem. In the case of this noun suffix group, there is no distinction between the nominative and accusative forms. The group follows the same inflection as ጸሐፊ፡ (see 4.2 above) with the exception that the endings *i*+የ and *i*+ኪ appear as short *ə*+የ and *ə*+ኪ. Notice the 1cs and 2fs have two forms.

TABLE 4.6: Plural Nouns with Possessive Suffixes

Translation	Nominative Form	Nom. Suffix Form	Accusative Form (identical form)	Acc. Suffix Form
My cities	አህጉሪየ፡/አህጉርየ፡	-i+የ -ə+የ	አህጉሪየ፡/አህጉርየ፡	-i+የ -ə+የ
Your cities	አህጉሪከ፡	ከ	አህጉሪከ፡	ከ
Your cities	አህጉሪኪ፡/አህጉርኪ፡	-i+ኪ -ə+ኪ	አህጉሪኪ፡/አህጉርኪ፡	-i+ኪ -ə+ኪ

(continued)

Translation	Nominative Form	Nom. Suffix Form	Accusative Form (identical form)	Acc. Suffix Form
His cities	አህጉሪሁ፡	-ሁ	አህጉሪሁ፡	-ሁ
Her cities	አህጉሪሃ፡	-ሃ	አህጉሪሃ፡	-ሃ
Our cities	አህጉሪነ፡	-ነ	አህጉሪነ፡	-ነ
Your cities	አህጉሪክሙ፡	-ክሙ	አህጉሪክሙ፡	-ክሙ
Your cities	አህጉሪክን፡	-ክን	አህጉሪክን፡	-ክን
Their cities	አህጉሪሆሙ፡	-ሆሙ	አህጉሪሆሙ፡	-ሆሙ
Their cities	አህጉሪሆን፡	-ሆን	አህጉሪሆን፡	-ሆን

Often in Gəʿəz, collective nouns inflect as singular nouns, e.g., ደቂቅየ፡ for ደቂቂየ፡. It should be noted here that regular plural forms often appear without the distinctive *i*, e.g., ሊቃኑ፡ for ሊቃኒሁ፡. On the contrary, some singular nouns that appear outwardly to be plural nouns may take the *i* of the plurals; in particular, those nouns with a long *ā* in the final syllable such as *-ā+n* or *-ā+t* (following a guttural, እኁ – brother; እኅት – brothers).

Four commonly occurring nouns in particular stand out when they appear with the pronominal suffix: father, father-in-law, brother, and mouth. Each form with a *u* vowel in the nominative and a long *ā* in the accusative.

TABLE 4.7: Father, Father-in-Law, Brother, Mouth

	Nom.	Acc.	Nom.	Acc.	Nom.	Acc.	Nom.	Acc.
1cs	አቡየ፡	አባየ፡	ሐሙየ፡	ሐማየ፡	እኁየ፡	እኃየ፡	አፉየ፡	አፋየ፡
2ms	አቡከ፡	አባከ፡	ሐሙከ፡	ሐማከ፡	እኁከ፡	እኃከ፡	አፉከ፡	አፋከ፡
2fs	አቡኪ፡	አባኪ፡	ሐሙኪ፡	ሐማኪ፡	እኁኪ፡	እኃኪ፡	አፉኪ፡	አፋኪ፡
3ms	አቡሁ፡	አባሁ፡	ሐሙሁ፡	ሐማሁ፡	እኁሁ፡	እኃሁ፡	አፉሁ፡	አፋሁ፡
3fs	አቡሃ፡	አባሃ፡	ሐሙሃ፡	ሐማሃ፡	እኁሃ፡	እኃሃ፡	አፉሃ፡	አፋሃ፡
1cp	አቡነ፡	አባነ፡	ሐሙነ፡	ሐማነ፡	እኁነ፡	እኃነ፡	አፉነ፡	አፋነ፡
2mp	አቡክሙ፡	አባክሙ፡	ሐሙክሙ፡	ሐማክሙ፡	እኁክሙ፡	እኃክሙ፡	አፉክሙ፡	አፋክሙ፡
2fp	አቡክን፡	አባክን፡	ሐሙክን፡	ሐማክን፡	እኁክን፡	እኃክን፡	አፉክን፡	አፋክን፡
3mp	አቡሆሙ፡	አባሆሙ፡	ሐሙሆሙ፡	ሐማሆሙ፡	እኁሆሙ፡	እኃሆሙ፡	አፉሆሙ፡	አፋሆሙ፡
3fp	አቡሆን፡	አባሆን፡	ሐሙሆን፡	ሐማሆን፡	እኁሆን፡	እኃሆን፡	አፉሆን፡	አፋሆን፡

One singular noun is worth mentioning here. The noun "hand" appears in the singular with the connecting vowel *ē* before the suffixes rather than the short *ə* vowel: እዴየ፡ እዴከ፡ እዴኪ፡ እዴሁ፡ እዴሃ፡ እዴነ፡ እዴክሙ፡ እዴክን፡ እዴሆሙ፡ እዴሆን.

4.6 Vocabulary

1. ዲበ፡ – on, upon, onto
2. ኀበ፡ – by, with, at, or near
3. ብእሲ፡ – man, husband (pl. ሰብእ፡)
4. ብእሲት፡ – woman, wife (pl. አንስት፡)
5. ሐመር፡ – (f./m.) boat or ship (pl. አሕማር)
6. መሥግር፡ – fisherman (pl. መሥግራን፡)
7. ሊቅ፡ – elder, chief (pl. ሊቃን፡ or ሊቃናት or ሊቃውንት፡)
8. ነቢይ፡ – prophet (pl. ነቢያት፡)
9. ገዳም፡ – (m.) wilderness (pl. ገዳማት፡)
10. ንግሥት፡ – queen (pl. ንግሥታት፡)
11. ሮጸ፡ – run
12. ጕየ፡ – flee
13. ገብአ፡ – return or go back
14. በጽሐ፡ – arrive
15. አርዌ፡ – beast, wild animal
16. ምስለ፡ – with, in the company of

4.7 Exercises

A. Translate the following:

1. መኑ፡ ውእቱ፡ መኰንንከ፡

2. አይቴ፡ ውእቱ፡ ቤተ፡ አቡክሙ፡

3. ዮሐንስ፡ መኰንኖሙ፡ ውእቱ፡

4. ዝንቱ፡ ውእቱ፡ እጐከ፡

5. ዝንቱ፡ ውእቱ፡ ቃላተ፡ አበዊነ፡

6. ዝንቱ፡ አርዌ፡ ምድር፡

7. መኑ፡ ውእቱ፡ ጸሐፊከ።

   _____

8. አይቴ፡ አቡከ።

   _____

9. እንታክቲ፡ ይእቲ፡ ወለተ፡ እኀትዬ።

   _____

10. እሉ፡ እሙንቱ፡ ውሉደ፡ እኁኪ።

    _____

B. Luke 2:1–4: Translate the following:

¹ወኮነ፡ በውእቱ፡ መዋዕል፡ ወፅአ፡ ትእዛዝ፡ እምኀበ፡ ቄሳር፡ ንጉሥ፡ ከመ፡ ይጻሐፍ፡ ኵሉ፡ ዓለም።

²ወውእቱ፡ ጸሐፍ፡ ቀዳሚ፡ ውእቱ፡ እመ፡ ቄሬዎስ፡ መስፍን፡ ለሶርያ።

³ወሐረ፡ ኵሉ፡ ሰብእ፡ ይጻሐፍ፡ በበ፡ ሀገሩ።

⁴ወዐርገ፡ ዮሴፍኒ፡ እምገሊላ፡ እምሀገረ፡ ናዝሬት፡ መንገለ፡ ይሁዳ፡ ኀበ፡ ሀገረ፡ ዳዊት፡ እንተ፡ ስማ፡ ቤተ፡ ልሔም፡ እስመ፡

እምሀገረ፡ ዳዊት፡ ወእምአዝማደ፡ ቤቱ፡ ውእቱ።

Chapter 5

CONSTRUCT NOUNS

5.1 The Noun Construct State

In Semitic languages, the use of the noun construct state is the standard way to form a genitive construction. The modified noun (N_1) is placed in the first position of the construct state while the modifying noun (N_2) is placed directly afterwards; no other word can intervene between the two. The modifying relationship between N_1 and N_2 is denoted in Gəʿəz by adding an ă vowel to the first noun (N_1) in the chain. The first noun is identified as "in construct" with the second noun. Construct noun chains can also occur with three or more nouns, but this is rare. Generally, when this occurs there will be a fixed expression as a subset to the chain, for example ቤተ፡ መቅደስ፡ – "house of the holy place, or temple," in the construct chain: ትድባበ፡ ቤተ፡ መቅደስ፡ – "pinnacle of the temple."

Plural noun construct chains are formed the same way–the addition of the -ă vowel (see table 5.1). Two additional key points should be offered concerning the construct. First, for nouns that end in the -i vowel, the construct is formed by changing i to ē. For example, ጸሐፊ፡ – "scribe" transforms to ጸሐፌ፡ ሕዝብ፡ – "scribe of the people." Second, nouns that end in long vowels (ā, ē, and o) do not transform in the construct chain: አርዌ፡ ገዳም፡ – "beast of the wilderness."

TABLE 5.1 GƏʿƏZ CONSTRUCT NOUNS

Noun Construct Chain	Translation
ንጉሠ፡ ሀገር፡	The/a king of the/a city[1]
ወልደ፡ ነጉሥ፡	The son of the king
ቃለ፡ ነቢይ	Voice/word of the prophet
ስመ፡ መልአክ፡	The name of the angel
ፍልሰተ፡ ባቢሎን	The Exile of Babylon
ሊቀ፡ ካህናት፡	The chief of the priests
መዓረ፡ ገዳም፡	Honey of the Wilderness
ጸሐፌ፡ ሕዝብ፡	Scribe of the people
ነገሥተ፡ ሀገር፡	The kings of the city
ውሉደ፡ ነጉሥ፡	The sons of the king
ቃላተ፡ ነቢይ	The words of the Prophet

5.2 Vocabulary

1. ዕፅ፡ – (m./f.) tree (pl. ዕፀው፡)
2. ፍኖት፡ – (f./m.) road, way, path (pl. ፍናው፡)
3. አርዌ፡ – (m./f.) animal, wild beast (pl. አራዊት፡)
4. ሰማይ፡ – (m./f.) heaven (pl. ሰማያት፡)
5. በረድ፡ – (m.) hail
6. ዝናም፡ – (m./f.) rain (pl. ዝናማት፡)
7. ቄጽል፡ – (m./f.) leaf or foliage (pl. አቆጽል፡)
8. ቤተ፡ ንጉሥ፡ – house of the king, palace
9. እንተ፡ – by way of, via
10. ታሕተ፡ – under, below
11. ውእቱ፡ – he, it, that
12. ዐርገ፡ – to ascend, come up
13. ኢ- – negative prefix to verbs

5.3 Exercises

A. Translate the following:

1. ወልደ፡ መሥግር።

2. ቃለተ፡ ነቢያት።

3. አራዊተ፡ ዝንቱ፡ ደብር።

4. አብያተ፡ መኳንንት።

5. ሊቀ፡ ጸሐፍት።

6. ጸሐፌ፡ ንጉሥ።

7. ነገረ፡ መኮንን።

8. ውሉደ፡ ጸሐፊ፡
___

9. ቃለ፡ ዝንቱ፡ መልአክ፡
___

10. አዋልደ፡ ውእቱ፡ መኰንን፡
___

B. Translate the following:

1. ወድቀ፡ ወልደ፡ ውእቱ፡ ብእሲ፡ እምውስተ፡ ዝንቱ፡ ዕፅ፡
___

2. ሐረት፡ (ት ending indicates 3fs verb ending) ወለተ፡ ንጉሥ፡ ኀበ፡ ውእቱ፡ ነቢይ፡
___

3. ኢወድቁ፡ አቅጽለ፡ ይእቲ፡ ዕፅ፡
___

4. ሮጹ፡ ውሉደ፡ መኰንን፡ ውስተ፡ ፍኖተ፡ ሀገር፡
___

5. ኢሐሩ፡ ሰብእ፡ ኀበ፡ ውእቱ፡ መኰንን፡
___

6. ዐርገ፡ ቃላተ፡ ነቢይ፡ ውስተ፡ ሰማይ፡
___

7. ወፅአ፡ መልአክ፡ እምውስተ፡ ሰማይ፡ ወበጽሐ፡ ኀበ፡ ቤተ፡ ይእቲ፡ ብእሲት፡
___

8. በጽሑ፡ መላእክተ፡ ሰማይ፡ ውስተ፡ ሀገር፡ ወነበሩ፡ ህየ፡
___

9. ወረደ፡ ዝናም፡ እምውስተ፡ ሰማይ፡ ወኢወረደ፡ በረድ፡
___

10. ወድቁ፡ አቅጽለ፡ ዕፀው፡ ውስተ፡ ፍኖት፡
___

C. John 1:1–5: Translate the following:

¹ቀዳሚሁ፡ ቃል፡ ውእቱ፡ ወውእቱ፡ ቃል፡ ኀበ፡ እግዚአብሔር፡ ውእቱ፡ ወእግዚአብሔር፡ ውእቱ፡ ቃል፡።

²ወዝንቱ፡ እምቀዲሙ፡ ኀበ፡ እግዚአብሔር፡ ውእቱ።

³ወኵሉ፡ ቦቱ፡ ኮነ፡ ወዘአንበሌሁሰ፡ አልቦ፡ ዘኮነ፡ ወኢምንትኒ፡ እምዘኮነ።

⁴ወዘሂ፡ ኮነ፡ በአንቲአሁ፡ ቦቱ፡ ሕይወት፡ ውእቱ፡ ወሕይወትሰ፡ ብርሃኑ፡ ለእጓለ፡ እመሕያው፡ ውእቱ።

⁵ወብርሃንሰ፡ ዘውስተ፡ ጽልመት፡ ያበርህ፡ ወያርኢ፡ ወጽልመትኒ፡ ኢይረክቦ፡ ወኢይቀርቦ።

Chapter 6

PREPOSITIONS

6.1 Role of Prepositions

A preposition links nouns, pronouns, and phrases to other words in a sentence while describing the relationship between these words. The word or phrase that the preposition introduces is called the object of the preposition. Prepositional phrases can function adjectively when it is modifying a noun or pronoun: "the man on the plane." A preposition usually indicates the temporal, spatial, or logical relationship of its object to the rest of the sentence as in the following examples:

- The book is *on* the table.
- The book is *in* the drawer.
- She held the book *over* the desk.
- She read the book *during* study hall.

In each of the preceding sentences, the preposition locates the noun "book" in space or in time.

A prepositional phrase is made up of the preposition, its object, and any associated adjectives or adverbs. A prepositional phrase can function as a noun, an adjective, or an adverb.

6.2 Identifying Prepositions

Most prepositions appear as separate words preceding the noun they govern.

ውስተ፡ ቤት፡ – "in/into/to the (a) house"
ዲበ፡ ደብር፡ – "on the (a) mountain"

Gəʿəz also includes inseparable prepositions much like biblical Hebrew or Aramaic. These prepositions are written in conjunction with the following word that it is governing.

በ – "in, with" – in reference to location, agent, or manner
ለ – "to, for" – in reference to the dative case
እም – "from" – instrument of action or the source of action

31

For example:

በቤት፡ – "in the/a house"
ለንጉሥ፡ – "for the/a king"
እምሀገር፡ – "from the/a city"

In addition, the preposition እም has an independent long version እምነ፡

እምነ፡ ሀገር፡ – "from the city"

TABLE 6.1: Prepositions

በ	in	በእንተ፡	in regard to
ለ	to, toward	ህየንተ፡	instead of
እምነ፡	from, out of	እንበለ፡ and ዘእንበለ፡	without, except
ኀበ፡	with, toward	መቅድመ፡	before, in preference to
እስከ፡	till, as far as, up to	ማዕዶተ፡	beyond, along
መትሕተ፡	underneath	ከመ፡	as, like
ዐውደ፡	about, around	ውስተ፡	in, into
እንተ፡	In the direction of	ላዕለ፡	upon, over, above
መልዕልተ፡	above, over, upon	ተክሰ፡	in place of
ዲበ፡	upon, above, over	ተውላጠ፡	for, in exchange for
መንገለ፡	toward, to	መንጸረ፡ and አንጸረ፡	over against
ምስለ፡	with, in the likeness of	ደኀረ፡	after, behind
ቀደመ፡	before	ማእከለ፡	in the midst of, between
መቅድመ፡	beyond, along	ታሕተ፡	below, under
ጠቃ፡ and ጥቃ፡	close to	አምላለ፡	like
ዉእደ፡	along	መጠነ፡ and አምጣነ፡	of the size of
ከወላ፡	behind	በዕብሬት፡	for the sake of
አፍአ፡	outside of	አመ፡	at the time of

6.3 Prepositions with Pronominal Suffixes

As we learned in chapter 4, pronominal suffixes are added to nouns, verbs, and in this case prepositions. As a point of grammar, a pronominal suffix resembles a pronoun, by specifying a person, place, or thing, while functioning primarily as another part of speech. The word *his* in the phrase *his choice* is a pronominal adjective. The following table identifies the various forms of the pronominal suffix with the prepositions እምነ፡, ዲበ፡, and ታሕተ፡.

TABLE 6.2: Prepositions and Pronominal Suffixes

P/G/N	Pronominal suffix	Preposition እምነ፡	Preposition ዲበ፡	Preposition ታሕተ
1 cs	የ	እምኔየ፡	ዲቤየ፡	ታሕቴየ፡
2 ms	ከ	እምኔከ፡	ዲቤከ፡	ታሕቴከ፡
2 fs	ኪ.	እምኔኪ፡	ዲቤኪ፡	ታሕቴኪ፡
3 ms	-u	እምኔሁ፡	ዲቤሁ፡	ታሕቴሁ፡
3 fs	-ā	እምኔሃ፡	ዲቤሃ፡	ታሕቴሃ፡
1 cp	ነ	እምኔነ፡	ዲቤነ፡	ታሕቴነ፡
2 mp	ከሙ	እምኔክሙ፡	ዲቤክሙ፡	ታሕቴክሙ፡
2 fp	ክን	እምኔክን፡	ዲቤክን፡	ታሕቴክን፡
3 mp	-o+ሙ	እምኔሆሙ፡	ዲቤሆሙ፡	ታሕቴሆሙ፡
3 fp	-o+ን	እምኔሆን፡	ዲቤሆን፡	ታሕቴሆን፡

Several other prepositions follow this pattern with a long *ē* as the "connecting vowel": ኀበ፡, ምስለ፡, ቅድመ፡, ማእከለ፡, መንገለ፡, ድኅረ፡, ላዕለ፡. It should be noted that on occasion these prepositions can occur without the long *ē* connecting vowel. This is the case with the word ማእከለ፡ – "in the midst of" with the third-person suffixes (e.g., በማእከሎሙ፡ – "in their midst" or "in the midst of them"). Three other prepositions follow their own peculiar pattern of formation; the student should attempt to memorize these forms:

a. ውስተ፡ ውስቴትየ፡ ውስቴትከ፡ ውስቴትኪ፡ ውስቴቱ፡ ውስቴታ፡ ውስቴትነ፡ ውስቴትክሙ፡ ውስቴትክን፡ ውስቴቶሙ፡ ውስቴቶን፡ (built on a singular noun ending in a consonant).

b. በእንተ፡ በእንቲአየ፡ በእንቲአከ፡ በእንቲአኪ፡ በእንቲአሁ፡ በእንቲአሃ፡ በእንቲአነ፡ በእንቲአክሙ፡ በእንቲአክን፡ በእንቲአሆሙ፡ በእንቲአሆን፡ (built on the stem በእንቲአ-, *bă'entiă-*).

c. ከመ፡ ከማየ፡ ከማከ፡ ከማኪ፡ ከማሁ፡ ከማሃ፡ ከማነ፡ ከማክሙ፡ ከማክን፡ ከማሆሙ፡ ከማሆን፡ (built on a singular noun ending in a vowel).

TABLE 6.3: Preposition ለ and Preposition በ with Prenominal Suffixes

P/G/N	Preposition ለ	Definition	Preposition በ	Definition
1 cs	ሊተ፡	To me	ብየ፡	by, with, in me
2 ms	ለከ፡	To you	ብከ፡	by, with, in you
2 fs	ለኪ፡	To you	ብኪ፡	by, with, in you
3 ms	ሎቱ፡	To him	ቦ፡ ቦቱ፡	by, with, in him
3 fs	ላቲ፡	To her	ባ፡ ባቲ፡	by, with, in her
1 cp	ለነ፡	To us	ብነ፡	by, with, in us

(continued)

P/G/N	Preposition ለ	Definition	Preposition በ	Definition
2 mp	ለክሙ፡	To you	ብክሙ፡	by, with, in you
2 fp	ለክን፡	To you	ብክን፡	by, with, in you
3 mp	ሎሙ፡	To you	ቦሙ፡	by, with, in them
3 fp	ሎን፡	To you	ቦን፡ ቦንቱ፡ ቦቶን፡	by, with, in them

6.4 Indicator of Possession

The preposition በ can also indicate possession or lack of possession. The object of possession generally appears in the accusative case like a direct object. The preposition is generally translated with the verb "have" with the relevant pronoun:

ብየ፡ ወርቀ፡ – "I have gold [lit. there is in me gold]"
ቦሙ፡ ኅብስተ፡ – "They have bread"
ብክሙ፡ ሃይማኖተ፡ – "You have faith"

If a noun appears in the sentence as the possessor of an item or items, then it must be used in apposition with the third-person suffix of the preposition:

ብእሲ፡ ቦቱ፡ ክልኤ፡ ውሉደ፡ – "a man has / had two sons [lit. there is in the man two sons]"
ብእሲት፡ ቦቲ፡ ክልኤተ፡ አምታተ፡ – "the woman has / had two husbands"

The lack of possession is shown with the addition of the prefix of negation አል፡

አልብየ፡ አልብከ፡ አልብኪ፡ አልቦ፡ አልቦቱ፡ – "I don't have"; "you (ms) don't have"; "you (fs) don't have"; "there is no"; "he doesn't have"
አልብነ፡ ማየ፡ – "we have no water (lit. there is no water with us)"
አልብክሙ፡ ሃይማኖተ፡ – "you have no faith"

The tense for the possession clause (have/had) can only be determined by the context of the passage.

6.5 Indicator of Existence

The third-person singular (f. or m.) ቦ፡ or ቦቱ፡ can indicate existence of something. It can also indicate the non-existence of an item with the addition of the negation አል፡, as in አልቦ፡ አልቦቱ፡

ቦ፡ ኅብስት(ተ)፡ – "there is bread"
አልቦ፡ ማይ፡/ማየ፡ – "there is no water"

34 Basics of Ancient Ethiopic

The በ፡, *bo* of existence or the አል of nonexistence plus the relative pronoun ዘ-, *ză* indicates an indefinite pronoun (this can also occur rarely with the plural form እለ፡). The combination of በ፡ ዘ- can be translated as "someone, something, no one, or nothing."

እመ፡ቦ፡ ዘኅደገ፡ ብእሲቶ፡ – "if someone divorces his wife"
አልቦ፡ ዘረከበ፡ ህየ፡ – "he found no one/nothing there"
አልቦ፡ ዘበልዑ፡ – "none of them ate"

The preposition/conjunction እንበለ፡ or ዘእንበለ፡ with አልቦ፡ indicates "only."

አልብነ፡ ዝየ፡ ዘእንበለ፡ ኅምስ፡ ኅብስት፡ – "We only have these five loaves"; ኅምስ፡ ኅብስት፡ could also be translated as an accusative – "we have but these five loaves"
አልቦ፡ ዘርእየ፡ ዘእንበለ፡ ብእሲቱ፡ "He saw only his wife"

6.6 Vocabulary

1. ኵሎ፡ ዕልተ፡ – (f./m.) every day, all day
2. መዓልት፡ – (m./f.) day
3. መዓልተ፡ – during the day
4. መዋዕል፡ – days
5. አሚር፡ – (m./f.) day, used only in certain fixed expressions ውእቱ፡/ይእተ፡ አሚረ፡ – (on that day)
6. ቀርበ፡ – to draw near, approach (ኀበ፡ ውስተ፡ ለ-)
7. ኀለፈ፡ – pass by
8. በከየ፡ – weep, mourn
9. ማእከለ፡ – among, in the midst of
10. እማእከለ፡ – from among
11. እስከ፡ – until, up to, as far as
12. ላዕለ፡ – on, upon, down onto, over, above, about, concerning
13. ቅድመ፡ – before (spatial); in the presence of; በቅድመ፡ – (adverb: previously, beforehand)
14. እኁ፡ (pl. አኀው፡) – brother
15. እኅት፡ (pl. አኃት፡) – sister
16. ብሔር፡ (pl. ቢሓውርት፡) – region, province, district
17. ምድር፡ ጽባሕ፡ – eastern region
18. ወንጌል፡ – gospel
19. ሞት፡ – death
20. ሰከበ፡ – lay, lay down
21. ሞተ፡ – die
22. ሰበከ፡ – preach
23. ሐዘነ፡ – be/become sad
24. እምዝ፡ – then, next, thereupon
25. ወይን – wine, vine, grapes
26. ድኅረ፡ – behind, in back of

6.7 Exercises

A. Translate the following:

1. በእንተ፡ አኃትየ፡

2. ዲበ፡ ዝንቱ፡ ወይን፡
_____

3. ዲበ፡ ወንጌልነ፡
_____

4. በማእከለ፡ አዕጻዳቲሁ፡
_____

5. ምስለ፡ አጎዊሁ፡
_____

6. እምነ፡ አዋልዲሃ፡
_____

7. እምነ፡ አምዳሪሆሙ፡
_____

8. ድኅረ፡ ምታ፡
_____

9. በእንተ፡ ሞቶሙ፡,
_____

10. ውስተ፡ ብሔረ፡ ጽባሕ፡
_____

11. ውስተ፡ በሓውርቲሆሙ፡
_____

12. እስከ፡ ውእቱ፡ ሴሊት፡
_____

13. እስከ፡ ዛቲ፡ ዕለት፡
_____

14. እስከ፡ ውእቱ፡ ምሴት፡
_____

B. Translate the following:

1. ገብረ፡ ዘንተ፡ ኵሎ፡ በእንቲአከሙ።

2. ሐነጹ፡ ዛኵላ፡ ሀገረ።

3. ገብኡ፡ ኵሎን፡ ውስተ፡ አብያቲሆን።

4. መጽኡ፡ ኵሎሙ፡ አሕዛብ፡ ኀቤሁ።

5. መጽኡ፡ እምኵሉ፡ በሐውርተ፡ ምድር።

6. መጽአ፡ ኀቤየ፡ ኵሎ፡ አሚረ።

7. ርእየ፡ ኵሎ፡ ሰማየ፡ በቅድሜሁ።

8. ረከቡ፡ ኵላ፡ አሕማሪሆሙ።

9. ሣጠ፡ ኀቤነ፡ ኵሎ፡ አዕጻዱሁ።

10. ነብሩ፡ ህየ፡ ኵሎ፡ ሌሊተ።

C. Translate the following:

1. ሐመረ፡ አቡየ።

2. ነገሥተ፡ አምዳሪሆሙ።

3. ነገረ፡ መላእክቲሁ፡

_____

4. ሊቃነ፡ ሕዝብነ፡

_____

5. ዝናማተ፡ ብሔሩ፡

_____

6. ቤተ፡ እኁየ፡

_____

7. ቃላተ፡ እምየ፡

_____

8. በሐውርተ፡ ምድሮሙ፡

_____

9. ሞተ፡ እኅትየ፡

_____

10. አራዊተ፡ ምድር፡

_____

11. አምታተ፡ አዋልዲሃ፡

_____

12. አግብርተ፡ ቤትነ፡

_____

13. አህጉረ፡ ምድርክሙ፡

_____

14. ቃላተ፡ ነቢያቲሆሙ፡

_____

15. አምዳረ፡ ጽባሕ፡

_____

Chapter 7

INTRODUCTION TO ETHIOPIC VERBS

7.1 Introduction

Gəʿəz exhibits three basic lexical types of verbs related to the main triliteral consonantal root system (three main root consonants). These lexical types are designated as G, D, and L according to the stem forms of the perfect verb. The G verb (Heb. *qal*) is the three-letter *simple root* in the stem vowel pattern–$C_1 ăC_2 ăC_3 ă$, e.g., ነበረ፡ – "he sat." The D verb (Heb. *piel*) is the three-letter root with the *doubling* of the second consonant (radical) plus the stem vowel pattern–$C_1 ăC_2 C2 ăC_3 ă$,[1] e.g., ነጸረ፡ – "he looked." The L verb (no Heb. equivalent) is the three-letter root plus the *lengthening* of the first stem vowel and the remaining stem vowel pattern–$C_1 āC_2 ăC_3 ă$, e.g., ባረከ፡ – "he blessed."

The designation G is for the German *Grundstamm* (basic stem). For any given three-letter root, only one of the above forms is usually in use.[2] However, quite a number of verbs may appear as either a G or D with no difference in meaning.

Gəʿəz verbs go through three stages or steps in forming what we see in the text. The three consonant root is formed in the verb by way of a particular vowel pronunciation, whereas nouns are formed by another vowel pronunciation. For example, the root ተክለ፡, *tkl* is identified as a verb when it is pronounced ተክለ፡ – "he planted" and the noun is pronounced ተክል፡ – "plant." The root must (1) be formed into its stem and then (2) it takes on its tense and mood and (3) it is given its person, gender, and number. The G stem has three other main derived stems from the *Grundstamm*, or "basic stem": the causative, designated C (CG, CD, CL, etc.), the reflexive, designated Gt, Dt, Lt, etc., and the causative-reflexive, designated CGt, CDt, etc. Like Hebrew, each of these has a simple action and an intensive action (often recognized by the doubling of a consonant in the root – አርሰሐሰሐ፡ – "utterly reproach again and again"–and, in addition, there is also a passive form.

---

1. Keep in mind the doubling of the radical in Gəʿəz is not marked in any way, unlike the *dagesh forte* in Hebrew, and only appears in the transliteration and not in the Gəʿəz script.
2. It should be noted here that Gəʿəz also exhibits quadriliteral (4) and quinquiliteral (5) consonant roots. These will be discussed in later chapters.

7.2 Quadriliteral Root Forms

Verbs formed from a quadriliteral root exhibit the consonant pattern of $C_1 \breve{a} C_2 C_3 \breve{a} C_4$-in the perfect of the basic stem, designated Q (see further ch. 37). The Q verb is formed with the simple root and the stem vowel pattern (see above, e.g., ተርጎመ፡ – "he translated"). When the second consonant of the quadriliteral root is a ወ, the ă vowel and the ወ contract to an o vowel, e.g., ሞቅሐ፡ – "he put in chains" from መወ·ቀሐ፡. Similarly, when the second consonant of the root is a ይ, the ă vowel and the ይ contract to an ē, e.g., ዴገነ፡ – "he pursued" from ደይገነ፡. Because of the long initial stem vowel, these verb types follow a similar inflection pattern as the L verbs discussed above.

7.3 G Verbs

G verbs appear the most often in Gəʿəz and have the largest array of inflection. There are two major types of G verbs based upon the perfect stem. As mentioned above, the first type follows the pattern of $C_1 \breve{a} C_2 \breve{a} C_3 \breve{a}$, e.g., ነበረ፡ – "he sat". The second type follows the pattern of $C_1 \breve{a} C_2 C_3 \breve{a}$ (no vowel between C_2 and C_3) which is represented by the verb ገብረ፡ – "he made." This distinction is only made in the third-person forms of the perfect.

7.4 Inflection of the Perfect Verb

The perfect suffixes are identical for all types of verbs (G, D, L, Q). These forms are what we would refer to as "strong" verbs in Hebrew. Any deviation of the form is due to the differences in the type of verb (ነበረ፡ versus ገብረ፡) or because of phonetic changes brought on by the presence of a guttural (አ ዐ ህ ሕ ኀ) in the root or the "vowel consonants" ወ and ይ. In addition, verbs whose first consonant is a guttural or "vowel consonant" conform to the regular pattern in the table below.

TABLE 7.1: Full Inflection of the Perfect Verb

P/G/N	G Verb	G Verb	D Verb	L Verb	Q Verb
3 ms	ነበረ፡	ገብረ፡	ነገረ፡	ባረከ፡	ተርጎመ፡
3 fs	ነበረት፡	ገብረት፡	ነገረት፡	ባረከት፡	ተርጎመት፡
2 ms	ነበርከ፡	ገበርከ፡	ነገርከ፡	ባረከ፡	ተርጎምከ፡
2 fs	ነበርኪ፡	ገበርኪ፡	ነገርኪ፡	ባረኪ፡	ተርጎምኪ፡
1 cs	ነበርኩ፡	ገበርኩ፡	ነገርኩ፡	ባረኩ፡	ተርጎምኩ፡
P/G/N	G Verb	G Verb	D Verb	L Verb	Q Verb
3 mp	ነበሩ፡	ገብሩ፡	ነገሩ፡	ባረኩ፡	ተርጎሙ፡
3 fp	ነበራ፡	ገብራ፡	ነገራ፡	ባረካ፡	ተርጎማ፡
2 mp	ነበርክሙ፡	ገበርክሙ፡	ነገርክሙ፡	ባረክሙ፡	ተርጎምክሙ፡
2 fp	ነበርክን፡	ገበርክን፡	ነገርክን፡	ባረክን፡	ተርጎምክን፡
1 cp	ነበርነ፡	ገበርነ፡	ነገርነ፡	ባረክነ፡	ተርጎምነ፡

7.5 The D stem

The D stem in Gəʿəz requires some special note; it has been referred to as the "intensive stem" in which the action of the verb is intensified by either frequent repetition or the eagerness of the one doing the action. It is identified by the doubling of the middle radical, or at times multiple radicals in the root, although the doubling of the middle radical is not seen in the Gəʿəz script, e.g., ነጸረ፡ – "he looked," and appears only in transliteration, năṣṣără. However, the doubling of multiple radicals of the root can been seen in the script, e.g., ነጠብጠብ፡ – "it dripped" from the root ነጠብ፡ – "it dropped." In addition, the D verb can express actions that continue on for some time, e.g., ሐለወ፡ – "he watched," ሐለየ፡ – "he turned over in his mind," and ኍለቈ፡ – "he numbered." Most of the D verbs carry the notion of an act that is performed carefully or with some zeal. The CD derived form of the D verb often translates in a similar fashion to the D verb but often in the sense of making or doing something, e.g., ሠነየ – "he was beautiful, was good," but አሠነየ፡ – "he beautified, he did good," ፈጸመ፡ – "he completed," but አፈጸመ፡ – "he rendered perfect," and ሐዘነ፡ – "he was deeply sad," but አሐዘነ፡ – "he inspired compassion." The D stem is also used to form denominatives which signify the bringing about of something or busying oneself with something. These verbs can often be formed from numerals, e.g., ሠለሰ፡ – "he did something a third time," ረብዐ፡ – "he formed four," and ዐሠረ፡ – "he gave a tithe."

7.6 Special Considerations

If the final consonant of the root is either a ቀ or ገ, the ከ of the personal endings is assimilated into the ቀ or ገ resulting in a doubling of the consonant. This doubling is only seen in the transliteration as it is not represented in the Ethiopic script. The word ዐረጉ፡ – "I went up," evolves from ዐረግኩ፡. Also, the word ወድቅኩ፡ – "I fell," shifts with the assimilation of the ከ to ወደቁ፡. The difficulty with this shift is that this form will look identical to that of the third-person plural forms. A comparable issue occurs with the words in which the final stem consonant is a ከ or a ኀ.

7.7 Vocabulary

1. ሕግ፡ (pl. ሕገግ፡) – law; በሕግ፡ – legally or lawfully
2. መጽሐፍ፡ (pl. መጻሕፍት፡) – book, document, writing, inscription
3. ልሳን፡ (pl. ልሳናት፡) – tongue or language; ልሳነ፡ ዮናናዊያን፡ – Greek; ልሳነ፡ ዕብራይስጥ፡ – Hebrew
4. በድን፡ (pl. አብድንት፡) – corpse
5. ነጸረ፡ – look or look at
6. ባረከ፡ – bless
7. ተርጐመ፡ – translate
8. አውያነ፡ – one who makes wine
9. ዐቀበ፡ – guard, keep watch on, take care of, observe or to keep (the law)
10. ቀበረ፡ – bury
11. ዐጸድ፡ – palace, enclosure, pen

12. ዐረቢ፡ – western
13. ዴገነ፡ – pursue or to chase

7.8 Exercises

A. Complete the following parsing chart:

Verb	Person	Gender	Number	Tense	Stem (G, D, L, Q)	Meaning
ነበርኩ፡						
ወረድኩ፡						
ረከብኩ፡						
ባረኩ፡						
ተከልኩ፡						
ቀረብነ፡						
ተርጐምኩ፡						

B. Translate the following:

1. ወደቁ፡ ዲበ፡ ምድር፡ ወሰከብኩ፡ ህየ፨

   _____

2. ተከልኩ፡ አውያነ፡ በውስተ፡ ዐጸድየ፨

   _____

3. ኢቀተልኩ፡ እሎንተ፡ ስብአ፨

   _____

4. ዐረጉ፡ አድባረ፡ በጽባሕ፨

   _____

5. ረከብኩ፡ በድነ፡ በውስተ፡ ፍኖት፨

   _____

6. ነበርኩ፡ ህየ፡ እስከ፡ ውእቱ፡ አሚር፨

   _____

7. ዐቀብኩ፡ ሕገጌሁ፡ መዓልተ፡ ወሌሊተ፨

   _____

42 Basics of Ancient Ethiopic

8. ወረድኩ፡ ውስተ፡ ሐይቅ፡ በምሴት።
   _____

9. ሐነጽኩ፡ ዘንተ፡ ቤተ፡ ለውሉድየ።
   _____

10. ባረኩ፡ ሕዝበ፡ ወእምዝ፡ ኃለፍኩ፡ እምነቤሆሙ።
    _____

C. Translate the following:

1. ኃለፍነ፡ እማእከሎሙ፡ እምድኅረ፡ ሞቱ፡ ለንጉሥሙ።
   _____

2. ሰከብነ፡ ህየ፡ እስከ፡ ጽባሑ።
   _____

3. ሐዘነ፡ ዲበ፡ ቃላቲሁ፡ ለመልአከ።
   _____

4. ነጸርነ፡ ኃበ፡ ሰማያት።
   _____

5. ገበርነ፡ ዘንተ፡ ኩሎ፡ በእንቲአክሙ።
   _____

6. ቀበርነ፡ በድኖ፡ ለአቡነ፡ ህየ።
   _____

7. ሰበክነ፡ ኩልነ፡ ውስተ፡ ኩሉ፡ በሐውርተ፡ ዛቲ፡ ምድር።
   _____

8. ዴገነ፡ ድኃሬሆሙ፡ ለደቂቅ፡ ሐይቀ።
   _____

9. ቀረብነ፡ ኃቤሆሙ።
   _____

10. ተርጐምነ፡ ዘንተ፡ መጻሕፍተ፡ እምልሳነ፡ ዐረቢ።
    _____

D. Translate the following:

1. በእንተ፡ ምንት፡ ኢዐቀብክሙ፡ ሕገግየ።

2. ተርጎመ፡ ዘንተ፡ መጻሕፍተ፡ እምልሳነ፡ ዮናናዊያን፡ ለልሳነ፡ ግዕዝ።

3. አይቴ፡ ቀበርክሙ፡ በድኖ፡ ለእኁክሙ።

4. አይቴ፡ ሰበከ፡ ወንጌሎ።

5. መነ፡ ባረከ፡ ወመነ፡ ኢባረከ።

6. ዘንተ፡ ገበርከ፡ በሕግ።

7. ተርጎምኩ፡ እሎ፡ ኩሎ፡ መጻሕፍተ፡ እምልሳነ፡ ዮናናዊያን።

8. ኀበ፡ አይ፡ ሀገር፡ ቀረብክሙ፡ ይእተ፡ ዕለተ።

9. በእንተ፡ ምንት፡ ሐዘንክሙ፡ ኩልክሙ።

10. ገብረ፡ ኩሎ፡ ሕገገ፡ እግዚአብሔር፡ እስከ፡ ዕለተ፡ ሞቱ።

Chapter 8

ADJECTIVES (PART 1)

8.1 Introduction

Adjectives are words that describe or modify a person or thing in the sentence. Gəʿəz has two principal types of adjectives: 1) those which derived from verbs (verbal adjectives), and 2) those which originated from nouns with the addition of the suffixes -ā+ዊ or -ā+ይ. The second type occurs rarely; we will discuss this later in the chapter. The first type, the verbal adjective, is closely associated with stative G verbs and some stative D verbs. These are the most common adjectives in Gəʿəz and are inflected for number, gender, and the addition of endings. There are four phonetic categories for these nouns: ቅቱል፡, ቀቲል፡, ቃትል፡, and ቀታል፡. Examples of each include 1) (ቅቱል፡) ክቡር፡ – "glorious or mighty" (from the verb ክብረ፡); 2) (ቀቲል፡) ጠቢብ፡ – "wise or prudent" (from the verb ጠበበ፡); 3) (ቃትል፡) ጻድቅ፡ – "righteous" (from the verb ጸድቀ፡); and 4) (ቀታል፡) ነዳይ፡ – "poor, indigent" (from the verb ነድየ፡). The most common of the four forms is the ቅቱል፡ but the inflection endings on ቃትል፡ are more easily recognized. This is a small group of adjectives, but it does include the ordinal numbers (e.g., ሣልስ፡ – "third") along with other frequently occurring adjectives (e.g., ባዕል፡ – "rich" and ኃጥእ፡ – "sinful"). The following table shows the inflection of this form of adjective for gender and number:

TABLE 8.1: Adjective inflection of the word ጻድቅ፡ "righteous"

Gender	Singular	Plural
Masculine	ጻድቅ፡	ጻድቃን፡
Feminine	ጻድቅት፡	ጻድቃት፡

If a stem ends in a ት፡ ድ፡ or ጥ፡ the ት፡ of the feminine singular ending is assimilated and does not appear in the Gəʿəz script. See for example: ባዕድ፡ – "other", fem. sing. form ባዕድ፡ from ባዕድት፡. Unlike the *dagesh forte* in Hebrew, there is no marker in Gəʿəz that indicates the assimilation of another consonant, so the reader must rely on context.

8.2 Attributive Adjectives

Attributive adjectives usually follow the noun they are modifying. Like Hebrew, they generally agree with the noun in gender and number if it is a personal noun. However, if the noun is impersonal then the position of the adjective and its agreement in gender and number can vary as in the following examples:

TABLE 8.2: Attributive Adjectives

Gender	Number	Ethiopic	Translation
Masculine	Singular	ንጉሥ፡ ጻድቅ፡፡	righteous king*
Masculine	Plural	ነገሥት፡ ጻድቃን፡፡	righteous kings
Feminine	Singular	ንግሥት፡ ጻድቅት፡፡	righteous queen
Feminine	Plural	ንግሥታት፡ ጻድቃት፡፡	righteous queens
Impersonal	-	ሀገር፡ ባዕድ፡፡	different city
Impersonal	-	አህጉር፡ ባዕዳን፡ / ባዕዳት፡፡	different cities

*Remember, these can be read as definite or indefinite phrases.

Adjectives also agree in case with the noun they are modifying:

ረከበ፡ ካልእተ፡ ፍኖተ፡፡ – "He found another road" (in this case accusative)

ጐዩ፡ ሀገረ፡ ባእደ፡፡ – "They fled to a different city."

If a descriptive adjective precedes the noun it is modifying, then it is usually there for emphasis. Other adjectives also precede the noun but are *not* emphatic in nature. These include demonstrative adjectives, cardinal and ordinal numbers, the term ኵል- – "each, every, all" and quantifying adjectives such as ዐቢይ፡ – "large" and ብዙኅ፡ – "many or much."

8.3 Demonstrative Adjectives

Demonstrative Adjectives normally precede the noun they are modifying. The adjectives ዝ and ዛ are written proclitically, e.g., ዝቤት፡ – "this house" and ዛሀገር፡ – "this city").

TABLE 8.3: Demonstrative Adjectives

Demonstrative Adjective	Masculine	Feminine
This	ዝ-, ዝንቱ፡	ዛ-, ዛቲ፡
That	ውእቱ፡	ይእቲ፡
These	እሉ-, እሎንቱ፡	እላ-, እላንቱ፡
Those	እሙንቱ፡	እማንቱ፡

If the demonstrative adjective is preceded by another possible proclitic like እም- then the እም- combines with the ዝ፡ to make one-word እምዝ፡ e.g., እምዝ፡ ቤት፡፡ – "from this house"

8.4 Adjectives in the *Qətul* Pattern

Adjectives formed in the *Qətul* pattern are the most common adjective pattern in Gəʿəz. Along with the related patterns formed from D verbs and L verbs, the G pattern has some changes when inflected. When the feminine ending ት is added, the *u* vowel of the final stem syllable of the masculine form shifts to an *ə*. For example, the masculine adjective ክቡር፡ – "mighty, glorious" shifts to ክብርት፡ in the feminine. Other examples include the masculine ቅዱስ፡, which shifts to ቀደስት፡ in the feminine – "holy," and the masculine ቡሩክ፡, which shifts to ቡርክት፡ in the feminine – "blessed."

When the masculine form ends in *-u+ይ*, the expected shift to *-ə+ይት* usually reduces to *-i+ት*. For example, the masculine adjective ኅሩይ፡ – "chosen, elect" shifts to ኅሪት፡ in the feminine. Other examples include the masculine ብሉይ፡ – "old, worn out" which shifts to ብሊት፡ in the feminine; the masculine እኩይ፡ – "bad, evil" shifts to እኪት፡ in the feminine.

When the second root consonant of the adjective is ወ, the ቅቱል፡ (*qətul*) pattern can at times be replaced with the ቅትል፡ (*qətəl*) pattern. When this occurs, the feminine form of the adjective appears, in some cases, like the masculine form in the Gəʿəz script. The masculine form ምዉት፡ / ሙት፡ – "dead" appears in the feminine form as ሙት[ት]፡. The masculine adjective ድዉይ፡ / ድውይ፡ – "ill, sick" shifts to ድውይት፡ in the feminine.

A similar shift happens when the third consonant is ወ. Words with the ending *-ə+ው* rather than *-u+ው*, are more consistent when it comes to this particular shift. The masculine adjective ዐልው፡ – "perverse, wicked" shifts to ዐሉት፡ in the feminine (with the ወ dropping out and the vowel on the ል shifting to ሉ).

The feminine plural of these adjectives is likely based on the masculine singular form, e.g., ክቡር፡ » fp ክቡራት፡ / ብሉይ፡ » fp ብሉያት፡ / ድውይ፡ » fp ድውያት፡. However, on occasion they do form off the feminine singular form that you would normally expect. Adjectives that end in a "dental" consonant – ድ፡ *d*, ት፡ *t* ጠ፡ *ṭ*, etc., appear not to take the feminine ት ending, but this is again a case of assimilation that does not appear in the Gəʿəz script. The masculine adjective ክቡድ፡ – "heavy" shifts to ክቢድ፡ in the feminine. The masculine adjective ሥጡጥ፡ – "torn" shifts to ሥጥጥ፡ in the feminine.

8.5   Adjectives as Predicates

Adjectives can appear in a predicate clause following two basic patterns. The first is described as the "pronoun subject" clause–the initial adjective (pred.) followed by the pronoun (subj.). The second is described as the "noun subject" clause–the initial adjective (pred.) followed by a possible third-person demonstrative pronoun (acting as the "to be" verb) followed by a noun (subj.).

Examples:

> ድውይ፡ አነ፡ – "I am ill."
> ጻድቃን፡ ንሕነ፡ – "We are righteous."
> እኩይ፡ ውእቱ፡ – "He is evil."
> እኩይ፡ ውእቱ፡ ምኩንን፡ – "The judge is evil."
> ቅድስት፡ ይእቲ፡ ሀገር፡ – "The city is holy."
> ጻድቃን፡ እሙንቱ፡ ነገሥት፡ – "The kings are just."
> ራትዓን፡ ነቢያት፡ – "The prophets are righteous."

The predicate adjective agrees in gender and number to the same extent as the attributive adjective. The predicate adjective clause is negated with the ኢ, hence ኢድውይ፡ አነ፡ "I am not ill."

8.6 Vocabulary

1. መኰንን፡ (pl. መኳንንት፡) – judge, high official
2. ቃል፡ (pl. ቃላት፡) – voice, word, sound
3. ነገር፡ (pl. ነገራት፡) – speech, account, thing
4. መልአክ፡ (pl. መላእክት፡) – angel, messenger
5. ጸሐፊ፡ (pl. ጸሐፍት፡) – scribe
6. ወልድ፡ (pl. ውሉድ፡) – son, child, boy
7. ወለት፡ (pl. አዋልድ፡) – daughter, girl
8. ሐይቅ፡ (pl. ሐይቃት፡) – seashore
9. ዕድ፡ (pl. ዕደው፡) – community of men
10. እም፡ (pl. እማት፡) – mother
11. አብ፡ (pl. አበው፡) – father
12. ምት፡ (pl. አምታት፡) – husband
13. ደቂቅ፡ – children, offspring
14. ንግሥት፡ (pl. ንግሥታት፡) – queen
15. አላ፡ – but
16. ዮሐንስ፡ – John
17. እግዚአብሔር፡ – God
18. አምላክ፡ – Lord
19. እስራኤል፡ – Israel
20. ስም፡ (pl. አስማት፡) – name, fame, reputation
21. ንዋይ፡ (pl. ንዋያት፡) – vessel, instrument
22. ሐዋርያ፡ (pl. ሐዋርያት፡) – apostle
23. ረድእ፡ (pl. አርዳእ አርድእት፡) – helper, disciple
24. ካልእ፡ (f. ካልእት፡) – other, another, associate
25. ባዕድ፡ (f. ባዕድ፡ pl. ባዕዳን፡) – other, different, alien
26. ኃጥእ፡ (f. ኃጥእት፡) – sinful, wicked; sinner (noun)
27. ራትዕ፡ (f. ራትዕት፡) – just, righteous
28. ረትዐ፡ – be righteous
29. ባዕል፡ (f. ባዕልት፡) – rich, wealthy
30. ብዕለ፡ – be rich
31. ጻድቅ፡ (f. ጻድቅት፡ pl. ጻድቃን፡) – righteous, just, true, faithful
32. ጸድቀ፡ – be righteous, faithful, true
33.ሰመየ፡ – name (something, someone)
34. መንፈስ፡ (pl. መንፈሳት፡) – spirit of various kinds
35. መንፈስ፡ ቅዱስ፡ – Holy Spirit
36. ልብስ፡ (pl. አልባስ፡) – clothing, garment
37. ወሬዛ፡ (pl. ወራዙት፡) – youth, young man
38. ትእምርት፡ – miracle
39. ዕልው፡ – evil
40. ምዉት፡ (pl. ምዉታን፡) – dead
41. ብሉይ፡ – old, worn out
42. ብዙኅ፡ – many, much
43. እኩይ፡ – evil, wicked
44. ሕዙን፡ – sad

8.7 Exercises

A. Translate the following:

1. ረድእ፡ ራትዕ፡

2. ነቢያት፡ ጻድቃን፡

3. ካልእ፡ ዕፅ፡

4. ካልእ፡ ንዋይ።
_____

5. ካልእ፡ ዐጸደ፡ ወይን።
_____

6. ብእሲት፡ ባዕልት።
_____

7. ውሉድ፡ ጻድቃን።
_____

8. ጸሐፍት፡ ኃጥኣን።
_____

9. መኰንን፡ ባዕል።
_____

10. ሊቃን፡ አበዐልት።
_____

11. ካልእት፡ ሐመር።
_____

12. ካልአን፡ ነቢያት።
_____

13. ነቢይ፡ ጻድቅ።
_____

14. ካልእት፡ ፍኖት።
_____

15. አዋልድ፡ ራትዓት።
_____

16. ሕዝብ፡ ኃጥኣን።
_____

17. አርዳእ፡ ጻድቃን።
_____

Adjectives (Part 1)

18. በሐውርት፡ ባዕድ።
___

19. ሐዋርያት፡ ራትዓን።
___

20. ነቢያት፡ ባዕዳን።
___

B. Translate the following:

1. ብዑላን፡ እሙንቱ፡ ሕዘቢ፡ ዝንቱ፡ ብሔር።
___

2. ዝውእቱ፡ ሕግ፡ ቅዱስ።
___

3. ዛቲ፡ ሀገር፡ እኪት፡ ይእቲ።
___

4. አነ፡ ድውይ፡ አነ፡ አንቲኑ፡ ድውይት፡ አንቲ፧
___

5. እኪት፡ ይእቲ፡ ዛበሲት።
___

6. ዕልዋን፡ እሙንቱ፡ አርዳኢሁ።
___

7. ብዙኃን፡ እሙንቱ፡ ኃጥኣን፡ ዝየ።
___

8. ቅድስት፡ ይእቲ፡ ዛቲ፡ ሀገር።
___

9. ምዉት፡ ምታ።
___

10. ለምንት፡ ሕዙን፡ አንተ፧
___

C. Translate the following:

1. ቀተልነ፡ ውእተ፡ ነቢየ፡ ዕልወ።

2. ነጸርክዎ፡ ለመጽሐፍ፡ ወርኢኩ፡ ከመ፡ ሕግ፡ ብሊት፡ ውእቱ።

3. ኢሰማዕነ፡ ለነገሩ፡ እኩይ።

4. ፈነዎ፡ ለረድኡ፡ ኀበ፡ ብእሲት፡ ድውይት።

5. ኮነት፡ እሙ፡ ብእሲተ፡ ብዕልተ።

6. ገብረ፡ ቅዱስ፡ ማርቆስ፡ ብዙነ፡ ተኣምረ።

7. ኢርኢክሙኑ፡ ተኣምራቲሁ፤

8. ነሥእዎ፡ ለንዋዩ፡ ለብእሲ፡ ብዑል።

9. ዝንቱ፡ ትእምርት፡ እመንፈስ፡ ቅዱስ፡ ውእቱ።

10. ገሥጸ፡ ወራዙተ፡ እኩያነ፡ በእንተ፡ ኀጢኣቶሙ።

11. ስሕቱ፡ እምሃይማኖት፡ ርትዕት።

12. ሤጥክዎ፡ ለሐመርየ፡ ብሊት።

13. ወረደ፡ መንፈስ፡ ቅዱስ፡ ላዕሌሁ።

14. ቀርቡ፡ ኀቤሁ፡ ሕዝብ፡ ብዙኃን።
    _____

15. መኑ፡ ተርጐመ፡ ሕገ፡ ብሊተ፡ ለልሳነ፡ ግዕዝ፤
    _____

16. ሐነጹ፡ ብዙኃነ፡ አብያተ።
    _____

17. ሰደድዎሙ፡ ለሰብእ፡ እኩይን።
    _____

18. ተከሉ፡ ብዙኃተ፡ ዕፀወ፡ ሀየ።
    _____

19. ሕዙን፡ ምታ፡ በእንቲአሃ።
    _____

20. ነሥእ፡ አልባሰ፡ ወጕየ፡ እምቤት።
    _____

Chapter 9

ADJECTIVES (PART 2)

9.1 Introduction

Two further patterns of adjectives exist in Gǝʿǝz, the *qătil* and the *qăttāl* patterns. The *qătil* pattern also includes the *qăttil* pattern derived from the D verbs. The *qătil* pattern consists of a comparatively few, though important, adjectives. Unlike the *qătul* adjectives, the *qătil* forms the feminine singular by replacing the stem vowel *i* with *ā* rather than adding ት. The masculine adjective ዐቢይ፡ – "great, large" shifts to the feminine form ዐባይ፡. Similarly, the masculine adjective ሐዲስ፡ – "new" shifts to the feminine form ሐዳስ፡. The feminine plural adjective may be formed from either the masculine or the feminine singular: ሐዲሳት፡ or ሐዳሳት፡.

A variant of the *qătil* occurs when the middle root consonant is a guttural; this appears in the *qǝtil* pattern. The masculine adjective ርሒብ፡ – "broad, wide" shifts to the feminine form ረሓብ፡. Many of the *qătil* adjectives have a feminine and masculine internal plural form *qātălt* along with an external plural form ($C_1 ăC_2 ăC_3 t$, e.g., ጠቢብ፡, ጠበብት፡ – "wise"). For example, the singular adjective ዐቢይ፡ – "great" has a plural form of ዐበይት፡ with plural nouns. Similarly, the masculine adjective በሊኅ፡ – "sharp" shifts to the plural form በላኅት፡. Likewise, the masculine adjective ጠቢብ፡ – "wise" shifts to the plural form ጠበብት፡.

9.2 The Adjective in the Comparative Position

The comparative in Gǝʿǝz is formed in a similar manner to that of biblical Hebrew with the addition of the preposition "from." In the case of Gǝʿǝz, the word እምነ፡ is added to the adjective. For example, እኩይ፡ ውእቱ፡ እምነ፡ ንጉሥ፡፡ "he is more evil than the king." In addition, the comparison may be made stronger by the addition of the adverb ፈድፋደ፡ – "much, much more": ጠቢብ፡ ውእቱ፡ ፈድፋደ፡ እምነ፡ እኁሁ፡፡ – "he is much wiser than his brother." All stative verbs whose predicate is preceded by እምነ፡ may be understood likewise: e.g., በዝኑ፡ ውእቱ፡ ሕዝብ፡ እምነ፡ ሕዝብነ፡፡ – "that people became more numerous than (from) our people."

Another adverb, ጥቀ፡, is used frequently to intensify an adjective; it can appear following or preceding the adjective. For example, ጥቀ፡ ድውይ፡ ውእቱ፡፡ or ድውይ፡ ጥቀ፡ ውእቱ፡፡ "He is very ill."

9.3 The Adjective Pattern *Qăttāl*

Adjectives of the *qăttāl* type follow no particular pattern in forming the feminine singular. It is possible to come across a form with no stem change, ቀታልት፡, a form with a change to a short *ă* final stem vowel from a long *ā* vowel, ቀተልት፡, or at times one might discover the masculine form being used for the feminine adjective. In Gə'əz script, feminine adjectives in this pattern are undifferentiated from the feminine singular of the *qătil* pattern (i.e., *qătāl*).

9.4 Adjectives Ending in *-ā+ዊ* and *-ā+ይ*

There are multiple adjectives that occur with these endings but are used rather infrequently. When used they are comparable to a preferred relative construction or a construct phrase. They are derived from an assortment of nouns and generally denote "of" or "pertaining to"; they often correspond to English adjectives ending in "-ly," e.g., ምድራዊ፡ – "worldly, of the world"; ሰማያዊ፡ – "heavenly, of heaven, divine." The inflection pattern is as follows:

TABLE 9.1: Inflection of "*-āwī*" Adjectives

Gender	Singular	Plural
Masculine	ሰማያዊ፡	ሰማያዊያን፡ / ሰማያውያን፡
Feminine	ሰማያዊት፡	ሰማያዊያት፡ / ሰማያውያት፡

Most of these adjectives may appear with the optional ending of *-ā+ይ*. They follow a regular pattern in their inflection: *-ā+ይ, -ā+ት, -ā+ያን, -ā+ያት*, e.g., ነዋይ፡.

TABLE 9.2: Inflection of "*-āy*" Adjectives

Gender	Singular	Plural
Masculine	ሰማይ፡	ሰማያን፡
Feminine	ሰማያት፡	ሰማያት፡

9.5 Miscellaneous Adjective Patterns

In addition to the adjectives discussed above and in the previous chapter, occasionally other patterns occur. These included the following examples:

a. The *qătl* form: አብድ፡ (f. አብድ፡; pl. አብዳን፡, አብዳት፡) – "foolish, ignorant", "fool."

b. The *qətāl* form: ሕያው፡ (f. ሕያውት፡; pl. ሕያዋን፡ / ሕያዋት፡) – "alive, living."

Adjectives may also appear in construct with a noun that follows; as such, the noun qualifies the meaning of the adjective. For example, in the phrase እኩየ፡ ልብ፡ – "evil of heart," we are told of the type of evil. Similarly, we are told what type of beauty in the phrase ሠናየ፡ ገጽ፡ – "beautiful in appearance."

In addition, any adjective in Gə'əz may be used as a substantive, an equivalent of the English "the one who is" or "those who are": the adjective ድዉይ፡ can be translated as "one who is sick" or "a sick person."

Likewise, in the plural ድዉያን፡ can be translated as "those who are sick" or "the sick ones." Adjectives in the feminine singular pattern of *qətəlt* are used particularly to describe inanimate things or abstract ideas in the sense of "that which is." The adjective እኪት፡ can be translated "that which is evil," or the adjective ርትእት፡ can be translated "that which is correct." As with all translation work, the context of the passage will assist greatly in translating these somewhat ambiguous terms or phrases.

9.6 Vocabulary

1. ዓመት፡ ዓም፡ (pl. ዓመታት፡) – year
2. ሥጋ፡ (pl. ሥጋት፡) – body, flesh, esp. of the flesh as opposed to the spirit
3. ሐብል፡ (pl. አሕባል፡) – rope, cord
4. ሕይወት፡ – life, lifetime
5. ሐዲስ፡ (f. ሐዳስ፡ pl. ሐደስት፡) – new (ሕግ፡ ሐዲስ፡ – New Testament)
6. ዐቢይ፡ (f. ዐባይ፡ pl. ዐቢየት፡) – big, large, important, great
7. ዓብየ፡ – be great
8. ጠቢብ፡ (f. ጠባብ፡ pl. ጠቢበት፡) – wise, prudent, skilled
9. ጠበ፡ – be wise
10. ልሂቅ፡ (f. ልህቅት፡) – adult, grownup, old
11. ልህቀ፡ – grow up
12. ነዊኅ፡, ነዋኅ፡ (f. ነዋኅ፡ pl. ነዋኅት፡) – high, tall, distant
13. ኖኅ፡ – be high
14. ፈድፋደ፡ – exceedingly, very much, greatly
15. ጥቀ፡ – very, extremely
16. ዓለም፡ (pl. ዓለማት፡) – world, eternity
17. ዓለማዊ፡ – worldly
18. መድኀን፡ (pl. መድኀናን፡) – savior, redeemer
19. እግዚእ፡ (f. እግዝእት or እግእት፡; pl. አጋእዝት፡) – lord, master, leader, chief
20. ምንዳቤ፡ – affliction, torment
21. ልብ፡ (pl. አልባብ፡) – heart, mind, intellect
22. ገጽ፡ (pl. ገጻት፡) – face, appearance
23. ሠናይ፡ (f. ሠናይት፡) – beautiful, fine, good
24. ሠነየ፡ – be beautiful, good
25. ነዳይ፡ (f. ነዳይት፡) – poor, destitute
26. ኄር፡ (f. ኄርት፡) – good, excellent
27. ሕያው፡ (f. ሕያውት፡) – alive, living
28. ምድራዊ፡ (f. ምድራዊት፡) – of the world, worldly
29. ብርሃናዊ፡ (f. ብርሃናዊት፡) – of or pertaining to light, radiant
30. ሰማያዊ፡ (f. ሰማያዊት፡) – heavenly, divine
31. መንፈሳዊ፡ (f. መንፈሳዊት፡) – of the spirit, spiritual
32. ሥጋዊ፡ – fleshly (not spiritual)
33. ወንጌላዊ፡ (f. ወንጌላዊት፡) – gospel (adj.), evangelist (n.)
34. ጽኑዐ / ጽኑእ፡ (f. ጽንዕት፡) – strong, powerful, harsh, severe, lasting
35. ጸንዐ፡ – be strong, lasting, severe

9.7 Exercises

A. Translate the following:

1. ልብስ፡ ሐዲስ፡

2. ባሕር፡ ዐቢይ፡

3. አርድእት፡ ጠቢባን።

4. ዋሬዛ፡ ነዊኅ።

5. ካህን፡ ዐቢይ።

6. ንዋይ፡ ሐዳስ።

7. ስም፡ ዐቢይ።

8. መናፍስት፡ እኩያት።

9. ደብር፡ ነዊኅ።

10. ኤጲስ፡ ቆጶስ፡ ጠቢብ።

11. ፍኖት፡ ነዋኅ።

12. ተአምር፡ ዐቢይት።

13. በሓውርት፡ ነዋኅት።

14. ሕገግ፡ ሐደስት።

15. መሣውእ፡ ዐቢይት።

B. Translate the following:

1. ነዋነት፡ አድባረ፡ ብሐርክሙ፡ እምአድባረ፡ ብሐርነ።
   _____

2. ዐቢይ፡ ዝንቱ፡ ቤት፡ እምኩሉ፡ አብያተ፡ ሀገር።
   _____

3. ብዑል፡ አቡከ፡ እም፡ አቡየ።
   _____

4. ነዊህ፡ አነ፡ እምእኑየ።
   _____

5. ልሂቅ፡ ዝንቱ፡ ሐዋርያ፡ እምካልአን፡ ሐዋርያት።
   _____

6. ልሂቅ፡ አንተ፡ እምኔየ።
   _____

7. ነዋህ፡ ይአቲ፡ እምኩሎን፡ አኃቲሃ።
   _____

8. ጠቢብ፡ አንተ፡ ፈድፋደ፡ እምነ፡ ካልአነከ።
   _____

9. ዝንቱ፡ ልብስ፡ ሐዲስ፡ ውእቱ፡ እምልብስየ።
   _____

10. ነዊህ፡ ፈድፋደ፡ እምዝየ፡ ውእቱ፡ ብሐሮሙ።
    _____

C. Translate the following:

1. ገጻቲሆሙ፡ ለወራዙት።
   _____

2. ወንጌሉ፡ ለእግዚአነ።
   _____

Adjectives (Part 2)

3. ነዳያነ፡ ዝንቱ፡ ዓለም።
_____

4. አሰማዒቲሆሙ፡ ለኔራን፡ ወለአኩያን።
_____

5. ምንዳቤሆሙ፡ ለክርስቲያን።
_____

6. አብያቲሆሙ፡ ለአጋእስቲነ።
_____

7. ቃላቲሁ፡ ለመድኃኔ።
_____

8. ገጹ፡ ለመንፈስ፡ ቅዱስ።
_____

9. መጻሕፍቲሆሙ፡ ለወንጌላዊያን።
_____

10. ሕይወታ፡ ለእግዝትነ።
_____

11. አልባቢሆሙ፡ ለዐቢይት።
_____

12. አስማቲሆሙ፡ ለሰማያውያን።
_____

13. ነገሮሙ፡ ለዕልዋን፡ ወኃጥኣን።
_____

14. ቃላቲሆሙ፡ ለጠቢብት።
_____

15. ሕይወቶሙ፡ ለቅዱሳን።
_____

16. ምንዳቤሆሙ፡ ለነዳያን፡ ወድውያን።
_____

17. ንዋዮሙ፡ ለዐቢይት፡ ወአብዕልት።

18. ጌራነ፡ ልብ።

19. ሠናያነ፡ ገጽ።

20. ጽኑዓነ፡ ልብ።

D. Translate the following:

1. ጽኑዓት፡ አህጉሪሆሙ፡ ወዐቢያት፡ እምአህጉሪከሙ።

2. ዛቲ፡ ፍኖት፡ ጥቀ፡ ነዋኅ፡ ይእቲ።

3. ሕዙነ፡ ገጽ፡ ውእቱ።

4. ጥቀ፡ ሕዙናን፡ እሙንቱ፡ አልባቢሆሙ፡ ለውሉዲሁ።

5. ሕያዋን፡ እሙንቱ፡ ወኢሙታን።

6. ነዳዬ፡ ልብ፡ ውእቱ፡ ወኢጠቢብ።

7. ሐይው፡ ዝንቱ፡ ቅዱስ፡ ሕይወተ፡ መንፈሳዊተ።

8. ሕያው፡ እግዚእነ፡ ወኢምዉት።

9. ጽንዕት፡ ይእቲ፡ ሃይማኖቱ።

10. ነዓያን፡ አርዳኢሁ፡ ወኢብዙኅ፡ ንዋዮሙ።
_____

11. ኔር፡ ልብከ፡ ወሠናይ፡ ገጽከ።
_____

12. ብእል፡ እግዚእየ፡ ፈድፋደ፡ እምአጋዝዝቲከሙ።
_____

Chapter 10

PERFECT GUTTURAL ROOTS

10.1 Perfect II Guttural Roots

As with the Hebrew verbs, the Gəʿəz verb system contains what are commonly called weak verbs because they have a weak consonant among the three or four root consonants. The first group we will encounter involves the perfect verbs with guttural consonants, similar to what we find in Hebrew. In Gəʿəz, we only need give consideration to the G verbs that have a guttural in the second (II) position. As a reminder, the Gəʿəz gutturals include the following consonants: አ፡ ዐ፡ ሀ፡ ኀ፡ ሐ፡. The weak G verbs exhibit two patterns–one that follows the $C_1ăC_2ăC_3ă$ consonant/vowel pattern ነበረ፡ such as ሰአለ፡ – "he asked, prayed," and a second that follows $C_1ăC_2C_3ă$ consonant/vowel pattern, the verb form of ገብረ፡, such as ክሕደ፡ – "he denied, rejected." The D and L verb types follow the expected patterns of inflection (see ch. 7). According to Lambdin, some D verbs form II Guttural roots and have a parallel G verb form. For example, the D verb መህረ፡, măhhără, has a G stem parallel in መህረ፡, măhără. This is likely due to the discontinuation of doubling of guttural consonants in the modern textual tradition but remains in the classical text traditions.[1] You will need to rely on the context of the passage to translate.[2] Compare the similarities to the strong G Verb declension patterns in table 10.2 below (also ch. 7).

TABLE 10.1: G-Stem II Guttural Verbs

PGN	To ask	PGN		PGN	To deny	PGN	
3ms	ሰአለ፡	3mp	ሰአሉ፡	3ms	ክሕደ፡	3mp	ክሕዱ፡
3fs	ሰአለት፡	3fp	ሰአላ፡	3fs	ክሕደት፡	3fp	ክሕዳ፡
2ms	ሰአልከ፡	2mp	ሰአልከሙ፡	2ms	ክሕድከ፡	2mp	ክሕድከሙ፡
2fs	ሰአልኪ፡	2fp	ሰአልክን፡	2fs	ክሕድኪ፡	2fp	ክሕድክን፡
1cs	ሰአልኩ፡	1cp	ሰአልነ፡	1cs	ክሕድኩ፡	1cp	ክሕድነ፡

10.2 Perfect III Guttural Roots

There are two basic groups of III Guttural verbs in Gəʿəz–the G-stem verb, which follows the $C_1ăC_2C_3ă$ consonant/vowel pattern ገብረ፡ and the D, L, and Q verbs, which follow the $C_1ăC_2əC_3ă$ consonant/vowel

---

1. Lambdin, *Introduction*, 53.
2. See Lambdin, *Introduction*, 53.

pattern ነስሐ፡; both groups have some variation in the vowels in the paradigm. In each case the stem vowel following the second consonant in the first- and second-person forms include the *ā* vowel.

TABLE 10.2: III Guttural Verbs (cf. ch. 7)

PGN	G Strong Verb	G-III Weak "to come"	D Strong Verb	D-III Weak "to raise, lift up"	L Strong Verb	Q/L-III Weak "to bind in chains"
3ms	ነበረ፡	መጽአ፡	ነገረ፡	ነስሐ፡	ባረከ፡	ሞቅሐ፡
3fs	ነበረት፡	መጽአት፡	ነገረት፡	ነስሐት፡	ባረከት፡	ሞቅሐት፡
2ms	ነበርከ፡	መጻእከ፡	ነገርከ፡	ነሳሕከ፡	ባረከ፡	ሞቃሕከ፡
2fs	ነበርኪ፡	መጻእኪ፡	ነገርኪ፡	ነሳሕኪ፡	ባረኪ፡	ሞቃሕኪ፡
1cs	ነበርኩ፡	መጻእኩ፡	ነገርኩ፡	ነሳሕኩ፡	ባረኩ፡	ሞቃሕኩ፡
3mp	ነበሩ፡	መጽኡ፡	ነገሩ፡	ነስሑ፡	ባረኩ፡	ሞቅሑ፡
3fp	ነበራ፡	መጽአ፡	ነገራ፡	ነስሐ፡	ባረካ፡	ሞቅሓ፡
2mp	ነበርክሙ፡	መጻእክሙ፡	ነገርክሙ፡	ነሳሕክሙ፡	ባረክሙ፡	ሞቃሕክሙ፡
2fp	ነበርክን፡	መጻእክን፡	ነገርክን፡	ነሳሕክን፡	ባረክን፡	ሞቃሕክን፡
1cp	ነበርነ፡	መጻእነ፡	ነገርነ፡	ነሳሕነ፡	ባረክነ፡	ሞቃሕነ፡

Note the following vowel changes due to the III Guttural:

a. In the G, D, and L III Guttural verbs in the 3ms/fs forms the middle vowel reduces from an *ă* in the strong to an *ə*.

b. In the G, D, and L verbs in the 2m/f s and 1cs forms the middle vowel lengthens from an *ă* in the strong to an *ā*.

c. In the G, D, and L verbs in the 3m/f p forms the middle vowel reduces from an *ă* in the strong to an *ə*.

d. In the G, D, and L verbs in the 2m/f p and 1cp forms the middle vowel lengthens from an *ă* in the strong to an *ā*.

e. In each case, the III Guttural maintains the strong verb vowel followed by the same personal endings.

10.3 Perfect III-ወ/ይ Roots

The G-stem verbs in this category follow two patterns of declension: the ነበረ፡, $C_1 ăC_2 ăC_3 ă$, and the ገብረ፡, $C_1 ăC_2 C_3 ă$. In the first- and second-person forms, on occasion when the final stem syllable closes, -ă+ወ can often contract to an *o* vowel and -ă+ይ can contract to an *ē* vowel, although this is less common. Unfortunately, these changes can be quite random and can occur in the G, D, L, and Q verbs.

TABLE 10.3: Perfect G-Stem III-ወ/የ Guttural Verbs

PGN	G strong Verb	III-ወ C₁ăC₂ăC₃ă "cross"	III-የ C₁ăC₂ăC₃ă "weep"	III-ወ C₁ăC₂C₃ă "be devastated"	III-የ C₁ăC₂C₃ă "drink"
3ms	ነበረ፡	ዐደወ፡	በከየ፡	ቢድወ፡	ሰትየ፡
3fs	ነበረት፡	ዐደወት፡	በከየት፡	ቢድወት፡	ሰትየት፡
2ms	ነበርከ፡	ዐደውከ፡ ዐዶከ፡	በከይከ፡ በኬከ፡	ቢደውከ፡ ቢዶከ፡	ሰተይከ፡ ሰቴከ፡
2fs	ነበርኪ፡	ዐደውኪ፡ ዐዶኪ፡	በከይኪ፡ በኬኪ፡	ቢደውኪ፡ ቢዶኪ፡	ሰተይኪ፡ ሰቴኪ፡
1cs	ነበርኩ፡	ዐደውኩ፡ ዐዶኩ፡	በከይኩ፡ በኬኩ፡	ቢደውኩ፡ ቢዶኩ፡	ሰተይኩ፡ ሰቴኩ፡
3mp	ነበሩ፡	ዐደዉ፡	በከዩ፡	ቢድዉ፡	ሰትዩ፡
3fp	ነበራ፡	ዐደዋ፡	በከያ፡	ቢድዋ፡	ሰትያ፡
2mp	ነበርክሙ፡	ዐደውክሙ፡ ዐዶክሙ፡	በከይክሙ፡ በኬክሙ፡	ቢደውክሙ፡ ቢዶክሙ፡	ሰተይክሙ፡ ሰቴክሙ፡
2fp	ነበርክን፡	ዐደውክን፡ ዐዶክን፡	በከይክን፡ በኬክን፡	ቢደውክን፡ ቢዶክን፡	ሰተይክን፡ ሰቴክን፡
1cp	ነበርነ፡	ዐደውነ፡ ዐዶነ፡	በከይነ፡ በኬነ፡	ቢደውነ፡ ቢዶነ፡	ሰተይነ፡ ሰቴነ፡

Note the following changes due to the III-ወ/የ verbs:

a. There are no changes in form between the strong G verb and the regular form of the III-ወ/የ verbs.

b. Vowel changes occur in the contracted 2 m/f s and p and the 1cs and 1cp forms of the verb.

c. Note the two possible forms in the III-ወ/የ verbs in the first- and second-person singular and plural forms. In the III-ወ verbs the -ă middle vowel along with the III-ወ contract to an *o* vowel followed by the personal endings. In the III-የ verbs, the middle *i* vowel contracts with the III-የ to form the *ē* vowel followed by the personal endings.

10.4 Perfect G-Stem with II Guttural and III-የ

Several G-verbs contain both II Guttural and a III-የ consonants as part of the root. They can appear as both the ነበረ፡, C₁ăC₂ăC₃ă form and the ገብረ፡, C₁ăC₂C₃ă form. The ነበረ፡ form follows the verb በከየ፡ – "to weep" in table 10.3. If the verb is of the ገብረ፡ form, then -ə+የ is replaced with the *i* vowel in the first and second person.

TABLE 10.4: Perfect G-Stem with II Guttural and III-የ

PGN	G Strong Verb	"to see"	PGN	G Strong Verb	"to see"
3ms	ነበረ፡	ርእየ፡	3mp	ነበሩ፡	ርእዩ፡
3fs	ነበረት፡	ርእየት፡	3fp	ነበራ፡	ርእያ፡
2ms	ነበርከ፡	ርኢከ፡	2mp	ነበርክሙ፡	ርኢክሙ፡
2fs	ነበርኪ፡	ርኢኪ፡	2fp	ነበርክን፡	ርኢክን፡
1cs	ነበርኩ፡	ርኢኩ፡	1cp	ነበርነ፡	ርኢነ፡

Perfect Guttural Roots   63

Note the following changes due to the II-Guttural and III-ዐ verbs:

a. The middle *ă* of the strong verb in the 3 s/p forms shifts to an *ə* vowel followed by the personal endings.

b. The middle *ă* of the strong verb in the 2 s/p and 1s/p forms shifts to an *i* vowel and the III-ዐ is dropped/assimilated followed by the personal endings.

10.5 Vocabulary

1. ሃይማኖት፡ – faith
2. ኅብስት፡ (pl. ኅባውዝ፡) – bread
3. ደም፡ (pl. ደማት፡) – blood
4. እድ፡ (pl. እደው፡) – hand
5. ጸሐፈ፡ – write
6. ሰአለ፡ – ask for
7. ውሕዘ፡ – flow
8. ስሕተ፡ – err, stray (from path or doctrine)
9. ከሕደ፡ – deny, repudiate
10. ገሠጸ፡ – rebuke, reproach
11. ሶበ፡ – when
12. አመ፡ – when
13. ማይ፡ (pl. ማያት፡) – water
14. ብርሃን፡ (pl. ብርሃናት፡) – light
15. ኃጢአት፡ (pl. ኃጣውእ፡ ኃጣይእ፡) – sin
16. ነሥአ፡ – raise, lift up
17. መርሐ፡ – lead, guide
18. ሰምዐ፡ – hear, hear of, obey
19. መልአ፡ (trans.) – fill with something
20. ፈርሀ፡ – be afraid
21. ነስሐ፡ – repent of
22. ከመ፡ (prep.) – like, as; (conj.) that
23. እስመ፡ – because, for, since
24. ባሕር፡ (pl. አብሕርት፡) – sea, ocean
25. እብን፡ (pl. እብን፡ አአባን፡) – stone
26. ፀሐይ፡ / ፀሐይ፡ (pl. ፀሐያት፡) – sun
27. ወርኅ፡ (pl. አውራኅ፡) – moon
28. ዐደወ፡ – cross (a goal)
29. አተወ፡ – go home, depart from home
30. ውዕየ፡ – be burned up, consumed by fire
31. ወደየ፡ – put, place, set
32. ሀለው፡ / ሀሎ፡ – exist or be
33. ፈነወ፡ – send

10.6 Exercises

A. Translate the following:

1. ሃይማኖቶሙ፡ ለክርስቲያን፡፡

   _____

2. ሃይማኖቶሙ፡ ለደቂቆሙ፡፡

   _____

3. ቢየሙ፡ ለወልድየ፡፡

   _____

4. ልሳኖሙ፡ ለመላእክት፡

5. እምእዬሁ፡ ለነቢይ፡

6. አደዊሃ፡ ለእነቱ፡

7. ደሙ፡ ለበድኑ፡

8. ሃይማኖቶሙ፡ ለአሀዊነ፡

9. ጎብስት፡ ወወይን፡

10. መጻሕፍቲሁ፡ ለጸሐፊ፡

B. Translate the following:

1. ወሶበ፡ ቦኡ፡ ሀገረነ፡ ውእተ፡ አሚረ፡ ቀተሉ፡ ኩሎሙ፡ ዕደወ፡

2. መጽኡ፡ ኀቤነ፡ ወሰአሉ፡ ወይነ፡ ወኅብስተ፡ እምኔነ፡

3. ወሶበ፡ ረከቡ፡ ክርስቲያነ፡ ቀተሉ፡ ሊቃኒሆሙ፡

4. ሶበ፡ ርእዩ፡ ደሞ፡ ለንጉሥ፡ ወጉዩ፡ እምቅድሜሁ፡

5. አሙ፡ ሞተ፡ ብእሲሃ፡ ኀለፈት፡ እምህየ፡ ወገብአት፡ ኀበ፡ ቤተ፡ አቡሃ፡

Perfect Guttural Roots

C. Translate the following:

1. ወሰበ፡ ረከቡነ፡ ወቀተሉ፡ ደቂቀነ፡ ወነሥኡ፡ አንስቲነ፡ ምስሌሆሙ፡፡

2. ሐዘነ፡ ውእተ፡ አሚረ፡ እስመ፡ ገብርነ፡ ዘንተ፡ ኃጢአተ፡፡

3. ወሰበ፡ ሰማዕነ፡ ዘንተ፡ ነገረ፡ ነሳሕነ፡ እምኲሎ፡ ኃጣውኢነ፡፡

4. አሞ፡ ቀርበት፡ ዕለተ፡ ሞቱ፡ ለአቡነ፣ ባረከነ፡ ወእምዝ፡ ኃለፈ፡ እምኀቤነ፡ ኃበ፡ አበዊሁ፡፡

5. ወሰበ፡ ነጸሩ፡ ውስተ፡ ሰማይ፡ ርእዩ፡ ብርሃነ፡ ወሰምዑ፡ ቃሎሙ፡ ለመላእክት፡፡

D. Translate the following:

1. ወሰበ፡ ርኢነ፡ ይእተ፡ ሐመረ፡ ወረድነ፡ ውስተ፡ ሐይቀ፡ ባሕር፡፡

2. ኢኮነ፡ ወርኀ፡ በይእቲ፡ ሌሊት፡ ወጐየይነ፡ ገዳመ፡ ምስለ፡ ደቂቅነ፡ ወአንስቲነ፡፡

3. ነጸርኩ፡ ኃበ፡ አድባር፡ ወርኢኩ፡ ብርሃነ፡ ከመ፡ ብርሃነ፡ ፀሐይ፡፡

4. ፈኖኩ፡ ዘንተ፡ ነቢየ፡ ኃቤክሙ፡ እስመ፡ ኢዐቀብክሙ፡ ሕገጌየ፡ ወስሕትክሙ፡፡

5. አሞ፡ ሀሎነ፡ ምስሌክሙ፡ ኢሰማዕክሙነ፡፡

6. ነበሩ፡ በውስተ፡ ሀገረ፡ ፀሐይ፡ እስከ፡ ሞቱ፡ ለውእቱ፡ ንጉሥ፣ ወእምዝ፡ አተዉ፡ ምድሮሙ፡፡

Chapter 11

THE PERFECT VERB WITH OBJECT SUFFIXES

11.1 Perfect Verbs with Object Suffixes

As with Hebrew, the pronominal object suffix is directly affixed to the transitive verb, thus making it the direct object of the verb. The verb object suffixes in the 1st and 2nd person are identical to the possessive suffixes affixed to nouns with the exception of the 1cs form.

TABLE 11.1: Strong Verb Object Suffixes

PGN	Form	Translation
3ms	-o / -ሁ	him
3fs	-ā / -ሃ	her
2ms	-ከ	you
2fs	-ኪ	you
1cs	-ኒ	me
3mp	-o+ሙ / -ሆሙ	them
3fp	-o+ን / -ሆን	them
2mp	-ከሙ	you
2fp	-ከን	you
1cp	-ነ	us

The object suffix attaches directly to the end of each verb form with some minor vowel changes to the final syllable of the verb due to the four possible vowel endings plus a consonant that may appear on verbs (ă, ā, u, i, or a silent vowel). For example, 3fs -ă+ት becomes -ă+ተ; 2fs ኪ becomes ከ; 2fp ከን becomes ከና or ከ and 1cp ነ becomes ና plus the suffixes (see more on 3rd person below).

TABLE 11.2: Strong Verb Plus Object Suffix

Verb PGN	1cs Suffix	2ms Suffix	2fs Suffix	1cp Suffix	2mp Suffix	2fp Suffix
3ms -ă	-ă+ኒ	-ă+ h	-ă+ኪ	-ă+ነ	-ă+ hሙ	-ă+ hን
3fs -ăት	-ă+ተኒ	-ă+ተh	-ă+ተኪ	-ā+ተነ	-ă+ተhሙ	-ă+ተhን
2ms -h	-hኒ	-	-	-hነ	-	-
2fs -ኪ	-hኒ	-	-	-hነ	-	-
1cs -ኩ	-ኩh	-ኩh	-ኩኪ	-	-ኩhሙ	-ኩhን
3mp -u	-u+ኒ	-u+h	-u+ኪ	-u+ነ	-u+hሙ	-u+hን
3fp -ā	-ā+ኒ	-ā+h	-ā+ኪ	-ā+ነ	-ā+hሙ	-ā+hን
2mp -hሙ	-hሙኒ	-	-	-hሙነ	-	-
2fp -hን	-hናኒ / -hኒ	-	-	-hናነ / --hና	-	-
1cp -ነ	-	-ናh	-ናኪ	-	-ናhሙ	-ናhን

When the object suffix is attached to the perfect verb, we form a complete sentence: subject (sometimes understood), verb, and object of the verb:

a. ባረhኒ፡ – "he blessed me"

b. ባረhተነ፡ – "she blessed us"

c. ባረኩኒ፡ – "they blessed me"

11.2 Perfect Verbs with 3rd Person Object Suffixes

Third-person suffixes are more complicated than 1st and 2nd person pronominal suffixes–there are more alterations made to the end of the verb form when attaching the suffix. As will be noted below there are varying rules that govern the form of the suffix and the verb. The following table lists the third-person object suffixes:

TABLE 11.3: Perfect Verbs Third-Person Object Suffixes

Suffix PGN	Suffix Ending	Suffix PGN	Suffix Ending
3ms	-o / -ሁ	3mp	-o+ሙ / -ሆሙ
3fs	-ā / ሃ	3fp	-o+ን / -ሆን

11.2.1 The following alterations occur to the verb endings:

a. Verb ending -ă remains -ă

b. Verb ending -ă+ተ becomes -ă+ተ

c. Verb ending -ህ remains -ህ

d. Verb ending -ሂ becomes -ህ

e. Verb ending -ሁ remains -ሁ

f. Verb ending -u remains -u

g. Verb ending -ā remains -ā

h. Verb ending -ክሙ remains -ክሙ

i. Verb ending -ክን becomes -ክና or -ክ

j. Verb ending -ን becomes -ና

11.2.2 From these alterations, the following patterns can be established:

a. If the verb ends in -ā, the suffixes attached are -ሁ, -ሃ, -ሆሙ, -ሆን

b. If the verb ends in -u or -ə, the suffixes attached are -o, -ā, -o+ሙ, -o+ን, this is done after changing the -u to -ə+ሞ, and -ə to -ə+የ

c. If the verb ends in -ă, drop the -ă and add -o, -ā, or -o+ሙ

11.2.3 These rules can be quite complicated as is illustrated in the table below:

TABLE 11.4: Variations of 3rd Person Object Suffixes

PGN of ă Verbs	Verbal Endings	3ms	3fs	3mp	3fp
3ms	-ă	-o	-ā	-o+ሙ	-o+ን
3fs	-ă+ት	-ă+ዮ	-ă+ታ	-ă+ቶሙ	-ă+ቶን
2ms	-ህ	-ህ -ሁ	-ህ -ሃ	-ሆሙ	-ሆን
2fs	-ሂ	-ሂዮ	-ሂያ	-ሂዮሙ	-ሂዮን
1cs	-ሁ	-ሁየ	-ሁያ	-ሁየሙ	-ሁየን
3mp	-u	-ə+የ	-ə+የ	-ə+የሙ	-ə+የን
3fp	-ā	-ā+ሁ	-ā+ሃ	-ā+ሆሙ	-ā+ሆን
2mp	-ክሙ	-ክሙየ	-ክሙያ	-ክሙየሙ	-ክሙየን

(continued)

PGN of ā Verbs	Verbal Endings	3ms	3fs	3mp	3fp
2fp	-ከን	-ከናሁ -ካሁ	-ከናሃ -ካሃ	-ከናሆሙ	-ከናሆን
1cp	-ነ	-ናሁ	-ናሃ	-ናሆሙ	-ናሆን

a. Note the two forms on the 2ms and 2fp verbs with 3ms and 3fs suffixes.

b. Keep in mind there may be variations depending on the vowel ending on the verb: see the following examples:

  i. A verb ending in *ā* with 1cs suffix: this would have to be ቀነዋ + ኒ, ቀነዋኒ, but then there is no unusual verb change

  ii. A verb ending in *o*, ቀፍሎ

11.3 Partitive Apposition

A. Both dative and accusative pronominal suffixes are often incorporated in reference to parts of the human body as the object of a transitive verb.
   a. ሰምዕዎ፡ ቃሎ። – "they heard his voice."
   b. ገሰሰቶ፡ ልብሶ። – "she touched his clothing."
   c. አሰርዎ፡ እደዊሁ። – "they bound his hands."
B. However, object suffixes can also be used with stative and intransitive verbs. They can have three functions when used in this mode:
   a. They can be used in a comparative construction:
      በዝኅነ፡ ውእቱ፡ ሕዝብ። – "that people became more numerous than us."
   b. If the subject is a body part or an inalienable attribute such as the "soul" or "one's reputation," a dative suffix can be added to the verb to support the possessive pronoun:
      መረረተኒ፡ ነፍስየ። – "my soul became bitter."
   c. It can also be translated as an appropriate prepositional phrase:
      በቀየቶ፡ – "she wept for him."

11.4 Vocabulary

1. ምስጢር፡ (pl. ምስጢራት፡) – mystery (emphasis on Eucharist)
2. ሲሳይ፡ – food, sustenance
3. ዘመድ፡ (pl. አዝማድ፡) – family, relatives, tribe
4. ነገረ፡ – say, tell
5. ነበበ፡ – speak to, tell
6. ወሀበ፡ – give

7. ለአከ፡ – send
8. ወሰደ፡ – lead, bring, take
9. መህረ፡ G – teach
10. መጠወ፡ – surrender, hand over
11. አመረ፡ – tell, show, indicate, make known
12. ዘ- – that, the fact that
13. በእንተ፡ ዘ- – because

11.5 Exercises

A. Translate the following:

1. ወሰደቶ፡ ለብእሲ፡ በውስተ፡ ቤታ፡ ወዐቀቦ፡ህየ፡ እስከ፡ ኀለፈት፡ ሌሊት፡፡

2. ወሀበ፡ ለነ፡ ሕይወተ፡ ሐዳሰ፡ ወሠናይተ፡፡

3. ሙኩ፡ መህረክሙ፡ በልሳነ፡ ግዕዝ፡፡

4. መጠውዋ፡ ለሀገሮሙ፡ ለውእቱ፡ ንጉሥ፡፡

5. ነገርክዎሙ፡ ከመ፡ መጻእኩ፡ እምካልእት፡ ሀገር፡፡

6. ነሥአ፡ ለወሬዛ፡ ምስሌሁ፡ እስመ፡ ዘመዱ፡ ውእቱ፡፡

7. ለምንት፡ ነገርከኒ፡ ሠናየ፡ ወገበርከ፡ እኩየ፡ ላዕሌየ፡፡

8. ለአኮ፡ ለወልዱ፡ ኀቤነ፡ ምስለ፡ ዝንቱ፡ መጽሐፍ፡፡

9. መህሮ፡ አቡሁ፡ ሃይማኖተ፡ ርትዕተ፡፡

10. ወሀብናሁ፡ ሲሳየ፡ ለፍኖት፡ ወፈኖናሁ፡ ውስተ፡ ገዳማተ፡ ውእቱ፡ ብሔር፡፡

11. ለአከ፡ ሎቱ፡ ወነገሮ፡ ከመ፡ ገብአ፡ እግዚአሙ፡ እምሐይቀ፡ ባሕር፡
    _____

12. ዝንቱ፡ ውእቱ፡ ምስጢር፡ ዐቢይ፡ ወቅዱስ፡
    _____

13. ወሰድዖ፡ ለዝንቱ፡ ቅዱስ፡ ኀበ፡ መኳንንተ፡ ሕዝብ፡
    _____

14. በእንተ፡ ምንት፡ ኢሰማዕክሙኒ፡ ቃላትየ፡
    _____

15. ገሠጾሙ፡ ወነገሮሙ፡ ከመ፡ ፈነዎ፡ እግዚአብሔር፡ ለወልዱ፡ ውስተ፡ ዓለም፡ በእንቲአነ፡ ኩልነ፡
    _____

16. ሰአልዖ፡ ኀብስተ፡ ወወሀቦሙ፡ እበነ፡
    _____

17. ነቢበክምዎኑ፡ ለዝንቱ፡ ወሬዛ፡ እስመ፡ ኀለፈ፡ ዘመዱ፡
    _____

18. ወፀአ፡ እምዘመድ፡ ዐቢይ፡ ወብዑል፡
    _____

19. መሀርከሙኑ፡ ለውሉዲከ፡ በእንተ፡ ወንጌሉ፡ ለእግዚእነ፡
    _____

20. ኢመጠውናሁ፡ ሀገረነ፡ ለውእቱ፡ ንጉሥ፡
    _____

B. Translate the following: 1 Enoch 86.1–6

¹ ወካዕበ፡ ርኢኩ፡ በአዕይንትየ፡ እንዘ፡ እነውም፡ ወርኢኩ፡ ሰማየ፡ መልዕልተ፡ ወነዋ፡ ኮከብ፡ አሐዱ፡ ወድቀ፡ እምስማይ፡ ወይትሌዐል፡ ወይበልዕ፡ ወይትረዐይ፡ ማእከለ፡ እልክቱ፡ አልህምት፡

² ወእምዝ፡ ርኢኩ፡ አልህምተ፡ ወጸሊማነ፡ ወናሁ፡ ኩሎሙ፡ ለጠዉ፡ ምዕያሞሙ፡ ወምርዓዮሙ፡ ወአጥዋሆሙ፡ ወአሐዙ፡ የሐይዉ፡ ጀለካላኡ፡

³ ወካዕበ፡ ርኪኩ፡ በራእይ፡ ወነጸርክዎ፡ ለሰማይ፡ ወነዋ፡ ርኢኩ፡ ከዋክብት፡ ብዙኃን፡ ወረዱ፡ ወተገድፉ፡ እምሰማይ፡ በኀቤ፡ ዝኩ፡ ኮከብ፡ ቀዳማዊ፡ ወማእከሰ፡ እልኩ፡ ጣዕዋ፡ አልህምተ፡ ኮኑ፡ ወምስሌሆሙ፡ ይትረዓይ፡ ማእከሎሙ።

⁴ ወነጸርክዎሙ፡ ወርኢኩ፡ ወነዋ፡ ኩሎሙ፡ አውፅኡ፡ ኃፍረታቲሆሙ፡ ከመ፡ አፍራስ፡ ወአሐዙ፡ ይዕረጉ፡ ዲባ፡ እጉልተ፡ አልህምት፡ ወጽንሳ፡ ኮሎን፡ ወወለዳ፡ ነጌያተ፡ ወአግማለ፡ ወአእዱገ።

⁵ ወኮሎሙ፡ አልህምት፡ ፈርህዎሙ፡ ወደንገፁ፡ እምኔሆሙ፡ ወአሐዙ፡ እንዘ፡ ይነዝሩ፡ በስነኒሆሙ፡ ወይውሕጡ፡ ወይወግኡ፡ በአቅርንቲሆሙ።

⁶ ወአሐዙ፡ እንከ፡ ይበልዕዎሙ፡ ለእልኩ፡ አልህምት፡ ወነዋ፡ ኩሎሙ፡ ውሉደ፡ ምድር፡ አሐዙ፡ ይርዐዱ፡ ወያድለቅልቁ፡ እምኔሆሙ፡ ወይንፈጹ፡ እምኔሆሙ።

Chapter 12

SPECIAL CONSTRUCTIONS

12.1 The ወልዱ፡ ለንጉሥ፡ Construction

This special construction denotes possession by a specific individual in which the possessor of the item is indicated first by the applicable pronominal suffix, in this case the third-person "-u," followed by the preposition ለ-.

a. ወልዱ፡ ለንጉሥ፡ – "the son of the king"

b. ቤታ፡ ለብእሲት፡ – "the house of the woman"

c. ፈቃዶሙ፡ ለነቢያት፡ – "the wish of the prophets"

There is little difference between this construction and the simple construction of ወልደ፡ ንጉሥ፡. However, the ወልዱ፡ ለንጉሥ፡ construction can only be used when the second noun denotes a particular individual or thing; translated only as "the king's son." The special relationship is identified with the *-u* pronominal suffix on the first noun ወልዱ፡ indicating "his son" *of the king*. Whereas the ወልደ፡ ንጉሥ፡ construction does not designate a definite noun in relation to the preceding noun, in this case the phrase can be translated as "a king's son," "the king's son," or a member of the royal court – a prince.

In addition, the ወልዱ፡ ለንጉሥ፡ can change the word order as in ለንጉሥ፡ ወልዱ፡ or it can be separated by other terms in the sentence ወልዱ፡ አንተ፡ ለንጉሥ፡ – "you are the son of the king." This construction with the ለ- can also be used to designate other close relationships between two nouns:

a. ሀጕላ፡ ለሀገር፡ – "the destruction of the city"

b. አድያሚሁ፡ ለዮርዳኖስ፡ – "the districts of the Jordan"

12.2 The Quantifier ኵል-

The term ኵል- translates as the English "each, every, all" (Heb. כל) and always requires the addition of a pronominal suffix: e.g., ኵልነ፡ – "all of us"; ኵሎሙ፡ – "all of them."

a. The term can also act in parallel to another pronominal form in the sentence:
   ለክሙ፡ ኵልክሙ። – "(to you) to all of you"
   ሐሩ፡ ኵሎሙ። – "all of them went"

b. The third-person masculine singular form of ኵል- can stand independently with the meaning of "everything, or everybody" (ኵሉ፡ or its accusative form ኵሎ፡):
   ኵሉ፡ ድልው። – "everything is ready"
   ወሀብኩ፡ ሎቱ፡ ኵሎ። – "I gave him everything"
   በገጸ፡ ኵሉ። – "in the presence of everyone"

c. The third-person forms can also be used in parallel before a non-personal singular or plural noun:
   ኵላ፡ ሀገር። – "all the city, the whole city, each city"
   ኵላ፡ አህጉር። – "all the cities"
   ኵላ፡ በሐውርት። – "all the districts"

d. Plural forms of personal nouns can take the singular or plural form of ኵል-
   ኵሉ፡ / ኵሎሙ፡ ነቢያት። – "all the prophets"

e. The demonstrative pronouns ዝ-/ዝንቱ፡ will often be found preceding ኵል-
   ዝንቱ፡ ኵሉ። – "all this"
   ዝኵሉ፡ ብሔር። – "this whole district, all of this district"

12.3 The ቀተሎ፡ ለንጉሥ። Construction

Along with the possibility of the use of the accusative alone to mark the direct object of a transitive verb, the ቀተሎ፡ ለንጉሥ። – "he killed the king" can be used to express the object pronominally in which the object of the verb is first expressed pronominally as "he killed him," followed by the preposition ለ- and the non-accusative form ቀተሎ፡ ለንጉሥ። – "he killed (him), the king." The phrase ቀተሎ፡ ለንጉሥ። is used when the object is specific and definite, whereas the simple accusative ቀተለ፡ ንጉሠ። can be used as a definite or indefinite direct object.

12.4 The Preposition አልቦ፡ . . . ዘእንበለ።

The preposition/conjunction እንበለ፡ or ዘእንበለ፡ is often used associated with the word አልቦ፡ in the possessive or existential contexts and usually translated as "only."

a. አልብነ፡ ዝየ፡ ዘእንበለ፡ ኀምስ፡ ኅብስት። – "we have here only five loaves"

b. አልቦ፡ ዘርእየ፡ ዘእንበለ፡ ብእሲቱ። – "he saw only his wife"

c. አልቦ፡ ዘወሀበ፡ ለነ፡ ዘእንበለ፡ ማይ። – "he gave us only water"

The preposition ዘእንበለ፡ can also be understood as a conjunction depending on the presence of a non-accusative or an accusative object, usually translated as "but."

12.5 Vocabulary

1. ሣእን፡ (pl. አሥእን፡ አሥአን፡ አሣእን፡) – shoe, sandal
2. ቶታን፡ (pl. ቶታናት፡) – shoelace
3. ዐጽቅ፡ (pl. አዕጹቅ፡ አዕጹቃት፡) – branch, palm branch
4. አይኅ፡ – the flood
5. ወገረ፡ G/D – throw, stone someone; ተወግረ፡ Gt/Dt – to be stoned; ተዋገረ፡ Glt – throw stones at one another
6. ገነዘ፡ G – prepare for burial; ተገንዘ፡ Gt – be prepared for burial; አንገዘ፡ CG – cause someone to be buried
7. በተከ፡ G – break; ተበትከ፡ Gt – break (intrans)
8. ተርፈ፡ / ተረፈ፡ G – remain, survive; አትረፈ፡ CG – leave behind
9. ኀሠሠ፡ G – seek, look for; ተኀሥሠ፡ Gt – seek for oneself; ተኃሠሠ፡ Glt – discuss with one another
10. ኀደገ፡ G – leave, divorce, abandon, forgive; ተኀድገ፡ Gt – be left, be divorced; ተኃደገ፡ Glt – divorce someone
11. እንበለ፡ / ዘእንበለ፡ – without, except for
12. በርናበ፡ – Barnabas
13. ጴጥሮስ፡ – Peter
14. ሮሜ፡ – Rome
15. እስክንድርያ፡ – Alexandria
16. ሕግ፡ ሕገግ፡ – law, the Law
17. በሕግ፡ – legally, lawfully
18. መጽሐፍ፡ (pl. መጻሕፍት፡) – book, document, scroll
19. ልሳን፡ (pl. ልሳናት፡) – tongue, language
20. በድን፡ (pl. አብድንት፡) – corpse
21. ዮናናዊያን፡ – the Greeks
22. አፍርንጅ፡ – the Romans
23. ዕብራዊያን፡ – the Hebrews
24. ግዕዝ፡ አግዓዚ፡ – the Ethiopians
25. ብሔረ፡ አግዓዚ፡ – Ethiopia
26. ነጸረ፡ – look, look at
27. ባረከ፡ – bless
28. ተርጕመ፡ – translate
29. ዐቀበ፡ – guard, keep, watch
30. ቀበረ፡ – bury, intern
31. ዴገነ፡ – pursue, chase

12.6 Exercises

A. Translate the following:

1. ኀበ፡ አይ፡ ሀገር፡ ቀረብከሙ፡ ይአቴ፡ ዕለተ።

   _____

2. ገብረ፡ ኵሎ፡ ሕገገ፡ እግዚአብሔር፡ እስከ፡ ዕለተ፡ ሞቱ።

   _____

3. በእንተ፡ ምንት፡ ሐዘንክሙ፡ ኵልክሙ።

   _____

4. ተርጐምኩ፡ እሉ፡ ኵሎ፡ መጻሕፍተ፡ እምልሳነ፡ ዮናናዊያን።

5. ዘንተ፡ ገብርከ፡ በሕግ።

6. አይቴ፡ ሰበከ፡ ወንጌሎ።

7. አየ፡ መጽሐፈ፡ ተርጐምከ፡ እምልሳነ፡ አፍርንጅ።

8. አይቴ፡ ቀበርክሙ፡ በድኖ፡ ለአጕክሙ።

9. መነ፡ ባረከ፡ ወመነ፡ ኢባረከ።

B. Translate the following:

1. ኃለፍነ፡ እንተ፡ ኀበ፡ ቤቱ፡ ወነጸርነ፡ ውስቴቱ።

2. ተርጐም፡ ዘንተ፡ መጻሕፍተ፡ እምልሳነ፡ ዮናናዊያን፡ ለልሳነ፡ ግዕዝ።

3. ሰደዱ፡ አራዊተ፡ እምህገር፡ ወዴገኑ፡ እምድኅሬሆሙ፡ እስከ፡ ምሴት።

4. ነበረ፡ በውስተ፡ ኢትዮጵያ፡ ምስለ፡ አግዓዚ።

5. ለምንት፡ ገበርኪ፡ ዘንተ።

6. ምንት፡ ነጸርክሙ።

7. በእንተ፡ ምንት፡ ኢበከያ፡ ዲበ፡ ሞቶሙ፡ ለአምታቲሆን።

8. ቀበሩ፡ አብድንቲሆሙ፡ ለአጎዊሆሙ።

_____

9. እፎ፡ ዐቀብከን፡ ውሉዲከን፡ በይአቲ፡ ዕለት።

_____

10. ጐየ፡ ውስተ፡ ብሔረ፡ ግዕዝ፡ ወበረ፡ ምስሌሆሙ።

_____

C. Translate the following: Jubilees 1.1–10. Students should consult the answer key as needed.

¹ ወኮነ፡ በቀደሚ፡ ዓመት፡ ዘፀአቶሙ፡ ለደቂቀ፡ እስራኤል፡ እምነ፡ ግብጽ፡ በወርኅ፡ ሣልስ፡ አመ፡ ዐሡሩ፡ ወሰዱሱ፡ ለውእቱ፡ ወርኅ፡ ተናገሮ፡ እግዚአብሔር፡ ለሙሴ፡ እንዘ፡ ይብል፡ ዕርግ፡ ኀቤየ፡ ውስተ፡ ደብር፡ ወእሁበከ፡ ክልኤ፡ ጽላተ፡ አብን፡ ዘሕግ፡ ወዘትእዛዝ፡ ዘመጠነ፡ ጸሐፍኩ፡ ታለብዎሙ።

² ወዐርገ፡ ሙሴ፡ ውስተ፡ ደብረ፡ እግዚአብሔር፡ ወነደረ፡ ስብሐተ፡ እግዚአብሔር፡ ውስተ፡ ደብረ፡ ሲና፡ ወጸለሎ፡ ደመና፡ ሰዱሰ፡ ዕለተ።

³ ወጸውዖ፡ ለሙሴ፡ በዕለተ፡ ሳብዕት፡ በማእከለ፡ ደመና፡ ወርእየ፡ ስብሐተ፡ እግዚኣብሔር፡ ከመ፡ እሳት፡ ዘይነድድ፡ ውስተ፡ ርእሰ፡ ደብር።

⁴ ወሀሎ፡ ሙሴ፡ ውስተ፡ ደብር፡ አርብዓ፡ ዕለተ፡ ወአርብዓ፡ ሌሊተ፡ ወአምሮ፡ እግዚኣብሔር፡ ዘቀዳሚ፡ ወዘኒ፡ ይመጽእ፡ ነገር፡ ኩፉሌ፡ ኩሉ፡ መዋዕላት። ወለሕግ፡ ወለስምዕ፡

⁵ ወይቤሎ፡ አንብር፡ ልብከ፡ ውስተ፡ ኩሉ፡ ነገር፡ ዘአነ፡ እነግረከ፡ በዝንቱ፡ ደብር፡ ወጸሐፍ፡ ውስተ፡ መጽሐፍ፡ ከመ፡ ይርአዩ፡ ትውልዶሙ፡ ከመ፡ ኢኀደግዎሙ፡ በእንተ፡ ኩሉ፡ እኩይ፡ ዘገብሩ፡ ለአስሕቶ፡ ሥርዓት፡ ዘአነ፡ አውርዕ፡ ማእከሌየ፡ ወማእከሌከ፡ ዮም፡ ለትውልዶሙ፡ በደብረ፡ ሲና።

⁶ ወይከውን፡ ከመዝ፡ አመ፡ ይመጽእ፡ ኩሉ፡ ዝነገር፡ ላዕሌሆሙ፡ ወያአምሩ፡ ከመ፡ ጸደቁ፡ እምኔሆሙ፡ በኩሉ፡ ፍትሐሙ፡ ወበኩሉ፡ ምግባሮሙ፡ ወያአምሩ፡ ከመ፡ ህልው፡ ኮንኩ፡ ምስሌሆሙ።

⁷ ወአንተኒ፡ ጸሐፍ፡ ለከ፡ ኩሎ፡ ዘቃለ፡ ዘአነ፡ አየዐለ፡ ዮም፡ እስመ፡ አአምር፡ ምረቶሙ፡ ወክሳዶሙ፡ ይቡሰ፡ ዘአንበለ፡ አብአሙ፡ ውስተ፡ ምድር፡ እንተ፡ መሐልኩ፡ ለአብርሃም፡ ወለይስሐቅ፡ ወለያዕቆብ፡ እንዘ፡ እብል፡ ለዘርእከሙ፡ እሁብ፡ ምድረ፡ እንተ፡ ትውሕዝ፡ ሐሊበ፡ ወመዓረ። ወይበልዑ፡ ወይጻግቡ፡

⁸ ወይትመየጡ፡ ኀበ፡ አምላከ፡ ነኪር፡ ኀበ፡ እለ፡ ኢያድኅንዎሙ፡ እምኩሉ፡ ምንዳቤሆሙ። ወትስምዕ፡ ዛቲ፡ ስምዕ፡ ለስምዕ፡

⁹ እስመ፡ ይረስዑ፡ ኩሎ፡ ትእዛዝየ፡ ኩሎ፡ ዘአነ፡ እኤዝዞሙ፡ ወየሐውሩ፡ ድኅረ፡ አሕዛብ፡ ወድኅረ፡ ርኩሶሙ፡ ወድኅረ፡ ኀሳሮሙ፡ ወይትቀነዩ፡ ለአማልክቲሆሙ፡ ወይከውንዎሙ፡ ማዕቀፈ፡ ወለምንዳቤ፡ ወለፃዕር፡ ወለመሥገርት፡

¹⁰ ወይትሐጐሉ፡ ብዙኃን፡ ወይትአኀዙ፡ ወይወድቁ፡ ውስተ፡ እደ፡ ፀር፡ እስመ፡ ኀደጉ፡ ሥርዓትየ፡ ወትእዛዝየ፡ ወበዓላተ፡ ኪዳንየ፡ ወሰንበታትየ፡ ወቅድሳትየ፡ ዘቀደስኩ፡ ሊተ፡ በማእከሎሙ። ወደብተራየ፡ ወመቅደስየ፡ ዘቀደስኩ፡ ሊተ፡ በማእከለ፡ ምድር፡ ከመ፡ እሢም፡ ስምየ፡ ላዕሌሁ፡ ወይኀድር።

Chapter 13

PRONOUNS (PART 1)

13.1 Personal Pronouns

The Personal Pronouns in Gəʿəz follow a similar pattern to that of Hebrew Pronouns. They identify person (1st, 2nd, 3rd), gender (masc. or fem.), and number (singular and plural). Each is designated by its own term as seen in the table below:

TABLE 13.1: Independent Personal Pronouns

PGN	Pronoun	Translation	PGN	Pronoun	Translation
1cs	አነ፡	I	1cp	ንሕነ፡	we
2ms	አንተ፡	you	2mp	አንቲ፡	you
2fs	አንትሙ፡	you	2fp	አንትን፡	you
3ms	ውእቱ፡	he, it, that	3mp	እሙንቱ፡	They, those
3fs	ይእቲ፡	she, it, that	3fp	እማንቱ፡	They, those

The third-person masculine and feminine plural have an additional form, equivalent to the 3cp form in Hebrew ውእቶሙ፡.

13.2 Pronouns in Non-Verbal Predicate

Gəʿəz pronouns can serve as the subject in a non-verbal predicate phrase: a Noun (as the predicate) and the Pronoun (as subject)–in this word order.

a. ብእሲ፡ አነ። – "I am a man"

b. ብእሲት፡ አንቲ። – "you are a woman"

c. መሠግር፡ ውእቱ። – "he is a fisherman"

d. መኳንንት፡ እሙንቱ። – "they are judges"

e. ነቢያት፡ ንሕኑ። – "we are prophets"

f. ኢየሩሳሌም፡ ይእቲ። – "it is Jerusalem"

At times the author may wish to emphasize the person in the phrase and the pronoun will appear before the predicate noun and also following it: አነ፡ ብእሲ፡ አነ። – "I am a man." How the emphatic nature of the double pronoun should be made in the translation is unclear, but something like "I am (that) man."

13.3   The "Neutralized Copula" ውእቱ፡

The word ውእቱ፡ is used to represent a form of the verb "be" in a sentence irrespective of the person, gender, or number of the personal subject pronoun.

a. አነ፡ ብእሲ፡ ውእቱ። – "I am a man"

b. አንተ፡ ብእሲ፡ ውእቱ። – "you are a man"

c. አነ፡ መኮንን፡ ውእቱ። – "I am a judge"

d. አንተ፡ መኮንን፡ ውእቱ። – "you are a judge"

e. አነ፡ ውእቱ፡ መኮንን። – "I am a judge" – note the word order of the copula can change and follow the subject pronoun.

The copula ውእቱ፡ can also be used in the predicate phrase involving two nouns. Two Gəʿəz nouns can form a predicate phrase three different ways:

Noun (1) + Noun (2)-ዮሐንስ፡ ሐዋርያ። – John is an apostle"
Noun (1) + Noun (2) + 3rd person pronoun – ዮሐንስ፡ ሐዋርያ፡ ውእቱ።
Noun (1) + 3rd person pronoun + Noun (2) – ዮሐንስ፡ ውእቱ፡ ሐዋርያ።

All three phrases can be translated as "John is an apostle." Generally speaking, the copula will agree in number and gender with the nouns if they are human beings but should be understood as "neutral" in the predicate.

13.4   The Demonstrative Pronouns (see ch. 8 for review of the demonstrative)

If the subject of the sentence is a demonstrative pronoun such as "this" or "these," the word order usually follows the Demonstrative Pronoun + 3rd person pronoun + noun.

a. ዝንቱ፡ ውእቱ፡ ኦሪት፡ ወነቢያት። – "this is the Law and the Prophets"

b. ዘቲ፡ ይእቲ፡ ወለተ፡ ንጉሥ። – "this is the daughter of the king"

c. እሉ፡ እሙንቱ፡ ውሉደ፡ ንጉሥ። – "These are the sons of the king"

The Gəʿəz plural demonstrative pronouns follow a similar pattern as the Hebrew demonstrative. They are masculine and feminine in gender and point to something nearby, "these," or something distant, "those."

TABLE 13.2: Plural Demonstratives

Masculine	እሉ፡ እሎንቱ፡	These (m.)
Feminine	እላ፡ እላንቱ፡	These (f.)
Masculine	እሙንቱ፡	Those (m.)
Feminine	እማንቱ፡	Those (f.)

13.5 Interrogative Pronouns

Interrogative pronouns are usually found at the beginning of a clause unless they are part of a construct noun sequence or are governed by a preposition. The common interrogative pronouns include:

መኑ፡ – "who?"	መነ፡ – "who?" (acc.)	እለ፡ መኑ፡ – "who?" (pl.)
ምንት፡ – "what?"	ምንተ፡ – "what?" (acc.)	
አይ፡ – "which?" (አያት፡ pl.)	አየ፡ – "which?" (acc.)	አያተ፡ – (acc. pl.)

The following examples reveal the normal syntax for interrogatives:

a. መኑ፡ ውእቱ፡ ዝንቱ፡ ብእሲ። – "who is this man?"

b. መነ፡ ቀተሉ። – "whom did they kill?"

c. ምንት፡ ውእቱ፡ ዝንቱ። – "what is this?"

d. ምንተ፡ ረከበ። – "what did he find?"

e. አይ፡ ሀገር፡ ዛቲ። – "which city is this?"

f. አየ፡ ሀገረ፡ ሐነጹ። – "which city did they build?"

g. ኀበ፡ መኑ፡ ጐዩ። – "to whom did they flee?"

h. ወልደ፡ መኑ፡ አንተ። – "whose son are you?"

i. በእንተ፡ ምንት፡ ሐረ፡ – "why did he go?"

j. እሊ፡ መኑ፡ እሙንቱ፡ – "who are they?"

13.6 Interrogative Adverbs

Like the interrogative pronouns, the adverbs usually are found at the beginning of a clause. The common interrogative adverbs include:

a. አይቴ፡ በአይቴ፡ – "where?"

b. እምአይቴ፡ – "whence?"

c. ማእዜ፡ – "when?"

d. እፎ፡ – "how?"

e. ለምንት፡ or በእንተ፡ ምንት፡ – "why?"

13.7 Interrogatives with ዘ-

The normal use of the interrogative can often be augmented with the use of ዘ-. The normal clause መኑ፡ ገብረ፡ ዘንተ፡ – "who did this?" can appear as the altered መኑ፡ ዘገብረ፡ ዘንተ፡. In this case the relative clause becomes the second part of the non-verbal clause. In addition to this alteration, the pronominal term ውእቱ፡ can be inserted into the clause: መኑ፡ ውእቱ፡ ዘገብረ፡ ዘንተ፡. This phrase could have several translations, but generally speaking, the reason appears to be emphatic on the part of the author. In this case, the ውእቱ፡ should be understood as the subject of the phrase: "It (ውእቱ፡) is who (መኑ፡), who (ዘ) did this?"

Interrogative adverbs also follow this emphatic construction similar to the interrogative pronouns. The following offer some examples:

a. እፎ፡ ዘኢሰምዑ፡ ለቃሉ፡ – "why did they not heed his words?"–lit. "this was how . . ."

b. በአይቴ፡ ዘረከብከ፡ መጽሐፈ፡ – "where did you find the book?"–lit. "this was where . . ."

13.8 Interrogatives with አኮ፡

All Gəʿəz interrogatives can be negated with the term አኮ፡. This is used to emphasize the part of the clause that is being negated.

አኮ፡ ህየ፡ ዘርእየኒ፡ – "it was not there that he saw me"–emphasizing the verb ህየ፡

The other negated form of a sentence can be expressed with አኮ፡ also:

ኢሐነጸ፡ ዝንቱ፡ ብእሲ፡ ቤቶ፡ ህየ፡ – "this man did not build his house there" can be expressed as አኮ፡ ህየ፡ ዘሐነጸ፡ ዝንቱ፡ ብእሲ፡ ቤቶ፡፡ or as አኮ፡ ቤቶ፡ ዘሐነጸ፡ ዝንቱ፡ ብእሲ፡ ህየ፡፡ – all translated similarly.

A positive form of this construction occurs rarely and is identified with the H prefixed to the verb in the phrase:

a. እሉኬ፡ ዘያረኩስ፡ እስም፡ ለሕዝብ፡፡ – "it is these things that defile the people."

b. በጸጋ፡ ዘነሣእከሙ፡፡ – "this was as a gift that you received."

አኮ፡ is also used to negate phrases in general:

a. አምላከ፡ ሕያዋን፡ ውእቱ፡ ወአኮ፡ አምላከ፡ ምዉታን፡፡ – "He is the Lord of the living and not the Lord of the dead."

b. ወባሕቱ፡ ፈቃደከ፡ ይኩን፡ ወአኮ፡ ፈቃድየ፡፡ – "However, may it be what you want and not what I want."

In addition, a contrasting phrase may follow an አኮ፡ H-formula that is introduced with the conjunction አላ፡ – "indeed"; here, the phrase አኮ፡ H- ("this is not that . . .) may appear with only the verb:

አኮ ዘሞተት፡ አላ፤ ትነውም፡፡ – "it is not that she is dead, indeed she only sleeps."

Finally, the phrases አኮ፡ ሁ፡ or አኮ፡ ኑ፡ like አልቦ፡ ኑ፡ can be used in rhetorical sentences to form a question from a statement; one that expects a positive response.

አኮ፡ ሁ፡ ሠናየ፡ ዘርዐ፡ ዘራእከ፡ ውስተ፡ ገራህት፤ – "Did you not sow good seed in the ground?"

13.9 Vocabulary

1. ሐይቅ፡ (pl. ሐይቃት፡) – shore of the lake
2. ዕድ፡ (ዕደው፡) – collective for men
3. እም፡ (እማት፡) – mother
4. አብ፡ (pl. አበው፡) – father
5. ቤተ፡ አብ፡ – family
6. ምት፡ (pl. አምታት፡) – husband
7. ደቂቅ፡ – children, offspring
8. ንግሥት፡ (pl. ንግሥታት፡) – queen
9. እግዚአብሔር፡ – God
10. አምላክ፡ – the Lord
11. እስራኤል፡ – Israel
12. አላ፡ – but (following a negative clause)
13. መዐት፡ – wrath
14. ጽቡር፡ – clay, mud
15. አጽበረ፡ ጽቡረ፡ CG – work clay
16. ዜና፡ (pl. ዜናት፡) – report, story, account
17. ጊዜ፡ (pl. ጊዜያት፡) – time
18. ኩሎ፡ ጊዜ፡ – always
19. ሞቅሕ፡ (pl. መዋቅሕት፡) – bonds, chains
20. ቤተ፡ ሞቅሕ፡፡ – prison

21. ሐተተ፡ – investigate; ተሐተተ፡ Gt – be investigated
22. ነግሠ፡ – become ruler, king; አንገሠ፡ CG – cause someone to rule
23. ህድአ፡ – quiet down; አህድአ፡ CG – pacify, make tranquil
24. ህዱእ፡ (adj.) – quiet, tranquil
25. ከሠተ፡ – reveal, uncover; ተከሥተ፡ Gt – be revealed, be uncovered
26. ሞቅሐ፡ – put in chains/imprison; ተሞቅሐ፡ Qt – be bound in chains; አሞቅሐ፡ CQ – have someone put in prison

13.10 Exercises

A. Translate the following:

1. ንሕነ፡ ነቢያተ፡ እግዚአብሔር፡ ንሕነ።

2. ዝውእቱ፡ ነቢዩ፡ እግዚአብሔር።

3. እሉ፡ እሙንቱ፡ ሰብአ፡ ዛቲ፡ ሀገር።

4. ዛቲ፡ ይእቲ፡ ፍኖተ፡ ገዳም።

5. እሉ፡ እሙንቱ፡ ደቂቀ፡ መኰንን።

6. እሉ፡ እሙንቱ፡ ሊቃነ፡ ሕዝብ።

7. ዝውእቱ፡ አምላከ፡ ሰማይ።

8. ዝንቱ፡ ውእቱ፡ ነገረ፡ አምላክ።

9. እላንቱ፡ እማንቱ፡ አንስተ፡ ንጉሥ።

10. እሉ፡ ሰብእ፡ እሙንቱ፡ አምታተ፡ እማንቱ፡ አንስት።

11. እሎንቱ፡ እሙንቱ፡ አምታተ፡ አንስት።

12. እሎንቱ፡ እሙንቱ፡ መኳንንት።

13. ዝውእቱ፡ ገዳም፣ ወእሉ፡ እሙንቱ፡ አራዊተ፡ ገዳም።

14. ዛቲ፡ ይእቲ፡ እም፡ እላንቱ፡ አዋልድ።

15. አንትሙ፡ ጸሐፍት፡ አንትሙ።

B. Translate the following:

1. ኢነበሩ፡ ውሉደ፡ ሀገር፡ ህየ፣ አላ፡ ሮጹ፡ ውስተ፡ ሐይቅ።

2. ኢጉዩ፡ አምታተ፡ አንስት፣ አላ፡ ነበሩ፡ ውስተ፡ ሀገር።

3. ገብኡ፡ እሙንቱ፡ ሰብእ፡ እምአድባር።

4. በኡ፡ ደቂቀ፡ ውእቱ፡ መኰንን፡ ኀበ፡ ንጉሥ።

5. ዐርገ፡ እምውስተ፡ ሐይቅ፡ ወበአ፡ ውስተ፡ ሀገር።

6. ገብአት፡ እም፡ ዝንቱ፡ ገብር፡ እምይእቲ፡ ሀገር።

7. በጽሐት፡ አሕማረ፡ እሙንቱ፡ መሥግራን፡ ኀበ፡ ሐይቅ።

8. ወረደ፡ በረድ፡ ወዝናም፡ ዲበ፡ አብያተ፡ ዛቲ፡ ሀገር።

9. ጉያ፡ እላ፡ አንስት፡ እምህገር።
   _____

10. በጽሐ፡ ዝንቱ፡ ንጉሥ፡ ምስለ፡ ንግሥት፡ ኀበ፡ ሀገር።
    _____

C. Translate the following: Jubilees 1.11–21.

[11] ወገብሩ፡ ሎሙ፡ ፍሥሐታተ፡ ወአሙ፡ ወግልፎ፡ ወሰገዱ፡ ዘዘ ዚአሆሙ፡ ለስሒት፡ ወይዘብሑ፡ ውሉዶሙ፡ ለአጋንንት፡ ወለኵሉ፡ ግብረ፡ ስሕተተ፡ ልቦሙ።

[12] ወእፌኑ፡ ኀቤሆሙ፡ ሰማዕተ፡ ከመ፡ አስምዕ፡ ሎሙ፡ ወኢይሰምዑ፡ ወሰማዕተኒ፡ ይቀትሉ፡ ወለእለሂ፡ የኃሥሡ፡ ሕገ፡ ይሰድድዎሙ፡ ወኵሎ፡ ያጠርዑ፡ ወይዌጥኑ፡ ለገቢረ፡ እኩይ፡ በቅድመ፡ አዕይንትየ፡

[13] ወእኀብእ፡ ገጽየ፡ እምኔሆሙ፡ ወእሜጥዎሙ፡ ውስተ፡ እደ፡ አሕዛብ፡ ለጊዋዊ፡ ወለሕብል፡ ወለተበልዖ፡ ወእሴስሎሙ፡ እማእከለ፡ ምድር፡ ወእዘርዎሙ፡ ማእከለ፡ አሕዛብ።

[14] ወይረስዑ፡ ኵሎ፡ ሕግየ፡ ወኵሎ፡ ትእዛዝየ፡ ወኵሎ፡ ፍትሕየ፡ ወይስሕቱ፡ ሠርቀ፡ ወሰንበተ፡ ወበዓለ፡ ወኢዮቤለ፡ ወሥርዓተ።

[15] ወእምዝ፡ ይትመየጡ፡ ኀቤየ፡ እማእከለ፡ አሕዛብ፡ በኵሉ፡ ልቦሙ፡ ወበኵሉ፡ ነፍሶሙ፡ ወበኵሉ፡ ኀይሎሙ፡ ወአስተጋብኦሙ፡ እማእከለ፡ ኵሉ፡ አሕዛብ፡ ወየኀሥሡኒ፡ ከመ፡ እትራከቦሙ፡ ሶበ፡ ኀሠሡኒ፡ በኵሉ፡ ልቦሙ፡ ወበኵሉ፡ ነፍሶሙ፡ ወእክሥት፡ ሎሙ፡ ብዙኀ፡ ሰላመ፡ በጽድቅ፡

[16] ወአፈልሶሙ፡ ተክለ፡ ርቱዕ፡ በኵሉ፡ ልብየ፡ ወበኵሉ፡ ነፍስየ፡ ወይከውኑ፡ ለበረከት፡ ወአኮ፡ ለመርገም፡ ወይከውኑ፡ ርእሰ፡ ወአኮ፡ ዘነበ።

[17] ወአሐንጽ፡ መቅደስየ፡ ማእከሎሙ፡ ወአኀድር፡ ምስሌሆሙ፡ ወእከውኖሙ፡ አምላከ፡ ወእሙንቱኒ፡ ይከውኑኒ፡ ሕዝብየ፡ ዘበአማን፡ ወዘበጽድቅ፡

[18] ወኢያኀድጎሙ፡ ወኢይትናከሮሙ፡ እስመ፡ አነ፡ እግዚአብሔር፡ አምላኮሙ።

[19] ወወድቀ፡ ሙሴ፡ በገጹ፡ ወጸለየ፡ ወይቤ፡ እግዚአ፡ አምላኪየ፡ ኢትኅድግ፡ ሕዝበከ፡ ወርስተከ፡ ለሐዊር፡ በስሕተተ፡ ልበሙ፡ ወኢትመጥዎሙ፡ ውስተ፡ እደ፡ አሕዛብ፡ ከመ፡ ይኩኑንዎሙ፡ ወከመ፡ ኢያግበርዎሙ፡ ከመ፡ ይኑጥኡ ለከ።

[20] ይትለዐል፡ እግዚአ፡ ምሕረትከ፡ ላዕለ፡ ሕዝብከ፡ ወፍጥር፡ ሎሙ፡ መንፈሰ፡ ርትዐ፡ ወኢይኩኖሙ፡ መንፈሰ፡ ቤልሐር፡ ለአስተዋድዮቶሙ፡ ቅድሜከ፡ ወለአዕቅጾቶሙ፡ እምኵሉ፡ ፍኖተ፡ ጽድቅ፡ ከመ፡ ይትሐጐሉ፡ እምቅድሙ፡ ገጽከ።

[21] ወእሙንቱ፡ ሕዝብከ፡ ወርስትከ፡ ዘባላሕከ፡ በኀይልከ፡ ዐቢይ፡ እምእደ፡ ግብጽ፡ ፍጥር፡ ሎሙ፡ ልበ፡ ንጹሐ፡ ወመንፈሰ፡ ቅዱሰ፡ ወኢይትዐጽጹ፡ በኃጢአቶሙ፡ እምይእዜ፡ ወእስከ፡ ለዓለም።

Chapter 14

PRONOUNS (PART 2)

14.1 Relative Pronouns and Relative Clauses

The Gəʿəz relative pronouns are as follows:

Masculine Singular: ዘ-
Feminine Singular: እንተ፡
Common Plural: እለ፡

The masc. sing. ዘ-form may be used instead of እንተ፡ and እለ፡ if they are not used in the absolute sense. Note that ዘ- must be attached to the following word: e.g., ብእሲ፡ ዘመጽአ፡ – "the man that/who came," but not so for እንተ፡ and እለ፡.

a. Relative clauses in which the relative pronoun is the subject of the clause present no special issues:
ብእሲ፡ ዘተሣየጠ፡ ቤትየ፡ – "the man who bought my house."
ብእሲት፡ እንተ፡ ወለደት፡ ወልደ፡ – "the woman who gave birth to the child."
ነቢያት፡ እለ፡ ተነበዩ፡ ህየ፡ – "the prophets who prophesied there."

b. However, when the relative pronoun is the direct object of the verb, it is indicated by a "resumptive pronoun" (referring to the subject) attached to the verb:
ብእሲ፡ ዘርእይዎ፡ (or ዘርእዮ፡) – "the man whom they saw."

c. If a relative pronoun appears in a prepositional relationship (e.g., in which, of which, to which) then there will likely be a resumptive pronoun present:
ሀገር፡ እንተ፡ ስማ፡ ኢየሩሳሌም፡ – "the city whose name is Jerusalem"
ብእሲ፡ ዘቀተልዎ፡ ለወልዱ፡ – "a man whose son they killed"
ምድር፡ ዘነበሩ፡ ውስቴታ፡ – "the land in which they settled"

d. A preposition may appear before the relative pronoun if there is no likelihood of ambiguity. This occurs most often with the preposition በ-:

መዋዕሊሁ፡ በዘአስተርአዮሙ፡ ኮከብ። – "the time <u>at which</u> the star appeared to them"

On rare occasion, the preposition በ- will appear following the relative pronoun:

ምድር፡ እንተ በጎቢ፡ መጻእነ። – "The land to which we have come" – the addition of the preposition ኅቢ፡ is likely being used as a point of clarification of the land.

e. The use of the relative clause as a noun is fairly frequent:

ዘሞተ፡ – "the one who died"
እለ፡ እምውስተ፡ ጸሐፍት። – "those who were from among the scribes"
እለ፡ ነበሩ፡ ህየ። – "those who had remained there"

f. Relative pronouns can function as the absolute in a construct noun relationship:

ዘለምጽ፡ – "a/the leper" or "the one of leprosy"
እንተ፡ ኦርዮ። – "the one (wife) of Uriah"
እለ፡ ስገል። – "diviners" or "those of divination"
እለ፡ ኣጋንንት። – "demoniacs" or "those of demons"

g. The relative pronoun ዘ-can be used in a similar way (usually not እንተ፡ or እለ፡) while appearing with the names of materials from which something is made:

መንበር፡ ዘወርቅ። – "the/a golden throne" or "a throne of gold"
ቅናት፡ ዘአነዳ። – "a/the leather belt" or "a belt of leather"

h. The above usage in (g.) resulted in ዘ- expressing the genitive case as a preposition "of." It most often functions in this way when an adjective, a proper name, or a suffix intervenes between the relative pronoun and the construct noun:

ወንጌል፡ ቅዱስ፡ ዘእግዚእነ። – "the holy gospel of our Lord"
ዐጸደ፡ ወይን፡ ዘሀግሪጾስ። – "the vineyard of Agrippa"
ቤተልሔም፡ ዘይሁዳ። – "Bethlehem of Judah"

i. The attributive relative clause may appear before or after the noun it is modifying:

ዘሞተ፡ ብእሲ። or ብእሲ፡ ዘሞተ። – "the man who died"
ዘወርቅ፡ መንበር። or መንበር፡ ዘወርቅ። – "the throne of gold"
ዘመጠነዝ፡ ሃይማኖት። or ሃይማኖት፡ ዘመጠነዝ። – "such faith"; lit. "faith that is to this extent"
ዘከመዝ፡ ሥልጣን። or ሥልጣን፡ ዘከመዝ። – "such authority"; lit. "authority that is like this"

j. On occasion the relative pronoun must be supplied in the translation when it does not appear but may be needed:

ብእሲ፡ ስሙ፡ ዮሐንስ። – "a man *whose* name is John"

14.2 Indefinite Pronouns

Indefinite pronouns are formed in Gəʿəz by attaching the suffixes -ሂ or -ኒ to the interrogatives መኑ፡ – "who?" or ምንት፡ – "what?". These usually appear in negative sentences:

a. ኢርእዩ፡ መነሂ፡ – "they saw no one" or "they didn't see anyone"

b. ኢገብረ፡ ምንተሂ፡ – "he did nothing" or "he didn't do anything"

To make the negation more emphatic, the pronoun has ወኢ-attached to it

a. ኢርእዩ፡ ወኢመነሂ፡ – "they saw no one at all"

b. ኢነገረ፡ ዘንተ፡ ወኢለመኑሂ፡ – "he told this to no one at all"

14.3 Independent Personal Pronouns

In addition to the subject personal pronoun forms in chapter 13, there are an additional three series of independent pronouns: subject, direct object, and possessive.

TABLE 14.1: Independent Subject Pronouns

PGN		PGN	
1cs	ለሊየ፡	1cp	ለሊነ፡
2ms	ለሊከ፡	2mp	ለሊከሙ፡
2fs	ለሊኪ፡	2fp	ለሊከን፡
3ms	ለሊሁ፡	3mp	ለሊሆሙ፡
3fs	ለሊሃ፡	3fp	ለሊሆን፡

The Subject forms are only used when there is a strong emphasis or contrast required in the clause. Generally, they stand in apposition to other pronominal markers such as verb subjects or other independent pronouns. They are best understood as the English intensive pronouns:

a. ርኢክዎ፡ ለሊየ፡ – "I myself saw him"

b. ውእቱ፡ ለሊሁ፡ እግዚእነ፡ ውእቱ፡ – "He himself is our God"

Rarely, the subject forms can be used to modify a noun: e.g., ለሊሁ፡ ቃልከ፡ – "your very / own word."
The direct object forms, shown below, are used for either emphasis: e.g., ኪያከ፡ ርኢነ፡ አኮ፡ ኪያሁ፡ – "We saw you, not him"; or as the direct object of the perfective active participle (here the ቀቲሎ፡ form); e.g., ኪያሁ፡ ቀቲሎ፡ጐየ፡ – "Having killed him, he fled."

TABLE 14.2: Independent Direct Object Pronouns

PGN		PGN	
1cs	ኪያየ፡	1cp	ኪያነ፡
2ms	ኪያከ፡	2mp	ኪያከሙ፡
2fs	ኪያኪ፡	2fp	ኪያክን፡
3ms	ኪያሁ፡	3mp	ኪያሆሙ፡
3fs	ኪያሃ፡	3fp	ኪያሆን፡

TABLE 14.3: Independent Possessive Pronouns

PGN	Masculine Singular Noun	Feminine Singular Noun	Plural Noun
1cs	ዚአየ፡	እንቲአየ፡	እሊአየ፡
2ms	ዚአከ፡	እንቲአከ፡	እሊአከ፡
2fs	ዚአኪ፡	እንቲአኪ፡	እሊአኪ፡
3ms	ዚአሁ፡	እንቲአሁ፡	እሊአሁ፡
3fs	ዚአሃ፡	እንቲአሃ፡	እሊአሃ፡
1cs	ዚአነ፡	እንቲአነ፡	እሊአነ፡
2mp	ዚአከሙ፡	እንቲአከሙ፡	እሊአከሙ፡
2fp	ዚአክን፡	እንቲአክን፡	እሊአክን፡
3mp	ዚአሆሙ፡	እንቲአሆሙ፡	እሊአሆሙ፡
3fp	ዚአሆን፡	እንቲአሆን፡	እሊአሆን፡

The possessive forms occur often and their pronominal status (mine, yours, his, hers) is important to note, i.e., a noun must appear in construct before the possessive pronoun:

a. ቤተ፡ ዚአየ፡ – "my house" or "the house of mine."

b. ብእሲተ፡ እንቲአየ፡ – "my wife" or "the wife of mine."

c. አግብርተ፡ እሊአየ፡ – "my servants" or "the servants of mine."

They may also be used in the predicate as true pronouns: ዝንቱ፡ ቤት፡ ዚአየ፡ ውእቱ፡ – "this house is mine." Often, possessive pronouns may be preceded by ዘ- which may indicate a relative pronoun: መጽሐፍ፡ ዘዚአየ፡ – "the book that is mine" or "my book." It can also indicate a nominalized relative pronoun: ይከውነነ፡ ዘዚአሁ፡ – "We shall possess that which is his."

14.4 The Phrase ቦ፡ ዘ- as an Indefinite Pronoun

The term ቦ፡ is often used in combination with the relative pronoun ዘ- (at times with አለ፡) and is translated as the English indefinite pronouns "someone, something, no one, or nothing." The relative pronoun ዘ- can act as either the subject or object of the clause.

እመ፡ ቦ፡ ዘኀደገ፡ ብእሲቶ፡። – "if (እመ፡) someone divorces his wife . . ."
አልቦ፡ ዘረከበ፡ ህየ፡። – "he found nothing there."
አልቦ፡ ዘረከበ፡ ወርቀየ፡። – "no one found my gold."

The positive forms of ቦ፡ ዘ- are used to articulate a related opposite idea.

ቦ፡ ዘቦአ፡ ሀገረ፡ ወቦ፡ ዘጕየየ፡። – "some entered the city and some fled."
ቦ፡ ዘቀተሉ፡ ወቦ፡ ዘኢቀተሉ፡። – "some they killed and some they did not kill."

14.5 Vocabulary

1. ፀምር፡ – wool, fleece
2. ጸጕር፡ – hair, fur, feathers
3. ወርቅ፡ – gold, money
4. ብሩር፡ (pl. ብሩራት፡) – silver
5. ኀጺን፡ (pl. ኀጸውንት፡) – iron, sword, weapon
6. ብርት፡ – copper
7. ገመል፡ (pl. ገመላት፡ አግማል፡) – camel
8. ቅናት፡ (pl. ቅናታት፡ ቅናውት፡) – belt
9. ማእስ፡ / ማዕስ፡ (pl. አምእስት፡ / አምዕስት፡) – skin, hide, leather
10. ሰይፍ፡ (pl. አስያፍ፡ አሰይፍት፡) – sword
11. መካን፡ (pl. መካናት፡) – place, locale
12. ተረስየ፡ Dt – put on a garment, clothe oneself
13. ተገብረ፡ Dt – labor, toil, work

14.6 Exercises

A. Translate the following:

1. ሀገር፡ እንተ፡ ነሥአዋ፡።

2. አንስት፡ እለ፡ ሐዘና፡ ዲቤሁ፡።

3. ሰብእ፡ እለ፡ ምኡ፡ ሀገረነ።

4. ፀምር፡ ዘሜጡ፡ ለነ።

5. ነገር፡ ዘሰማዕናሁ።

6. ሕዝብ፡ ዘዐደዎ፡ ለባሕርነ።

7. አርዳእ፡ እለ፡ ሀለዉ፡ ምስሌሁ።

8. ወርቅ፡ ዘነሥኡኒ፡ እምቤትየ።

9. ንጉሥ፡ እኩይ፡ ዘፈርሁ፡ እምቅድሜሁ።

10. ኃጥአን፡ እለ፡ ነስሑ፡ እምኃጢአቶሙ።

11. ብፁዕ፡ ዘገብረ፡ ዘንተ፡ ሰይፈ፡ እምኔሁ።

12. ብርሃን፡ ዘመልአ፡ ውስተ፡ ሰማይ።

13. መልአክ፡ ዘመርሐነ፡ እምገዳም።

14. አግማል፡ ዘተሣየጥነ፡ እምኔቤሁ።

15. ውሉድ፡ እለ፡ ሞቱ፡ በደዌ።

16. መሥግር፡ ዘሜጠ፡ ዛተ፡ ሐመረ።

17. ብእሲ፡ ጠቢብ፡ ዘገብረ፡ ዘንተ፡ ሰይፈ።

18. መጻሕፍት፡ ዘውዕዩ፡ ወአተ፡ አሚረ።

19. ፍኖት፡ እንተ፡ ስሕትነ፡ እምኔሃ።

20. ሃይማኖት፡ ዘከሕድዋ።

B. Translate the following:

1. ቤት፡ ዘእብን።

2. ቅናት፡ ዘማእስ።

3. መሥዋዕት፡ ዘጎብስት፡ ወወይን።

4. ሐመር፡ እንተ፡ ዕፅ።

5. ደመና፡ ዘብርሃን።

6. ንዋይ፡ ዘወርቅ።

7. አስይፍት፡ እንተ፡ ብርት።

8. አልባስ፡ ዘጸጉረ፡ ገመል።

9. ሰይፍ፡ ዘኃጺን።

10. ዐጽፍ፡ ዘዐምር።
_____

C. Translate the following:

1. ረከብነ፡ ዘንተ፡ መካነ፡ እኩየ፡ ፈድፋደ፡ ወኢነበርነ፡ ውስቴቱ።
_____

2. ኢገባእኩ፡ ሀገረ፡ እንተ፡ ኃበ፡ ወፃእኩ።
_____

3. ኢወደይኩ፡ ወርቀየ፡ ውስተ፡ ውእቱ፡ መካን።
_____

4. ተንሥአ፡ እምኀበ፡ ነበረ፡ ወዴገነ፡ ድኃሬነ።
_____

5. አመ፡ ሠሉስ፡ ለወርኅ፡ ኃለፉ፡ እምኀቤነ።
_____

6. መጽአ፡ ኃበ፡ ቆምነ፡ ወተስእለነ፡ በእንተ፡ ፍኖተ፡ ባሕር።
_____

7. በጻሕነ፡ ዝየ፡ አመ፡ ኮነ፡ አቡነ፡ መኰንነ፡ ብሔር።
_____

8. አመ፡ መጻእክሙ፡ ኃበ፡ መካን፡ ኃበ፡ ሀሎ፡ ኢርኢክምዎኑ።
_____

9. ሀሎነ፡ ምስሌሁ፡ እስከ፡ አመ፡ ሞተ፤ ወእምዝ፡ ገባእነ፡ ኃበ፡ ሐነጽነ፡ ቤተነ።
_____

10. ኢተናገርነ፡ እምአመ፡ ገሠጽሁ፡ በእንተ፡ ዘገብረ።
_____

Chapter 15

MEDIO-PASSIVE VERBS

15.1 Medio-Passive Verbs

In Gəʿəz, active transitive verbs that fall in the G, D, L, or Q categories can be converted to a medio-passive verb by adding the prefix ተ- in the perfect forms.

TABLE 15.1: Medio-Passive Forms

Verb Form	Active Verb	Translation	Verb Form	Passive Verb	Translation
G	ቀተለ፡	He killed	Gt	ተቀትለ፡	He was killed
D	ፈነወ፡	He sent	Dt	ተፈነወ፡	He was sent
L	ባረከ፡	He blessed	Lt	ተባረከ፡	He was blessed
Q	ተርጐመ፡	He translated	Qt	ተተርጐመ፡	It was translated

15.2 Gt Medio-Passive Verbs

The Gt verbs follow a similar consonant/vowel pattern, ተ+C_1ăC_2C_3ă, in both the ነበረ፡, *nabara* and ገብረ፡, *gabra* verb types. An alternate pattern exists with some verbs, in particular those with I Guttural roots, ተ+C_1ăC_2C_3ă፡ ተሕንጸ፡ (alternate form: ተ+C_1ăC_2ăC_3ă፡ ተሐነጸ፡). Verbs in the II Guttural form follow the ገብረ፡ (*gabra*); for example: ተጽሕፈ፡.

TABLE 15.2: Gt Weak Medio Passive Verbs

Root Sound		Translation	Root Sound		Translation
I Guttural	ተሐንጸ፡	He was killed	II-ወ	ተመውእ፡	He was defeated
II Guttural	ተጽሕፈ፡	It was built	II-የ	ተሠይመ፡	He was appointed
III Guttural	ተሰምዐ፡	It was heard	III-ወ	ተወርወ፡	He cast himself down
I-ወ	ተወልደ፡	He was born	III-የ	ተሰምየ፡	He was named

The declension patterns for Perfect Gt verbs follow the general patterns of the G weak verbs (see ch. 10).

TABLE 15.3: Patterns for Weak Gt Verbs

PGN	I Gutt	II Gutt	III Gutt	I-W
3ms	ተሐንጸ፡	ተጽሕፈ፡	ተሰምዐ፡	ተወልደ፡
3fs	ተሐንጸት፡	ተጽሕፈት፡	ተሰምዐት፡	ተወልደት፡
2ms	ተሐንጽከ፡	ተጽሕፍከ፡	ተሰማዕከ፡	ተወለድከ፡
2fs	ተሐንጽኪ፡	ተጽሕፍኪ፡	ተሰማዕኪ፡	ተወለድኪ፡
1cs	ተሐንጽኩ፡	ተጽሕፍኩ፡	ተሰማዕኩ፡	ተወለድኩ፡
3mp	ተሐንጹ፡	ተጽሕፉ፡	ተሰምዑ፡	ተወልዱ፡
3fp	ተሐንጻ፡	ተጽሕፋ፡	ተሰምዓ፡	ተወልዳ፡
2mp	ተሐንጽክሙ፡	ተጽሕፍክሙ፡	ተሰማዕክሙ፡	ተወለድክሙ፡
2fp	ተሐንጽክን፡	ተጽሕፍክን፡	ተሰማዕክን፡	ተወለድክን፡
1cp	ተሐንጽነ፡	ተጽሕፍነ፡	ተሰማዕነ፡	ተወለድነ፡
PGN	**II-W**	**III-W**	**II-Y**	**III-Y**
3ms	ተመውአ፡	ተወርወ፡	ተሠይመ፡	ተሰምየ፡
3fs	ተመውአት፡	ተወርወት፡	ተሠይመት፡	ተሰምየት፡
2ms	ተመዋእከ፡	ተወረውከ፡	ተሠየምከ፡	ተሰመይከ፡
2fs	ተመዋእኪ፡	ተወረውኪ፡	ተሠየምኪ፡	ተሰመይኪ፡
1cs	ተመዋእኩ፡	ተወረውኩ፡	ተሠየምኩ፡	ተሰመይኩ፡
3mp	ተመውኡ፡	ተወርዉ፡	ተሠይሙ፡	ተሰምዩ፡
3fp	ተመውኣ፡	ተወርዋ፡	ተሠይማ፡	ተሰምያ፡
2mp	ተመወእክሙ፡	ተወረውክሙ፡	ተሠየምክሙ፡	ተሰመይክሙ፡
2fp	ተመወእክን፡	ተወረውክን፡	ተሠየምክን፡	ተሰመይክን፡
1cp	ተመወእነ፡	ተወረውነ፡	ተሠየምነ፡	ተሰመይነ፡

15.3 Usage of the Gt Passive Verbs

Authors generally use the passive form of the G verb in order to leave the agent of the action of the verb unidentified. The active subject is usually added with the prepositions በ-, በኀበ፡, or እምኀበ፡. The preposition በ- would usually indicate "instrument" (a tool being used) if there is no human agent involved.

a. Gt verbs can also be read as reflexive or middle voice in meaning. These occasions require close attention. The following verbs fall into this category:

  i. ተዐደወ፡ – "transgress" (from ዐደወ፡ "transgress"); if "transgress a law," then it appears with እም-; if it is against a person, then it appears with ላዕለ፡.

  ii. ተዐቀበ፡ – "guard oneself against" (from ዐቀበ፡፡ "guard, keep watch"); followed by እምነ፡ or an object suffix.

iii. ተረክበ፡ – "be found" (from ረከበ፡ "find"); it follows the same meaning as ኮነ፡, it may be followed by a predicate noun or adjective in the accusative, e.g., ተረክበ፡ ጻድቀ፡ – "he was found to be righteous.

iv. ተርእየ፡ "appear or seem to be" (from ርእየ፡ "see"); it may follow similar rules as ተረክበ፡ in which it may be followed by a predicate noun or adjective in the accusative, e.g., ተርእየ፡ ጻድቀ፡ – "he appeared to be righteous."

b. Most Gt verbs follow the meaning of a simple passive of the G transitive verbs from which it is derived.

TABLE 15.4: Gt Verbs Derived from G Verbs

Gt Form	Translation	G Form	Translation
ተፈርሀ፡	he was feared	ፈርሀ፡	he feared
ተገብረ፡	it was done	ገብረ፡	he made/did
ተሐንጸ፡	it was built	ሐንጸ፡	he built
ተመርሐ፡	he was led	መርሐ፡	he led
ተመውአ፡	he was defeated	መውአ፡	he defeated
ተነግረ፡	it was spoken	ነገረ፡	he spoke
ተቀብረ፡	he was buried	ቀብረ፡	he buried
ተቀትለ፡	he was killed	ቀትለ፡	he killed
ተሰብከ፡	it was preached	ሰብከ፡	he preached

c. Some Gt verbs are not derived from a G verb or their meanings do not exactly correspond.

TABLE 15.5: Gt Verbs with No Corresponding G Verb or Meaning

Gt Form	Translation	G Form	Translation
ተነበበ፡	be read	ነበበ፡	speak / tell
ተልእከ፡	serve	ለአከ፡	send a message
ተምዕዐ፡	become angry	No G verb	
ተሐሥየ፡	rejoice	No G Verb	

d. Two Gt verbs have their own distinct irregularities

The verb ተነሥአ፡ – "be taken up" is the passive of ነሥአ፡ – "take up." The form ተነሥአ፡ is inflected as if derived from a Q verb root and is reflexive in meaning – "get up, arise, or to rise from the dead." If used with ላዕለ፡, it can be understood as "rise up against."

The verb ተምዕዐ፡ follows the same irregularities as ተነሥአ፡ but due to the two gutturals in the II and III positions, it has two other stem forms: 1) ተምዕዐ፡ 2) ተምዐ፡ 3) ተመዔ፡; each of these follow the expected declension patterns of the corresponding gutturals.

15.4 Vocabulary

1. ተዝካር፡ – memorial, feast, commemoration
2. ደመና፡ (pl. ደመናት፡) – cloud
3. ግብር፡ (pl. ግብራት፡ ግበር፡) – deed, act, work, liturgy
4. ገብር፡ (pl. አግብርት፡) – slave, servant
5. ምዕራፍ፡ (pl. ምዕራፋት፡) – quiet place, resting place, chapter of a book
6. ምቅሠፍት፡ (pl. ምቅሠፋት፡) – punishment, beating, divine punishment
7. መቅደስ፡ – temple, sanctuary
8. ቤተ፡ መቅደስ። – Jerusalem Temple
9. ቤተ፡ ልሔም። – Bethlehem
10. ኢየሱስ፡ ክርስቶስ። – Jesus Christ
11. ወለደ፡ Gt: ተወልደ፡ – bear a child; Gt: be born
12. ሜጠ፡ – turn away, divert; ተመይጠ፡ Gt – turn around, return, be converted
13. ተሐሠየ፡ / ተሐሥየ፡ Gt – rejoice
14. ተምዕዐ፡ / ተምዐ፡ (at: ላዕለ፡ ዲበ፡ በእንተ፡) Gt – become angry
15. አምነ፡ – be true, believe; ተአመነ፡ / ተአምነ፡ Gt – be believed, have faith in, confess sins

15.5 Exercises

A. Translate the following:

1. መኑ፡ ተሠይመ፡ ኤጲስ፡ ቆጶስ፡ ዲበ፡ ብሔርከ።

2. ተሠየጥኩ፡ በአደዊሆሙ፡ ለእሎንቱ፡ ሰብእ።

3. ተፈራህኩ፡ በእንተ፡ ስምየ፡ ዐቢይ።

4. ይእተ፡ አሚረ፡ ተተክለት፡ ሃይማኖት፡ ጽንዕት፡ በልቡ።

5. ተጽሕፈ፡ ዝንቱ፡ መጽሐፈ፡ ሕገግ፡ በመዋዕለ፡ አበዊነ።

6. ለመኑ፡ ተገብረት፡ ዛቲ፡ ሐመር።

7. ማእዜኑ፡ ተመዋእከሙ፡ ወተኃሣእከሙ።

8. ተመራሕነ፡ ውስተ፡ ፍኖት፡ ርትዕት።

9. ተሰደድነ፡ እምአብያቲነ፡ ወእምነበ፡ አዝማዲነ።

10. ተመውኡ፡ ሕዝብነ፡ ወተነሥአት፡ ሀገርነ።

B. Translate the following:

1. ሰደድዎ፡ ለመድኅንነ።

2. ጸሐፉ፡ አስማቲሆሙ፡ ውስቴቱ።

3. ገብረ፡ አምላክ፡ ዘንተ፡ ዓለመ።

4. ሰማዕነ፡ ቃለ፡ ምንዳቤሁ።

5. መርሕዎ፡ ለወሬዛ፡ ዝየ።

6. ፈራህኩ፡ ውእተ፡ ነገረ።

7. ቀበርዎ፡ ለሥጋሁ፡ ምስለ፡ ዘመዱ።

8. ቀተልዎ፡ ለእግዚአሙ።

9. ሤጥነ፡ ኵሎ፡ አሕባሊነ።

10. ወሀብዎ፡ ሲሳየ፡ ወልብሰ።
_____

C. Translate the following:

1. ተሰመይኩ፡ ስመ፡ ዮሐንስሃ፡ በስም፡ እኍ፡ አቡየ።
_____

2. በይእቲ፡ ዕለት፡ ተረክብኩ፡ ዕልወ፡ ወተሰደድኩ፡ እማእከሎሙ።
_____

3. ተዐቀብት፡ ሀገርነ፡ ወኢተነሥአት።
_____

4. ወእምድኅረዝ፡ ተልእከ፡ በቤተ፡ መቅደስ፡ ኩሎ፡ መዋዕለ፡ ሕይወቱ።
_____

5. ተመልአ፡ ሰማይ፡ ብርሃነ፡ ወተሰምዐ፡ ቃለ፡ መላእክት።
_____

6. ተነብበ፡ ዝንቱ፡ ኩሉ፡ መጽሐፍ፡ በቤተ፡ መቅደስ፡ ይእተ፡ አሚረ።
_____

7. ሶበ፡ ተዐደነ፡ ውእተ፡ ደብረ፡ ወበጸሕነ፡ ሀገሮሙ፤ ነበርነ፡ ህየ፡ ኩላ፡ ዓመተ።
_____

8. ተመልአ፡ ሰማይ፡ ደመናተ፡ ወወረደ፡ ዝናም፡ ወበረድ።
_____

9. ተልእከዎ፡ ለዝንቱ፡ ቅዱስ፡ እስከ፡ ዕለተ፡ ሞቱ።
_____

10. ዛቲ፡ ዕለት፡ ተዝካረ፡ ሞቱ፡ ለቅዱስ፡ ማርቆስ።
_____

Chapter 16

GLT RECIPROCAL VERBS

16.1 Gəʿəz Verbs of Reciprocity

The G verb category contains many verbs that are considered reciprocal, which indicates a mutual interchange between two parties. These verbs are marked with a ተ- prefix with a lengthening of the stem vowel to an $ā$ between C_1 and C_2. The vocalization would look like this: ተ-$C_1āC_2ăC_3ă$, e.g., ተቃረበ፡ – "approach one another, have sexual intercourse." They occur infrequently, but many verbs could be formed in this manner. The Glt verbs can be divided into two categories: group 1, those verbs whose meanings are fairly predictable from the general idea of reciprocity (table 16.6); and group 2, those verbs in which one must pay particular attention to the context when it comes to deriving its meaning (table 16.2).

TABLE 16.1: Group 1 Glt Reciprocal Verbs, with Predictable Meanings

Glt Verb Form	Translation	G (Gt) Verb Form	Translation
ተባከየ፡	weep together	በከየ፡	weep, cry
ተካሐደ፡ (concerning: በእንተ፡)	argue with	ከሐደ፡	deny, repudiate
ተቃረበ፡	approach one another, have sexual intercourse	ቀርበ፡	draw near
ተራወጸ፡	run together	ሮጸ፡	run
ተናጸረ፡	look at one another	ነጸረ፡	look, look at
ተቃተለ፡	kill one another	ቀተለ፡	kill
ተራአየ፡ (ገጸ፡ በገጽ፡)	see one another (face to face)	ርእየ፡	see
ተማዕዐ፡	get mad at one another	ተምዕዐ፡	become angry, enraged
ተሳአለ፡	find out by asking around	ሰአለ፡	ask for
ተሳምዐ፡	hear / understand one another	ሰምዐ፡	hear/obey

In addition, Glt verbs should not be mistaken for Lt verbs which they resemble, rather one must remember these verbs are linked to G or Gt verbs.

TABLE 16.2: Group 2 Glt Reciprocal Verbs, with Special Meanings

Glt Verb Form	Translation	G Verb Form	Translation
ተባጽሐ፡	bring someone before a judge	በጽሐ፡	arrive, happen
ተባውአ፡	intrude	ቦአ፡	enter
ተጋብአ፡	gather, assemble	ገብአ፡	come, go back
ተራከበ፡	congregate/join	ረከበ፡	find, come upon
ተናገረ፡ / ተናበበ፡	speak	ነገረ፡ / ነበበ፡	say, tell
ተማየጠ፡	buy	ሤጠ፡	sell
ተዋለደ፡	procreate	ወለደ፡	bear a child
ተኃለፈ፡	wander to and fro	ኀለፈ፡	pass by, through
ተቃወመ፡	oppose, stand against	ቆመ፡	arise, stand
ተፋነወ፡	bid farewell	ፈነወ፡	send

16.2 Glt Verbs of Repeated Action

Some Glt verbs follow other Semitic verb *binyanim* in that certain forms suggest a repeated action by the subject. For example, the verb ተዋለደ፡ – "be multiplied with offspring" suggests continual procreation, not a one-time event; while the verb ተኃለፈ፡ – "wander to and fro" doesn't mean go for a short walk to see something, but to wander back and forth as if pacing. The Hebrew verb התלהך, "he wandered back and forth, or paced about" carries a similar repeated (iterative) action. There are no corresponding reciprocal forms of the D or L verbs in Gəʿəz although some D or L verbs have Glt derivatives. There are Q verbs that have a corresponding Qlt form with the $\bar{a}$ vowel between the second and third root consonants (ተC_1ăC_2āC_3ă); e.g., ተሰናአወ፡ – "be in accord or in mutual agreement" from the root ሰነአወ፡.

16.3 Vocabulary

1. ትእዛዝ፡ (pl. ትእዛዛት፡) – order, command, edict
2. በትእዛዘ፡ – at the command of
3. ኪዳን፡ (pl. ኪዳናት፡) – pact, treaty, covenant
4. ኪዳን፡ ብሊት፡ / ኪዳን፡ ብሉይ፡ – Old Testament
5. ኪዳን፡ ሐዲስ፡ – New Testament
6. ምስል፡ (pl. ምስል፡ ምስላት፡ አምሳል፡) – likeness, form, image
7. በአምሳለ፡ – in the likeness of
8. ዐጽፍ፡ (pl. ዐጽፋት፡ / አዕጽፍት፡) – tunic, cloak, mantle
9. ሱታፌ፡ / ሱታፍ፡ – companion, associate
10. ጸብእ፡ (pl. አጽብእ፡ / ጸብአት፡) – war, battle
11. ተካየደ፡ Glt – make a treaty, pact, or covenant
12. ጸብአ፡ – fight; ተጻብአ፡ Glt – fight one another

13. ዖደ፡ – go around, surround
14. ረድአ፡ – help someone; ተረድአ፡ Gt – be helped; ተራድአ፡ Glt – help one another
15. ተሳተፈ፡ Lt – associate with; share something
16. ተሰናአወ፡ Qlt – come to an agreement
17. በከመ፡ – prep. according to, in accordance with
18. በበይናቲ፡ (with suffix pronouns) – prep. among, between – used with Glt verbs of reciprocal action.

16.4 Exercises

A. Translate the following:

1. ተባውኡነ፡ ወተከሉ፡ እኪተ፡ በማእከሌነ።

2. ወጽኡ፡ ተዋለዱ፡ ወመልኡ፡ ኮላ፡ ምድረ።

3. ተሣየጥክዎ፡ እምብእሲ፡ ብዑሎ።

4. ወሰበ፡ ተባከየ፡ ተፋነውዎ፡ ለወልደሙ።

5. አሙኑ፡ ተሣየጥከ፡ ዘንተ፡ መጽሐፈ፡ ብለዮ።

6. ተሐሥዮ፡ በግብራቲሁ፡ ዐበይት፡ ወተፈሥሑ፡ በቃላቲሁ፡ ጠበብት።

7. ተመየጥነ፡ ወተጋባእነ፡ ውስተ፡ ቤቱ፡ ለመኮንን።

8. ተባጽሕዎሙ፡ ለእሎንቱ፡ ስድስቱ፡ ሰብእ፡ ኀበ፡ መኮንን።

9. ተቃወሙ፡ ላዕሌሆሙ፡ ወሰደድዎሙ፡ እማእከሎሙ።

10. በእንተ፡ ምንት፡ ተሳተፍክሞሙ፡ ለአኩያን።

11. ተጋብኡ፡ ሰብእ፡ ዘመዱ፡ ወተሰናአዉ፡ በእንተ፡ ንዋዩ፡

12. ወእምድኅረ፡ ተስዴ፡ ተኃለፉ፡ እምብሔር፡ ለብሔር፡

13. ተራከብኩ፡ ምስለ፡ ዝንቱ፡ ቅዱስ፡ ወተልእክዎ፡

14. ሶበ፡ ዘንተ፡ ተናበቡ፡ ተምዓዕነ፡ ወተባሕናሁ፡ ቅድመ፡ ካህን፡ ዐቢይ፡

15. እፎ፡ ተባውእዎ፡ ኃጥአን፡ ወእኩያን፡ ለሕዝብነ፡

16. ተራከቡ፡ ሕዝብ፡ ወገብሩ፡ ተዝካረ፡ ንጉሦሙ፡ ምዉት፡

17. ተናገረ፡ ምስሌሃ፡ ወተሣየጠ፡ ውእተ፡ መጽሐፈ፡ ቅዱሰ፡ እምኔሃ፡

18. ወሶበ፡ ተአመረ፡ ትምእርት፡ ተጋብነ፡ ለጸብእ፡

B. Translate the following:

1. ጠቢብ፡ ውእቱ፡ ወሠናይ፡ ጥቀ፡ አምሳሊሁ፡

2. ዝንቱ፡ መጽሐፍ፡ በእንተ፡ አጽባተ፡ አበዊነ፡ ውእቱ፡

3. ያዶ፡ ደመና፡ ከመ፡ ዐጽፍ፡ ብርሃናዊ፡

4. እምንት፡ ገብርከ፡ ዝንተ፡ ዐጽፈ፡

5. ተርእዮ፡ ለነ፡ በአምሳለ፡ መልአከ፡ ብርሃናዊ፡

6. ዝንቱ፡ ረድእ፡ ኮነ፡ ሱታፌሁ፡ ለእግዚእነ።

7. በአምሳለ፡ መኑ፡ ገብረ፡ እግዚአብሔር፡ ብእሴ።

8. ያድነ፡ ውስተ፡ ውእቱ፡ ብሔር፡ ብዙኅ፡ አውራኅ።

9. ተካየደ፡ እግዚአብሔር፡ ምስለ፡ ሕዝቡ፡ ክልኤ፡ ኪዳናተ፡ አሐቲ፡ ተሰምየት፡ ኪዳነ፡ ብሊተ፡ ወካልእት፡ ተሰምየት፡ ኪዳነ፡ ሐዳሰ።

10. ኢሀለወ፡ ሱታፌ፡ እግዚአብሔር፡ አሐዱ፡ ውእቱ።

C. Matthew 8:1–17. Translate the following passage.

¹ ወእንዘ፡ ይወርድ፡ እምደብር፡ ተለውዎ፡ ሰብእ፡ ብዙኃን።

² ወናሁ፡ መጽአ፡ አሐዱ፡ ብእሲ፡ ዘለምጽ፡ ወቀርበ፡ ኃቤሁ፡ ወሰገደ፡ ሎቱ፡ እንዘ፡ ይብል፣ እግዚአ፡ እመሰ፡ ፈቀድከ፡ ትክል፡ አንጽሖትየ።

³ ወሰፍሐ፡ እየሁ፡ ወገሠሦ፡ ወይቤሎ፣ እፈቅድ፡ ንጻሕ፤ ወንጽሐ፡ እምለምጹ፡ በጊዜሃ።

⁴ ወይቤሎ፡ እግዚአ፡ ኢየሱስ፡ ዑቅ፡ ኢትንግር፡ ወኢለመኑሂ፡ ወባሕቱ፡ ሑር፡ ወአፍትን፡ ርእሰከ፡ ለካህን፡ ወአብእ፡ መባእከ፡ በእንተ፡ ዘነጻሕከ፡ በከመ፡ አዘዘ፡ ሙሴ፡ ከመ፡ ይኩን፡ ስምዐ፡ ላዕሌሆሙ።

⁵ ወበዊአ፡ ቅፍርናሆም፡ መጽአ፡ ኃቤሁ፡ መስፍን፡ ምእት።

⁶ ወይቤሎ፣ እግዚአ፡ ብቋዕኒ፡ ቀልዔየ፡ ድውይ፡ ወይሰክብ፡ ውስተ፡ ቤተ፡ ወመፃጕዕ፡ ወጥቀ፡ ፅዑር።

⁷ ወይቤሎ፡ እግዚአ፡ ኢየሱስ፣ ነየ፡ እመጽአ፡ አነ፡ ወአፌውሶ።

⁸ ወአውሥአ፡ ሐቤ፡ ምእት፡ ወይቤ፡ እግዚአ፡ ኢይደልወኒ፡ ከመ፡ አንተ፡ ትባአ፡ ታሕተ፡ ጠፈርየ፣ ዳእሙ፡ በል፡ ቃለ፡ ወየሐዩ፡ ወልድየ።

⁹ እስመ፡ አነሂ፡ ብእሲ፡ መኰንን፡ አነ፡ ወብየ፡ ሐራ፡ እለ፡ እኤንን። ወእብሎ፡ ለዝ፡ ሑር፡ ወየሐውር፡ ወለካልኡ፡ ነዓ፡ ወይመጽእ፡ ወለገብርየኒ፣ ግበር፡ ዘንተ፡ ወይገብር።

¹⁰ ወሰሚዖ፡ እግዚእ፡ ኢየሱስ፡ አንከረ፡ ወይቤሎሙ፡ ለእለ፡ ይተልውዎ፣ አማን፡ እብለክሙ፡ ኢረከብኩ፡ ዘመጠነዝ፡ ሃይማኖት፡ በውስተ፡ ኵሉ፡ እስራኤል።

¹¹ ወባሕቱ፡ እብለክሙ፡ ብዙኃን፡ ይመጽኡ፡ እምሥራቅ፡ ወእምዕራብ፡ ወይረፍቁ፡ ምስለ፡ አብርሃም፡ ወይስሐቅ፡ ወያዕቆብ፡ በመንግሥተ፡ ሰማያት።

¹² ወለውሉደ፡ መንግሥትሰ፡ ያወፅእዎሙ፡ ውስተ፡ ጸናፌ፡ ጽልመት። ህየ፡ ሀሎ፡ ብካይ፡ ወሐቅየ፡ ስነን።

¹³ ወይቤሎ፡ እግዚእ፡ ኢየሱስ፡ ለውእቱ፡ ሐቤ፡ ምእት፡ ሑርኬ፡ ወበከመ፡ ተአመንከ፡ ይኩንከ፣ ወሐየወ፡ ወልዱ፡ በይእቲ፡ ሰዓት፣ ወገቢአ፡ መስፍን፡ ውስተ፡ ቤቱ፡ ረከቦ፡ ለቀልጔሁ፡ ሐይዎ።

¹⁴ ወበዊአ፡ እግዚእ፡ ኢየሱስ፡ ቤቶ፡ ለጴጥሮስ፡ ረከባ፡ ለሐማቱ፡ ጴጥሮስ፡ እንዘ፡ ትሰክብ፡ ትፈዕን።

¹⁵ ወገስሳ፡ እዴሃ፡ ወኀደጋ፡ ፈንታ፡ ወተንሥአት፡ ወተልእኮሙ።

¹⁶ ወምሴተ፡ ከዊዎ፡ አምጽኡ፡ ኀቤሁ፡ ብዙኃነ፡ እለ፡ አጋንንት፡ ወአውፅአሙ፡ በቃሉ፡ ወፈወሰ፡ ኵሎ፡ ድውያነ።

¹⁷ ከመ፡ ይትፈጸም፡ ቃለ፡ ኢሳይያስ፡ ነቢይ፡ ዘይቤ፡ ውእቱ፡ ነሥአ፡ ደዌነ፡ ወጾረ፡ ሕማመነ።

Chapter 17

NUMBERS AND CARDINAL ADVERBS

17.1 Cardinal Numbers

Cardinal numbers in Gəʿəz usually precede the object that is being counted. The number 1 is usually the only number in which agreement in gender with the object is present. Masculine numbers two through ten end with an accented ቱ. The accusative form of the masculine numbers two through ten end with an accented ተ. It is quite common for an author to generalize the numbers in -ቱ፡ for all occasions. Note the vowel ending difference for the number 1 in its common and accusative forms – *u* and *ă*: አሐዱ፡ and አሐደ፡, respectively. Note that each number does have its own Gəʿəz symbol (see left column, table 17.1).

TABLE 17.1: Masculine Cardinal Numbers

Number	Common Form	Accusative Form
One ፩፡	አሐዱ፡	አሐደ፡
Two ፪፡	ክልኤቱ፡	ክልኤተ፡
Three ፫፡	ሠለስቱ፡	ሠለስተ፡
Four ፬፡	አርባዕቱ፡	አርባዕተ፡
Five ፭፡	ኀምስቱ፡	ኀምስተ፡
Six ፮፡	ስድስቱ፡	ስድስተ፡
Seven ፯፡	ሰብዑቱ፡	ሰብዐተ፡ / ሰብዑተ፡
Eight ፰፡	ሰማንቱ፡	ሰማንተ፡ / ሰማኒተ፡
Nine ፱፡	ጽዑቱ፡	ጽዑተ፡ / ተስዑቱ፡
Ten ፲፡	ዐሠርቱ፡	ዐሠርተ፡

Note the masculine numbers 7–9 have variant forms in the accusative: 7 ሰብዑቱ፡, 8 ሰማኒቱ፡, and 9 ተስዑቱ፡. The variant form ክልኤ፡ is used for both masculine and feminine forms of the number 2.

TABLE 17.2: Feminine Cardinal Numbers

Number	Common Form	Accusative Form
One ፩፡	አሐቲ፡	አሐተ፡
Two ፪፡	ክልኤቲ፡	ክልኤተ፡
Three ፫፡	ሠላስ፡	ሠላስ፡
Four ፬፡	አርባዕ፡	አርባዕ፡
Five ፭፡	ኀምስ፡	ኀምስ፡
Six ፮፡	ስሱ፡	ስሱ፡
Seven ፯፡	ሰብዑ፡	ሰብዑ፡
Eight ፰፡	ሰማኒ፡	ሰማኒ፡
Nine ፱፡	ትስዑ፡	ትስዑ፡
Ten ፲፡	ዐሥሩ፡ / ዐሥር፡	ዐሥሩ፡ / ዐሥር፡

Note in table 17.2, those common forms ending in *u* have no different accusative forms (6, 7, 9, and 10). The feminine number 10 has a variant form in the common and accusative: ዐሥር፡.

The number usually agrees in case with the object being counted which can be either singular or plural:

a. አሐዱ፡ ብእሲ፡ – "one/a certain man"; አሐቲ፡ ብእሲት፡ – "one/a certain woman"; ክልኤቱ፡ አብያት፡ – "two houses"

b. ክልኤቲ፡ ሀገር፡ – "two cities"; ክልኤ፡ ደመና፡ – "two clouds"; ሠለስቱ፡ ወርኀ፡ – "three months/moons"

c. ኀምስ፡ ዕለት፡ – "five days"; ስሱ፡ አንስት፡ – "six females"; ሰብዑቱ፡ ሰብአ፡ – "seven people."

Numbers do not generally appear in construct. If it is the case, the number and the object are usually separated by እም-, so ሠለስቱ፡ እምአርዳኢሁ፡ – "three of his disciples," lit. "three from his disciples."

17.2 Ordinal Numbers

As in other Semitic languages, in Gəʿəz the ordinal numbers including the number three are derived from the same root as the cardinal numbers above. The root pattern is $C_1āC_2əC_3$, ቃትል፡ with the feminine form adding the ት, $C_1āC_2əC_3ት$, ቃትልት፡. The accusative forms add the *ă* vowel to the ending of the masculine number, e.g., ቀዳመ፡ rather than ቀዳሚ፡. The masculine ordinal "first" is ቀዳሚ፡, while the feminine form is ቀዳሚት፡. The ordinal "second" is the odd one out as it can appear in four forms: ካልእ፡ (f. ካልእት፡) is generally used when there are only two objects being numbered; the other three forms include ዳግም፡ (f. ዳግምት፡); ካዕብ፡ (f. ካዕብት፡); ባዕድ፡; the last one, ባዕድ፡, has a secondary meaning of "other" or "foreign."

TABLE 17.3: Ordinal Numbers 3–10

Ordinal Number	Masculine	Feminine
Third	ሳልስ፡	ሳልስት፡
Fourth	ራብዕ፡	ራብዕት፡
Fifth	ኀምስ፡	ኀምስት፡
Sixth	ሳድስ፡	ሳድስት፡
Seventh	ሳብዕ፡	ሳብዕት፡
Eighth	ሳምን፡	ሳምንት፡
Ninth	ታስዕ፡	ታስዕት፡
Tenth	ዓሥር፡	ዓሥርት፡

a. The ordinal numbers, apart from ካልእ፡, can appear with the adjectival suffixes -$\bar{a}$+ዊ፡ or -$\bar{a}$+ይ፡. In addition, the ordinal adjectives generally precede the object noun:

  i. ሣልስ፡ አንቀጽ፡፡ – "a/the third gate"

  ii. ራብዓዊ፡ ብእሲ፡፡ – "a/the fourth man"

  iii. ሳብዓዊት፡ ሀገር፡፡ – "a/the seventh city"

b. It should be noted that the feminine ordinals of $\bar{a}$+ይ፡ ordinals are formed with -i+ት፡ suffixes: ሣልሲት፡ ብእሲት፡፡ – "a/the third woman." The term ዓሥራት፡ "tithe" is also derived from the ordinal stem ዓሥር፡.

c. A further group of ordinals is used specifically to identify time, such as hours of the day and days of the week or month and can also replace the regular cardinal numbers when units of time are being counted. These numbers follow the pattern of $C_1\breve{a}C_2uC_3$, ቀቱል፡፡

  i. በዐሡር፡ ዕለት፡፡ – "on the tenth day of the month"

  ii. ሠሉስ፡ ሌሊት፡፡ – "the third night"

  iii. ረቡዕ፡ ለወርኁ፡፡ – "the fourth (day) of the month"

  iv. ነበረ፡ ህየ፡ ሠሉስ፡ ዕለተ፡፡ – "he stayed there three days"

Note at times the nouns for hour, day, week, or month are implied based on the context and need to be added to the translation.

17.3 Numbers Above Ten (10)

The numbers 11–19 retain gender distinction; they are designated as 10 plus 1–9. The masculine form of 10 in these numbers is ዐሠርቱ፡ and the feminine form is ዐሡሩ፡. The numbers are read, for example, as "ten and one" and so on.

TABLE 17.4: Numbers 10–19

Number	Masculine	Feminine
11	ዐሠርቱ፡ ወአሐዱ፡	ዐሡሩ፡ ወአሐቲ፡
12	ዐሠርቱ፡ ወክልኤቱ፡	ዐሡሩ፡ ወክልኤ፡
13	ዐሠርቱ፡ ወሠለስቱ፡	ዐሡሩ፡ ወሠላስ፡
14	ዐሠርቱ፡ ወአርባዕቱ፡	ዐሡሩ፡ ወአርባዕ፡
15	ዐሠርቱ፡ ወኃምስቱ፡	ዐሡሩ፡ ወኃምስ፡
16	ዐሠርቱ፡ ወስሱቱ፡	ዐሡሩ፡ ወስሱ፡
17	ዐሠርቱ፡ ወስብዑቱ፡	ዐሡሩ፡ ወስብዑ፡
18	ዐሠርቱ፡ ወሰማኒቱ፡	ዐሡሩ፡ ወሰማኒ፡
19	ዐሠርቱ፡ ወትጽዑቱ፡	ዐሡሩ፡ ወትጽዑ፡

17.4 The Tens Numbers 20–90

The numbers 20–90 are based on the corresponding units with the ending -ā with the exception of 20 which uses the number 10 as its base. You will notice the similarities to the corresponding Hebrew numbers in this category.

TABLE 17.5: The Numbers 20–90

Number	Gəʿəz	Number	Gəʿəz	Number	Gəʿəz
20	ዕሥራ፡	50	ኃምሳ፡	80	ሰማንያ፡
30	ሠላሳ፡	60	ስሳ፡	90	ተስዓ፡ ትስዓ፡
40	አርብዓ፡	70	ሰብዓ፡		

The tens are usually unmodified for gender and case but the single digits that are added such as 20 and 1 usually retain the gender of the noun being counted: ዕሥራ፡ ወአሐዱ፡ / አሐቲ፡ – 11; ዕሥራ፡ ወክልኤቱ፡ / ክልኤ፡ – 2. The number 100 is expressed as ምእት፡ (pl. አምእት፡) and the number 1000 is usually expressed as 10 hundred: ዐሠርቱ፡ ምእት፡, 2000 is expressed as 20 hundred and so on.

17.5 Cardinal Adverbs

When the numbers "three" to "ten" are identified as adverbs, they follow the pattern of $C_1əC_2C_3ă$ (ቅትሉ፡) in the accusative. These denote, for example, three times.

TABLE 17.6: Cardinal Adverbs

Number		Number	
Three times	ሥልሰ፡	Seven times	ስብዐ፡
Four times	ርብዐ፡	Eight times	ስምነ፡
Five times	ኃምሰ፡	Nine times	ትስዐ፡
Six times	ስድሰ፡	Ten times	ዐሥረ፡

These forms of numbers are also used in place of feminine cardinal numbers, so as you can see the number system in Gəʿəz can be quite complicated. The word for "once" may be expressed as አሐተ፡ or ምዕረ፡ and the term for "twice" is ካዕበ፡ or ዳግመ፡; it can also carry the sense of "again or a second time."

17.6 Names of Months in Ethiopic Calendar

The Ethiopic calendar consists of twelve months of thirty days plus a thirteenth month of five days or six in a leap year. The first of the year occurs on September 11 on the Western calendar, except in the year before a Western leap year, when the first of the year is the 12th of September, and the corresponding Western dates for each month shift by one day until the February leap day:

TABLE 17.7: Ethiopian Months

Month	Dates	Month	Dates
መስከረም፡	Sept. 11–Oct. 10	ሚያዝያ፡	Apr. 9–May 8
ጥቅምት፡	Oct. 11–Nov. 9	ግንቦት፡	May 9–June 7
ኅዳር፡	Nov. 10–Dec. 9	ሠኔ፡	June 8–July 7
ታኅሣሥ፡	Dec. 10–Jan. 8	ሐምሌ፡	July 8–Aug. 6
ጥር፡	Jan. 9–Feb. 7	ነሐሴ፡	Aug. 7–Sept. 5
የካቲት፡	Feb. 8–Mar. 9	ጳጉሜን፡	Sept. 6–Sept. 10
መጋቢት፡	Mar. 10–Apr. 8		

17.7 Vocabulary

*__Note:__ you should include all the numbers discussed in the chapter in your vocabulary.

1. ደዌ፡ (pl. ደዌያት፡) – sickness, illness, disease
2. ድንግል፡ (pl. ደናግል፡) – virgin, celibate monk
3. አነዳ፡ – skin, hide, leather
4. ሐብለ፡ አነዳ፡ – thong
5. ስብሐት፡ (pl. ስብሐታት፡) – praise, hymn of praise
6. ኀሳር፡ (pl. ኀሳራት፡) – poverty, wretchedness

7. ፈወሰ: D – cure, heal; ተፈወሰ: Dt – be healed, cured
8. ተነበየ: Dt – prophesy (to: ለ; against: ላዕለ፡)
9. ወሰከ: D – add (to: ዲበ፡ ላዕለ፡), increase, augment; ተወሰከ: Dt – be added to
10. ተፈሥሐ: Dt – rejoice (in: በ-, በእንተ፡, ላዕለ፡, ዲበ፡)
11. ቤዘወ: Q/L – redeem (with: በ-; from: እም-); ተቤዘወ: Qt – be redeemed; redeem oneself

17.8 Exercises

A. Translate the following:

1. በዳግም፡ ወርኅ፡ ዐደዉ፡ ስድስተ፡ ደብረ።

2. ወሰድዎሙ፡ ለእሎንቱ፡ ሠለስቱ፡ ሰብእ፡ ኀበ፡ ንጉሥ።

3. ነበርነ፡ ምስሌሆሙ፡ ዐሥሩ፡ ዓመተ።

4. ኢታምዕዐ፡ ካዕበ።

5. ሴጥክዎ፡ ሠለስተ፡ ሐብለ።

6. ውእተ፡ ወርኅ፡ ሐነጹ፡ ክልኤተ፡ ዐቢየ፡ አብያተ።

7. ለአከ፡ ኀቤየ፡ ክልኤ፡ መላእክተ።

8. ኢነገርኩክሙኑ፡ ዘንተ፡ ስልሰ፤ ለምንት፡ ኢሰማዕክሙኒ።

9. ገበርኩ፡ ክልኤተ፡ ንዋየ።

10. አመረነ፡ ኀምስተ፡ ምስጢረ፡ ቅዱሰ።

11. መጽአ፡ ኅቤነ፡ አሐዱ፡ እምዘመዱ።

12. ገብአ፡ ኀቡ፡ ቤትዮ፡ ርብዐ፡ ወኢረከብኒ፡ ምዕረ።

13. ሜጥነ፡ እሎንተ፡ አርባዕተ፡ ውሉደ፡ ኀበ፡ ቤቶሙ።

14. ሤመ፡ ተስዐተ፡ ዲያቆነ፡ ወኀምስተ፡ ቀሲሰ፡ ዲቤሆሙ።

15. ወሀቦሙ፡ ሲሳየ፡ ለሰማኒ፡ ዕለት።

16. ተቤዘወ፡ አዝማዲሁ፡ ኀምሰ።

17. በቀዳሚት፡ ዓመቱ፡ ሞአ፡ ኀምሰ፡ አህጉረ።

18. መሀርዎ፡ በዐሥርቱ፡ ልሳናት።

19. ነበሩ፡ ምስሌነ፡ ስድስተ፡ አውራኅ።

20. ዝንቱ፡ ተነበ፡ ሎሙ፡ ዳግሙ።

B. Matthew 5:1–10. Translate the following passage.

በእንተ፡ ብፁዓን።

¹ ወርእዮ፡ ብዙኃነ፡ አሕዛበ፡ ዐርገ፡ ውስተ፡ ደብር፡ ወነቢሮ፡ ቀርቡ፡ ኀቤሁ፡ አርዳኢሁ።

² ወከሠተ፡ አፉሁ፡ ወመሀሮሙ፡ እንዘ፡ ይብል።

³ ብፁዓን፡ ነዳያን፡ በመንፈስ፡ እስመ፡ ሎሙ፡ ይእቲ፡ መንግሥተ፡ ሰማያት።

⁴ ብፁዓን፡ እለ፡ ይላሕዉ፡ ይአዜ፡ እስመ፡ እሙንቱ፡ ይትፈሥሑ፡፡

⁵ ብፁዓን፡ የዋሃን፡ እስመ፡ እሙንቱ፡ ይወርስዋ፡ ለምድር፡፡

⁶ ብፁዓን፡ እለ፡ ይርኅቡ፡ ወይጸምኡ፡ ለጽድቅ፡ እስመ፡ እሙንቱ፡ ይጸግቡ፡፡

⁷ ብፁዓን፡ መሓርያን፡ እስመ፡ እሙንቱ፡ ይትመሐሩ፡፡

⁸ ብፁዓን፡ ንጹሓነ፡ ልብ፡ እስመ፡ እሙንቱ፡ ይሬአይዎ፡ ለእግዚአብሔር፡፡

⁹ ብፁዓን፡ ገባርያነ፡ ሰላም፡ እስመ፡ እሙንቱ፡ ውሉደ፡ ለእግዚአብሔር፡ ይሰመዩ፡፡

¹⁰ ብፁዓን፡ እለ፡ ይሰደዱ፡ በእንተ፡ ጽድቅ፡ እስመ፡ ሎሙ፡ ይእቲ፡ መንግሥተ፡ ሰማያት፡፡

Chapter 18

CAUSATIVE VERBS

18.1 Causative Verbs CG, CD, CL, CQ

The causative verbs are derived from the base verbs G, D, L, and Q. The Gəʿəz causative verb is marked by a prefixed አ-as seen in the following table:

TABLE 18.1 CAUSATIVE VERBS

Verb Class	Verb	Meaning	Derived Class	Verb	Meaning
G	ገብአ፡	come back	CG	አግብአ፡	bring back
D	ሠነየ፡	be beautiful	CD	አሠነየ፡	make beautiful
L	ማሰነ፡	perish	CL	አማሰነ፡	destroy
Q	ደንገፀ፡	be disturbed	CQ	አደንገፀ፡	disturb

The CG occurs the most often of the four types of causative verbs. The base pattern of the Perfect is $ăC_1C_2ăC_3ă$ with alterations to the verbs with III Guttural and II-ወ/የ. With the III Guttural verbs the vowel preceding C_3 and can be read as either a silent vowel (silent *shewa* in Hebrew) as in መጽአ፡, *mătsă* or the short ə as in ከሐነ፡, *năsăḥă*. The norm of CG verbs is for the short ə as in the form of መጽአ፡ which would read አምጽአ፡.

a. The causative II-ወ will generally lose the II radical of the root as in the verb ቆመ፡ from the verb ቀወመ፡. As a result, this verb declines as follows:

3ms	አቀመ፡	3mp	አቀሙ፡
3fs	አቀመት፡	3fp	አቀማ፡
2ms	አቀምከ፡	2mp	አቀምከሙ፡
2fs	አቀምኪ፡	2fp	አቀምክን፡
1cs	አቀምኩ፡	1cp	አቀምነ፡

b. If the verb is a II-ወ and a III Guttural, the ă on the I consonant shifts to the short ə vowel in the 3m/3f singular forms as in the declension as seen for the verb ቦአ፡. The first- and second-person, singular and plural forms have a long *ā* vowel on the I consonant and a short *ə* on the III consonant followed by the personal endings. The 3m/f plural forms have the short *ă* vowel and the personal endings attach to the III consonant. The II consonant drops out in all instances.

3ms	አብአ፡	3mp	አበኡ፡
3fs	አብአት፡	3fp	አበኣ፡
2ms	አቀምከ፡	2mp	አባእክሙ፡
2fs	አባእኪ፡	2fp	አባእክን፡
1cs	አባእኩ፡	1cp	አባእነ፡

c. If the verb is a II-ዐ, it follows the normal pattern of the lengthening of the I consonant vowel to *ē* throughout the paradigm. The III consonant vowel varies from a short "ă" vowel in the 3m/f sing. and a short *ē* on the III consonant in the 1st and 2nd person s/p forms. The 3m/f plural forms have the endings attached to the III consonant. The II-ዐ is lost throughout the declension as seen in the verb ሤመ፡ – "he appointed":

3ms	አሤመ፡	3mp	አሤሙ፡
3fs	አሤመት፡	3fp	አሤማ፡
2ms	አሤምከ፡	2mp	አሤምክሙ፡
2fs	አሤምኪ፡	2fp	አሤምክን፡
1cs	አሤምኩ፡	1cp	አሤምነ፡

18.2 The Meaning of Causative CG Verbs

The CG verb is derived from the stative G verbs and is principally factitive. So, አብደ፡ – "he was mad" is stative, and አአበደ፡ – "he made something/someone mad" is causative. Generally, the meaning of the G verb will be incorporated to some degree into the CG causative verb, although as we will see, that is not always the case. All the verbs in the following lists are transitive and take the direct object in the accusative. Causative verbs do not normally take dative pronominal suffixes.

The following is a listing of common CG verbs and should be put to memory:

1. አአከየ፡ – "make something bad"; (toward: ላዕለ፡ ዲበ፡)
2. አዐበየ፡ – "make great, increase"
3. አብዐለ፡ – "make rich"
4. አብለየ፡ – "age, make old"
5. አብዝኀ፡ – "multiply, make numerous"
6. አድወየ፡ – "make ill"
7. አፍርሀ፡ – "frighten"
8. አሕየወ፡ – "restore to life, heal, cure"
9. አሕዘነ፡ – "make sad"
10. አንደየ፡ – "reduce to poverty"
11. አኖኀ፡ አንገ፡ – "extend, put forth"
12. አርትዐ፡ – "make right, correct"
13. አጽደቀ፡ – "make righteous, just"
14. አጽንዐ፡ – "make firm, grasp strongly"; በልቡ፡ – "learn by heart"
15. አጠበበ፡ – "make wise"

Other intransitive verbs that appear as CG verbs carry the idea of causing or permitting someone or something to perform a particular act. Often with verbs of motion, the direction of motion is quite ambiguous, resulting in a variety of English translations. The CG verb አእተወ፡ from the G verb አተወ፡ "to go home" can be translated "to send someone home," "to permit someone to go home," or "to bring something home." All of these can be understood as an action caused by someone to someone or something.

1. አዕደወ፡ – "bring, lead, or take across"
2. አዕረገ፡ – "bring, lead, or take up"
3. አያደ፡ – "lead or take around"
4. አብከየ፡ – "move to tears"
5. አብጽሐ፡ – "bring"
6. አብአ፡ – "bring, lead, or take in"
7. አግብአ፡ – "bring, lead, or take back"
8. አጕየየ፡ – "put to flight"
9. አልሀቀ፡ – "raise, rear" (children)
10. አምዕዐ፡ – "enrage"
11. አምጽአ፡ – "bring, offer, cause to happen"
12. አሞተ፡ / አሙተ፡ – "let die, put to death"
13. አንበረ፡ – "set, place, deposit"
14. አቅረበ፡ – "cause to approach, to offer"
15. አቀመ፡ – "set up, establish, to confirm truth"
16. አሮጸ፡ – "cause to run"
17. አስሐተ፡ – "lead astray, to lead into sin"
18. አስከበ፡ – "cause to lie down"
19. አውዐየ፡ – "burn something up, scorch"
20. አውደቀ፡ – "drop, let fall"
21. አውፅአ፡ – "bring, lead, take forth"
22. አውሐዘ፡ – "cause to flow" (esp. tears)
23. አውረደ፡ – "bring, send, lead down"
24. አኅለፈ፡ – "cause to pass"

When CG verbs are turned into a negative statement and the negative prefix ኢ. is added to the prefix አ, the expected ኢአ, ’iă is transformed into ኢየ, ’iyă: e.g., ኢየሐዘነነ፡ ውእቱ፡ – "He did not make us sad."

18.3 Causative CG Verbs Derived from Transitive G Verbs

Causative transitive verbs are in essence doubly transitive: the subject causes someone to do something. The personal object usually appears as a suffix on the verb; thus, hiding the accusative case of the object: e.g., አርአየነ፡ መጽሐፈ፡፡ – "he caused us to see the book." It is also quite normal for the first object of the two in the sentence to be omitted from the Gəʿəz and your translation must be amended appropriately:

a. አቅተለ፡ ውእተ፡ ነቢየ፡፡ – "he caused someone to kill that prophet."

b. አስምዐ፡ ትእዛዞ፡፡ – "he made known his decree" ("he caused someone to hear his decree").

The following is a listing of common CG verbs that come from transitive G verbs and should be put to memory:

1. አአመነ፡ – "convert"
2. አዕደወ፡ – "lead or take across"
3. አዕቀበ፡ – "hand someone something"
4. አግበረ፡ – "make or order someone to do or make something"
5. አሕነጸ፡ – "have built"

6. አክሐደ፡ – "contradict, not believe"
7. አሞአ፡ / አምአ፡ – "make someone victorious"
8. አንበበ፡ – "read, recite"
9. አንሥአ፡ – "raise, cause to rise"
10. አንጸረ፡ – "look"
11. አቅበረ፡ – "cause, allow, order someone to bury someone"
12. አቅተለ፡ – "cause or order someone to kill someone"
13. አርአየ፡ – "show someone something, to reveal"
14. አርከበ፡ – "cause someone to find something"
15. አስምዐ፡ – "announce, summon as a witness"
16. አስመየ፡ – "be well known, famous"
17. አጽሐፈ፡ – "cause someone to write"
18. አውለደ፡ – "cause someone to bear a child"

18.4   Causative CD, CL, and CQ Verbs

The CD, CL, and CQ verbs are derived from D, L, and Q verbs and occur less frequently than CG verbs. The causative CD verb አአመረ፡ follows the form of the D stem verb አመረ፡ – "he made known" in all tenses but the perfect; there it is replaced with the form አአመረ፡ in which the vowel of the I consonant shortens to the ə vowel. Four other verbs should be noted due to their frequency: አገበረ፡ – "make someone do something"; አነስሐ፡ – "lead someone to repentance"; አሠነየ፡ – "adorn, or array"; and አቤዘወ፡ – "have someone redeemed."

18.5   Notes on the Gəʿəz Verbal System

The primary lexical types of verbs G, D, L, and Q, and their medio-passive, reciprocal, and causative derivatives make up a group of parallel systems. Now and again, there is no base verb from which a particular verb form derives. In addition, a transitive and intransitive relationship appears between the causative and the medio-passive verbs. Some examples include the following verbs:

CG/Gt	አአመረ፡ ተአምረ፡ – "know/be known"
	አምዕዐ፡ ተምዕዐ፡ – "enrage/be enraged"
CD/Dt	አሠፈወ፡ ተሠፈወ፡ – "give hope/have hope"
CQ/Qt	አመንደበ፡ ተመንደበ፡ – "afflict/be afflicted"

It is possible that one of the derived systems can form denominative verbs (verbs derived from a noun) that are outside of the derived system due to specialized meanings. The verb አስመየ፡ – "he was famous" is one example. The expected meaning of a CG form of the verb አስመየ፡ from the G verb ሰመየ፡ would be translated "he caused to name," but it is derived from the denominative form of the adjective ስሙይ፡ – "famous."

18.6 Vocabulary

1. እሳት፡ – fire
2. ነፍስ፡ (pl. ነፍሳት፡) – soul, spirit, breath
3. አረሚ፡ (adj. አረማዊ፡) – pagans, heathens, non-Christians
4. መንክር፡ (pl. ምንክራት፡) – miracle, marvel, wonder
5. እግር፡ (pl. እገር፡ አእጋር፡) – foot
6. አንቀጽ፡ (pl. አናቅጽ፡) – gate
7. ትርጓሜ፡ (pl. ትርጓማት፡) – translation, interpretation
8. ጥንት፡ – beginning
9. ነድ፡ – flame
10. መንገለ፡ – to, toward, in the direction of
11. አጥመቀ፡ CG – baptize; ተጠምቀ፡ Gt – be baptized
12. ነደ፡ – burn; አንደደ፡ CG – set fire; ተናደደ፡ Glt – burn with mutual passion
13. አዕረፈ፡ intrans. CG – rest, find rest; trans. – give rest
14. አፍቀረ፡ CG – love; ተፈቅረ፡ Gt – be loved; ተፋቀረ፡ Glt – love one another
15. አመንደበ፡ CQ – afflict, oppress; ተመንደበ፡ Qt – be oppressed, afflicted
16. አሰፈወ፡ CD – promise; ተሰፈወ፡ Dt – hope for, expect, look forward to
17. ፈጠረ፡ – create, fabricate; ተፈጥረ፡ Gt – be created
18. ሰሐበ፡ – pull, drag, draw, attract; ተሰሕበ፡ Gt – be pulled
19. ሰገደ፡ – bow down
20. ጠፍአ፡ – go out (a light, fire); አጥፍአ፡ CG – extinguish, destroy, annihilate
21. አእመረ፡ CG – know, understand, comprehend; ተአምረ፡ Gt – be known, be understood

18.7 Exercises

A. Translate the following:

1. አውደቀ፡ ዕፀ፡ ወወደዮ፡ ውስተ፡ እሳት።

2. ሞተ፡ አቡሁ፡ ወአልህቆ፡ እሙ፡ አቡሁ፡ ብእሲ፡ ጌር፡ ወጠቢብ።

3. ጠፍአት፡ እሳት፡ በመቅደሰ፡ ጣዖቶሙ።

4. ተሰሕብነ፡ ኃቤሁ፡ በእንተ፡ መንክራት፡ ዘገብረ።

5. እፎ፡ አጥፋእከሙ፡ ዛተ፡ እሳተ።

6. ነበረ፡ በማእከለ፡ አረጊ፡ ወሰገድ፡ ለጣዖቶሙ።

7. ሰሐብኩ፡ ቃልየ፡ እስከ፡ ምሴት፡ ወእምዝ፡ ኀለፍኩ፡ እምነቤሆሙ።

8. በሰሙን፡ አእመርነ፡ ከመ፡ መጠወ፡ አቡነ፡ ነፍሶ።

9. አብዝኀ፡ ሲሳየነ፡ ወኢነዴይነ።

10. አብዝኀ፡ ተአምረ፡ ወመንክራተ፡ ወእምኑ፡ ብዙኃን፡ በወንጌሉ።

11. ሰሐብዎ፡ ውስተ፡ ሀገር፡ እስከ፡ መልአ፡ ደሙ፡ ውስተ፡ ኩሉ፡ ፍናዊሃ።

12. አውፅኡ፡ ኃጺነ፡ ወብርተ፡ እምአድባረ፡ ብሔሮሙ፡ ወሤጥዎ፡ ለሰብእ፡ ባዕዳን።

13. ፈጠረ፡ እግዚአብሔር፡ ሰማየ፡ ወምድረ።

14. ሰገዱ፡ ሎቱ፡ ወወሀብዎ፡ ወርቀ፡ ወብሩረ።

15. ሰሐበነ፡ ገጹ፡ ሠናይ፡ ወነገሩ፡ ጠቢብ።

16. አእመርኩ፡ ሐገከ፡ ወተፈሣሕኩ፡ በቃላቲሁ።

17. አውደቀ፡ ቤቶሙ፡ ዲቤሆሙ፡ ወአመቶሙ።

18. ተፈጥረ፡ ዝንቱ፡ ዓለም፡ በእንቲአክሙ፡ ወበእንተ፡ ደቂቅክሙ።

19. አጥፍኡ፡ አህጉሪሁ፡ ወነሥኡ፡ ሕዝቦ፡ አግብርተ።

20. ሶበ፡ ሰምዑ፡ ነገሮ፣ አአመሩ፡ እስመ፡ መድኃኖሙ፡ ውእቱ።

B. Translate the following:

1. ወአምጽኡ፡ መላእክት፡ ሲሳየ፡ ለማልክ፡ ጼዴቅ፣ ወኮነ፡ ልብሱ፡ አነዳ፡ ወቅናቱ፡ ዘማእስ፣ ወነበረ፡ ህየ፡ ወተልእከ፡ ቅድመ፡ ሥጋ፡ አቡነ፡ አዳም፡ ኀበ፡ ተሐንጸ፡ ምዕራፉ።

2. ፈነዎ፡ ኖኅ፡ ለሴም፡ ወልዱ፡ ምስለ፡ ሥጋ፡ አቡነ፡ አዳም፡ ወአንበሮ፡ በማእከለ፡ ምድር፡ እንተ፡ ይእቲ፡ ውስተ፡ ኢየሩሳሌም።

3. አውፅአሙ፡ መኰንን፡ ለእሙንቱ፡ ሰብእ፡ ወአቅተሎሙ፡ ቅድመ፡ ኵሉ፡ ሕዝብ።

4. ወአም፡ ተመይጠ፡ አብርሃም፡ እምስብእ፣ እምድኃረ፡ ሞአ፡ ነገሥተ፡ ኀለፈ፣ እንተ፡ ኀበ፡ ሀገረ፡ ሳሌም፡ (ዘውእቱ፡ ኢየሩሳሌም፡ በከመ፡ ትርጓሜሆሙ፡ ለጠቢባነ፣) ወአቅረበ፡ ሎቱ፡ መልክ፡ ጼዴቅ፡ (ዘተሰምየ፡ ካህነ፡ ወንጉሠ፡ ሳሌም፡ ውስተ፡ ሕግ፡ ብሊት፡) ኅብስተ፡ ወወይነ፡ ወአብርሃም፡ ወሀበ፡ ዓሥራተ፡ እምኵሉ፡ ንዋዩ።

5. አይቴ፡ አቀበር፡ ንጉሥ፡ አብድንቲሆሙ፡ ለእለ፡ ተቀትሉ፡ ሰብእ።

6. ረዳእኩሁ፡ ለዝንቱ፡ ነዳይ፡ ወወሀብኩሁ፡ ሲሳየ፡ ወልብሰ።

7. አውለደ፡ ብዙኀ፡ ውሉደ፡ ወአዋልደ፡ ወበዝኀ፡ ዘመዱ፡ እምካልኣን፡ አዝማድ፡ ዘውእቱ፡ መካን።

8. ሙት፡ ነገሥት፡ እለ፡ ተጸብአሙ፡ አብርሃም።

9. በዛቲ፡ ትእምርት፡ አርአየነ፡ መስጢረ፡ ቅዳሴ፡ ዘሕግ፡ ሐዳስ።

10. አርከቦ፡ እግዚአብሔር፡ ለአብርሃም፡ ብዙኀ፡ ንዋየ፡ ውስተ፡ ግብጽ።

11. ዝንቱ፡ ውእቱ፡ አሰማዕቲሆሙ፣ ለአለ፡ አስመዩ፡ በውእቱ፡ ጸብአ።

_____

12. ነሥአ፡ ሴም፡ ለመልክ፡ ጼዴቅ፡ አምቤተ፡ አቡሁ፡ ወመርሐሙ፡ መልአከ፡ እግዚአብሔር፡ እስከ፡ በጽሐ፡ ሳሌምሃ፤ ወተሠይመ፡ መልክ፡ ጼዴቅ፣ ካህነ፡ ወነሥአ፡ አአባነ፡ ወአዕረገ፡ ዲቤሆሙ፡ መሥዋዕተ፡ በኅብስት፡ ወወይን፡ ዘወረደ፡ ሎቱ፡ እምሰማይ፡ ከመ፡ ትእምርተ፡ ምስጢረ፡ ሕግ፡ ሐዳስ።

_____

_____

_____

C. Luke 2:1–14. Please translate the passage.

¹ወኮነ፡ በውእቱ፡ መዋዕል፡ ወፅአ፡ ትእዛዝ፡ አምኀበ፡ ቄሳር፡ ንጉሥ፡ ከመ፡ ይጸሐፍ፡ ኵሉ፡ ዓለም።

²ወውእቱ፡ ጸሐፍ፡ ቀዳሚ፡ ውእቱ፡ አመ፡ ቄሬኔዎስ፡ መስፍን፡ ለሶርያ።

³ወሐረ፡ ኵሉ፡ ሰብእ፡ ይጸሐፍ፡ በበ፡ ሀገሩ።

⁴ወዐርገ፡ ዮሴፍኒ፡ እምገሊላ፡ እምሀገረ፡ ናዝሬት፡ መንገለ፡ ይሁዳ፡ ኀበ፡ ሀገረ፡ ዳዊት፡ እንተ፡ ስማ፡ ቤተ፡ ልሔም፡ እስመ፡ እምሀገረ፡ ዳዊቲ፡ ወእምአዝማደ፡ ቤቱ፡ ውእቱ።

⁵ወሐረ፡ ይጸሐፍ፡ ምስለ፡ ማርያም፡ እንተ፡ ፈኀሩ፡ ሎቱ፡ ብእሲተ፡ እንዘ፡ ፅንስት፡ ይአቲ።

⁶ወእምዝ፡ እንከ፡ እንዘ፡ ህለዉ፡ ህየ፡ በጽሐ፡ ዕለተ፡ ወሊዶታ።

⁷ወወለደት፡ ወልደ፡ ዘበኩራ፡ ወአሰረቶ፡ መንኮብያቲሁ፡ ወአስከበቶ፡ ውስተ፡ ጎል፡ እስመ፡ አልቦሙ፡ መካነ፡ ውስተ፡ ማኅደሮሙ።

⁸ወሀለዉ፡ ኖሎት፡ ውስተ፡ ውእቱ፡ ብሔር፡ ወይተግሁ፡ ወይሐልዉ፡ ወየዐቅቡ፡ መራዕዮሙ፡ ሌሊተበ፡ ዕብሬቶሙ።

⁹ወናሁ፡ ቆመ፡ መልአከ፡ እግዚአብሔር፡ ኀቤሆሙ፡ ወስብሐተ፡ እግዚአብሔር፡ በረቀ፡ ላዕሌሆሙ፡ ወፈርሁ፡ ዐቢየ፡ ፍርሀተ።

¹⁰ወይቤሎሙ፡ መልአክ፡ ኢትፍርሁ፡ እስመ፡ ናሁ፡ እዜንወክሙ፡ ዐቢየ፡ ዜና፡ ፍሥሓ፡ ዘይከውን፡ ለኩሉ፡ ሕዝብ።

¹¹እስመ፡ ናሁ፡ ተወልደ፡ ለክሙ፡ ዮም፡ መድኀን፡ ዘውእቱ፡ ክርስቶስ፡ እግዚእ፡ ቡሩክ፡ በሀገረ፡ ዳዊት።

¹²ወከመዝ፡ ትእምርቱ፡ ለክሙ፡ ትረክቡ፡ ሕፃነ፡ እሱረ፡ መንኮብያቲሁ፡ ስኩብ፡ ውስተ፡ ጎል።

¹³ወግብተ፡ መጽኡ፡ ምስለ፡ ውእቱ፡ መልአክ፡ ብዙኀ፡ ሐራ፡ ሰማይ፡ ይሴብሕዎ፡ ለእግዚአብሔር፡ ወይብሉ።

¹⁴ስብሐት፡ ለእግዚአብሔር፡ በሰማያት፡ ወሰላም፡ በምድር፡ ለእጓለ፡ እመ፡ ሕያው፡ ሥምረቱ።

Chapter 19

THE INFINITIVE

19.1 Base Forms of Gəʿəz Infinitive Verbs

The infinitive verb form articulates the concept of the action of a verb without the characteristic of tense or person. As a result, it carries the range of meaning of abstract or conceptual words, while also maintaining verbal characteristics. Each of the four types of Gəʿəz verbs, G, D, L, and Q (quadriliteral root), has its own way of forming the infinitive. In addition, each has a passive form Gt, Dt, Lt, and Qt and also a causative form CG, CD, CL, and CQ. The infinitive of all verb types, D, L, and Q, apart from G, is formed from the perfect. Each perfect form replaces the final stem vowel $ă$ with an $ə$ and adds an o to the end. For example, the D verb ነጸረ፡, *năṣṣără* would appear in the infinitive as ነጽሮ፡, *năṣṣəro*. The infinitive is capable of having objects of its own. When a pronominal suffix is added to the infinitive, the ending becomes $o+t$, ነጽሮት፡ + the suffix. In the case of the L verb infinitive, the verb ባሬከ፡ transforms to ባርኮ፡ and for the Q verb infinitive, the verb ተርጎመ፡ transforms to ተርጉሞ፡. This change occurs in all three forms: active, passive, and causative.

19.2 The G Verb Infinitive Base

The G verb infinitive base form is ቀቲል፡ but it offers variations in the various root types, e.g., II Guttural, III-ወ/የ, etc. The II Gutturals shift from ቀቲል፡ to ቀቲል፡. On occasion the i vowel may be replaced by the $ə$ vowel in II- and III-ወ/የ verbs, e.g., ርእይ፡ to ርእይ፡. When a pronominal suffix is added to the infinitive, the additional -$o+t$ is added to the infinitive, e.g., ቀቲል፡ transforms to ቀቲሎት፡ + the pronominal suffix. The following is a list of possible G verb infinitives. The last four examples reveal the possible changes with II Guttural, III-ወ/የ:

1. ነቢር፡ – "to sit"
2. ገቢር፡ – "to do"
3. ዐሪግ፡ – "to ascend"
4. ኀሊይ፡ – "to seek"
5. ስኢል፡ – "to seek"
6. ስሕት፡ – "to err"
7. መጺእ፡ – "to come"

8. በጺሐ፡ – "to arrive"
9. ርኢይ፡ / ርአይ፡ – "to see"
10. ቀዊም፡ / ቀዉም፡ – "to stand"
11. ሠይጥ፡ / ሠይጥ፡ – "to sell"
12. በኪይ፡ / በከይ፡ – "to weep"
13. ወሪድ፡ – "to descend"

19.3 Use of the Infinitives

A. The Gəʿəz infinitive is most often used as the accusative that completes other verbs. There are several verbs in which this occurs with frequency: ክህለ፡ – "be able"; ረስዐ፡ – "forget (to do)"; ስእነ፡ – "be unable"; ፈርሀ፡ – "be afraid (to do)"; ኀደገ፡ – "stop (doing)"; ከልአ፡ – "prevent (from doing)"; አበየ፡ – "refuse (to do)."

Examples:

i. ኢክህልነ፡ በዊአ፡ – "we were not able to enter"

ii. ስእኑ፡ ሐዊረ፡ – "they were unable to go"

iii. ረሳዕኩ፡ገቢአ፡ – "I forgot to return"

iv. ፈርሀ፡ ነቢረ፡ ህየ፡ – "he was afraid to remain there"

v. ከልአኒ፡ ወፂአ፡ – "he prevented me from leaving"

vi. አበይኩ፡ ጕይየ፡ – "I refused to flee"

vii. ኀደጉ፡ መጺአ፡ ኀቤነ፡ – "they stopped coming to us"

B. A further set of verbs are used with infinitives and are usually translated as adverbs. Some examples include the following:

i. ቀደመ፡ – "do first or beforehand"

ii. አብዝኀ፡ – "do frequently"

iii. አፍጠነ፡ – "do quickly"

iv. ጐንደየ፡ – "do late"

v. ኀብረ፡ – "do together"

vi. ደገመ፡ – "do again or continually"

With these verbs, the adverbial aspects with the infinitive are quite clear.
Examples:

i. ቀደምኩ፡ በጺሐ፡ or (በጻሕኩ፡) – "I arrived first"

ii. ኀበርነ፡ ተገበሮ፡ or (ተገበርነ፡) – "we worked together"

iii. ደገመ፡ መጺአ፡ or (መጽአ፡) – "he came again"

iv. አብዝኁ፡ ተቃትሎ፡ or (ተቃተሉ፡) – "they fought together frequently"

v. ጐንደይኩ፡ በጺሐ፡ or (በጻሕኩ፡) – "I arrived late"

C. In the case of transitive verbs, the infinitive generally is in construct with the object noun: ስእነ፡ ቀቲለ፡ ወልዶ፡ – "he was unable to kill his son"; ኀብሩ፡ ሐኒጸ፡ ሀገር፡ – "they built the city together." If the object is separated from the infinitive in the sentence structure, then the accusative infinitive must be used: ዘንተ፡ ብእሴ፡ ኢክህለ፡ ቀቲለ፡ – "as for this man, he was unable to kill."

D. The pronominal objects of the infinitive are identified with pronominal suffixes as on a noun in the accusative. For example: ቀቲሎትየ፡ – "to kill me"; ቀቲሎተከ፡ – "to kill you"; ቀቲሎቶ፡ – "to kill him." A secondary form may also be used for noun objects: e.g., the construction ቀተሎ፡ ለንጉሥ፡ – "to kill the man" can be expressed as ቀቲሎቶ፡ ለዝንቱ፡ ብእሲ፡ – "to kill this man."

E. Infinitive transitives and intransitives may also function as gerunds and can be suffixed by the subjective-genitive pronominal suffix depending on the context: e.g., ቀቲሎትከ፡ – "*your* killing"; በከዮቱ፡ – "*his* weeping." Some infinitives appear as ordinary nouns: e.g., አሚን፡ – "faith, belief."

19.4 Vocabulary

1. ክህለ፡ / ከህለ፡ – be able, prevail against (+ obj. suff.); ተክህለ፡ Gt – be possible (+ inf.); አክህለ፡ CG – enable, to make able; can take the personal objective suffix in the dative
2. ስእነ፡ – be unable; ተስእነ፡ Gt – be impossible (+ inf.); can take the personal objective suffix in the dative: ተስእነኒ፡ ሐዊረ፡ – it was impossible for me to go
3. ከልአ፡ – prevent, withhold; ተከልአ፡ Gt – abstain (from)
4. ደገመ፡ – do something again (+inf.)
5. ቀደመ፡ – go before, precede; አቅደመ፡ CG – put or place first, to happen or exist; ተቀድመ፡ Gt – occur, take place first; ተቃደመ፡ Glt – go/come out to meet
6. ፈጠነ፡ – be swift, quick; አፍጠነ፡ CG – hurry or hasten (+ inf.)
7. ፍጡን፡ – swift, quick

8. ኅብረ: / ኃብረ: – connected to or associated with; አኅበረ: CG – associate; ተኃብረ: Gt – associate with someone
9. ጐንደየ: – last, remain; delay, tarry; አጐንደየ: CG – put off, delay, defer; ተጐናደየ: Qlt – delay in doing

19.5 Exercises

A. Translate the following:

1. ዐቢይ፡ አአምሮቱ፡ እምአአምሮትነ፡ ፈድፋደ።

2. አከሀለነ፡ ትእዛዙ፡ ገቢአ፡ ሀገረነ።

3. ሶበ፡ ኃለፈ፡ ማየ፡ አይኅ፡ ቀደም፡ ተከለ፡ ኖኅ፡ ዐጸደ፡ ወይን።

4. ኅብሩ፡ ላዕሌየ፡ ለቀቲሎትየ፣ ወባሕቱ፡ ከሀልኩ፡ ጐይየ፡ እምኔሆሙ።

5. ፈጠነከ፡ ውሒዘ፡ ህየ፡ ወኢተከሀለነ፡ ዐዲወ።

6. ቀደም፡ ዐሪገ፡ ውስተ፡ ደብር፣ ወድኃረ፡ ዐርጉ፡ አርዳኢሁ።

7. ቀደም፡ በዊአ፣ ወበአነ፡ እምድኃሬሁ።

8. ጐንደየ፡ ገብሩ፡ ገቢአ፡ ሀገረ።

9. ወረደ፡ ዝናም፡ ወኢከሀለት፡ እሳት፡ ነዲደ።

10. ውእተ፡ ጊዜ፡ ተስእናሙ፡ ጐይየ።

11. አበዩ፡ ትእዛዛቲሁ፡ ወደገሙ፡ ስሒተ፡ እምፍኖት፡ ርትዕት።

12. ኀበርነ፡ ኩልነ፡ ሐኒጸ፡ አብያተ፡ ሐዲሰ።

13. ደገሙ፡ አመንድቦቶሙ፡ ለክርስቲያን።

14. ተስእነ፡ ቀሪበ፡ ኀበ፡ አናቅጸ፡ ሀገር።

15. ተናገርነ፡ በእንተ፡ ተመይጦቶሙ፡ ለአሕዛብ፡ ውስተ፡ አሚነ፡ እግዚእነ።

16. ኀብረ፡ ነገሩ፡ ምስለ፡ ዜና፡ ዘሰማዕነ፡ እመልአከ፡ ንጉሥ።

17. ለምንት፡ አኀበርክሙ፡ ዘንተ፡ ጣዖተ፡ እኩየ፡ ምስለ፡ እግዚአብሔር፡ ወቤቱ።

18. ኢጐንደየ፡ ሞቱ።

19. አቅደሙ፡ ነገሩ፡ ዘንተ፡ ነቢያት፡ በመዋዕለ፡ አበዊነ።

20. እምድኀረ፡ ተአምነ፡ ኀጢአቶ፥ ተከህለ፡ ምተጠምቆ።

B. Mark 7:24–37. Translate the following:

[24] ወተንሥአ፡ እምህየ፡ ሐረ፡ ብሔረ፡ ጢሮስ፡ ወሲዶና፡ ወበአ፡ ቤተ፡ ወኢፈቀደ፡ ያእምሮ፡ መኑሂ፡ ወስእነ፡ ተከብቶ።

[25] ወእምዝ፡ ሰምዐት፡ ብእሲት፡ በእንቲአሁ፡ እንተ፡ ጋኔን፡ እኩይ፡ አኀዛ፡ ላቲ፡ ወለታ፡ ወበአት፡ ወሰገደት፡ ሎቱ፡ ታሕተ፡ አገሪሁ።

[26] ወአረማዊት፡ ይእቲ፡ ብእሲት፡ ወሲሮፊኒቂስ፡ ይእቲ፡ ወሰአለቶ፡ ያውፅአ፡ ጋኔነ፡ እምወለታ።

[27] ወይቤላ፡ እግዚእ፡ ኢየሱስ፡ ኅድጊ፡ ቅድመ፡ ምዕረ፡ ይጽገቡ፡ ውሉድ፡ እስመ፡ ኢኮነ፡ ሠናየ፡ ነሢአ፡ ኅብስተ፡ ውሉድ፡ ወውሂብ፡ ለከለባት።

[28] ወተሠጥወቶ፡ ወትቤሎ፥ እወ፡ እግዚእ፡ ከለባትኒ፡ ይበልዑ፡ በታሕተ፡ ማእድ፡ ፍርፋራተ፡ ዘያወድቁ፡ ደቂቅ።

²⁹ ወይቤላ፥ በእንተ፡ ዝቃልኪ፡ ሑሪ፡ ወፅአ፡ ውእቱ፡ ጋኔን፡ እምወለትኪ።

³⁰ ወሐረት፡ ወአተወት፡ ቤታ፡ ወረከበታ፡ ለወለታ፡ ለብስታ፡ ወትነብር፡ ዲበ፡ ዐራታ፡ ወንደጋ፡ ጋኔና።

³¹ ወንሊፆ፡ ካዕበ፡ እምጢሮስ፡ ሐረ፡ እንተ፡ ሲዶና፡ ላዕለ፡ ገሊላ፡ ማእከለ፡ ዐሥርቱ፡ አህጉር።

³² ወአምጽኡ፡ ኅቤሁ፡ በሃመ፡ ወጽሙመ፡ ወአስተብኁዕዎ፡ ከመ፡ ይደይ፡ እዴሁ፡ ላዕሌሁ።

³³ ወአግሐሦ፡ እምነበ፡ ሰብእ፡ በባሕቲቶሙ፡ ወወደየ፡ አጻብዒሁ፡ ውስተ፡ እዘኒሁ፡ ወተፍአ፡ ወገሰሰ፡ ልሳኖ።

³⁴ ወነጸረ፡ ሰማየ፡ ወአስተምሐረ፡ ወይቤሎ፡ ኤፍታሕ፡ ተረኅው፡ ብሂል።

³⁵ ወሶቤሃ፡ ተከሥታ፡ እዘኒሁ፡ ወተፈትሐ፡ ማእሰረ፡ ልሱ፡ ወተናገረ፡ ርቱዐ።

³⁶ ወገሠጾሙ፡ ኢይንግሩ፡ ወኢለመኑሂ፡ ወአምጣነ፡ ይከልአሙ፡ ውእቱ፡ ፈድፋደ፡ ይነግሩ፡ ሎቱ።

³⁷ ወፈድፋደ፡ ያነክሩ፡ እንዘ፡ ይብሉ፡ ኩሎ፡ ሠናየ፡ ገብረ፡ ለጽሙማን፡ ያሰምዖሙ፡ ወለበሃማን፡ ያነብቦሙ።

Chapter 20

PARTICIPLES

20.1 Perfect Active Participles

Each verb in the Gǝʿǝz language has a perfect active participle that reflects the person, gender, and number of the participle, much like nouns, thus, they are often referred to as verbal nouns. The participle stem is derived from the infinitive form of the verb with the final stem vowel being an *i* rather than the *e* between the C_2 and C_3 radicals of the root. So the form of the perfect active participle is $C_1ăC_2iC_3$ (note the G verb infinitive is already an *i* vowel; cf. ch. 19).

TABLE 20.1: Perfective Active Participle Forms

Stem	Infinitive form	Stem	Infinitive form	Stem	Infinitive form	Stem	Infinitive form
G	ቀቲል-	D	ቀቲል-	L	ቃቲል-	Q	ተርጒም-
Gt	ተቀቲል-	Dt	ተቀቲል-	Lt	ተቃቲል-	Qt	ተተርጒም-
CG	አቅቲል-	CD	አቀቲል-	CL	አቃቲል-	CQ	አተርጒም-

20.2 Perfect Active Participle Inflection

The perfect active participle is inflected like a noun in the accusative and is used to articulate that the action of the participle was completed prior to the time of the action of the main verb in the clause. Thus, the participle is a subordinate clause, like the English temporal clause that begins with "when" or "after" or "having," as in the participle phrase "having eaten, he took a walk in the garden." These participle forms are generally found in Gǝʿǝz preceding the main verb, but can be found following it also: e.g., ነቢርየ፡ ተናገርኩ፡ ምስሌሆሙ። – "having sat down, I spoke with them," or a better English translation: "I sat down and spoke with them." As can be seen in this example, and the one to follow, the noun subject in Gǝʿǝz also belongs to the subordinate phrase "having sat down": ነቢሮ፡ ኢየሱስ፡ ነገሮሙ። – "having sat down, Jesus said to them" or "Jesus sat down and spoke to them." It should be noted that a suffixed object pronoun will not be found attached to this form. The object noun is reflected with the accusative noun or with the preposition ለ, lă: e.g., ቀቲልየ፡ ብእሴ፡/ለብእሲ፡ ጐየይኩ። – "having slain the man, I fled," or "I slayed the man and fled."

The perfect active participle may also be used to complement another element in a clause or perhaps, while acting as an absolute, the complete clause. For example:

1. ረከቡኒ፡ ነቢርየ፡ህየ። – "after (I) having sat there, they found me," or "they found me seated there."
2. ረከቡ፡ ቤቶ፡ ወዲቆ። – "they found his house, after (it) having collapsed" or "they found his house in ruins."
3. ተመዋእ፡ ሀገርነ፡ ጉየይነ። – "we fled after our city was defeated."

The perfect active participle is not negated. A negative expression appears as a subordinate clause with the words ሶበ፡ or እንዘ፡ plus the perfect form: ወእንዘ፡ ኢረከበ፡ ማየ፣ ኃለፈ። – "and having found no water, he continued on his way" or "and without finding water, he continued on his way."

TABLE 20.2: G Stem Active Participle Declension

PGN	Participle form	Meaning	PGN	Participle form	Meaning
3ms	ቀቲሎ፡	He, having killed	3mp	ቀቲሎሙ፡	They, having killed
3fs	ቀቲላ፡	She, having killed	3fp	ቀቲሎን፡	They, having killed
2ms	ቀቲለከ፡	You, having killed	2mp	ቀቲለከሙ፡	You, having killed
2fs	ቀቲለኪ፡	You, having killed	2fp	ቀቲለክን፡	You, having killed
1cs	ቀቲልየ፡	I, having killed	1cp	ቀቲለነ፡	We, having killed

a. Note in each case the I consonant includes the *ă* vowel followed by the II consonant with the *i* vowel.

b. The III consonant in the 3ms, 3mp/fp has the *o* vowel with the plural forms having the expected suffixes.

c. The 3fs III consonant has the *ā* vowel signifying the 3fs form.

d. The 2nd person s/p and the 1cp forms have the *ă* vowel followed by endings.

20.3 Perfect Passive Participle Inflection

There is also a passive form/meaning of the transitive active verb; if the stem is passive, then the translation/meaning is passive.

TABLE 20.3: G Stem Passive Participle Declension

PGN	Participle form	Meaning	PGN	Participle form	Meaning
3ms	ተቀቲሎ፡	He, having been killed	3mp	ተቀቲሎሙ፡	They, having been killed
3fs	ተቀቲላ፡	She, having killed	3fp	ተቀቲሎን፡	They, having been killed
2ms	ተቀቲለከ፡	You, having been killed	2mp	ተቀቲለከሙ፡	You, having been killed
2fs	ተቀቲለኪ፡	You, having been killed	2fp	ተቀቲለክን፡	You, having been killed
1cs	ተቀቲልየ፡	I, having been killed	1cp	ተቀቲለነ፡	We, having been killed

a. Note each form has a ተ prefix followed by the I consonant with an *ă* vowel and the II Consonant with the *i* vowel.

b. The III consonant follows the same vowel pattern as the active participle.

20.4 Vocabulary

1. ላህም፡ (pl. አልህምት፡) – bull, cow
2. ጽንፍ፡ – edge, margin, hem, shore
3. አጽናፍ፡ ምድር፡ – ends of the earth
4. ጻማ፡ ዓጋ፡ (pl. ጻማት፡ ዓጋት፡) – labor, toil, work
5. ክሳድ፡ / ክሣድ፡ (pl. ክሳዳት፡ ክሳውድ፡ ክሣውድ፡) – neck
6. ሰላም፡ – safety, peace
7. በሰላም፡ – safely, in peace
8. ነፋስ፡ (pl. ነፋሳት፡) – wind
9. አሰረ፡ – tie up, bind; ተአሰረ፡ Gt – be tied up, bound
10. ፈትሐ፡ – untie, loosen, to let loose, set free, to forgive (sins), to pass judgment; ተፈትሐ፡ Gt – be loosened; አፍትሐ፡ CG – bring judgment to; ተፋትሐ፡ Glt – engage in a legal case with
11. አኀዘ፡ – seize, grasp, hold; ተአኀዘ፡ Gt – be seized, grasped; አአኀዘ፡ CG – order someone held; ተአኀዘ፡ Glt – be involved in battle with (see 22.4 for the inceptive use of this verb with the infinitive)
12. መጠረ፡ – cut, cut off; ተመጥረ፡ Gt – be cut, to be cut off
13. ጽሙ፡ – secretly
14. ጽሚተ፡ – in secret
15. በጽሚት፡ – in private

20.5 Exercises

A. Translate the following:

1. ተፈዋሳ፡ እምደዌሃ፡ ተፈሥሐት፡ ፈድፋደ፡ ወአምነት፡ በወንጌል፡ ዘሰበከ፡ ቦቱ።

2. አፍጢኖ፡ ተንሥአ፣ ደገናሙ።

3. ንዲኅ፡ አባሁ፡ ወእም፣ ገብረ፡ ምስለ፡ ውእቱ፡ ብእሲ፡ ቅዱስ።

4. ከዊኖ፡ ነፋስ፣ ኢይክህልኩ፡ ሐዊረ፡ ውስተ፡ ባሕር።

5. ተነሢኦን፡ አንስት፡ እምአምታቲሆን፡ በከደ፡ ወአበደ፡ ተገብሮ።

6. ሐነጹ፡ ሎሙ፡ ቤተ፡ ክርስቲያን፡ ውስተ፡ መካነ፡ ዐጸደ፡ አልህምት፡ ኀበ፡ ጽንፈ፡ ባሕር።

7. ወጊሮሙ፡ ኃጻውንቲሆሙ፡ ዲበ፡ ምድር፤ አበዩ፡ ወኢአ፡ ጸብአ።

8. ከዊኖ፡ ምሴተ፤ ነበርነ፡ ህየ፡ ወኢሐርነ፡ እስከ፡ ጽባሕ።

9. መጺአሙ፡ ጽሚተ፡ በሌሊት፤ ኀበርነ፡ ምስሌሆሙ፡ ላዕለ፡ ውእቱ፡ ንጉሥ፡ እኩይ።

10. ፈነዎሙ፡ ለመላእክቲሁ፡ ውስተ፡ አጽናፈ፡ ምድር፡ ምስለ፡ ዝንቱ፡ ዜና።

11. ሀዲአ፡ ነፋስ፡ ተከህሎሙ፡ ዐሪገ፡ ውስተ፡ ሐመሮሙ።

12. በአይ፡ ጻጋ፡ ዘከህሉ፡ ቀቲሎቶ።

13. ተእኒዞ፤ ተወድየ፡ ውስተ፡ ቤተ፡ ሞቅሐ።

14. ተስእነኒ፡ ነቢረ፡ ህይ፡ በሰላም፡ እስመ፡ ኢያፍቀሩኒ፡ ሕዝብ፤ ወአመንደቡኒ።

15. አሲሮሙ፡ ሐብለ፡ ውስተ፡ ክሳዱ፤ ወሰድዎ፡ እንተ፡ ፍኖት፡ ከመ፡ ላህም።

16. በጺሐሙ፡ ጽንፈ፡ ባሕር፤ ኢክህሉ፡ ዐዲዋቶ፡ በእንተ፡ ነፋስ፡ ዐቢይ።

17. ሶበ፡ ረከብናሆሙ፡ ተአሲሮሙ፤ መተርነ፡ አሕባሊሆሙ፡ ወፈታሕናሆሙ።

18. ተበቲኮ፡ ዐጽቅ፡ ዘነበረ፡ ዲቤሁ፤ ወድቀ፡ ዲበ፡ ምድር፡ ወተቀትለ።

19. ገቢረነ፡ ሰላመ፡ ምስሌሆሙ፥ ኢጸባእናሆሙ።

20. ተሣዴጦ፡ ላህመ፥ ወሰዶ፡ ኀበ፡ ዐጸዱ።

B. Matthew 6:1–24. Translate the following:

¹ ወባሕቱ፡ ዑቁ፡ ምጽዋተክሙ፡ ኢትግበሩ፡ ለዐይነ፡ ሰብእ፡ ከመ፡ ታስተርእዩ፡ ሎሙ፡ ወእመ፡ አኮሰ፡ ዐስበ፡ አልብክሙ፡ በኀበ፡ አቡክሙ፡ ዘበሰማያት።

² ሶቤሃ፡ ትገብሩ፡ ምጽዋተክሙ፡ ኢትንፍሑ፡ ቀርነ፡ ቅድሜክሙ፡ በከመ፡ መድልዋን፡ ይገብሩ፡ በምኲራብት፡ ወበአስካኀት፡ ከመ፡ ይትአኰቱ፡ እምኀበ፡ ሰብእ፡ አማን፡ እብለክሙ፡ ሐጕሉ፡ ዐሴቶሙ፡

³ ወአንተሰ፡ ሶበ፡ ትገብር፡ ምጽዋተከ፡ ኢታእምር፡ ፀጋምከ፡ ዘተገብር፡ የማንከ።

⁴ ከመ፡ በኅቡእ፡ ይኩን፡ ምጽዋትከ፡ ወአቡከ፡ ዘይሬእየከ፡ ዘበኅቡእ፡ ይዕሰየከ፡ ክሡተ።

⁵ ወሶበሂ፡ ትጼልዩ፡ ኢትኩኑ፡ ከመ፡ መድልዋን፡ እስመ፡ እሙንቱ፡ ያፈቅሩ፡ በምኲራብት፡ ወውስተ፡ መዓዝነ፡ መራኅብት፡ ቀዊሞ፡ ወጸልዮ፡ ከመ፡ ያስተርእዩ፡ ለሰብእ፥ አማን፡ እብለክሙ፡ ነጕሉ፡ ዐሴቶሙ።

⁶ ወአንተሰ፡ ሶበ፡ ትጼሊ፡ ባእ፡ ቤተከ፡ ወዕፁ፡ ኆኅተከ፡ ወጸሊ፡ ለአቡከ፡ ሰማያዊ፡ በኅቡእ፥ ወአቡከ፡ ዘይሬእየከ፡ በኅቡእ፡ የዓሥየከ፡ ክሡተ።

⁷ ወእንዘ፡ ትጼልዩ፡ ኢዘንግዑ፡ ከመ፡ አሕዛብ፡ እስመ፡ ይመስሎሙ፡ በአብዝኆ፡ ንባሙ፡ ዘይሰምዖሙ።

⁸ ኢትትመሰልዎሙኬ፡ እስመ፡ የአምር፡ አቡክሙ፡ ሰማያዊ፡ ዘትፈቅዱ፡ ዘእንበለ፡ ትጽአልዎ።

⁹ አንትሙሰ፡ ሶበ፡ ትጼልዩ፡ ከመዝ፡ በሉ፥ አቡነ፡ ዘበሰማያት፡ ይትቀደስ፡ ስምከ፥

¹⁰ ትምጻእ፡ መንግሥትከ፥ ወይኩን፡ ፈቃደከ፡ በከመ፡ በሰማይ፡ ከማሁ፡ በምድር።

¹¹ ሲሳየነ፡ ዘለለ፡ ዕለትነ፡ ሀበነ፡ ዮም።

¹² ኅድግ፡ ለነ፡ አበሳነ፡ ወጌጋየነ፡ ከመ፡ ንሕነኒ፡ ንኅድግ፡ ለዘአበሰ፡ ለነ።

Participles 135

¹³ ኢታብኦነ፡ እግዚአ፡ ውስተ፡ መንሱት፡ አላ፡ አድኅነነ፡ ወባልሐነ፡ እምክሱ፡ እኩይ፤ እስመ፡ ዚአከ፡ ይእቲ፡ መንግሥት፡ ኀይል፡ ወስብሐት፡ ለዓለም፡ ዓለም፡ አሜን።

¹⁴ እስመ፡ ለእመ፡ ኀደግሙ፡ ለሰብእ፡ አበሳሆሙ፡ የኀድግ፡ ለክሙኒ፡ አቡክሙ፡ ሰማያዊ፡ አበሳክሙ።

¹⁵ ወእመሰ፡ ኢኀደግሙ፡ ለሰብእ፡ አበሳሆሙ፡ አቡክሙኒ፡ ሰማያዊ፡ ኢያኀድግ፡ አበሳክሙ።

¹⁶ ወሶብሂ፡ ትጸውሙ፡ ኢትኩኑ፡ ከመ፡ መደልዋን፡ እስመ፡ እሙንቱ፡ ይትመጸዉ፡ ወይቄጽሩ፡ ገጾሙ፡ ወያማስኑ፡ ከመ፡ ያእምር፡ ሰብእ፡ ከመ፡ ጾሙ፤ አማን፡ እብለክሙ፡ ነሥኡ፡ ዕሤቶሙ።

¹⁷ ወአንትሙሰ፡ ሶበ፡ ትጸውሙ፡ ቅብኡ፡ ርእስክሙ፡ ወሕጽቡ፡ ገጸክሙ።

¹⁸ ከመ፡ ኢታሰተርኢ፡ ሰብእ፡ ከመ፡ ጾምክሙ፡ እንበለ፡ አቡክሙ፡ ማዕመረ፡ ኅቡአት፡ ወአቡክሙ፡ ዘይሬእየክሙ፡ በኅቡእ፡ የዐሲየክሙ፡ ክሡተ።

¹⁹ ኢትዝግቡ፡ ለክሙ፡ መዝገበ፡ ዘበምድር፡ ኀበ፡ ይበሊ፡ ወይማስን፡ ወኀበ፡ ፃዴ፡ ወቀነቀኔ፡ ያማስኖ፡ ወኀበ፡ ሰረቅት፡ ይከርዮ፡ ወይሰርቅዎ።

²⁰ አላ፡ ዝግቡ፡ ለክሙ፡ መዝገበ፡ ዘበሰማያት፡ ኀበ፡ ኢይበሊ፡ ወኢይማስን፡ ወኀበ፡ ኢያማስኖ፡ ፃዴ፡ ወቀንቀኔ፡ ወኀበ፡ ሰረቅት፡ ኢይከርዮ፡ ወኢይሰርቅዎ።

²¹ እስመ፡ ኀበ፡ ሀሎ፡ መዝገብክሙ፡ ህየ፡ ይሄሉ፡ ልብክሙኒ።

²² ማኀቶቱ፡ ለሥጋከ፡ ዐይንከ፡ ውእቱ፡ እምከመ፡ ዐይንከ፡ ብሩህ፡ ወስፉሕ፡ ውእቱ፡ ኩሉ፡ ሥጋከ፡ ብሩህ፡ ይከውን፤

²³ ወእመሰ፡ ዐይንከ፡ ሐማሚ፡ ውእቱ፡ ኩሉ፡ ሥጋከ፡ ጽልመተ፡ ይከውን፤ ወስበ፡ ብርሃን፡ ዘላዕሌከ፡ ጽልመት፡ ውእቱ፡ ጽልመትከ፡ እፎ፡ ብርሃን፡ ይከውነከ።

²⁴ ኢይክል፡ አሐዱ፡ ገብር፡ ለክልኤ፡ አጋእዝት፡ ተቀንዮ፡ ወእመ፡ አኮሰ፡ አሐደ፡ ይጸልእ፡ ወካልአ፡ ያፈቅር፡ ወእመ፡ አኮ፡ ለአሐዱ፡ ይትኤዘዝ፡ ወለካልኡ፡ ኢይትኤዘዝ፤ ኢትክሉኬ፡ ተቀንዮ፡ ለእግዚአብሔር፡ ወለንዋይ።

Chapter 21

THE IMPERFECT

21.1 Imperfect Strong G Verbs

In this lesson we will learn the third inflected form of the Gəʿəz G verbs: the imperfect. The Gəʿəz imperfect, as in the Hebrew, notes an incomplete action that can be translated in the present or future tense in English (e.g., Gen 32:14 – "*he set apart a gift* [ዘይወስድ፡ ለዔሳው፡] which he could send to Esau"). The imperfect can also be used to indicate an ongoing present action (e.g., Matt 11:4 – "*Tell John* [ዘትሰምዑ፡ ወዘትሬአዩ፡] what you are (at this moment) hearing and seeing").

Thus far we have learned the perfect participle. The remaining two stems include the subjunctive and the imperative (see chs. 22, 23). The lexical base forms of the verbs, G, D, L, and Q and some of the derived verbal types (e.g., the causative G verbs) also have verbal nouns (ch. 24) and adjectives (ch. 25) that occur quite frequently and follow an expected pattern similar to portions of the verbal system.

21.2 Pattern for the Imperfect G Verb

The inflection of the imperfect G verb is accomplished through the use of suffixes and prefixes. The primary verb pattern appears as $C_1 \check{a} C_2 C_2 \partial C_3$, e.g., ነብር፡. As you will see below, the prefixes ይ-, ት-, አ-, and ን- are similar phonetically to those found on Hebrew imperfect verbs.

TABLE 21.1: G Verb Imperfect Inflection

PGN	Verb Form	Meaning	PGN	Verb Form	Meaning
3ms	ይዘክር፡	he will remember	3mp	ይዘክሩ፡	they will remember
3fs	ትዘክር፡	She will remember	3fp	ይዘክራ፡	they will remember
2ms	ትዘክር፡	You will remember	2mp	ትዘክሩ፡	you will remember
2fs	ትዘክሪ፡	you will remember	2fp	ትዘክራ፡	You will remember
1cs	አዘክር፡	I will remember	1cp	ንዘክር፡	We will remember

    a. Note the similar vowel pattern with the three consonants in the singular forms, the only difference being the addition of the Imperfect suffix *i* on the 2fs.

b. The plural forms hold the same vowel pattern as the singular in consonants I and II, while the III consonant adjusts due to the addition of the Imperfect suffixes.

c. The 3fs and 2ms forms are identical, and context will determine the meaning.

21.3 Negating the Imperfect Verb Forms

As with other verb forms, the imperfect is negated with the prefixed አ. The አ of the first-person singular form አዘክር፡ appears as a ይ, thus, ኢይዘክር፡ – "I will not remember," which can be confused with the 3ms form; therefore, you must rely on the context of the sentence (see ch. 18).

21.4 Other Oddities of the Imperfect Verb Form

If the second and third radicals of the verb are the same, the inflected forms that end in a vowel reflect an optional shortening of the verb form: e.g., the verb ነበበ፡ in the 3mp can appear as ይነቡ፡ for ይነብቡ፡, or ትነቡ፡ for ትነብቡ፡. This may be compared to some degree to what happens with some geminates in biblical Hebrew.

21.5 The Imperfect and Object Suffixes

The object suffixes are attached to the imperfect with a "connecting" vowel (-ā-, -i-, -u-).[1] If the stem ends with an unvocalized consonant, then the connecting vowel ă is employed with first-and second-person object suffixes, hence አዘክረከ፡ – "I will remember you." The third-person suffixes for these verb types use just the vowel form of the suffix, e.g., -ሁ, -ሃ, -ሆሙ፡ ትዘክራ፡ – "she will remember her." If the verb ends in the feminine formative of -i, the -i can be reduced to a short ə when attaching the first- or second-person suffixes: ትዘክርኒ፡ – "you (f.) will remember me." The third-person object suffix for these verbs use only the vowel forms (-o, -ā, -o+ሙ, -o+ን): ትዘክሮሙ፡ – "she will remember them." For the verb that normally ends in -u, the first and second object suffixes attach directly to the verb form: ይዘክሩኒ፡ – "they will remember me." The third-person object suffixes for these verbs use only the vowel forms (-o, -ā, -o+ሙ; -o+ን): ይዘክርዎሙ፡ – "they will remember them."

TABLE 21.2 IMPERFECT OBJECT SUFFIXES

PGN	Form Ending -i/ə	Form Ending -u	Form Ending -ā	PGN	Form Ending -i/ə	Form Ending -u	Form Ending -ā
3ms	-ə+ሁ	-ዮ	-ā+ሁ	3mp	-ə+ዮሙ	-ዮሙ	-ā+ሆሙ
3fs	-ə+ሃ	-ዋ	-ā+ሃ	3fp	-ə+ዮን	-ዮን	-ā+ሆን
2ms	-ə+ከ	-u+ከ	-ā+ከ	2mp	-ə+ከሙ	-u+ከሙ	-ā+ከሙ
2fs	-ə ኪ	-u+ኪ	-ā+ኪ	2fp	-ə+ክን	-u+ክን	-ā+ክን
1cs	-i+ኒ / ə+ኒ	-u+ኒ	-ā+ኒ	1cp	-ə+ነ	-u+ነ	-ā+ነ

---

1. Cf. Lambdin, *Introduction*, 144.

21.6 Independent Uses of the Imperfect

The imperfect has four general uses in Gəʿəz. As mentioned previously, these generally indicate an action that is incomplete in the mind of the author. For the verb ይነብር፡, these uses include – 1) simple future: "he will sit"; 2) durative: "he was, is, will be sitting"; 3) habitual: "he used to sit," "he regularly sits," "he sits as a habit," "he will sit"; 4) general present: የዐቢ፡ – "he is great"; this category is usually a subsection of the durative or habitual use, but it occurs regularly in relative clauses and is used in place of a corresponding adjective with some verbs.

a. ይመጽእ፡ ዘየዐቢ፡ እምኔየ፡፡ – "One who is greater than I shall come."

b. እሳት፡ ዘይነድድ፡፡ – "a burning flame," ("a flame, the one that is burning").

With the habitual and durative uses of the imperfect, the tense of the verb is usually determined by context. The use of certain constructions suggest that the imperfect should be read in the past tense. One of the most common constructions is the use of the verb ኮነ፡ (to be, become) in the expression ወኮነ፡ ሰበ፡ (and while . . .):

a. ኮነ፡ ይነብር፡ ህየ፡፡ – "he was sitting there" ("he used to sit there")

b. ወኮነ፡ ሰበ፡ ይነብር፡ ህየ፡፡ – "and while he was sitting there . . ."

21.7 Dependent Uses of the Imperfect

The dependent use of the imperfect occurs most often with the conjunction እንዘ፡ – "when or while" and the imperfect in these cases is best understood as an adjectival gerund.

a. It can be used to modify the subject:
ነበረ፡ እንዘ፡ ይነብብ፡፡ – "he sat speaking."

b. It can be used to modify the object:
ረከብዎ፡ ለብእሲ፡ እንዘ፡ ይነብር፡ ህየ፡፡ – "they found the man sitting there."

c. It can function as a dependent clause:
ወእንዘ፡ ይበኪ፡ ኤርምያስ፡ ለሕዝብ፡ አውዕእዎ፡፡ – "And as Jeremiah wept for the people, they led him away."

Often the እንዘ፡ does not appear in the construction:
ነበረ፡ ይነብብ፡፡ – "he sat speaking."
ርእየ፡ ብእሴ፡ ይቀርብ፡፡ – He saw the man approaching."

When the imperfect appears in this construction it should always be considered durative, which indicates an extended action alongside the action of the main verb. In addition, the word order may be changed for emphasis. If so, one will find other elements that are identified by the እንዘ፡ preceding it:

ረከቦ፡ ውስተ፡ መቃብር፡ እንዘ፡ ይነብር። – "He found him dwelling among the tombs."

21.8 Vocabulary

1. ኆኅት፡ (pl. ኆኅታት፡ / ኃዋኅው፡) – door, doorway
2. መስኮት፡ (pl. መሳኩው፡) – window
3. አረጋይ፡ (f. አረጊት፡ pl. አእሩግ፡) – old person
4. አረጋዊ፡ (f. አረጋዊት፡ pl. አረጋውያን፡) – old person
5. ዘከረ፡ – remember, mention; ተዘከረ፡ Gt – be remembered
6. ከብረ፡ – be glorious, magnificent; አክበረ፡ CG – make glorious
7. ክቡር፡ (f. ክብርት፡) – glorious
8. ረኵሰ፡ – be unclean, impure; አርኰሰ፡ CG – pollute, contaminate, defile
9. ርኩስ፡ (f. ርኵስት፡) – unclean
10. ፈለሰ፡ – separate, go away, depart, emigrate; አፍለሰ፡ CG – send away, deport, exile; ተፋለሰ፡ Glt – wander as exiles
11. አርኀወ፡ CG – open; ተርኀወ፡ Gt – be opened
12. ርኁው፡ – open (adj.)
13. ወኮነ፡ ሶበ፡ – and when; and while (used with imperfect)

21.9 Exercises

A. Translate the following:

1. ኮኑ፡ ይሰግዱ፡ ለጣዖት፡ ዘእብን፡ ወዘዕፅ።

2. እፎ፡ ንፈልስ፡ እምዛቲ፡ ምድር፡ ሠናይት።

3. አገብር፡ ሰላመ፡ ምስለ፡ ሕዝበ፡ ዛቲ፡ ሀገር።

4. አልቦ፡ ዘይጠብብ፡ ዘእንበለ፡ ሃይማኖት።

5. ንስድዶሙ፡ ለክርስቲያን፡ እማእከለነ።

6. ውእተ፡ ጊዜ፡ አከሥት፡ ለከሙ፡ ነገሮ።
   _____

7. ውስተ፡ አይ፡ መካን፡ ትነብራ።
   _____

8. እቀርብ፡ ኅቤከ፡ በምሴት።
   _____

9. ማኑ፡ ይጻድቅ፡ በቅድመ፡ እግዚአብሔር።
   _____

10. እተክል፡ አውያንየ፡ ዝየ፡ ኅበ፡ አልቡ፡ ነፋስ።
    _____

11. ትመትርኑ፡ አዕጹቀ፡ እምዕፅ።
    _____

12. አይቴ፡ ዘትረክቢ፡ ወልደኪ።
    _____

13. ይነድድ፡ ዝንቱ፡ እሳት፡ ኩሎ፡ ጊዜ።
    _____

14. ኮኑ፡ ይነብሩ፡ ውስተ፡ ጽንፈ፡ ባሕር።
    _____

15. ንሰብክ፡ ወንጌሎ፡ እስከ፡ አጽናፈ፡ ምድር።
    _____

16. መኑ፡ ይዘክር፡ ስምየ፡ እምድኅረ፡ ሞትኩ።
    _____

17. ለመኑ፡ ትነግርዮ፡ ዘንተ፡ ዜና።
    _____

18. አልቡ፡ ዘይተርፍ፡ እምድኅረ፡ ውእቱ፡ ምንዳቤ።
    _____

19. ትረክቡ፡ አልህምቲክሙ፡ ኅበ፡ ዐጻድዮ።
    _____

20. ንቀብር፡ ምስለ፡ አበዊሁ።
    _____

21. ይከብር፡ ስምከ፡ አምስመ፡ እኍከ።
    _____

22. ይቀትሉነ፡ እሎንቱ፡ ሰብእ።
    _____

23. መኑ፡ ዘይነግሥ፡ ህየንቴከ።
    _____

24. በአይ፡ ጻጋ፡ ንቀትል፡ ዘንተ፡ ጻድቀ።
    _____

B. 1 Enoch 6.1–7. Translate the following:

¹ ወኮነ፡ እምዘ፡ በዝኁ፡ ውሉደ፡ ሰብእ፡ በእማንቱ፡ መዋዕል፡ ተወልዳ፡ ሎሙ፡ አዋልድ፡ ሥናያት፡ ወላሕያት፡

² ወርእዩ፡ ኪያሆን፡ መላእክት፡ ውሉደ፡ ሰማያት፡ ወፈተዉዎን፡ ወይቤሉ፡ በበይናቲሆሙ፡ ንዑ፡ ንኅረይ፡ ለነ፡ አንስተ፡ እምውሉደ፡ ሰብእ፡ ወንለድ፡ ለነ፡ ውሉደ።

³ ወይቤሎሙ፡ ሰምያዛ፡ ዘውእቱ፡ መልአኮሙ፡ እፈርህ፡ ዮጊ፡ ኢትፈቅዱ፡ ይትገበር፡ ዝንቱ፡ ግብር፡ ወእከውን፡ አነ፡ ባሕቲትየ፡ ፈዳየ፡ ለዛቲ፡ ኃጢአት፡ ዐባይ።

⁴ ወአውሥኡ፡ ሎቱ፡ ኵሎሙ፡ ወይቤሎ፡ መሐላ፡ ንምሐል፡ ኵልነ፡ ወንትዋገዝ፡ በበይናቲነ፡ ከመ፡ ኢንሜጥ፡ ለዛቲ፡ ምክር፡ ወንግበራ፡ ለዛቲ፡ ምክር፡ ግብረ።

⁵ አሜሃ፡ መሐሉ፡ ኵሎሙ፡ ኅቡረ፡ ወአውገዙ፡ ኵሎሙ፡ በበይናቲሆሙ፡ ቦቱ።

⁶ ወከኑ፡ ኵሎሙ፡ ወወረዱ፡ ውስተ፡ አርዲስ፡ ዝውእቱ፡ ድማሁ፡ ለደብረ፡ አርሞን፡ ወጸውዕዎ፡ ለደብረ፡ አርሞን፡ እስመ፡ መሐሉ፡ ቦቱ፡ ወአውገዙ፡ በበይናቲሆሙ።

⁷ ወዝንቱ፡ አስማቲሆሙ፡ ለመላእክቲሆሙ፡ ሰምያዛ፡ . . .

C. Matthew 25:31–46. Please translate the following passage.

³¹ ወአመ፡ ይመጽእ፡ ወልደ፡ እጓለ፡ እመሕያው፡ በስብሓቲሁ፡ ወኵሎሙ፡ መላእክቲሁ፡ ምስሌሁ፡ አሜሃ፡ ይነብር፡ ውስተ፡ መንበረ፡ ስብሓቲሁ።

³² ወይትጋብኡ፡ ኵሎሙ፡ አሕዛብ፡ ቅድሜሁ፡ ወይፈልጦሙ፡ ዘዘ፡ ዚአሆሙ፡ ከመ፡ ኖላዊ፡ ይፈልጥ፡ አባግዐ፡ እምአጣሊ።

³³ ወያቀውም፡ አባግዐ፡ በየማን፡ ወአጣሊ፡ በጸጋም።

³⁴ አሜሃ፡ ይብል፡ ንጉሥ፡ ለእለ፡ በየማን፡ ንዑ፡ ቡሩካኒሁ፡ ለአቡየ፡ ትረሱ፡ መንግሥተ፡ ዘአስተዳለው፡ ለክሙ፡ እምቅድመ፡ ዓለም።

³⁵ እስመ፡ ርኅብኩ፡ ወአብላዕሙኒ፡ ጸማእኩ፡ ወአስተይክሙኒ፡ ወነግድ፡ ኮንኩ፡ ወተወከፍክሙኒ።

³⁶ ዕራቁ፡ ወአልበስክሙኒ፡ ደወይኩ፡ ወሐጽክሙኒ፡ ተሞቃሕኩ፡ ወነበብክሙኒ።

³⁷ አሜሃ፡ ያወሥኡ፡ ጻድቃን፡ ወይብሉ፡ እግዚአ፡ ማእዜ፡ ርኢናከ፡ ርኁበ፡ ወአብላዕናከ፡ ወጽሙአ፡ ወአስተይናከ።

³⁸ ወማእዜ፡ ርኢናከ፡ እንግዳከ፡ ወተወከፍናከ፡ ወዕራቀ፡ ወአልበስናከ።

³⁹ ወድዉየከ፡ ወሐወጽናከ፡ ወሙቁሐከ፡ ወነበብናከ።

⁴⁰ ወያወሥእ፡ ንጉሥ፡ ወይብሎሙ፡ አማን፡ እብለክሙ፥ ኵሎ፡ ዘገበርክሙ፡ ለአሐዱ፡ እምእሉ፡ ንኡሳን፡ አኃውየ፡ እለ፡ የአምኑ፡ ብየ፡ ሊተ፡ ገበርክሙ።

⁴¹ ወእምዝ፡ ይብሎሙ፡ ለእለ፡ በጸጋም፥ ሑሩ፡ ርጉማን፡ ውስተ፡ እሳት፡ ዘለዓላም፡ ዘድልው፡ ለሰይጣን፡ ወለመላእክቲሁ።

⁴² እስመ፡ ርኅብኩ፡ ወኢያብላዕክሙኒ፡ ጸማእኩ፡ ወኢያስተይክሙኒ።

⁴³ ወነግደ፡ ኮንኩ፡ ወኢተወከፍክሙኒ፡ ዕራቁ፡ ወኢያልበስክሙኒ፡ ደወይኩ፡ ወኢሐጻክሙኒ፡ ተሞቃሕኩ፡ ወኢነበብክሙኒ።

⁴⁴ አሜሃ፡ ያወሥኡ፡ እለ፡ በፀጋም፡ እንዘ፡ ይብሉ፥ እግዚአ፡ ማእዜ፡ ርኢናከ፡ ርኁበ፡ ወጽሙአ፡ ወእንግዳ፡ ወዕራቀ፡ ወድዉየ፡ ወተሞቁሐ፡ ወኢታልአክናከ።

⁴⁵ ወእምዝ፡ ያወሥአሙ፡ ንጉሥ፡ እንዘ፡ይብል፥ አማን፡ እብለክሙ፥ ዘኢገበርክሙ፡ ለአሐዱ፡ እምእሉ፡ ንኡሳን፡ ሊተ፡ ኢገበርክሙ።

⁴⁶ ወየሐውሩ፡ እሉሂ፡ ውስተ፡ ኵነኔ፡ ዘለዓላም፡ ወጻድቃንሰ፡ ውስተ፡ ሕይወት፡ ዘለዓላም።

Chapter 22

THE SUBJUNCTIVE

22.1 The Subjunctive G Strong Verbs

The subjunctive is generally used to imply the intention of performing an action such as orders, wishes, or desires, some subordinate clauses, or with some compound tenses. The pattern of the subjunctive has two forms: prefix (ይ-, ት-, እ-, ን-) + ə-C_1C_2əC_3 + possessive suffix, and prefix (ይ-, ት-, እ-, ን-) + ə-C_1C_2ăC_3 + possessive suffix. In each case the stem vowel is determined by the lexical from of the verb and has no predictable pattern. In the list that follows, one can see a connection with the ክብረ፡ verb type and the ə vowel subjunctive. A similar connection can be seen with the ገብረ፡ verb type and the ă vowel subjunctive, although there are many exceptions along with some verbs appearing in both forms.

TABLE 22.1: Subjunctive Verb Forms

Verbal Base Form	Imperf.	Subj.	Subj. Translation	Verbal Base Form	Imperf.	Subj.	Subj. Translation
በተከ፡	ይበትክ፡	ይብትክ፡	Let him break	ቀደመ፡	ይቀድም፡	ይቅድም፡	Let him precede
ደገመ፡	ይደግም፡	ይድግም፡	May it be done again	ቀርበ፡	ይቀርብ፡	ይቅረብ፡	Let him approach
ፈለሰ፡	ይፈልስ፡	ይፍልስ፡	Let him depart	ቀተለ፡	ይቀትል፡	ይቅትል፡	Let him kill
ፈጠረ፡	ይፈጥር፡	ይፍጥር፡	Let him devise	ረከበ፡	ይረክብ፡	ይርከብ፡ / ይርከብ፡	May he find
ገብረ፡	ይገብር፡	ይግብር፡	Let him work	ረኵሰ፡	ይረኵስ፡	ይርኵስ፡ / ይርከስ፡	Let him be unclean
ገነዘ፡	ይገንዝ፡	ይግንዝ፡	Let him prepare (it) for burial	ሰበከ፡	ይሰብክ፡	ይስብክ፡	Let him preach
ክብረ፡	ይከብር፡	ይክበር፡	Let him be glorious	ሰደደ፡	ይሰድ፡ / ይሰድድ፡	ይስድድ፡	May he banish
ከሠተ፡	ይከሥት፡	ይክሥት፡	Let him reveal (it)	ሰከበ፡	ይሰክብ፡	ይስክብ፡ / ይርከብ፡	Let him lie down
ነበበ፡	ይነብ፡ / ይነበብ፡	ይንበብ፡	Let him speak	ሰገደ፡	ይሰግድ፡	ይስግድ፡	May he bow down

Verbal Base Form	Imperf.	Subj.	Subj. Translation	Verbal Base Form	Imperf.	Subj.	Subj. Translation
ነበረ፡	ይነብር፡	ይንበር፡	Let him sit	ጸድቀ፡	ይጸድቅ፡	ይድደቅ፡ / ይጽደቅ፡	May he be righteous
ነደደ፡	ይነድ፡	ይንድድ፡ / ይንደድ፡	Let it burn	ተከለ፡	ይተከል፡	ይትከል፡	Let him plant
ነገረ፡	ይነግር፡	ይንግር፡	May he say	ተርፈ፡	ይተርፍ፡	ይትረፍ፡ / ይትርፍ፡	May he remain
ነግሠ፡	የነግሥ፡	ይንግሥ፡ / ይንገሥ፡	May he become king	ጠበበ፡	ይጠብ፡	ይጥበብ፡ / ይጥበብ፡	May he be wise
ቀበረ፡	ይቀብር፡	ይቅብር፡/ ይቅበር፡	Let him bury	ዘከረ፡	ይዘክር፡	ይዝከር፡	May he remember

22.2 Inflection of the Subjunctive

The inflection of the subjunctive verb form is identical to the imperfect verb form.

PGN	Subjunctive Form	Translation	PGN	Subjunctive Form	Translation
3ms	ይቅትል	Let him kill	3mp	ይቅትሉ፡	Let them kill
3fs	ትቅትል፡	Let her kill	3fp	ይቅትላ፡	Let them kill
2ms	ትቅትል፡	May you kill [him]	2mp	ትቅትሉ፡	May you kill [him]
2fs	ትቅትሊ፡	May you kill [him]	2fp	ትቅትላ፡	May you kill [him]
1cs	እቅትል፡	Let me kill	1cp	ንቅትል፡	Let us kill

22.3 Subjunctive with the Object Suffixes

The object suffixes are added to the subjunctive form in the same manner as the imperfect verb form ending in a vowel (see section 21.5 in ch. 21). For the subjunctive forms that end in a consonant, the second-person object suffix is applied directly to the subjunctive without a connecting vowel. Third-person suffixes usually appear in their contracted forms with the expected ሀ dispensed. For example:

ይቅትሎ፡ – "let him kill him"; ይቅትላ፡ – "let him kill her"; ይቅትልከ፡ – "let him kill you" (m); ይቅትልኪ፡ "let him kill you" (f); ይቅትለኒ፡ – "let him kill me";
ይቅትሎሙ፡ – "let him kill them" (m); ይቅትሎን፡ – "let him kill them" (f); ይቅትልክሙ፡ – "let him kill you" (m); ይቅትልክን፡ – "let him kill you" (f); ይቅትለነ – "let him kill us."

22.4 Function of the Subjunctive Verb

a. Independent Use:

When the subjunctive is the verb of the main clause it generally translates as a cohortative or jussive force:

እንግር፡ – "let me speak"
ትርከብዎ፡ – "may you find him"
ኢንስከብ፡ – "let us not lie down"

On occasion, the preposition ለ may be attached to the subjunctive to reflect the positive sense:

ለይንበር፡ – "let him remain"

When the second-person subjunctive is negated, it is translated as the negative imperative:

ኢትንብር፡ ህየ፡ – "do not sit here"
ኢትቅትሎ፡ – "do not kill him"

b. Dependent Use

When the subjunctive is subordinated to another verb, it generally expresses purpose or result. This can occur with or without the conjunction ከመ፡, for example:

ቀርቡሁ፡ ከመ፡ ይስግዱ፡ ሎቱ፡ – "they approached him in order to bow down to him."

When paired with a number of other verbs, the other verb often functions as an auxiliary verb when followed by a subjunctive. Some examples of these verbs include ፈቀደ፡ – "want or wish"; አኀዘ፡ – "begin"; ወጠነ፡ – "begin"; መከረ፡ – "decide to"; ኃደገ፡ – "permit, allow." In these instances, the subjunctive is translated as an infinitive:

ፈቀደ፡ ከመ፡ ይንበር፡ ህየ፡ – "he wanted to remain there"
ወጠነ፡ ንቅረብ፡ – "we began to approach"
መከረ፡ ከመ፡ ይቅትለኒ፡ – "he decided to kill me"

With the verb ኃደገ፡ – "permit, allow," one can expect the subject of the subordinate clause to be present:

ኃደገ፡ ለብእሲ፡ ከመ፡ ይንበር፡ – "he allowed <u>the man</u> to remain."

The combination of the conjunction ከመ፡ + ኢ- can be translated as "in case":

ጐየይኩ፡ (አጐዪ፡) ከመ፡ ኢይርከቡኒ፡ – "I fled (shall flee) in case they will find me"

c. Further Uses of the Subjunctive

The subjunctive often appears following the conjunctions (ዘ)እንበለ፡ and አምቅድመ፡ generally translated as "before":

ነገሮሙ፡ <u>ዘእንበለ፡</u> ይፍልሱ፡ – "he spoke to them <u>before</u> they left"

The subjunctive often follows the impersonal verb ደለወ፡ (imperfect form: ይደልዉ፡), which is translated as "befitting, suitable, or proper" or "should":

ኢይደልወኒ፡ ከመ፡ እቅረብ፡ ሎቱ፡ – "it is not befitting that I approach him," or "I shouldn't approach him."

When the subjunctive follows the predicate adjective መፍትው፡ – "it is necessary" or "must," it is translated as follows:

መፍትው፡ ከመ፡ ንቅብሮ፡ – "it is necessary that we bury him," "we must bury him."

22.5 Vocabulary

1. እንስ፡ (pl. እንሳት፡) – young animal
2. እንስ፡ እመሕያው፡ – humankind (lit. "offspring of the mother of the living" – the offspring of Eve)[1]
3. ድርህም፡ (pl. ድርህማት፡ ደራህም፡) – drachma, denarius
4. ኍልቍ፡ / ኍልቁ፡ (pl. ኍለቍ፡) – number, amount
5. አልቦ፡ ኍልቌ፡ – there is no limit, innumerable
6. ፈቀደ፡ – want, wish, desire (subj. ይፍቅድ፡); ተፈቀደ፡ Gt – be wanted, be desired
7. መከረ፡ – plan, propose, decide on (subj. ይምክር፡); አምከረ፡ CG – advise, give counsel to; ተማከረ፡ Glt – take counsel together (used with ምስለ፡) – deliberate and decide to + subj.
8. ደለወ፡ – weigh, be useful, suitable; ተደለወ፡ Gt – be weighed
9. ወጠነ፡ – to begin; ተወጠነ፡ Gt – to be begun
10. አዘዘ፡ D – order, command + subj.; ተአዘዘ፡ Dt – obey
11. መፍተው፡ – it is necessary, fitting, proper, obligatory

22.6 Exercises

A. Translate the following:

1. አምጽአ፡ ለነ፡ እንስ፡ ላህም፡

2. ተቃረብነ፡ ከመ፡ ንግበር፡ ሰላመ፡

3. ደለወ፡ ወርቀ፡ ወብሩረ፡ ወአንበሮ፡ በቅድሜየ፡

---

[1]. Jan Dochhorn, "Die Menschen als 'Kinder der Mutter der Lebenden' – eine etymologische Parallele zu êm kol-chaj in Gen 3,20 aus dem Altäthiopischen," *Zeitschrift für Althebraistik* 12 (1999): 2–20.

4. ኢይትረፍ፡ ወኢአሐዱ፡ እምኔሆሙ።
   _____

5. ለምንት፡ ኢተአዘዝከሙ፡ ሊተ፡ ሶበ፡ አአመርከሙ፡ ትእዛዝየ።
   _____

6. መፍትው፡ ከመ፡ ትዝክሩ፡ ነገርየ።
   _____

7. ተማከሩ፡ ከመ፡ ይፍልሱ፡ እምዝየ፡ ምስለ፡ አዝማዲሆሙ።
   _____

8. ኢተራከብነ፡ ምስሌሆሙ፡ ከመ፡ ኢንርኩስ።
   _____

9. ሰሚያሙ፡ ዘንተ፣ ወጠኑ፡ ተቃትሎ።
   _____

10. ተሣየጥኩ፡ ዘንተ፡ መጽሐፈ፡ እምኔሃ፡ በሠለስቱ፡ ድርህም።
    _____

11. መፍትው፡ ኩሎ፡ ጊዜ፡ ለተአዝዞ፡ ለእግዚእከ።
    _____

12. ዝንቱ፡ ቅዱስ፡ ውእቱ፡ ኅምስቱ፡ አምኁልቆሙ፡ ለሊቃነ፡ ጳጳሳት።
    _____

13. ሶበ፡ ተናገሩ፡ ምስሌነ፣ ኢፈቀድነ፡ ንንግሮሙ፡ ወኢምንተኒ።
    _____

14. አዘዘነ፡ ከመ፡ ንግበር፡ ሎቱ፡ ዐባየ፡ ሐመረ።
    _____

15. አልቦ፡ ጐልቌ፡ እኩያን፡ ውስተ፡ መካን።
    _____

16. ውሂቡ፡ ሊተ፡ ደራህመ፡ ወርቅ፡ ተሣየጥኩ፡ ሲሳየ፡ ወልብሰ፡ ለዘመድየ።
    _____

17. መፍትው፡ ከመ፡ ንግበር፡ በከመ፡ አዘዙነ።
    _____

18. አንበበ፡ ለነ፡ ዘንተ፡ መጽሐፈ፡ ከመ፡ ንዝክር፡ ግበረሆሙ፡ ለቅዱሳን፡።
_____

19. አዘዝክዎሙ፡ ከመ፡ ይቅበሩ፡ ሙታኒሆሙ፡።
_____

20. አምከርክዎ፡ ከመ፡ ይክሥት፡ ሎሙ፡ ዘንተ፡ ነገር።
_____

21. ጥቀ፡ ብዙኅ፡ ውእቱ፡ ኁልቄ፡ ደራህም፡ ዘተረክበ፡ ውስተ፡ ቤቱ።
_____

22. ተረከቡ፡ እንዘ፡ ይነብሩ፡ ምስለ፡ አቡሆሙ፡።
_____

23. መከረ፡ ይንበር፡ ዝየ፡ ምስሌነ፡።
_____

24. መጽአ፡ መድኃንነ፡ ውስተ፡ ዓለም፡ በእንተ፡ እንለ፡ እመሕያው፡።
_____

B. Jubilees 10.1–17. Translate the following:

[1] ወበሱባዔ፡ ሣልስ፡ ዘኢዮቤልዉ፡ ዝኑቱ፡ አኀዙ፡ አጋንንት፡ ርኩሳን፡ ያስሕትዎሙ፡ ለደቂቀ፡ ውሉደ፡ ኖኅ፡ ወያዕብድዎሙ፡ ወያሕጕልዎሙ፡።

[2] ወመጽኡ፡ ውሉደ፡ ኖኅ፡ ኀበ፡ ኖኅ፡ አቡሆሙ፡ ወነገርዎ፡ በእንተ፡ አጋንንት፡ እለ፡ ያስሕቱ፡ ወይጼልሉ፡ ወይቀትሉ፡ ውሉደ፡ ውሉዱ።

[3] ወጸለየ፡ ኖኅ፡ ቅድመ፡ እግዚአብሔር፡ አምላኩ፡ ወይቤ፡ አምላከ፡ መናፍስት፡ ዘውስተ፡ ኵሉ፡ ዘሥጋ፡ ዘገበርከ፡ ምስሌየ፡ ምሕረተ፡ ወአድኅንኬ፡ ወውሉድየሂ፡ እምነ፡ ማየ፡ አይኅ፡ ወኢገበርከ፡ ከመ፡ እኀልቅ፡ ከመ፡ ገበርከ፡ ለውሉደ፡ ሐጕል፡ እስመ፡ ዐቢይ፡ ሣህልከ፡ ላዕሌየ፡ ወዐብይት፡ ምሕረትከ፡ ላዕለ፡ ነፍስየ፡ ይትለዐል፡ ሣህልከ፡ ላዕለ፡ ውሉደ፡ ውሉድየ።

[4] ወኢይምብሉ፡ መናፍስት፡ እኩያን፡ ላዕሌሆሙ፡ ከመ፡ ኢያማስንዎሙ፡ እምነ፡ ምድር፡ ወአንተኒ፡ ባርከኒ፡ ኪያየ፡ ወውሉድየ፡ ንልሃቅ፡ ወንብዛኅ፡ ወንምልአ፡ ለምድር።

⁵ወአንተ፡ ታአምር፡ ዘእመ፡ ገብሩ፡ ትጉሃኒከ፡ አበዊሆሙ፡ ለእሉ፡ መንፈስ፡ በመዋዕልየ፡ ወዝኒ፡ መናፍስት፡ እለ፡ ሀለዉ፡ በሕይወት፡ ዕጽምሙ፡ ወአንዙሙ፡ ውስተ፡ መካነ፡ ደይን፡ ወኢያማስኑ፡ ውስተ፡ ውሉደ፡ ገብርከ፡ አምላኪየ፡ እስመ፡ ፀዋጋን፡ እሙንቱ፡ ወለአማስኖ፡ ተፈጥሩ።

⁶ወኢይመብሉ፡ በመንፈስ፡ ሕያዋን፡ እስመ፡ አንተ፡ ባሕቲትከ፡ ታአምር፡ ኮነሆሙ፡ ወኢይትባዕሑ፡ ላዕለ፡ ውሉደ፡ ጻድቃን፡ እምይእዜ፡ ወእስከ፡ ለዓለም።

⁷ወይቤለነ፡ አምላክነ፡ ከሙ፡ ንእሰር፡ ኩሎ።

⁸ወመጽአ፡ መልአከ፡ መናፍስት፡ መስቴማ፡ ወይቤ፡ እግዚአ፡ ፈጣሪ፡ አትርፍ፡ እምኔሆሙ፡ ቅድሜየ፡ ወይስምዑ፡ ቃልየ፡ ወይገብሩ፡ ኩሎ፡ ዘእቤሎሙ፡ እስመ፡ ለእመ፡ ኢተርፉ፡ ሊተ፡ እምውስቴቶሙ፡ ኢይክል፡ ገቢረ፡ ስልጣነ፡ ፈቃድየ፡ ውስተ፡ ውሉደ፡ ሰብእ፡ እስመ፡ አሙንቱ፡ ውእቶሙ፡ ለአማስኖ፡ ወለአስሕቶ፡ ቅድመ፡ ኩነኔየ፡ እስመ፡ ዓቢይ፡ እከዮሙ፡ ለውሉደ፡ ሰብእ።

⁹ወይቤ፡ ይትረፉ፡ ቅድሜሁ፡ ዓሥራቶሙ፡ ወተስዓቶ፡ መክፈልተ፡ ያውርዱ፡ ውስተ፡ መካነ፡ ደይን።

¹⁰ወለአሐዱ፡ እምኔነ፡ ይቤ፡ ከመ፡ ንምህሮ፡ ለኖኅ፡ ኩሎ፡ ፈውሶሙ፡ እስመ፡ ያአምር፡ ከመ፡ አኮ፡ በርትዕ፡ ዘየሐውሩ፡ ወአኮ፡ በጽድቅ፡ ዘይትባአሱ።

¹¹ወገበርነ፡ በከመ፡ ኩሉ፡ ቃሉ፡ ወኮሎ፡ እኩያነ፡ እለ፡ ይሰውጡ፡ አሰርነ፡ ውስተ፡ መካነ፡ ደይን፡ ወዐሥራቶሙ፡ አተረፍነ፡ ከመ፡ ይኩንኑ፡ ቅድመ፡ ሰይጣነ፡ ዲበ፡ ምድር።

¹²ወፈውስ፡ ደዊሆሙ፡ ኮሎ፡ ነገርናሁ፡ ለኖኅ፡ ምስለ፡ አስሕቶቶሙ፡ ከመ፡ ይፈውስ፡ በዕፀ፡ ምድር።

¹³ወጸሐፈ፡ ኖኅ፡ ኩሎ፡ ዘከመ፡ መሀርናሁ፡ በመጽሐፍ፡ በኩሉ፡ ትዝምደ፡ ፈውስ፡ ወተዐጽዉ፡ መናፍስት፡ እኩያን፡ እምድኅሬሆሙ፡ ለውሉደ፡ ኖኅ።

¹⁴ወወሀበ፡ ኩሎ፡ መጻሕፍተ፡ ዘጸሐፈ፡ ለሴም፡ ወልዱ፡ ዘይልህቅ፡ እስመ፡ ኪያሁ፡ ያፈቅር፡ ፈድፋደ፡ እምኮሉ፡ ውሉዱ።

¹⁵ወኖኅ፡ ኖዐ፡ ምስለ፡ አበዊሁ፡ ወተቀብረ፡ ውስተ፡ ሉባር፡ ደብር፡ በምድረ፡ አራራት።

¹⁶ተስዕተ፡ ምእተ፡ ወኃምሳ፡ ዓመተ፡ ፈጸመ፡ በሕይወቱ፡ ዐሠርተ፡ ወተስዓተ፡ ኢዮቤልዉ፡ ወክልኤ፡ ሱባዔ፡ ወኃምስተ፡ ዓመተ።

[17] ዘአፈድፈደ፡ ሐዩወ፡ ዲበ፡ ምድር፡ እምውሉደ፡ ሰብእ፡ በአንተ፡ ጽድቁ፡ ዘባቲ፡ ፍጹም፡ በጽድቁ፡ ዘእንበለ፡ ሄኖክ።

እስመ፡ ግብሩ፡ ለሄኖክ፡ ፍጥረት፡ ውእቱ፡ ለስምዕ፡ ለትዝምደ፡ ዓለም፡ ከመ፡ ይንግር፡ ኵሎ፡ ግብረ፡ለትውልደ፡ ትውልድ፡

በዕለተ፡ ደይን።

Chapter 23

THE IMPERATIVE

23.1 Imperative Strong G Verbs

The Gəʿəz imperative signals a command from someone to someone to do something. The Gəʿəz imperative verb is formed from the subjunctive verb forms. Starting with the subjunctive, you need to delete the subjunctive prefix and insert the *ə* vowel between C₁ and C₂ radicals of the root, while the *ă* or *ə* vowel remains. So the form of the imperative is $C_1 \partial C_2 \breve{a} C_3$: the subjunctive ይንብር፥, *yənbăr*, becomes the imperative ንበር፥, *nəbăr*. The frequent lexical variation between the *ă* and the *ə* between the C₂ and C₃ in the subjunctive is also found in the imperative.

TABLE 23.1: Imperative Forms–Sit!

2ms	ንበር፥	2mp	ንበሩ፥
2fs	ንበሪ፥	2fp	ንበራ፥

The imperative inflects for number and gender using the same endings as the second-person forms of the subjunctive and the imperfect verbs.

TABLE 23.2: Imperative with 1cs Object Suffixes

ቅትለኒ፥	"kill me"	ቅትሉኒ፥	"kill me"
ቅትሊኒ፥	"kill me"	ቅትላኒ	"kill me"

Like the subjunctive verb, the imperative verb also takes the object suffixes, but only the 1st or 3rd person suffixes, which are applied in the same way as the imperfect verb forms.

23.2 The Agent Noun ቀታሊ፥

The agent noun signifies someone or something that performs a regular, customary action of the verb. The majority of G verbs can form the agent noun. The pattern is as follows: $C_1 \breve{a} C_2 \bar{a} C_3 i$ as in ቀታሊ፥ – "the one who kills," or "killer." The agent noun appears in the 3ms (ቀታሊ፥), 3fs (ቀታሊት፥), 3mp (ቀታልያን፥), and 3fp (ቀታልያት፥), as well as in a common plural form (ቀተልት፥).

TABLE 23.3: Agent Nouns

	Masculine	Translation	Feminine	Translation
Singular	ጸሓፊ፡	"the one who writes" [writer]	ጸሓፊት፡	"the one who writes" [writer]
Plural	ጸሓፍያን፡	"the ones who write" [writers]	ጸሓፍያት፡	"the ones who create" [writers]

a. This verb form is generally treated as a noun and therefore may stand in construct with another noun. If this is the case, then a vowel change occurs at the end from an *i* vowel to an *ē* vowel.

   i. ፈጣሪ፡ changes to ፈጣሬ፡, as in ፈጣሬ፡ ምድር፡ – "creator of the world" – always refers to God.

   ii. ጸሓፊ፡ changes to ጸሓፌ፡, as in ጸሓፌ፡ ዝንቱ፡ መጽሐፍ፡ – "the writer of this book" or "the one who writes this book."

b. In some situations, the accusative noun is used if the verbal nature of the agent noun requires it: ሰአሊ፡ ሕይወተ፡ – "one who asks for life."

c. Agent nouns can also be used in apposition and function as an adjective: ንሕነ፡ ፈጣሪ፡ ዘንተ፡ ምድር፡ "we, the ones who create this world." Other examples include:
   ነባቢ፡ – talkative, boastful, garrulous
   ነዳዲ፡ – burning, blazing as in fire, wrath, or lust

d. The agent noun is not used with a significant number of verbs. If this is the case, then the relative phrase ዘይቀትል፡ is used; it is formed from ዘ + the imperfect verb.

e. The ordinal ቀዳሚ፡ – "first" offers some special situations in translation. As an adjective, it is generally translated as "first, previous, prior, or antecedent." As a noun it can be translated as "the ancient ones," "men of old," "those who came before or first." It can also signify the rank of an individual such as "nobles" or "princes." In addition, ቀዳሚ፡ can mean "beginning," "the first or best of anything." As an adverb, ቀዳሚ፡, and ቀዳሚሁ፡, as well as the accusative, ቀዳሜ፡, are translated "at first," "in the beginning," or "previously".

23.3 Frequent Agent Nouns

These should be committed to memory.

1. ፈቃዲ፡ – "one actively seeking something" (irregular pl. ፈቀድ፡, a contraction from ፈቀድት፡ – "necromancer")
2. ፈጣሪ፡ – "Creator" (always refers to God)
3. ገባሪ፡ (pl. ገበርት፡) – "maker, craftsman"
4. መካሪ፡ – "counselor, advisor"
5. ነባሪ፡ – "household servant"

6. ነጋሢ፡ (pl. ነገሥት፡) – "king, ruler, one who rules"
7. ቀታሊ፡ (pl. ቀተልት፡) – "murderer, killer, one who kills"
8. ሰባኪ፡ – "preacher"
9. ሰዳዲ፡ – "persecutor, exorcist"
10. ተራፊ፡ – "survivor"
11. ገባር፡ – (as a collective): "workers, laborers" (follows the pattern $C_1 \breve{a} C_2 \bar{a} C_3$, ቀታል፡)

23.4 Vocabulary

1. ጥራዝ፡ (pl. ጥራዛት፡) – fragment of a book
2. ነኪር፡ (f. ነካር፡ pl. ነከርት፡) – strange, alien, foreign, strange, wonderful
3. ክርስቲያናዊ፡ – Christian
4. ሠምረ፡ (subj. ይሥመር፡) – take delight, be please with; አሥመረ፡ CG – please, delight + obj. suff.
5. ፀንሰ፡ (subj. ይፅንስ፡ ይፀነስ፡) – become pregnant by (እም-); ተፀንሰ፡ Gt – be conceived
6. ዘበጠ፡ (subj. ይዝብጥ፡) – beat, whip; ተዘበጠ፡ Gt – be whipped, or beaten; ተዛበጠ፡ Glt – beat one another; ዘባጢ፡ – fighter
7. ገደፈ፡ (subj. ይግድፍ፡) – throw, cast, discard; ተገድፈ፡ Gt – be thrown away, to be discarded
8. ፄወወ፡ Q/L – take captive, exile; ተፄወወ፡ Qt – be taken captive
9. ቀዲሙ፡ (adv.) – first, at first, previously; እምቀዲሙ፡ – before this, from the beginning

23.5 Exercises

A. Translate the following:

1. ወሬዛ፡ ዘባጢ፡

2. ቀዳሚ፡ ወራዙቲከሙ፡

3. ነበርተ፡ ቤቱ፡

4. መጻሕፍተ፡ ቀደምት፡

5. ነጋሢ፡ ጻድቅ፡

6. መዐት፡ ነዳዲት፡

7. ቀዳሚሁ፡ ለዓለም።

8. ቀተልት፡ ዕልዋን።

9. ሊቃነ፡ ገባር።

10. ሰባኪ፡ ነባቢ።

11. ገበርተ፡ ሰላም።

12. ትእዛዘተ፡ ቀደምተ፡ ሀገር።

13. ገባረ፡ ንጉሥ።

14. ገባሬ፡ ብርት።

15. አርዌ፡ ነባቢ።

16. ፈጣሬ፡ ሰማይ።

17. ፈቃዴ፡ ንዋይ፡ ዓለማዊ።

18. ቀታሊ፡ ጽኑዕ።

19. ሰዳዬ፡ ክርስቲያን።

20. ቀዳሜ፡ ወራዙቲከሙ።

21. መካሪ፡ ጠቢብ።

22. ሰዳዬ፡ መናፍስት፡ እኩያን።

23. ፈጣሪነ።

24. ገባሬ፡ ሕግ።

25. አረጋዪ፡ ነባቢ።

B. Translate the following:

1. ኢትፍልስ፡ እምየ፡ ኀቤሁ፣ ንበር፡ ምስሌየ።

2. ንግሩነ፡ ዘትመክሩ፡ አንትሙ፡ ከመ፡ ትግበሩ።

3. ግድፍ፡ ዘንተ፡ ልብሰ፡ ብሉየ፡ ውስተ፡ እሳት።

4. ክሥት፡ ሊተ፡ ዘነገርከ።

5. ኢትግድፍ፡ መጻሕፍተ፡ ዘቦቱ፡ ቃለ፡ እግዚአብሔር።

6. ቅድመኒ፡ አንተ፡ እስም፡ አይደለወኒ፡ ከመ፡ አነ፡ እቅድምከ።

7. ንግሩኒ፡ ኍልቈ፡ ሰብእ፡ ቀተልት፡ እለ፡ መጽኡ፡ ላዕሌክሙ።

8. ንበር፡ ዝየ፡ ምስሌየ፡ ወኢትንብብ።

9. ግንዝዎ፡ ለበድኑ፡ በአልባስ፡ ሠናይት፡ ወቅብርዎ፡ ኀበ፡ አመርኩክሙ።

10. ስድዱ፡ ቀተልተ፡ ወዘባጥኖ፡ አማእከሌክሙ።

11. ስግዱ፡ ለአምሳልየ፡ ከመ፡ ኢይቅትልክሙ።

12. ንብብ፣ ገብርየ፣ ወአነ፡ አገብር፡ ዘሰአልከ።

13. ዝከሪ፡ ቃልየ፡ ወኢትንግሪ፡ ወኢለሙኑሂ።

14. ኢትዝብጦ፣ እስመ፡ ብእሲ፡ ራትዕ፡ ወኄር፡ ውእቱ።

C. 1 Enoch 15.1–12. Translate the following:

¹ ወአውሥአኒ፡ ወይቤለኒ፡ ወለቃሉ፡ ሰማዕኩ፡ ኢትፍራህ፡ ሄኖክ፡ ብእሲ፡ ጻድቅ፡ ወጸሐፌ፡ ጽድቅ፡ ቅረብ፡ ዝየ፡ ወስማዕ፡ ቃልየ።

² ወሐር፡ በሎሙ፡ ለትጉሃነ፡ ሰማይ፡ እለ፡ ፈነዉከ፡ ትስአል፡ በእንቲአሆሙ፡ አንትሙ፡ መፍትው፡ ትስአሉ፡ በእንተ፡ ሰብእ፡ ወአኮ፡ ሰብእ፡ በእንቲአክሙ።

³ በእንተ፡ ምንት፡ ኀደግሙ፡ ሰማየ፡ ልዑለ፡ ወቅዱሰ፡ ዘለዓለም፡ ወምስለ፡ አንስት፡ ሰከብክሙ፡ ወምስለ፡ አዋልደ፡ ሰብእ፡ ረኰስክሙ፡ ወነሣእክሙ፡ ለክሙ፡ አንስተ፡ ወከመ፡ ውሉደ፡ ምድር፡ ገበርክሙ፡ ወወለድክሙ፡ ውሉደ፡ ረዓይተ።

⁴ ወአንትሙሰ፡ ቅዱሳን፡ መንፈሳውያን፡ ሕያዋን፡ ሕይወት፡ ዘለዓለም፡ ቢዴ፡ አንስት፡ ረኰስክሙ፡ ወበደመ፡ ሥጋ፡ አውለድክሙ፡ ወበደመ፡ ሰብእ፡ ፈተውክሙ፡ ወገበርክሙ፡ ከመ፡ እምቱ፡ ይገብሩ፡ ሥጋ፡ ወደመ፡ እለ፡ እመንቱ፡ ይመውቱ፡ ወይትሃጐሉ።

⁵ በእንተዝ፡ ወሀብክዎሙ፡ አንስቲያ፡ ከመ፡ ይዝርኡ፡ ላዕሌሆን፡ ወይትወለዱ፡ ውሉደ፡ በላዕሌሆን፡ ከመ፡ ከማሁ፡ ኢይንትግ፡ ግብር፡ በላዕሌሆን፡ ቢዴ፡ ምድር።

⁶ ወአንትሙሰ፡ ቀዳሚ፡ ኮንክሙ፡ መንፈሳዊያነ፡ ሕያዋነ፡ ሕይወት፡ ዘለዓለም፡ ዘኢይመውት፡ ለኩሉ፡ ትውልደ፡ ዓለም፡፡

⁷ ወበእንተዝ፡ ኢረሰይኩ፡ ለክሙ፡ አንስቲያ፡ እስመ፡ መንፈሳዊያነ፡ ሰማይ፡ ውስተ፡ ሰማይ፡ መሐድሪሆሙ፡፡

⁸ ወይእዜኒ፡ ረዓይት፡ እለ፡ ተወልዱ፡ እመናፍስት፡ ወሥጋ፡ መንፈሳተ፡ እኩያን፡ ይሰመይ፡ በዲበ፡ ምድር፡ ወውስተ፡ ምድር፡ ይከውን፡ መሐድሪሆሙ፡፡

⁹ ወይፍሳት፡ እኩያን፡ ወጽኡ፡ እምሥጋሆሙ፡ እስመ፡ እምልዕልት፡ ተፈጥሩ፡ (ወ)እምቅዱሳን፡ ትጉሃን፡ ኮኑ፡ ቀዳሚቶሙ፡ ወቀዳሚ፡ መሰረት፡ መንፈሰ፡ እኩየ፡ ይከውኑ፡ በዲበ፡ ምድር፡ ወመንፈሰ፡ እኩያን፡ ይሰመይ፡፡

¹⁰ መንፈሳተ፡ ሰማይ፡ ውስተ፡ ሰማይ፡ ይከውን፡ መኃድሪሆሙ፡ ወመንፈሳተ፡ ምድር፡ ዘተወልደ፡ በዲበ፡ ምድር፡ ውስተ፡ ምድር፡ መኃድሪሆሙ፡፡

¹¹ ወመንፈሰ፡ ሬዐይትኒ፡ ደመናተ፡ እለ፡ ይገፍዑ፡ ወያማስኑ፡ ወይወድቁ፡ ወይትባአሱ፡ ወይደቅቁ፡ ዲበ፡ ምድር፡ ወጋዘ፡ ይገብሩ፡ ወኢምንተኒ፡ ዘይበልዑ፡ እክለ፡ ወይጻምኡ፡ ወይትዐቀፉ፡፡

¹² ወይትነሥኡ፡ እሎንቱ፡ ነፍሳት፡ ዲበ፡ ውሉደ፡ ሰብአ፡ ወዲበ፡ አንስት፡ እስመ፡ ወፅኡ፡ (እምኔሆሙ፡፡).

Chapter 24

VERBAL ADJECTIVE ቀቱል፡

24.1 The Verbal Adjective ቀቱል፡

The pattern ቀቱል፡ ($C_1 \partial C_2 u C_3$) is the most common form used for adjectives with stative G verbs. Verbal adjectives are formed from the same pattern used for transitive G verbs and in addition for several intransitive active verbs. The voice of the adjective depends on the verb from which it was derived.

a. With active transitive verbs, the verbal adjective usually corresponds to the English passive perfect participle: the adjective has experienced the action of the verb, e.g., ብቱክ፡ – "broken."

b. With active intransitive verbs, the verbal adjective is resultative – the state that resulted from the action of the verb and corresponds to the English perfect active participle, e.g., ቀቡር፡ – "buried, burying, having buried."

c. With stative verbs, the verbal adjective is the simple adjective, e.g., ሕዙን፡ "sad."

The occurrence of verbal adjectives is low due to the preferred use of relative clauses with a finite verb. The list below offers the verbal adjectives in the ቀቱል፡ form that have been previously presented:

a. Transitive active verbs (received action):

1. ብቱክ፡ – "broken"

2. ቀቡር፡ – "buried"

3. ፍጡር፡ – "created"

4. ቀቱል፡ – "slain"

5. ግቡር፡ – "worked, made, finished"

6. ስዱድ፡ – "expelled, exiled"

7. ግኑዝ፡ – "prepared for burial"

8. ትኩል፡ – "planted, implanted"

9. ክሡት፡ – "uncovered, bare, open eyes"

10. ዝቡጥ፡ – "beaten"

11. ግዱፍ፡ – "thrown, cast, rejected"

12. ዝኩር፡ – "mentioned, remembered"

13. ጥሙቅ፡ – "baptized" (አጥመቀ፡ C)

14. ፍቁር፡ – "beloved" (አፍቀረ፡ C)

b. Intransitive Active Verbs (resultative):

1. ፅንስት፡ – "pregnant"

2. ፍሉስ፡ – "exiled, in exile"

3. ንቡር፡ – "sitting, seated, residing"

4. ንዱድ፡ – "burning"

5. ንጉሥ፡ – "king"

6. ቅሩብ፡ – "near, nearby, adjacent" (with ለ, ኀበ); "at hand"

7. ስጉድ፡ – "prostrate in worship"

8. ስኩብ፡ – "lying down"

9. ሥሙር፡ – "pleasing, nice, pleasant" (with ለ, በኀበ)

10. ትሩፍ፡ – "excellent, outstanding" (f. ትርፍት፡ pl. ትሩፋት፡) – can be used as virtue, excellence

c. Stative Verbs–see previous vocabulary lists given as adjectives

24.2 ቅቱል፡ Adjectives as Adverbs

Adjectives in the ቅቱል፡ form with a prefixed በ- or at times in the accusative case function as adverbs:

በፍጡን፡ = ፍጡነ፡ – quickly, swiftly, soon
በከሡት፡ = ከሡተ፡ – openly, publicly

24.3 Additional Notes on Adjectival Complements

a. When used to complement a subject or object, the adjective may be introduced by the conjunction: እንዘ፡ – "while, when." It can be used to describe the state of a subject: እንዘ፡ ድውይ፡ ነበርኩ፡ ውስተ፡ ቤትየ፡ – "I remained at my home while ill."

b. The conjunction እንዘ፡ can also be used to modify other elements of a sentence. It can be used alongside a non-verbal clause: ርኢኩ፡ ብእሴ፡ እንዘ፡ ይቡስ፡ እዴሁ፡ – "I saw a man while his hand was being withered."

c. The adjective may also have attached personal pronominal suffixes to complement the subject or the object:
  ሐረ፡ ሕዙኑ፡ – "He went away sad"
  ሐርኩ፡ ሕዙንየ፡ – "I went away sad"
  ረከብዎ፡ ሕያዎ፡ – "They found him alive"

d. The case and the suffix attached to the adjective depend on the status of the word in which it stands in opposition:
  Nominative example: ኢትወፅእ፡ ሕያውከ፡ – "You will not leave alive"
  Accusative example: ኢይነሥኡከ፡ ሕያወከ፡ – "They will not take you alive"

24.4 Vocabulary

1. ነጐድጓድ፡ (pl. ነጐድጓዳት፡) – thunder
2. መብረቅ፡ (pl. መባርቅት፡) – lightning
3. አስሐትዮ፡ – ice, hail, snow, frost
4. ማስነ፡ – be ruined, destroyed; perish; become corrupt, rotten; አማስነ፡ CL – corrupt, destroy, wipe out; ተማስነ፡ Lt – passive of CL
5. ደክመ፡ (subj. ይድክም፡ ይድከም፡) – be tired, weary, feeble, infirm; አድከመ፡ CG – causative; ድኩም፡ (f. ድክምት፡) – tired, weary, weak, feeble, ill
6. ፀርፈ፡ / ፀረፈ፡ (subj. ይፀርፍ፡) – blaspheme (ላዕለ, ላ, against)
7. ፀራፍ፡ (adj.) – blasphemous, wicked, impious; n. ፀራፊ፡ pl. ፀራፍያን፡ – blasphemer
8. ቄረ፡ / ቀረረ፡ – be cold, cool; to cool off (anger); አቀረረ፡ CG – causative
9. ቁሪር፡ (f. ቀራር፡) – cold, cool

10. መስለ፡ (subj. ይምስል፡) – resemble, be like (with acc. dir. obj.); seem, appear as (with obj. suff. of person). Can appear as accusative of predicate noun or adjective: ይመስለኒ፡ ፍኖት፡ ርቱዐ፡ – the road seems straight to me; or with the preposition ከመ፡ ይመስለኒ፡ ከመ፡ ወርኅ፡ – it looks like the moon to me. Can also be impersonal: it seems (with obj. suffix of person + ከመ፡/ዘ- with perf. or imperf.); አምሰለ፡ CG – regard as, hold equivalent to (two accusatives, or acc. + ከመ፡)

24.5 Exercises

A. Translate the following:

1. ዕፁ፡ ቅርብት፡ ለቤትነ።

2. ንዋይ፡ ብሉይ፡ ወግዱፍ።

3. ወልድየ፡ ፍቁር።

4. ቶታን፡ ብቱክ።

5. ገጽ፡ ክሡት።

6. አረጋይት፡ ስክብት፡ ዲበ፡ ምድር።

7. ቃል፡ ዐቢይ፡ ከመ፡ ነጐድጓድ።

8. ገመል፡ ፍጥንት፡ ወጽንዕት።

9. ብእሲ፡ ፀሩፍ።

10. አልባስ፡ ግዱፍ።

11. ብድን፡ ቅቡር።

12. ስም፡ ዝኩር።

13. ካህን፡ ጻድቅ፡ ወትሩፍ።

14. ስም፡ ዝከርት፡ ውስተ፡ ዝንቱ፡ መጽጥፍ።

15. ነዳይ፡ ዝቡጥ።

16. አረጋይ፡ ድኩም።

17. አሣእን፡ ግዱፋን።

18. ሥጋ፡ ግኑዝ።

19. ብእሲት፡ ፅንስት።

20. ብሔር፡ ቅሩብ፡ ለባሕር።

21. ሕዝብ፡ ስጉድን፡ ቅድመ፡ ጣዖቶሙ።

22. አረጊት፡ ክርስቲያናዊት።

23. ሕዝብ፡ ፍሉሳን።

24. ወሬዛ፡ ቅቱል።

25. ጎጻን፡ ግቡር።

Verbal Adjective ቅቱል፡   163

26. ሀገር፡ ንብርት፡ ዲበ፡ ዳብር።

27. ማይ፡ ቄሪር፡ ከመ፡ አስሐትያ።

28. ጥራዝ፡ ግዱፍ፡ ውስተ፡ ፍኖት።

29. ዜና፡ ነኪር፡ ወፅሩፍ።

30. መብረቅ፡ ፍጡን።

31. ውሉድ፡ ጥሙቃን።

32. ብእሲ፡ ዝቡጥ።

33. ዕልው፡ ስዱድ።

34. ቃል፡ ሥሙር፡ ለእለ፡ ሰምዕዎ።

35. ሰይፍ፡ ትክልት፡ በእግሩ።

B. Job 1:6–12. Translate the following:

⁶ወእምድኅረ፡ ይአቲ፡ ዕለት፡ መጽኡ፡ መላእክተ፡ እግዚአብሔር፡ ወቆሙ፡ ቅድመ፡ እግዚአብሔር፡ ወመጽአ፡ ሰይጣን፡ ምስሌሆሙ።

⁷ወይቤሎ፡ እግዚአብሔር፡ ለሰይጣን፡ እምአይቴ፡ መጻእከ፡ ወተሰጥዎ፡ ሰይጣን፡ ለእግዚአብሔር፡ ወይቤ፡ አድከዋ፡ ለኵላ፡ ምድር፡ ወአንሶሰውኩ፡ ታሕተ፡ ሰማይ፡ ወመጻእኩ።

⁸ወይቤሎ፡ እግዚአብሔር፡ ለሰይጣን፡ ኁቅ፡ አልቦ፡ ዘትሔሊ፡ ላዕለ፡ ቀልጌዮ፡ ኢዮብ፡ እስመ፡ አልቦ፡ ከማሁ፡ በዲበ፡ ምድር፡ ብእሲ፡ ንጹሕ፡ ወጻድቅ፡ ወፈራሄ፡ እግዚአብሔር፡ ወይትገሀሥ፡ እምኵሉ፡ ምግባር፡ እኩይ።

⁹ ወተሰጥወ፡ ሰይጣን፡ ቅድመ፡ እግዚአብሔር። ወይቤ፣ ቡኁ በከንቱ፡ ያመልኮ፡ ኢዮብ፡ ለእግዚአብሔር።

¹⁰ አኮኑ፡ እስመ፡ አንተ፡ መላእከ፡ ሎቱ፡ እምውስጡ፡ ወእምአፍአሁ፡ ቤቶ፡ ወኮሎ፡ ዘአውዳሂ። ወባረክ፡ ተግባረ፡ አደዊሁ፡ ወአብዛኅከ፡ እንስሳሁ፡ ዲበ፡ ምድር።

¹¹ ወባሕቱ፡ ፈኑ፡ እዴከ፡ ወግሰስ፡ ኮሎ፡ ዘቦ፡ ወዳእሙ፡ ውስተ፡ ገጽከ፡ ይባርከከ።

¹² ወእምዝ፡ ይቤሎ፡ እግዚአብሔር፡ ለሰይጣን፣ ናሁኬ፡ ኮሎ፡ ዘቦ፡ መጠውኩከ፡ ውስተ፡ እዴከ፡ ዳእሙ፡ ኪያሁ፡ ኢትግስስ። ወወጽአ፡ ሰይጣን፡ እምነበ፡ እግዚአብሔር።

C. Job 2:1–8. Translate the following:

¹ ወእምዝ፡ እምድኅረ፡ ይእቲ፡ ዕለት፡ መጽኡ፡ መላእክተ፡ እግዚአብሔር፡ ወቆሙ፡ ቅድመ፡ እግዚአብሔር፡ ወመጽአ፡ ሰይጣን፡ ማእከሎሙ።

² ወይቤሎ፡ እግዚአብሔር፡ ለሰይጣን፣ እምአይቴ፡ መጻእከ፡ አንተ፡ ወይቤ፡ ሰይጣን፡ ሶሐ፡ ቅድመ፡ እግዚአብሔር፣ ሐርኩ፡ ታሕተ፡ ሰማይ፡ ወአንሶሰውኩ፡ ኮልሄ፡ ወመጻእኩ።

³ ወይቤሎ፡ እግዚአብሔር፡ ለሰይጣን፣ ኡቅኬ፡ ለቀሃልዔየ፡ ኢዮብ፡ እስመ፡ አልቦ፡ ዘከማሁ፡ በውስተ፡ ምድር፡ ብእሲ፡ የዋህ፡ ወጻድቅ፡ ወንጹሕ፡ ወፈራሄ፡ እግዚአብሔር፡ ወይትገሐሥ፡ እምኮሉ፡ ምግባር፡ እኩይ፡ ወዓዲ፡ የዋህ፡ ወአንተሰ፡ ትቤ፡ ታህጉሎ፡ ንዋዮ፡ በከንቱ።

⁴ ወተሰጥዎ፡ ሰይጣን፡ ለእግዚአብሔር፡ ወይቤ፣ ቤዛ፡ ማእስ፡ ማእስ፡ ኮሎ፡ ዘአጥረየ፡ ይሁብ፡ ስብአ፡ ቤዛ፡ ነፍሱ።

⁵ ወባሕቱ፡ ፈኑ፡ እዴከ፡ ወግሰስ፡ አዕጽምቲሁ፡ ወሥጋሁ፡ ወዳእሙ፡ ውስተ፡ ገጽከ፡ ይባርከከ።

⁶ ወይቤሎ፡ እግዚአብሔር፡ ለሰይጣን፣ ናሁ፡ መጠውኩካሁ፡ ውስተ፡ እዴከ፡ ዳእሙ፡ ነፍሶ፡ ዑቅ።

⁷ ወወፅአ፡ ሰይጣን፡ እምነበ፡ እግዚአብሔር፡ ወአኃዞ፡ ለኢዮብ፡ ዝልጋሴ፡ እኩይ፡ እምእግሩ፡ እስከ፡ ርእሱ።

⁸ ወነሥአ፡ ገልዐ፡ ወአሐዘ፡ ይሀክክ፡ ቀሥሎ፤ ወነበረ፡ አፍአ፡ እምሀገር፡ ወሰበ፡ ውስተ፡ መሬት፡ ወሐመድ።

Chapter 25

VERBAL NOUNS

25.1 The Verbal Noun or Participle

Practically all Gəʿəz G verbs have a noun that is closely associated with the action or quality that is defined by the verbal root. The verbal noun has all the properties of a regular noun but none of the properties of the verb. The English verbal noun is the present participle form of the verb, but this is not always the case with the Gəʿəz verbal nouns. The verbal noun can have singular and plural forms. In Gəʿəz there is no single pattern for verbal nouns; in fact, they can form in as many as a dozen patterns. There are seven primary patterns that you should be aware of: ቅትለት፡, ቅትል፡, ቅተል፡, ቅታል፡, ቀተል፡, ቀታል፡, and ቀትል፡. As you will see below, the meaning of a verbal noun can be abstract, ፍቅር፡ – "love", or concrete, ተክል፡ – "tree or plant."

25.2 The ቅትለት፡ Pattern

The ቅትለት፡ is the most common category of verbal nouns and can be formed from a number of active verbal roots. Notice this category for the majority of the nouns contains four radicals. The following is a list of verbal nouns formed from strong G verb roots:

ብትከት፡ – "breaking, fracture, rupture"
ፀርፈት፡ – "blasphemy"
ፍልሰት፡ – "wandering, exile, death"
ፍጥረት፡ – "act of creation, species, nature"
ግብረት፡ – "form, shape, way something is made"
ግንዘት፡ – "preparation for burial"
ንብረት፡ – "sitting down, position, way of life, dwelling"
ንደት፡ – "flame, burning"
ቅትለት፡ – "killing, murder"
ርክበት፡ – "finding, acquisition"
ስብከት፡ – "preaching, proclamation"
ስደት፡ – "exile, persecution"
ስግደት፡ – "prostration, adoration"

ሥምረት፡ – "favor, approval, consent"

ሥጥቀት፡ – "cutting, splitting"

ጥምቀት፡ – "baptism"

ዝብጠት፡ – "beating, whipping"

All plural forms that occur have the -ā+ት ending.

25.3 The ቅትል፡ Pattern

Notice this pattern is all short vowels:

ፅንስ፡ – "pregnancy" (also "fetus")

ፍቅር፡ – "love"

ግብር፡ – "deed, act, etc." (see vocab in chapter 15), also rarely, as an adverb "necessarily"

ክብር፡ – "glory, honor, magnificence"

ምክር፡ – "plan, counsel, advice"

ንግሥ፡ – "reign, rule"

ርኵስ፡ – "uncleanness, something unclean"

ቍር፡ – "cold, coldness"

ጽድቅ፡ – "justice"; ገብረ፡ ጽድቀ፡ – "do justice"; ኢኮነ ጽድቀ፡ – "it is not just to . . ."

በጽድክ፡ – "rightly, justly"

ዝክር፡ – "mention, memory, commemoration"

All plural forms that occur have the -ā+ት ending.

25.4 The ቅተል፡ Pattern

The ቅተል፡ pattern follows the root form of $C_1 \partial C_2 \breve{a} C_3$. The lone example here is ጥበብ፡ – "wisdom."

25.5 The ቅታል፡ Pattern

This pattern follows the $C_1 \partial C_2 \bar{a} C_3$:

ንባብ፡ – "speech, manner of speech"

ትራፍ፡ – "remainder, residue, overflow"; ትራፋተ፡ ነገሥት፡ is the book of Chronicles in the Old Testament (lit., "the remainder of the writings of the kings")

ድካም፡ – "weariness, infirmity, weakness"

ምታር፡ – "weariness, fragment, segment"

All plural forms that occur have the -ā+ት ending.

Verbal Nouns

25.6 The ቀተል፡ Pattern

This pattern follows the $C_1 \breve{a} C_2 \breve{a} C_3$:

> ነገር፡ – "speech, account, narrative"
> ቀብር፡ – "burial, funeral"
> ተረፍ፡ – "overflow, remainder" (see ትራፍ፡ above)

All plural forms that occur have the $-\bar{a}+ት$ ending.

25.7 The ቀታል፡ Pattern

This pattern follows the $C_1 \breve{a} C_2 \bar{a} C_3$:

> ፈቃድ፡ – "desire, wish"
> ነፋስ፡ – "wind"

25.8 The ቀትል፡ Pattern

The final category appears more often with concrete nouns than verbal nouns.

> ቀትል፡ – "killing, fight, battle" (ገብረ፡ ቀትለ፡ ምስለ፡ – "to fight a battle with")
> ተክል፡ (pl. ተክላት፡) – "a plant, tree"; (ዐጸደ፡ አትክልት፡ – "orchard, grove of trees"); in a figurative sense: ተክለ፡ ጽድቅ፡ – "plant of righteousness"

With these two nouns the concrete meaning can stand alongside an abstract meaning for the word. It should be noted that the noun patterns presented above can be derived nouns that are not verbal nouns based on its form. Each noun should be checked in the lexicon and its individual context. In addition, verbal nouns can vary in gender (m., f.) and usually appear in the plural with the ending of $-\bar{a}+ት$.

25.9 The Cognate Accusative

Verbal nouns are normally interpreted as ordinary nouns and should not present particularly difficult translation issues. At times, however, the verbal noun can be used as the object of its cognate verb as a point of emphasis. This does not affect the construction of the verb as is seen in the following examples:

> ዘበጥዎ፡ ዝብጠተ፡ ዕጹበ፡ – "they beat him severely" (a severe beating)
> ገነዝዎ፡ ለበድኑ፡ ግንዘተ፡ ሠናየ፡ – "They prepared his corpse splendidly for burial"
>   (a splendid preparation)

25.10 Vocabulary

1. ግዕዝ፡ (pl. ገዕዛት፡) – mode of life, manner; nature, quality, essential nature (of persons and things)
2. ጸሎት፡ (pl. ጸሎታት፡) – prayer(s)
3. አጽባዕት፡ (pl. አጻብዕ፡) – finger, toe
4. እዝን፡ (pl. እዘን፡ አእዛን፡) – ear
5. ዐይን፡ (pl. አዕይንት፡) – eye; ሰብአ፡ ዐይን፡–spies
6. ጸልመ፡ / ጸለመ፡ (subj. ይስለም፡ ይስልም፡) – grow dark, grow blind; ጸልመ፡ ገጹ፡ – he became angry; (አጸለመ፡ CG – he was made blind); ጽሉም፡ – dark, obscured; ጸሊም፡ (f. ጸላም፡); ጽልመት፡ – darkness; መዋዕለ፡ ጽልመት፡ – days of wane; አመ፡ X-u ለጽልመተ፡ Y – pm the X-day of the month of Y
7. ሠጠቀ፡ (subj. ይሥጥቅ፡) – cut, split; ተሠጥቀ፡ Gt – be cut or split; ሥጡቅ፡ (passive participle) – cut, split; ሥጥቀት፡ (noun) – cutting, splitting
8. ኃደረ፡ – reside, dwell, inhabit; ኃደረ፡ ላዕሉ፡ – reside in, possess as in demons; አኃደረ፡ CG – be made to dwell; ተኃድረ፡ Gt – be inhabited; ተኃደረ፡ Glt – live together
9. ዐሠበ፡ / ዐሥበ፡ (subj. ይዐሥብ፡ / ይዕሥብ፡) – be hard, difficult; ዕሡብ፡ – harsh, difficult; በዕሡብ፡ – with difficulty

25.11 Exercises

A. Translate the following:

1. ገነዝዎ፡ ግንዘተ፡ ሠናየ፡ ወቀበርዎ፡ በዐቢይ፡ ክብር፡።

2. በእንተ፡ ምንት፡ መተርዎ፡ አጻብዒሁ፡ ለዝንቱ፡ ብእሲ፡።

3. ተሰደ፡ እምነቤሆሙ፡ በእንተ፡ ፀርፈቱ፡ እኩይ፡።

4. ወእምዝ፡ ሜጦ፡ ለውእቱ፡ ቅዱስ፡ እምስደቱ፡።

5. ነገራ፡ ለንግሥት፡ በእንተ፡ ንብረቱ፡ ለውእቱ፡ ንጉሥ፡ ወበእንተ፡ ክብረ፡ ቤቱ፡ ወኮሉ፡ ግዕዙ፡።

6. ኢክህለነ፡ ተኃድሮ፡ ምስሌሆሙ፡ በእንተ፡ ርኩሶሙ፡።

7. ሀድአት፡ ምድርኒ፡ እምቅትለት፡ ወእመቅሠፍት፡ በጊዜ፡ ንግሡ፡።

8. ሶበ፡ ተሰምዐ፡ ቃሉ፡ ብትከተ፡ አዕጹቅ፣ ወሮጽነ፡ ፍጡነ፡ እምታሕተ፡ ዕፀው።
___

9. ሶበ፡ ሰምዑ፡ ጸሎታቲሆሙ፡ ለክርስቲያን፣ ተምዕዑ፡ ፈድፋደ፡ ወአዘዙሙ፡ ለአግብርቲሁ፡ ከመ፡ ይዝብጥዎሙ፡ ወይቅትልዎሙ።
___

10. ምንተ፡ ገብረ፡ እግዚአብሔር፡ እምድኅረ፡ ፍጥረተ፡ አቡነ፡ አዳም።
___

11. ተርእየነ፡ ግብረተ፡ አልባሲሁ፡ ኪረ፡ ጥቀ።
___

12. ወእምድኅረ፡ ነገነ፡ ምክሮ፣ ኃበርነ፡ ምስሌሁ።
___

13. አይቴ፡ ዘንደርክሙ፡ በመዋዕለ፡ ፍልሰትክሙ።
___

14. ንንብር፡ ዝየ፡ እስከ፡ ይቁርር፡ ንደተ፡ መዐዐት፡ ዘውስተ፡ ልቡ።
___

15. ተናገረ፡ ምስሌነ፡ በእንተ፡ ርክበተ፡ መጽሐፍ፡ ብሉይ፡ ውስተ፡ ቤተ፡ መቅደስ።
___

B. Translate the following:

1. ቀበር፡ ክቡር።
___

2. ጥበብ፡ ትርፍት።
___

3. ጥምቀተ፡ እንሊሆሙ።
___

4. በእንተ፡ ክብረ፡ ነገሥት።
___

5. ክሡተ፡ እዝን፡ ወፍጡነ፡ አእምሮ።
___

6. በሥምረተ፡ እግዚአሙ።
   _____

7. ፀንሳ፡ ለወለቱ።
   _____

8. በከመ፡ ፈቃዱ፡ ለአቡሁ።
   _____

9. ስግደቶሙ፡ ለጣዖት።
   _____

10. ግብራት፡ እኩያት፡ ዘንደርት።
    _____

11. አትክልት፡ ብቱካን፡ እምነበ፡ በረድ።
    _____

12. ስብከተ፡ ወንጌል፡ ዘመድኅንነ።
    _____

13. ርክበተ፡ ደራህም፡ ብሩር።
    _____

14. ፍቅሩ፡ ለወልዱ።
    _____

C. Acts 2:1–13. Translate the following:

¹ ወአመ፡ ተፈጸመ፡ መዋዕለ፡ ጰንጠቈስቴ፡ እንዘ፡ ሀለዉ፡ ኵሎሙ፡ ኅቡረ፡ አሐተኔ።

² መጽአ፡ ግብተ፡ እምሰማይ፡ ድምፅ፡ ከመ፡ ድምፀ፡ ነፋስ፡ ዓውሎ፡ ወመልአ፡ ኵሎ፡ ቤተ፡ ኀበ፡ ሀለዉ፡ ይነብሩ።

³ ወአስተርአይዎሙ፡ ልሳናት፡ ክፉላት፡ ከመ፡ እሳት፡ ዘይትከፈል፡ ወነበረ፡ ዲበ፡ ኵሎሙ። ወተመልኡ፡ ኵሎሙ፡ መንፈሰ፡ ቅዱሰ።

⁴ ወመልኡ፡ ኵሎሙ፡ መንፈሰ፡ ቅዱሰ ወአንዙ፡ ይንብቡ፡ ዘዘዚአሆሙ፡ በነገረ፡ ኵሉ፡ በሐውርት። በከመ፡ ወሀቦሙ፡ መንፈስ፡ ቅዱስ፡ ይንብቡ።

⁵ ወሀለዉ፡ በኢየሩሳሌም፡ ሰብአ፡ ጌራን፡ አይሁድ፡ ይነብሩ፡ እምኲሉ፡ አሕዛብ፡ ዘመትሕተ፡ ሰማይ።

⁶ ወሰሚያሙ፡ ዘነተ፡ ቃለ፡ ተጋብኡ፡ ኮሉሙ፡ ድንጉፂሀሙ፡ እስመ፡ ሰምዕዎሙ፡ ይነብቡ፡ ኮሉሙ፡ በነገረ፡ በሓውርቲሆሙ።

⁷ ወደንገፁ፡ ወአንክሩ፡ ወይቤሉ፡ አኮኑ፡ ሰብአ፡ ገሊላ፡ እሉ፡ ኮሉሙ።

⁸ እፎኑ፡ እንከ፡ ንሰምዖሙ፡ ይነብቡ፡ በነገረ፡ ኮሉ፡ በሓውርቲነ፡ እንዘ፡ ፍጥረትነ፤

⁹ ጶርቴ፡ ወሜድ፡ ወኢላሜጤ፡ ወእለኒ፡ ይነብሩ፡ ማእከለ፡ አፍላግ፡ ይሁዳ፡ ወቀጳዶቅያ፡ ወፍኖጦስ፡ ወእስያ።

¹⁰ ወፍርግያ፡ ወጵንፍልያ፡ ወግብፅ፡ ወደወለ፡ ልብያ፡ ወእለሂ፡ እምቀርኔን፡ ወእለሂ፡ መጽኡ፡ እምሮሜ፡ አይሁድ፡ ወፈላስያን። ወእለ፡ እምቀርጤስ፡ ወዓረብ።

¹¹ ወናሁ፡ ንሰምዖሙ፡ ይነብቡ፡ በነገረ፡ በሓውርቲነ፡ ዕበያቲሁ፡ ለእግዚአብሔር።

¹² ወደንገፁ፡ ኮሉሙ፡ ወታዕኡ፡ ዘይብሉ፡ ወዘይነብቡ፡ ወተባህሉ፡ በበይናቲሆሙ፥ ምንትኑ፡ እንጋ፡ ዝ።

¹³ ወመንፈቆሙ፡ ሰሐቅዎሙ፡ ወይብሉ፥ እሉስ፡ ፀዕረ፡ ጸግቡ፡ ወሰከሩ።

Chapter 26

SPECIAL NOUNS

26.1 Nouns of Place in the ም+C₁C₂āC₃ Pattern

Nouns of place appear in two principal forms with a prefixed ም- and are derived from G verbs. The first and most common type of these nouns appear in the pattern ም +$C_1C_2āC_3$ (ምቅታል፡). The noun usually identifies where the action of the verb is taking place or has taken place. Below are several common words that are derived from the G verb:

ምንዳድ፡ – "furnace, oven"
ምስጋድ፡ – "temple, shrine"
ምጥማቅ፡ – "baptistry or a pool"
ምንባር፡ – "residence, base, foundation, where something is placed"
ምቅራብ፡ – "neighborhood"
ምስካብ፡ – "bed, couch"

Some words that follow this ም+$C_1C_2āC_3$ pattern have developed specialized meanings over time and should be memorized individually:

ምግባር፡ – "custom, business practice, behavior"
ምርካብ፡ – "salary for performing one's job, acquisition"
ምንባብ፡ – "section of a text (pericope), a section of text set out for public reading"

These nouns can be either masculine or feminine and the plurals usually have the ending -ā+ት.

26.2 Nouns in the መ+C₁C₂ăC₃ Pattern

Nouns that appear in this pattern (መቅተል፡) carry a wider range of meaning rather than just place. Other meanings include nouns of instrument and nouns of action. The context must be studied closely to determine the correct translation of these nouns. Some of these nouns have appeared in previous chapter vocabulary lists: መንፈስ፡ – "a spirit," መልአክ፡ – "messenger, prince, angel," መብራቅ፡ – "lightning," መካን፡ – "location." Other common nouns in this pattern include the following:

መግነዝ፡ – "burial material"
መንበር፡ (pl. መናብርት፡) – "throne, chair"
መርኆ፡ (pl. መራኁት፡) – "key"
ተትከል፡ (pl. መታክል፡) – "stake, peg"

Some of these verbs regularly appear with a final -ት፡ added to the forms listed above in 26.2:

መሥዋዕት፡ – "sacrifice, altar"
መቅሠፍት፡ – "punishment, beating"
መቃብርት፡ – "grave, tomb"
ማንበርት፡ – "way of life, condition" (see መንበር፡ – dwelling, position, place of residence)

26.3 Nouns in the መ+C_1C_2əC_3 Pattern

The nouns that follow the መ+C_1C_2əC_3, መቅትል፡ also መቅትልት፡, have two separate functions: 1) they act as agent nouns (see ch. 23) for the CG verbs; and 2) they act as derived nouns from G verbs. They have a corresponding meaning to the መቅተል፡ forms:

መትከል፡ – "stake, peg" (see above መትከል፡)
መንግሥት፡ (pl. መንግሥታት፡) – "kingdom", መንግሥተ፡ ሰማያት፡ – "kingdom of heaven"

26.4 Vocabulary

1. ነፍሰ፡ – blow (as in the wind); አነፈሰ፡ CG – breathe something out (like fire)
2. በረቀ፡ (subj. ይብርቅ፡) – flash as lightning; አበረቀ፡ CG – cause lightning
3. ቀሠፈ፡ (subj. ይቅሥፍ፡) – beat or whip; ተቀሥፈ፡ Gt – be beaten; ቅሡፍ፡ – beaten, afflicted; ቅሥፈት፡ – punishment, affliction
4. ሰቀለ፡ (subj. ይስቅል፡) – suspend, hang up, crucify; ተሰቅለ፡ Gt – be crucified; ስቅለት፡ – crucifixion; መስቀል፡ (pl. መሳቅል፡) – cross
5. ርእስ፡ (pl. አርእስት፡) – head, summit, chief. Can occur with suffix as a reflexive or intensive pronoun: ቀተለ፡ ርእሶ፡ – he killed himself
6. ገነት፡ (pl. ገነታት፡) – garden, Eden
7. ሥራይ፡ (pl. ሥራያት፡) – medicine, herbs, incantations, spells, magic
8. ሰብአ፡ ሥራይ፡ – wizards, witches, dealers in spells
9. ጋኔን፡ (pl. አጋንንት፡) – evil spirit, demon; ዘጋኔን፡ (pl. እለ፡ አጋንንት፡) – one possessed by an evil spirit

26.5 Exercises

A. Translate the following:

1. ጸውያሙ፡ ለሰደድ፡ ወአዘዘሙ፡ ከመ፡ ይስድድዎ፡ ለጋኔን፡ ዘነደረ፡ ላዕለ፡ ወልዱ፣ ወባሕቱ፡ ኢክህሉ፡ ሰዲዶቶ።

2. አምጽኡ፡ ሎቱ፡ ሥራየ፡ ነኪረ፡ እምአጽናፈ፡ ምድር፣ ወባሕቱ፡ ኢክሁሉ፡ ፈውሶ፡ እምደዌሁ፡ ዕጹብ።

3. ተጋብኡ፡ ኀቢ፡ ምጥማቅ፡ ዘቅሩብ፡ ለቤተ፡ ንጉሥ።

4. እምድኅረ፡ አንፈስነ፡ እምጸማነ፣ ዳግም፡ አጎዝነ፡ ጊቢረ።

5. ወደየ፡ ጥራዘ፡ መጽሐፍ፡ ውስተ፡ ምንዳድ።

6. ተቀሥፉ፡ እሎንቱ፡ ሕዝብ፡ ኃጥአን፡ በእሳት፡ ወአእባን፡ ዘወረዱ፡ ላዕሌሆሙ፡ እምሰማይ።

7. ዝንቱ፡ ዕፅ፡ ውእቱ፡ እመስቀል፡ ዘተሰቅለ፡ አየሱስ፡ ዲቤሁ።

8. አውፅኡ፡ ሐዋርያት፡ አጋንንተ፡ በስመ፡ እግዚእነ፡ ኢየሱስ፡ ክርስቶስ፡ (ሎቱ፡ ስብሐት)።

9. ሰምዐ፡ እግዚአብሔር፡ ለጸሎተ፡ ነቢይ፣ ወአሰምዐ፡ ቃለ፡ ነጎድጓዱ፡ ወአብረቀ፡ መባርቅቲሁ፡ በውስተ፡ ሰማይ፡ ጸሊም።

10. እምድኅረ፡ ስቅለቱ፡ ለመድኃኒነ፣ ጐየ፡ አርዳኢሁ፡ ከመ፡ ኢይርከብዎሙ፡ ሰብአ፡ ሀገር፡ ወይቅሥፍዎሙ።

11. ሀደሩ፡ አበዊነ፡ ቀዳምት፡ ውስተ፡ ገነት፡ ሡናይ፡ ፈድፋደ፣ ወባሕቱ፡ ተወደዉ፡ ላዕለ፡ እግዚአብሔር፡ ወውእቱ፡ አዘዘሙ፡ ለመላእክቲሁ፡ ከመ፡ ይስድድዎሙ፡ ለአበዊነ፡ እምውስተ፡ ገነት፡ ኀበ፡ መካን፡ ዘጽልመት።

12. ንንበር፡ ቅሩብ፡ ለምንዳድ፣ እስመ፡ ወጠነ፡ ነፋስ፡ ቄሪር፡ ነፊሰ።

13. ርእሰ፡ ዝንቱ፡ ደብር፡ መንበሩ፡ ለእግዚብሔር፡ ውእቱ።

14. በእንተ፡ ምንት፡ ኢከሀለ፡ ወሪደ፡ እምዳበ፡ መስቀል፨
    _____

15. ስቁል፡ ሕይወትየ፡ በትእዛዘ፡ ንጉሥከ፨
    _____

16. ጸውዖሙ፡ ለሰደድ፡ ወአዘዞሙ፡ ከመ፡ ይስድድዎ፡ ለጋኔን፡ ዘንደረ፡ ላዕለ፡ ወልዳ፣ ወባሕቱ፡ ኢከሀሉ፡ ሰዲዶቶ፨
    _____

17. ኮሎ፡ አሚረ፡ አንበቡ፡ ለነ፡ አሐደ፡ ምንባበ፡ እመጽሐፍ፡ በእንተ፡ ሕይወተ፡ ቅዱሳን፨
    _____

18. ሶበ፡ በጽሑ፡ ውእተ፡ መካነ፡ ርእዮ፡ ኮሎሙ፡ ክርስቲያን፡ ስቁላነ፡ ዲበ፡ መሳቅል፡ በትእዛዘ፡ ውእቱ፡ ነጉሥ፡ ዐለው፨
    _____

19. ሰከበ፡ ዲበ፡ ምስካቡ፡ ወተደወየ፨
    _____

20. ቀተሎቶ፡ ለውእቱ፡ ብእሲ፡ እኩይ፡ በመትከል፡ ዘዐፅ፨
    _____

B. Translate the following:

1. መቅበርት፡ ከሡት፨
   _____

2. መፍትው፡ ከመ፡ አቅሥፍከ፨
   _____

3. ኢኮነ፡ ጽድቀ፡ ለፀውዖቶሙ፨
   _____

4. እዝን፡ ምትርት፡ እምርእሱ፨
   _____

5. ጥበበ፡ ጠቢባን፨
   _____

6. መንገለ፡ ርእሰ፡ ደብር፨
   _____

7. መጽአኒ፡ ድካም፡ ወስእንኩ፡ ሐዊረ፡ በእግር።

8. ነዳይ፡ ቅሡፍ፡ ወስዱድ።

9. አትክልት፡ ነዊኃን፡ ወጽኑዓን።

10. ምንባረ፡ መስቀል።

11. አምከርክዎሙ፡ ከመ፡ ይፍልሱ።

12. እኮ፡ ዝንቱ፡ ሥራይ፡ ዘፈወሰ።

13. ብእሲ፡ ምቱረ፡ እድ።

14. ምትረተ፡ ርእሱ።

15. አማሰኑ፡ ዐጸደ፡ አትክልት።

16. አመረነ፡ ፍኖተ፡ በአጽባዕቱ።

17. ጸልማ፡ አዕይንቲሁ፡ ወኢክህለ፡ ርእየ።

18. ፀራፊ፡ ምቱረ፡ ልሳን።

19. መጽሐፍ፡ ሥጡቅ፡ ወጋዱፍ።

20. በጽምረተ፡ ሊቃ፡ ጳጳሳት።

Special Nouns 177

21. ዘእንበለ፡ ፈቃድ፡፡
___

22. ዐረጉ፡ ውስተ፡ ርእሰ፡ ደብር፡፡
___

C. Mark 5:1–20. Translate the following:

¹ ወበጺሐሙ፡ ማዕዶተ፡ ባሕር፡ ጎበ፡ ብሔረ፡ ጌርጌሴኖን፡፡

² ወወሪዶ፡ እምሐመር፡ ተቀበሎ፡ ሰቤሃ፡ ብእሲ፡ ወቪአ፡ እመቃብር፡ ዘኩይ፡ ጋኔን፡ ላዕሌሁ፡፡

³ ወይነብር፡ ውስተ፡ መቃብር፡ ወስእንዎ፡ አጽዮቶ፡ በመቅሕትኒ፡ እንዘ፡ ዘልፈ፡ ይሞቅሕዎ፡ ወአልቦ፡ ዘይክል፡ አድክሞቶ፡፡

⁴ እስመ፡ መዋቅሕቲኒ፡ ይሰብር፡ ወሰናስለኒ፡ ይቀጠቅጥ፡ ወየዐቅብዎ፡ ደቅ፡፡

⁵ ወዘልፈ፡ የዐወዩ፡ መዐልተ፡ ወሌሊተ፡ በውስተ፡ መቃብር፡ ወበውስተ፡ አድባር፡ ወጌምድ፡ ሥጋሁ፡ በአብን፡፡

⁶ ወሶበ፡ ርእዮ፡ ለእግዚእ፡ ኢየሱስ፡ እምርሑቅ፡ ሮጸ፡ ወሰገደ፡ ሎቱ፡፡

⁷ ወጸርሐ፡ በዐቢይ፡ ቃል፡ ወይቤ፤ ምንተ፡ ብየ፡ ምስሌከ፡ ኢየሱስ፡ ወልደ፡ እግዚአብሔር፡ ልዑል፡ አምሕለከ፡ በእግዚአብሔር፡ ከመ፡ ኢትሣቅየኒ፡፡

⁸ እስመ፡ ይቤሎ፡ ለውእቱ፡ ጋኔን፤ እኩይ፡ ፃእ፡ እምላዕሌሁ፡፡

⁹ ወተስእሎ፡ እግዚእ፡ ኢየሱስ፡ ወይቤሎ፤ መኑ፡ ስምከ፡ ወይቤሎ፡ ውእቱ፡ ጋኔን፡ ሌጌዎን፡ ስምየ፡ እስመ፡ ብዙኃን፡ ንሕነ፡፡

¹⁰ ወአስተብቍዖ፡ ብዙኅ፡ ከመ፡ ኢይስድዶ፡ አፍአ፡ እምብሔር፡፡

¹¹ ወቦ፡ህየ፡ መራዕየ፡ አሕርው፡ ብዙኅ፡ ይትረዐይ፡ መንገለ፡ ደብር፡፡

¹² ወአስተብቍዕዎ፡ ብዙኃን፡ ወይቤልዎ፤ እመሰ፡ ታወፅአነ፡ ፈንወነ፡ ውስተ፡ አሕርው፡ ከመ፡ ንባእ፡ ላዕሌሆሙ፡፡

¹³ ወአብሐሙ፡ እግሲእ፡ ኢየሱስ፡ ወወጺአሙ፡ እመንቱ፡ አጋንንት፡ ቦኡ፡ ላዕለ፡ አሕርው፡ ወአብዱ፡ ውእቱ፡ መራዕይ፡ ወጸድፉ፡ ውስተ፡ ባሕር፡ ወኮኑ፡ መጠነ፡ ዕሥራ፡ ምእት፡ ወሞቱ፡ በውስተ፡ ባሕር፡

¹⁴ ወገዕዩ፡ ኖሎት፡ ወዜነዊ፡ ለአህጉር፡ ወለአዕጻዳት፡ ወወፅኡ፡ ይርአዩ፡ ዘኮነ፡

[15] ወመጽኡ፡ ኀበ፡ እግዚእ፡ ኢየሱስ፡ ወረከብዎ፡ ለዘጋኔን፡ አኀዘ፡ እንዘ፡ ይነብር፡ ወልቡሒ፡ ገብአ፡ ወልቡስ፡ ልብሶ፡ ለዝኩ፡ ዘአኀዞ፡ ሌጌዎን፡ ወፈርሁ።

[16] ወዜነውዎሙ፡ እለ፡ ርእዩ፡ ዘከመ፡ ኮነ፡ ዘጋኔን፡ ወዘበእንተ፡ አሕርው።

[17] ወአኀዙ፡ ያስተብቍዕዎ፡ ከመ፡ ይፃእ፡ እምደወሎሙ።

[18] ወዐሪጎ፡ ሐመረ፡ አስተብቍዮ፡ ውእቱ፡ ዘጋኔን፡ ይሐር፡ ምስሌሁ።

[19] ወከልአ፡ እግዚእ፡ ኢየሱስ፡ ወይቤሎ፡ ሑር፡ ቤተከ፡ ኀበ፡ እሊአከ፡ ወንግር፡ ኮሎ፡ ዘገብረ፡ ለከ፡ እግዚአብሔር፡ ወተሣሀለከ።

[20] ወሖረ፡ ወአኀዘ፡ ይስብክ፡ በዐሥሩ፡ አህጉር፡ ኮሎ፡ ዘገብረ፡ ሎቱ፡ እግዚእ፡ ኢየሱስ፡ ወአንከሩ፡ ኮሎሙ።

Chapter 27

I GUTTURAL G VERBS (REMAINING FORMS)

27.1 Remaining Forms of I Guttural G Verbs

We previously covered the perfect G verbs from guttural roots in chapter 10 (you should review if needed). In this chapter we will cover the remaining imperfect, subjunctive, imperative, and infinitive verb forms that contain a guttural consonant in the I consonant position. As you will see in the table below, the vowel for the imperfect prefix shifts from the ə to the ă. The first table, 27.1, presents the strong verb forms for comparison to the guttural verbs we will discuss in the chapters to follow.

TABLE 27.1: Strong Verb Paradigm

PGN	Perfect	Imperfect	Subjunctive	Imperative
3ms	ነገረ፡	ይነግር፡	ይንግር፡	—
3fs	ነገረት፡	ትነግር፡	ትንግር፡	—
2ms	ነገርከ፡	ትነግር፡	ትንግር፡	ንግር፡
2fs	ነገርኪ፡	ትነግሪ፡	ትንግሪ፡	ንግሪ፡
1cs	ነገርኩ፡	እነግር፡	እንግር፡	—
3mp	ነገሩ፡	ይነግሩ፡	ይንግሩ፡	—
3fp	ነገራ፡	ይነግራ፡	ይንግራ፡	—
2mp	ነገርክሙ፡	ትነግሩ፡	ትንግሩ፡	ንግሩ፡
2fp	ነገርክን፡	ትነግራ፡	ትንግራ፡	ንግራ፡
1cp	ነገርነ፡	ንነግር፡	ንንግር፡	—

TABLE 27.2: I Guttural Forms

Perfect	Meaning	Infinitive	Imperfect	Subjunctive	Imperative
አምነ፡	Believe	አሚን፡	የአምን፡	ይአምን፡	አመን፡
አሰረ፡	Bind	አሲር፡	የአስር፡	ይአስር፡	አስር፡
ዐቀበ፡	Guard	ዐቂብ፡	የዐቅብ፡	ይዐቅብ፡	ዐቀብ፡

Perfect	Meaning	Infinitive	Imperfect	Subjunctive	Imperative
ዐርገ፡	Go up	ዐሪግ፡	የዐርግ፡	ይዕርግ፡ / ይዕረግ፡	ዕርግ፡ / ዕረግ፡
ዐጸበ፡ / ዐጸብ፡	Be harsh	ዐጺብ፡	የዐጽብ፡	ይዕጽብ፡ / ይዕጸብ፡	–
ሐነጸ፡	Build	ሐኒጽ፡	የሐንጽ፡	ይሕንጽ፡	ሕንጽ፡
ሐተተ፡	Investigate	ሐቲት፡	የሐትት፡	ይሕትት፡	ሕትት፡
ሐዘነ፡	Be sad	ሐዚን፡	የሐዝን፡	ይሕዝን፡ / ይሕዘን፡	ሕዝን፡ / ሕዘን፡
ነበረ፡	Join with	ነቢር፡	የነብር፡	ይነብር፡	ነብር፡
ነደገ፡	Divorce	ነዲግ፡	የነድግ፡	ይነድግ፡	ነድግ፡
ነደረ፡	Reside	ነዲር፡	የነድር፡	ይነድር፡	ነድር፡
ነለፈ፡	Deport	ነሊፍ፡	የነልፍ፡	ይነልፍ፡	ነልፍ፡
ነሠሠ፡	Desire	ነሢሥ፡	የነሥሥ፡	ይነሥሥ፡	ነሥሥ፡

a. Note the I Guttural in the verb maintains the ă as in the strong perfect.

b. The imperfect offers the most changes from the strong verb. The imperfect prefix ይ lengthens to the short ă vowel and the I Guttural maintains the short ă also.

c. The imperfect II and III consonants of the root shifts from the ă vowel to the short ə vowel.

d. The subjunctive forms also have vowel changes some of which depend on the category of the verb– ነበረ፡ or ከተረ፡. The II consonant in the ነበረ፡ verb maintains the ă vowel (see ነበር፡ above), while the II consonant in the ከተረ፡ verb reduces to short/silent ə vowel. This change may also be due to the general variability of the vowel in the subjunctive verb forms.

e. The subjunctive III consonant has the reduced ə vowel in all verbs.

f. Note the two options for a few of the subjunctive verbs (ዐርገ፡, ዐጸበ፡, and ሐዘነ፡).

g. The imperative forms follow the vocalization of the subjunctive less the subjunctive prefix.

h. Note the i stem vowel on the infinitive forms.

TABLE 27.3: I Guttural Perfect Paradigm (አምነ፡)

PGN	Perfect Forms	PGN	Perfect Forms
3ms	አምነ፡	3mp	አምኑ፡
3fs	አምነት፡	3fp	አምና፡
2ms	አመንከ፡	2mp	አመንክሙ፡
2fs	አመንኪ፡	2fp	አመንክን፡
1cs	አምኩ፡	1cp	አመንነ፡

TABLE 27.4: I Guttural Imperfect Paradigm

PGN	Imperfect Forms	PGN	Imperfect Forms
3ms	የአምን፡	3mp	የአምኑ፡
3fs	ተአምን፡	3fp	የአምና፡
2ms	ተአምን፡	2mp	ተአምኑ፡
2fs	ተአምኒ፡	2fp	ተአምና፡
1cs	እአምን፡	1cp	ነአምን፡

TABLE 27.5: I Guttural Subjunctive Paradigm

PGN	Subjunctive Forms	PGN	Subjunctive Forms
3ms	ይእመን፡	3mp	ይእምኑ፡
3fs	ትእመን፡	3fp	ይእምና፡
2ms	ትእመን፡	2mp	ትእምኒ፡
2fs	ትእምኒ፡	2fp	ትእምና፡
1cs	እእመን፡	1cp	ንእመን፡

TABLE 27.6: I Guttural Imperative Paradigm

PGN	Imperative Forms	PGN	Imperative Forms
2ms	እመን፡	2mp	እመኑ፡
2fs	እመኒ፡	2fp	እመና፡

The infinitive form of the paradigm verb appears as አሚን፡ (note the *i* stem vowel following the second radical): – "to believe."

27.2 I Guttural Causative Verb (አምነ፡)[1]

In the basic paradigm in table 27.7, note the slight change in the first root አ in the shift from simple causative to intensive causative in each of the forms: perfect, imperfect, subjunctive, and imperative.

TABLE 27.7: I Guttural Causative Verb[1]

	Simple Causative Action	Translation	Causative of the Intensive	Translation
Perfect	አአመነ፡	made to believe	አዐረየ፡	made to be equal
Imperfect	ያአምን፡	will be made to believe	ያዔሪ፡	will be made to be equal
Subjunctive	ያእምን፡	may he be made to believe	ያዕሪ፡	may he be made equal
Imperative	አአምን፡	make him believe	አዐሪ፡	make him equal

---

1. See ch. 18 for discussion on causative verbs.

The simple causative verb is used when someone or something is made to do something. In the case of the example in the chart above, አአምነ፡ can be translated as "caused to believe" or "made to believe." The column on the right represents the causative form of an intensive verb which is normally intransitive, but as a causative it becomes active in translation with a causative effect.

27.3   I Guttural Reflexive Verbs

The reflexive verb in Gəʿəz functions much like the Hithpael verb in Hebrew; the subject(s) is performing the action to herself or the action can be reciprocal between two or more subjects. Note the prefixed ተ or ት on the root along with the expected imperfect and subjunctive prefixes.

TABLE 27.8: I Guttural Reflexive Verb (አምነ፡)

	Simple Reflexive Action	Intensive Reflexive Action
Perfect	ተአምነ፡ / ተአመነ፡	ተአመነ፡
Imperfect	ይትአመን፡	ይትኤመን፡
Subjunctive	ይትአመን፡	ይትአመን፡
Imperative	ተአመን፡	ተአመን፡

27.4   I Guttural Causative Reflexive Verbs

The causative reflexive suggests a subject is being made to perform an action on herself/himself/itself; at times the subject is causing herself to perform the action on herself. As you can imagine this can create some translation issues for the beginning Gəʿəz student. However, these verb forms are easily identified due to the special prefixes they carry. All forms include a ተ or ታ prefix attached to the root along with an አስ prefix in the perfect and imperative forms, and a ያስ prefix in the imperfect and subjunctive forms.

TABLE 27.9: I Guttural Causative-Reflexive Verb (አምነ፡)

	Simple Causative-Reflexive Action	Intensive Causative-Reflexive Action
Perfect	አስተአመነ፡ / አስታእመነ፡	አስተአመነ፡
Imperfect	ያስታእምን	ያስተአምን
Subjunctive	ያስተአምን፡	ያስተኤምን፡
Imperative	አስታእምን፡	አስተአምን፡

27.5   I Guttural Verbal Adjectives in the ቅቱል፡ Pattern

A verbal adjective is generally the equivalent of a passive participle. It has both verbal and adjectival characteristics. A verbal adjective can modify a noun, but also it can act as an adverb as will be seen in the examples below:

እሙን፡ – faithful, trustworthy
እሙነ፡ – (adverb) truly
እሱር፡ – bound, tied, captive

ዕቁብ፡ – under guard, reserved
ዕቅብት፡ f. (pl. ዕቁባት፡) – concubine
ዕጹብ፡ – harsh, difficult
ኅኑጽ፡ – built, constructed
ኅቡር፡ – joined, associated; ኅቡረ፡ – (adverb) together, jointly
ኅዱግ፡ – abandoned, divorced
ኅዱር፡ – residing, dwelling
ኅሉፍ፡ – crossing, passing

27.6   I Guttural ቀታሊ፡ Agent Nouns[2]

አማኒ፡ – the one who believes; faithful (adj.)
ዐቃቢ፡ (f. ዐቀብት፡) – guard, watch over; ዐቃቢ፡ ገነት፡ – keeper of the garden
ሐናጺ፡ – architect, builder
ኀባዚ፡ – baker
ኅዳሪ፡ (pl. ኅደርት፡) – guest, sojourner
ኅላፊ፡ (pl ኅለፍት፡) – passerby, one passing by

27.7   I Guttural Verbal Nouns[3]

እስረት፡ – binding, tying
እምነት፡ – faith, belief
አማን፡ – truth; (adj.) አማኒ፡ – true, faithful; በአማን፡ (adv.) – truly, in truth
ዕቅብት፡ – guarding, keeping vigil
ዕርገት፡ – ascent, assumption into heaven
ዕጽብ፡ ዐጸብ፡ – harshness, difficulty
ሕንጽ፡ / ሕንጸት፡ / ሕንጻ፡ – building, construction
ሐተታ፡ – investigation, interrogation
ሕዘን፡ – sadness, grief
ኅብረት፡ – union, association, accord
ኅድገት፡ – remission (of debts)
ኅድጋት፡ / ኅዳጋት፡ – divorce
ኅድረት፡ – residing, dwelling
ኅሠሣ፡ (pl. ኅሠሣት፡) – wish, desire

27.8   I Guttural Nouns from the Pattern መቅተል(ት)፡

Note with the I Guttural nouns of this pattern, the vowel with the ማ prefix is the long ā before the first guttural, although there are words that have variations to this rule. e.g., ማእመን፡.

---

2. See ch. 23.
3. See ch. 25.

ማአመን፡ / ምእመን፡ / ማእምን፡ (adj.) – believing, faithful (one)
ማእሰር፡ (pl. ማእሰርት፡) – bond, chain, a vow
ማዕቀብ፡ (pl. መዓቅብ፡) – guard, guard house
ማዕርግ፡ (pl. መዓርግ፡) – place of ascent, stairs, ladder
ማሕተት፡ – testimony, witness
ማኅበር፡ – congregation, crowd, gathering, monastery, convent
ማኅደር፡ (pl. መኃድር፡) – dwelling place, room, cell

27.9 I Guttural Nouns from the Pattern ምቅታል፡

Note with the I Guttural nouns of this pattern, the vowel with the ም prefix is the short *ə* before the first guttural:

ምኅላፍ፡ – a place of crossing or passing through
ምዕራግ፡ – place of ascent

27.10 Vocabulary

1. ማሃይምን፡ (f. ማሃይምንት፡) – faithful (one), believer
2. ዐርበ፡ / ዕርበ፡ (ይዕረብ፡ ይዕርብ፡) – set (e.g., the sun); አዕረበ፡ CG – cause to set
3. ዐረብ፡ – west (direction)
4. ዐርብ፡ – Friday (ዕለተ፡ ዐርብ፡። ዐርብ፡ ዕለት፡።)
5. ዐርቢ፡ / ዐረባዊ፡ – western, Arabian; ምዕራብ፡ / ምዕርብ፡ ፀሓይ፡። – the west
6. ኀፈረ፡ / ኀፍረ፡ (ይኀፍር፡) – be ashamed; ተኀፍረ፡ – be put to shame
7. ኀፍረት፡ (pl. ኀፍረታት፡) – shame, impropriety
8. ሐመ፡ / ሐመመ፡ (ይሕምም፡ ይሕመም፡) – be ill, suffer illness or pain; አሕመመ፡ CG – afflict with illness
9. ኀፀበ፡ (ይኅፅብ፡) – wash; ተኀፅበ፡ Gt – wash oneself; ኅፁብ፡ – washed; ኅፅበት፡ – washing, ablution; ምኅፃብ፡ – bath, place for bathing
10. ሐወፀ፡ D – inspect, look at, visit
11. ዓዲ፡ (adv.) – still, yet, again
12. ሰኔት፡ (ዕለት፡) – the next day; ሳኔታ፡ – the next day; በሳኔታ፡ – on the next day

27.11 Exercises

A. Translate the following:

1. ኀደርት፡ በማእከሌሆሙ፡ ንሕነ፡ ወባሕቱ፡ ነዐቅብ፡ ሕገጊከሙ፡ በአማን፡።

2. ማእኮ፡ ኀሉፋኒሆሙ፡ ውስተ፡ ባሕር፡ በአሕማሪሆሙ፡።

3. ጻድቃን፡ እሙንቱ፡ ወጽኑዓን፡ በዕበተ፡ ሕግ።
_____

4. አዘዛሙ፡ ለዐቀብት፡ ከመ፡ ይእስርዎ።
_____

5. ተጋብኡ፡ ኩሎሙ፡ አሕዛበ፡ ምድር፡ ከመ፡ ይሕንጹ፡ ዐቢየ፡ ቤተ፡ ለነጋሢሆሙ።
_____

6. መፍትው፡ ከመ፡ ትዕቀቡ፡ ኩሎ፡ ሕገገ፡ ዘወሀብኩከሙ።
_____

7. ተስእልክዎ፡ ለንላፈ፡ በእንተ፡ ፍኖተ፡ ባሕር።
_____

8. በእንተ፡ ምንት፡ ዝንቱ፡ ሐዘን፡ ወልድየ።
_____

9. አማኒ፡ እሙን፡ አንተ፣ ወበእንተ፡ ዘአመንከ፡ ዘእንበለ፡ ይንግሩከ፡ በእንተ፡ ተአምርየ፡ ወመንክራትየ፣ ገብርኩ፡ መካነ፡ ዕቁብ፡ ለከ፡ ርእስከ፡ ውስተ፡ ቤተ፡ አቡየ፡ ዘበሰማያት።
_____

10. ኀሠሡ፡ ከመ፡ ይኅልፉ፡ እንተ፡ ማእከለ፡ ምድርነ።
_____

11. ለይሕትቱ፡ መጻሕፍተ፡ ሕገጊሆሙ፣ ወእምድኅረ፡ ሐተታሆሙ፡ ለይንግሩነ፡ ምንት፡ ረከቡ፡ ውስቴቶሙ።
_____

12. አቡሁ፡ ዐቃቤ፡ ሥራይ፡ ስሙይ፡ ውእቱ።
_____

13. አልብነ፡ ምዕራፈ፡ ኀበ፡ ነሀድር፡ ምስለ፡ ደቂቅነ።
_____

14. ወሀባ፡ መጽሐፈ፡ ኀድጋት፡ ወሰደዳ፡ እምውስተ፡ ቤቱ።
_____

15. ተገብሩ፡ ኀቡረ፡ በሕንጻሃ፡ ለዛቲ፡ ሀገር፡ ክብርት።
_____

16. ኃድጉኒ፡ ከመ፡ እኅበር፡ ምስሌክሙ።

17. ኢትሕዘኒ፡ ወለትዮ፡ እስመ፡ ኢሞተ፡ ምትኪ፡ በጽብእ።

18. ርእዮ፡ ንጉሥ፡ ከመ፡ ጐዩ፡ ዐቀብተ፡ ሥጋሁ፡ ወድቀ፡ ዲበ፡ ሰይፉ፡ ወቀተለ፡ ርእሶ።

19. እመኑ፡ ቦቱ፡ ወትረክቡ፡ ሕይወተ፡ ዘለዓለም።

20. ዝንቱ፡ ምንባብ፡ ውእቱ፡ በእንተ፡ ዕገቱ፡ ለነቢይ፡ ውስተ፡ ሰማይ።

21. ኢትኃብኡ፡ ገቢረ፡ ምስለ፡ ኃፉራነ፡ ዝንቱ፡ መካን።

22. አሲሮሙ፡ ዐቃቤ፡ አንቀጽ፡ ወበዊአሙ፡ ቤተ፡ ንጉሥ፡ በጽሚት፡ ቀተልዎሙ፡ ለዐቀብተ፡ ርእሱ፡ ለንጉሥ፡ ወሰደድዎሙ፡ ለዘመደ፡ መንግሥት፡ ውስተ፡ ፍኖት።

23. በእብተ፡ እምነትከ፡ ኢያንድገከ።

24. እምአይ፡ ዐቃቤ፡ ወይን፡ ተሣየጥከ፡ ዘንተ፡ ወይነ፡ ጌር፡ ፈድፋደ፡ ውእቱ።

25. ፈራህነ፡ ከመ፡ ኢይጸብነ፡ ጸጋ።

B. Translate the following:

1. ፈትሐ፡ መኣስዕሆሙ፡ ለእሱሩን።

2. አልቦ፡ ዘኢያንፍር፡ በይእቲ፡ ዕለት።

3. ተማከሩ፡ ከመ፡ ይቅትልዎ፡ ሶበ፡ ወረደ፡ ኀበ፡ ምንጻብ።
   _____

4. አተወ፡ ብሔሮሙ፡ እምቅድመ፡ ይዕረብ፡ ፀሐይ።
   _____

5. በእንተ፡ ምንት፡ ኢተአምና፡ ብየ።
   _____

6. አቀም፡ ብዙኀ፡ መዓቅብተ፡ ውስተ፡ አምዳር፡ ዘሞአ።
   _____

7. ለምንት፡ አሕመምከኒ፡ ዘንተ፡ ሕማመ፡ ዕጹበ።
   _____

8. በሳኒታ፡ ኀለፈ፡ እምዝንቱ፡ ዓለም፡ ወቦአ፡ ውስተ፡ ማኀበር፡ ቅዱሳን።
   _____

9. ተአሰርዎ፡ በአሕባል፡ ጽኑዕ።
   _____

10. ተቃደምናሆሙ፡ ውስተ፡ ምዕራገ፡ ሀገር፡ ወኢኃደግናሆሙ፡ ከመ፡ ይቅርቡ፡ ኀበ፡ አናቅጸ፡ ሀገር።
    _____

11. ተነጸብኩ፡ እደዊየ፡ ወገጽየ፡ በማይ፡ ቄሪር፡ ዘዝንቱ፡ ምጥማቅ።
    _____

12. በእንተ፡ ምንት፡ ከላእከኒ፡ ሐውጾቶሙ፡ ለድዉያን፡ ወሕሙማን።
    _____

13. ሰአልናሁ፡ ኀድገተ፡ ኀጣውኢነ።
    _____

14. ፈቀድኩ፡ ኀሊፈ፡ እንተ፡ ማእከለ፡ ማኀበሮሙ፣ ወኢወሁቡኒ፡ ምኀላፈ።
    _____

15. እንዘ፡ ዓዲከሙ፡ ምስሌነ፡ እነግረከሙ፡ በእንተ፡ መንግሥተ፡ ሰማያት።
    _____

16. ዓዲ፡ ሰዱስ፡ ወአኀልፍ፡ እምኔከሙ።
    _____

17. ጸውዐ፡ ሐናጼ፡ ወነገሮ፡ ምክሮ፡ ለሕንጸተ፡ ቤተ፡ ሐዲስ።

18. ሰማዕነ፡ ማሕተተክሙ፡ ላዕለ፡ ዝንቱ፡ ብእሲ፡ ወባሕቱ፡ ኢረከብነ፡ ኀጢአተ፡ ቦቱ።

19. ገብአ፡ ሀገረ፡ ወሐወጸ፡ ቤተ፡ ክርስቲያን፡ ዘሐነጹ፡ ውስተ፡ ጽንፈ፡ ባሕር።

20. ርእየ፡ ዐቢየ፡ ማዕርገ፡ እንዘ፡ ምንባሩ፡ ዲበ፡ ምድር፡ ወርእሱ፡ ውስተ፡ ሰማይ።

C. Jubilees 17.15–18. Translate the following:

[15] ወኮነ፡ በሱባዔ፡ ሳብዕ፡ በቀዳሚ፡ ዓመት፡ በወርኅ፡ ቀዳሚ፡ በዝ፡ ኢዮቤልዩ፡ አመ፡ ዐሡሩ፡ ወሰኑዩ፡ ለዝ፡ ወርኅ፡ ኮኑ፡ ቃላት፡ በሰማያት፡ በእንተ፡ አብርሃም፡ ከመ፡ ውእቱ፡ መሃይምን፡ በኵሉ፡ ዘይትናገር፡ ወያፈቅሮ፡ ኢግዚአብሔር፡ እስመ፡ በኵሉ፡ ምንዳቤ፡ ኮነ፡ ምእመነ።

[16] ወመጽአ፡ መኰንን፡ መስቴማ፡ ወይቤ፡ ቅድሜሁ፡ ለአምላክ፡ ናሁ፡ አብርሃም፡ ያፈቅሮ፡ ለይስሐቅ፡ ወልዱ፡ ወያስተኤድም፡ ኪያሁ፡ እምኵሉ፡ በሎ፡ ያዕርግ፡ ጽንሐሐ፡ ዲበ፡ ምሥዋዕ፡ ወአንተ፡ ትሬኢ፡ ለእመ፡ ይገብር፡ ዘንተ፡ ቃለ፡ ወተአምር፡ ለእመ፡ መሃይምን፡ ውእቱ፡ በኵሉ፡ ዘታሜክሮ።

[17] ወእግዚአብሔር፡ ያአምር፡ ከመ፡ መሃይምን፡ አብርሃም፡ በኵሉ፡ ምንዳቤ፡ ዘይቤሎ፡ እስመ፡ አመሮ፡ በምድሩ፡ ወበመግባሩ፡ ወበዐባር፡ ወአመሮ፡ በብዕለ፡ ነገሥት፡ ወአመሮ፡ ካዕበ፡ በብእሲቱ፡ እንዘ፡ ትትህፀድ፡ ወበከስበት፡ ወአመሮ፡ በይስማዔል፡ ወበአጋር፡ አመቱ፡ አመ፡ ፈነዎሙ።

[18] ወበኵሉ፡ በዘአመክሮ፡ ተረክበ፡ ምእመነ፡ ወኢተአንተለ፡ ነፍሱ፡ ወኢጉንደየ፡ ገቢሮቶ፡ እስመ፡ ምእመን፡ ወመፍቀሬ፡ እግዚአብሔር፡ ውእቱ።

Chapter 28

G VERBS WITH II GUTTURAL ROOTS

28.1 G Verbs with II Guttural Roots

In this chapter (see ch. 10 for the perfect) we will examine the remaining forms of the II Guttural verbs. These forms include the imperfect, subjunctive, imperative, and infinitive. The II Guttural roots for the imperfect follow this consonant/vowel pattern: ይ+$C_1\partial G_2\partial C_3$ (ይልአh፡ – "he will inscribe"). The subjunctive follows the pattern ይ+$C_1\partial G_2\ŭC_3$ (ይልአh፡ – "he may inscribe"). The imperative follows the pattern $C_1\ŭG_2\ŭC_3$ (ሰአh፡ – "(you) inscribe!"). Students should compare the strong paradigm in chapter 27.

TABLE 28.1: II Guttural Perfect Paradigm (ሰአh፡)

PGN	Perfect Forms	PGN	Perfect Forms
3ms	ሰአh፡	3mp	ሰአኩ፡
3fs	ሰአhት፡	3fp	ሰአካ፡
2ms	ሰአhh፡	2mp	ሰአhhሙ፡
2fs	ሰአhኪ፡	2fp	ሰአhhን፡
1cs	ሰአhኩ፡	1cp	ሰአhነ፡

Note the perfect II Guttural maintains the ă vowel in the I and III consonants and retains the perfect personal suffixes.[1]

TABLE 28.2: II Guttural Imperfect Paradigm (ሰአh፡)

PGN	Imperfect Forms	PGN	Imperfect Forms
3ms	ይልአh፡	3mp	ይልአኩ፡
3fs	ትልአካ፡	3fp	ይልአካ፡
2ms	ትልአh፡	2mp	ትልአኩ፡
2fs	ትልአኪ፡	2fp	ትልአካ፡
1cs	አልአh፡	1cp	ንልአh፡

---

1. If needed, students should review the two forms of the G verbs in chapter 7, *gabra* and *nabara*.

a. Note the II Guttural imperfect retains the strong verb prefixes rather than the shift to the ă vowel in the I Gutturals.

b. The I and II consonants have the short ə vowels and the III consonant adjusts according to the personal suffixes.

TABLE 28.3: II Guttural Subjunctive Paradigm (ለአከ፡)

PGN	Subjunctive Forms	PGN	Subjunctive Forms
3ms	ይልአከ፡	3mp	ይልአኩ፡
3fs	ትልአከ፡	3fp	ይልአካ፡
2ms	ትልአከ፡	2mp	ትልአኩ፡
2fs	ትልአኪ፡	2fp	ትልአካ፡
1cs	እልአከ፡	1cp	ንልአከ፡

a. Note the II Guttural subjunctive prefixes follow the strong verb pattern.

b. The II Guttural consonant shifts from the short ə vowel in the strong verb to the ă vowel, while the III consonant adjusts according to the endings.

TABLE 28.4: II Guttural Imperative Paradigm (ለአከ፡)

PGN	Imperative Forms	PGN	Imperative Forms
2ms	ለአከ፡	2mp	ለአኩ፡
2fs	ለአኪ፡	2fp	ለአካ፡

a. The infinitive form of the paradigm verb appears as ለኢከ፡ (Note the *i* stem vowel following the second radical): – "to inscribe."

b. The I consonant in the imperative shifts from the short ə vowel in the strong verb to the ă vowel.

c. The II Guttural consonant also has the ă vowel and the III consonant adjusts according to the personal endings.

28.2 II Guttural Causative Verbs (ለአከ፡)

In the basic paradigm in table 28.5, note the shift in the simple causative from the final ከ in the Perfect to the final ክ in the imperfect, subjunctive, and imperative. In addition, note the two possible forms of the perfect intensive causative with the shift from ለ to ሰ; also note the variation of the first consonant ሰ in the imperfect, subjunctive, and imperative.

G Verbs with II Guttural Roots 191

TABLE 28.5: II Guttural Causative Verbs

	Simple Causative Action	Intensive Causative Action
Perfect	አልአከ፡	አለአከ፡ / አልአከ፡
Imperfect	ያልአከ፡	ያሌአከ፡
Subjunctive	ያልአከ፡	ያልአከ፡
Imperative	አልአከ፡	አልአከ፡

28.3 II Guttural Reflexive Verbs

As mentioned previously, the reflexive verb in Gəʿəz functions much like the Hithpael verb in Hebrew; the subject(s) is performing the action to herself, or the action can be reciprocal between two or more subjects. Note the prefixed ተ or ት to the root on the simple reflexive along with the expected imperfect and subjunctive prefixes.

TABLE 28.6: II Guttural Reflexive Verbs (ግዕዝ፡)

	Simple Reflexive Action	Intensive Reflexive Action
Perfect	ተገዐዘ፡ / ተግዐዘ፡	ተገዐዘ፡ / ተግዐዘ፡
Imperfect	ይትገዐዝ፡	ይጌዐዝ፡
Subjunctive	ይትገዐዝ፡	ይገዐዝ፡
Imperative	ተገዐዝ፡	ተገዐዝ፡

TABLE 28.6: II Guttural Causative-Reflexive Verbs (ግዕዝ፡)

	Simple Causative-Reflexive Action
Perfect	አስተግዐዘ፡ አስተገዐዘ፡
Imperfect	ያስተግዐዝ፡
Subjunctive	ያስተግዐዝ፡
Imperative	አስተግዐዝ፡

28.4 Irregular Forms

There are two verbs that offer some difficulty in their formation: አኀዘ፡ (note it is also a I Guttural) – "seize, grasp, or hold" and ክህለ፡ – ("be able [to do something]")

Perf. አኀዘ፡   Imperf. ይአኀዝ፡ / ይእኀዝ፡   Subj. የአኀዝ፡   Impv. አኀዝ፡
Perf. ክህለ፡   Imperf. ይክል፡ (note loss of the middle root)   Subj. ይክሀል፡   Impv. ክህል፡

There are a number of II Gutturals of this form that adopt an *ē* vowel following the first consonant in place of the short *ə* vowel. However, there is no consistent pattern as to why this occurs.

28.5 II Guttural Verbal Adjectives in the ቅቱል፡ Pattern[2]

A verbal adjective is generally the equivalent of a passive participle. It has both verbal and adjectival characteristics. A verbal adjective can modify a noun, but also it can act as an adverb as will be seen in the examples below:

ብዑል፡ – rich, wealthy[3]
ጽሑፍ፡ – written
ስሑት፡ – led into error
ስኡን፡ – impotent, powerless
ልኡክ፡ – sent (one), apostle, messenger
ምሁር፡ – learned (person), expert
እኁዝ፡ – captive, held, possessed; እኁዝ፡ አጋንንት፡ – possessed by a demon

28.6 II Guttural ቀታሊ፡ Agent Nouns[4]

ጸሓፊ፡ – scribe
ከሓዲ፡ – infidel, non-believer
ክሃሊ፡ – powerful, capable ክሃሊ፡ ኩሉ፡ – omnipotent (strong in all things) ክሃሊ፡ + ለ + infinitive – "capable of"
አጋዚ፡ – owner, master, lord

28.7 II Guttural Verbal Nouns[5]

ጽሕፈት፡ – act of writing
ስእለት፡ – request, prayer
ስሕተት፡ – error, sin
ክሕድ፡ – lack of faith, heresy, rebellion
ክሕደት፡ – denial, apostasy
ልህቀት፡ – old age
ላእክ፡ (pl. ላእካን፡) – servant
አነዝ፡ / አነዚ፡ – pledge, pawn

---

2. See ch. 24.
3. The derivatives of this word create some difficulty for translators. As noted here the noun is translated "rich, wealthy." An adjective from the noun, ባዕል፡, also means "rich or wealthy." A closely associated noun ባዕል, written the same as the adjective ባዕል፡ is translated as "owner, master, lord." An additional noun በዓል፡, is translated as "feast or festival." The final form to consider is the verbal noun ብዕል፡ it is translated as "riches or wealth."
4. See ch. 23.
5. See ch. 25.

28.8 Nouns with a Prefixed መ-

There are several nouns from the II Guttural group that are formed with the prefixed መ-. Three prominent nouns should be noted due to their frequent appearance in various texts. These should be committed to memory.

መጽሐፍ፡ (pl. መጻሕፍት፡) – book, document, writing
መልህቅት፡ (pl. መልህቃት፡ መላህቅት፡ መልህቅታት፡) – elders, seniors, persons of older age
መልእክት፡ (pl. መልእካታት፡) – epistle, letter, service, office, function

28.9 The Verb ብህለ፡ – "Say"

This particular verb can create some difficulty when one comes across it in a text. Due to its frequent use to introduce direct speech, it is important to put this paradigm to memory. It is formed in the perfect with a distinctive prefix much like the imperfect while at the same time for all of the paradigm forms the middle consonant ህ is dropped in the conjugation. In addition, in half of the forms the final ለ is also dropped. As will be seen below the imperfect, subjunctive, and imperative are also irregular with the loss of the ህ consonant.

TABLE 28.7: The Verb ብህለ፡ Perfect Paradigm

PGN	Verb Form	Translation	PGN	Verb Form	Translation
3ms	ይቤ፡	He said	3mp	ይቤሉ፡	They said
3fs	ትቤ፡	She said	3fp	ይቤላ፡	They said
2ms	ትቤ፡	You said	2mp	ትቤሉ፡	You said
2fs	ትቤሊ፡	You said	2fp	ትቤላ፡	You said
1cs	እቤ፡	I said	1cp	ንቤ፡	We said

Imperfect form (3ms): ይብል፡ – "he will say"; subjunctive form (3ms); ይበል፡ – "may he say"; imperative form (2ms): በል፡ – "(you) say." The inflection for each of these follows the normal pattern. The imperfect of ብህለ፡ paired with the term እንዘ፡ (while, when, as) indicates direct speech will follow:

ወይቤሎ፡ እንዘ፡ ይብል፡ – "and while speaking, he said to him" translated "he said to him, '...'"
ወሰአልክዎ፡ እንዘ፡ እብል፡ – "and when speaking, I asked him" translated "I asked him, '...'"
ወነገርዎ፡ እንዘ፡ ይብሉ፡ – "and while speaking, they said to him" translated "they spoke to him, '...'"

The other derived forms of the verb ብህለ፡ form regularly: Gt, ተብህለ፡ – "be spoken of"; Glt, ተባህለ፡ – "speak with one another"; CG, አብለ፡ – "cause to speak" (note the loss of the ህ).

28.10 Vocabulary

1. መዕበል፡ / ማዕብል፡ (pl. ማዕበላት፡) – wave, flood
2. ፍሬ፡ (pl. ፍሬያት፡ / ፍርያት) – fruit

3. ንእሰ፡ (Subj. ይንአስ፡) – be small, young; አንአሰ፡ CG – make small
4. ንኡስ፡ (f. ንእስት፡) – small, little; young
5. ነአስ፡ – young girl; ንእስ፡ – childhood
6. ንስቲት፡ – small or little amount, found in construct chain; ንስቲተ፡ ኅብስት፡ – a little bread; as an adjective ሀገር፡ ንስቲት፡ – a small village, town
7. ርሕቀ፡ (Subj. ይርሐቅ፡) – be distant, remote (spatial or temporal); አርሐቀ፡ CG – remove, to delay; ተራሐቀ፡ Glt – separate mutually (from)
8. ርሑቅ፡ – far away, remote
9. ርሕቀት፡ – a period of time or a measure space
10. ምሕረ፡ / መሐረ፡ (Subj. ይምሐር፡) – have mercy upon; አምሐረ፡ CG – cause to have mercy; ተምሕረ፡ Gt – be shown mercy
11. ምሕረት፡ – mercy, pity
12. መሓሪ፡ – one who is merciful
13. ጥዕመ፡ / ጠዐመ፡ (Subj. ይጥዐም፡ / ይጠዕም፡) – taste, experience; አጥዐመ፡ CG – give to someone to taste or experience
14. ጥዑም፡ – tasty, delicious
15. ጣዕም፡ – a taste, flavor (e.g., vanilla)
16. ልህቀ፡ – grow older (mature), grow in size, grow up, reach puberty
17. ሰወረ፡ D – hide, conceal; ተሰወረ፡ Dt – be hidden
18. ናሁ፡ – behold
19. ንዐ፡ – come!; impv. base. forms: 2ms, ነዓ፡; 2fs, ንዒ፡; 2mp, ንዑ፡; 2fp ነዓ
20. ኦ – O! (vocative particle); ኦንጉሥ፡ – O king!; እግዚኦ፡ – O Lord!

28.11 Exercises

A. Translate the following:

1. ጣዕመ፡ ሞት፡፡

2. አንዘ፡ ጽኑዕ፡፡

3. መጽሐፍ፡ ጽሑፍ፡ በጽሕፈት፡ ሠናይ፡፡

4. ብዕለ፡ ውእቱ፡ ንጉሥ፡ ከቡር፡፡

5. በዓለ፡ መስቀል፡፡

6. አኃትየ፡ መላህቅት፡

7. ዘእንበለ፡ ምሕረት፡

8. ማዕበለ፡ ማይ፡

9. ጣዕም፡ ዝንቱ፡ ፍሬ፡

10. አረጋይ፡ ምሁረ፡ ሕግ፡

11. አኃዜ፡ ዓለም፡

12. መልእክተ፡ ጳውሎስ፡ ኀበ፡ ሰብአ፡ ሮሜ፡

13. መላህቅተ፡ እስራኤል፡

14. ሐመር፡ ንእስት፡

15. እግዚእ፡ ከሃሊ፡ ለረዲኦተነ፡

16. ፍሬ፡ ሠናይ፡

17. ማዕበለ፡ ዝናም፡

18. አረጋት፡ ድክምት፡ ወስእንት፡

19. ነጋሢ፡ አኃዚ፡

20. ካሕዶሙ፡ ለእሎንቱ፡ ዐልዋን።

21. ላእከ፡ እሙን።

22. አስማዒሆሙ፡ ለላእካኒሁ።

23. እግዚእ፡ መሓሪ።

24. ፍሬ፡ ጥዑም።

25. እምንእሱ፡ እስከ፡ ልህቃቱ።

26. ወሬዛ፡ እኁዘ፡ ጋኔን።

27. ክሕደተ፡ ስሑታን።

28. ቅትለተ፡ ከሓድያን።

29. ተክል፡ ንኡስ።

30. ነጉድጓድ፡ ርሑቅ።

31. ንስቲተ፡ ፍሬ።

32. ሕይወት፡ ዘአንበሎ፡ ስሕተት።

33. ሰብእ፡ እኁዛን፡ ውስተ፡ ቤተ፡ ሞቅሕ።

G Verbs with II Guttural Roots

34. በልህቃቲሁ፡ ለአቡነ፡
_____

35. ብሔር፡ ርሑቅ፡
_____

36. መልእክተ፡ ዝንቱ፡ ካህን፡ ጻድቅ፡
_____

37. ብእሲ፡ ጥዑም፡ ንባብ፡
_____

38. በዕለ፡ ሐመር፡
_____

39. ንስቲተ፡ ማይ፡ ቄሪር፡
_____

B. Jubilees 5.1–20. Translate the following:

¹ ወኮነ፡ አም፡ ወጠኑ፡ ደቂቀ፡ እጓለ፡ እመሕያው፡ ይብዝኁ፡ ዲበ፡ ገጸ፡ ኩላ፡ ምድር፡ ወአዋልድ፡ ተወልዳ፡ ሎሙ፡፡ ወርእይዎን፡ መላእክተ፡ እግዚአብሔር፡ በሐቲ፡ ዓመት፡ ዘኢዮቤልዩ፡ ዝንቱ፡ እስመ፡ ሠናያት፡ ለርኢይ፡ እማንቱ፡ ወነሥእዎን፡ ሎቶን፡ ሎሙ፡ አንስቲያ፡ እምኩሎሙ፡ እለ፡ ኀረዩ፡ ወወለዳ፡ ሎሙ፡ ውሉደ፡ ወእሙንቱ፡ ረዐይት፡፡

² ወልህቀት፡ ዐመፃ፡ ዲበ፡ ምድር፡ ወኮሉ፡ ዘሥጋ፡ አማሰነት፡ ፍኖታ፡ እምሰብእ፡ እስከ፡ እንስሳ፡ ወእስከ፡ አራዊት፡ ወእስከ፡ አዕዋፍ፡ ወእስከ፡ ኩሉ፡ ዘያንሱሱ፡ ውስተ፡ ምድር፡ ኩሎሙ፡ አማስኑ፡ ፍኖቶሙ፡ ወሥርዓቶሙ፡፡ ወአኀዙ፡ ይትባልዑ፡ በበይናቲሆሙ፡ ወዐመፃ፡ ልህቀት፡ በዲበ፡ ምድር፡ ወኮሉ፡ ኅሊና፡ አእምሮ፡ ለኩሎሙ፡ እጓለ፡ እመሕያው፡ ከመዝ፡ እኩይ፡ ኩሎ፡ መዋዕለ፡፡

³ ወርእያ፡ እግዚአብሔር፡ ለምድር፡ ወናሁ፡ ማሰነት፡ ወአማሰነት፡ ኩላ፡ ዘሥጋ፡ ሥርዓታ፡ ወአእከዩ፡ ኩሎሙ፡ ቅድመ፡ አዕይንቲሁ፡ ኩሉ፡ ዘሀሎ፡ ውስተ፡ ምድር፡፡

⁴ ወይቤ፡ ይደመስሶ፡ ለሰብእ፡ ወኩሉ፡ ዘሥጋ፡ በመልዕልተ፡ ገጸ፡ ምድር፡ ዘፈጠረ፡፡

⁵ ወኖኅ፡ ባሕቲቱ፡ ረከበ፡ ሞገሰ፡ በቅድመ፡ አዕይንቲሁ፡፡

⁶ ወዲበ፡ መላእክቲሁ፡ እለ፡ ፈነወ፡ ውስተ፡ ምድር፡ ወተምዐ፡ ፈድፈደ፡ ይሥርዖሙ፡ እምኮኩ፡ ሥልጣኖሙ፡ ወይቤለኒ፡ ከመ፡ ንስሮሙ፡ ውስተ፡ መዓምቅቲሃ፡ ለምድር፡ ወናሁ፡ እሙንቱ፡ አሱራን፡ ማእከሎሙ፡ ወብሕትዋን።

⁷ ወዲበ፡ ውሉዶሙ፡ ወዕለ፡ ቃል፡ እምቅድሙ፡ ገጹ፡ ከመ፡ ይምሐዖሙ፡ በሰይፍ፡ ወያስስሎሙ፡ እምታሕተ፡ ሰማይ።

⁸ ወይቤ፡ ኢይነብር፡ መንፈስየ፡ ዲበ፡ ሰብእ፡ ለዓለም፡ እስመ፡ እሙንቱ፡ ሥጋ፡ ወይኩን፡ መዋዕሊሆሙ፡ ምእተ፡ ወዕሥራ፡ ዓመት።

⁹ ወፈነወ፡ ሰይፎ፡ ማእከሎሙ፡ ከመ፡ ይቅትሉ፡ አሐዱ፡ አሐዱ፡ ቢጾሙ፡ ወወጠኑ፡ ይቅትሉ፡ ዝንቱ፡ ዘንተ፡ እስከ፡ ወድቁ፡ ኩሎሙ፡ ውስተ፡ ሰይፍ፡ ወተደምሰሱ፡ እምነ፡ ምድር።

¹⁰ ወአበዊሆሙሰ፡ ይኔጽሩ፡ ወእምድኅረዝ፡ ተአስሩ፡ ውስተ፡ ማዕምቅቲሃ፡ ለምድር፡ እስከ፡ ዕለተ፡ ደይን፡ ዐባይ፡ ለከዊነ፡ ኩኔ፡ ዲበ፡ ኩሎሙ፡ እለ፡ አማሰኑ፡ ፍናዊሆሙ፡ ወምግባሪሆሙ፡ ቅድመ፡ እግዚአብሔር።

¹¹ ወደምሰሰ፡ ኩሎ፡ እመካኖሙ፡ ወኢተርፈ፡ አሐዱ፡ እምኔሆሙ፡ ዘኢኩነነ፡ በኩሉ፡ አከዮሙ።

¹² ወገብረ፡ ለኩሉ፡ ግብሩ፡ ፍጥረተ፡ ሐዲሰ፡ ወጻድቅተ፡ ከመ፡ ኢያአብሱ፡ በኩሉ፡ ፍጥረቶሙ፡ እስከ፡ ለዓለም፡ ወይጸድቅ፡ ኩሉ፡ በበትዝምዱ፡ ኩሎ፡ መዋዕለ።

¹³ ወኮነ፡ ኩሎሙ፡ ተሠርዑ፡ ወተጽሕፉ፡ ውስተ፡ ጽላተ፡ ሰማይ፡ ወአልቦ፡ ዐማፂ፡ ወኮሎሙ፡ እለ፡ ይትዐደዉ፡ እምፍኖቶሙ፡ በእንተ፡ ተሠርዖት፡ ሎሙ፡ ከመ፡ ይሑሩ፡ ባቲ። ወለእመ፡ ኢሐሩ፡ ባቲ፡ ተጽሕፈ፡ ኮነ፡ ለኩሉ፡ ፍጥረት፡ ወለኩሉ፡ ትዝምድ።

¹⁴ ወአልቦ፡ ምንትኒ፡ ዘበሰማይ፡ ወዘበምድር፡ ወውስተ፡ ብርሃን፡ ወውስተ፡ ጽልመት፡ ወበሲኦል፡ ወውስተ፡ ቀላይ። ወውስተ፡ መጽልም፡ ወኩሉ፡ ኩኔሆሙ፡ ሥሩዕ፡ ወጽሑፍ፡ ወቀሩጽ።

¹⁵ በእንተ፡ ኩሉ፡ ለዐቢይ፡ በከመ፡ ዕበዩ፡ ወለንኡስሂ፡ በከመ፡ ንእሱ፡ ወለለ፡ አሐዱ፡ በከመ፡ ፍኖቱ፡ ይኴንኖ።

¹⁶ ወኢኮነ፡ ውእቱ፡ ዘይኔሥአ፡ ገጸ፡ ወኢኮነ፡ ውእቱ፡ ዘይነሥእ፡ ሕልያነ፡ እመ፡ ይቤ፡ ይግበር፡ ኮነ፡ ለለ፡ አሐዱ፡ ወአሐዱ፡ እመ፡ ወህበ፡ ኩሎ፡ ዘውስተ፡ ምድር፡ ኢይኔሥአ፡ ገጸ፡ ወኢይትሜጠ፡ እምኑሁ፡ እስመ፡ መኰንነ፡ ጽድቅ፡ ውእቱ።

[17] ወዲበ፡ ደቂቀ፡ እስራኤል፡ ተጽሕፈ፡ ወተሠርዐ፡ እም፡ ተመይጡ፡ ኃቤሁ፡ በጽድቅ፡ የኃድግ፡ ኵሎ፡ አበሳሆሙ፡ ወይሰሪ፡ ኵሎ፡ ኃጢአቶሙ።

[18] ተጽሕፈ፡ ወተሠርዐ፡ ይትመሐር፡ ለኵሉ፡ እለ፡ ይትመይጡ፡ እምኵሉ፡ ጌጋዮሙ። ምዕረ፡ ለዓመት።

[19] ወዲበ፡ ኵሎሙ፡ እለ፡ አማሰኑ፡ ፍናዊሆሙ፡ ወምክሮሙ፡ እምቅድመ፡ አይኅ፡ ኢተንሥአ፡ ገጾሙ፡ ዘእንበለ፡ ሴኖ፡ ባሕቲቱ፡ እስመ፡ ተንሥአ፡ ሎቱ፡ ገጹ፡ በእንተ፡ ውሉዳ፡ እለ፡ አድኃኖሙ፡ እምነ፡ ማየ፡ አይኅ፡ በእንቲአሁ፡ እስመ፡ ጻድቅት፡ ይአቲ፡ ልቡ፡ በኵሉ፡ ፍናዊሁ። በከመ፡ እዘዝ፡ በእንቲአሁ፡ ወኢተዐደወ፡ እምኵሉ፡ ዘሥሩዕ፡ ሎቱ።

[20] ወይቤ፡ እግዚአብሔር፡ ይደመስስ፡ ኵሎ፡ ዘዲበ፡ የብስ፡ እምሰብእ፡ እስከ፡ እንስሳ፡ እስከ፡ አረዊት፡ ወእስከ፡ አዕዋፍ፡ ወእስከ፡ ዘይትሐወስ፡ ዲበ፡ ምድር።

Chapter 29

G VERBS WITH III GUTTURAL ROOTS

29.1 III Guttural Root Verbs

In this chapter (see ch. 10 to review the perfect) we will examine the remaining forms of the III Guttural verbs, e.g., በጽሐ፡ – "arrive"). These forms include the imperfect, subjunctive, imperative, and infinitive. The III Guttural roots for the imperfect follow this consonant/vowel pattern: ይ+$C_1 \breve{a} C_2 \partial G_3$, ይበጽሕ፡– "he will arrive"). The subjunctive follows the pattern ይ+$C_1 \partial C_2 \bar{a} G_3$, ይምጻእ፡– "he may arrive." The imperative follows the pattern $C_1 \partial C_2 \bar{a} G_3$, ምጻእ፡– "(you) arrive!"

TABLE 29.1: Perfect III Guttural Paradigm (በጽሐ፡)

PGN	Perfect Forms	PGN	Perfect Forms
3ms	በጽሐ፡	3mp	በጽሑ፡
3fs	በጽሐት፡	3fp	በጽሓ፡
2ms	በጻሕከ፡	2mp	በጻሕክሙ፡
2fs	በጻሕኪ፡	2fp	በጻሕክን፡
1cs	በጻሕኩ፡	1cp	በጻሕነ፡

a. Note the I consonant maintains the $\breve{a}$ vowel throughout the paradigm.

b. The II consonant in the 3s/p forms are terminal and thus have the silent ∂ vowel, while the first- and second-person s/p forms have the $\bar{a}$ vowel.

c. The III consonant adjusts according to personal endings, but in the majority of occurrences it has the short ∂ vowel (2ms, 2fs, 1cs, 2mp, 2fp, 1cp).

TABLE 29.2: III Guttural Imperfect Paradigm (በስሐ፡)

PGN	Imperfect Forms	PGN	Imperfect Forms
3ms	ይበጽሕ፡	3mp	ይበጽሑ፡
3fs	ትበጽሕ፡	3fp	ይበጽሓ፡
2ms	ትበጽሕ፡	2mp	ትበጽሑ፡
2fs	ትበጽሒ፡	2fp	ትበጽሓ፡
1cs	እበጽሕ፡	1cp	ንበጽሕ፡

a. Note the III Guttural imperfect follows the same vowel pattern as the imperfect strong verb.

b. They use the same prefixes and the I, II, consonant vowels are the same and the III consonant adjusts according to the personal suffixes.

TABLE 29.3: III Guttural Subjunctive Paradigm (በጽሐ፡)

PGN	Subjunctive Forms	PGN	Subjunctive Forms
3ms	ይብጻሕ፡	3mp	ይብጽሑ፡
3fs	ትብጻሕ፡	3fp	ይብጽሓ፡
2ms	ትብጻሕ፡	2mp	ትብጽሑ፡
2fs	ትብጽሒ፡	2fp	ትብጽሓ፡
1cs	እብጻሕ፡	1cp	ንብጻሕ፡

a. The III Guttural subjunctive verb makes significant vowel adjustments in the paradigm

b. It maintains the strong subjunctive prefixes and personal endings.

c. The I consonant remains with the short *ə* vowel throughout the paradigm but the II consonant in the 3ms, 3fs, 2ms, 1cs, and 1 cp all adopt the long *ā* vowel.

d. The remaining forms (2fs, 3mp, 3fp, 2mp, and 2fp) retain the short *ə* vowel.

e. The III consonant adjusts according to the personal suffixes.

TABLE 29.4: III Guttural Imperative Paradigm (በጽሐ፡)

PGN	Imperative Forms	PGN	Imperative Forms
2ms	ብጻሕ፡	2mp	ብጽሑ፡
2fs	ብጽሒ፡	2fp	ብጻሓ፡

a. The infinitive form of the paradigm verb appears as በጺሕ፡ (Note the *i* stem vowel following the second radical): – "to arrive."

b. The III Guttural imperative follows a similar pattern to the subjunctive less the prefix.

c. Note that in the 2fs form the II consonant has the short *ə* vowel rather than the *ā* in the rest of the singular forms. In addition, the 1cp II consonant has the *ā* vowel, while the II consonant in the other plural forms has the *ə* vowel.

29.2   III Guttural Causative Verbs (አብጽሐ፡)

In the basic paradigm in table 29.5, note the shift in the simple causative form the final ሐ in the perfect to the final ሕ in the imperfect, subjunctive, and imperative. In addition, note the variation of the first consonant ብ/ቢ and ·ብ/ብ in the imperfect, subjunctive, and imperative of the simple and intensive forms.

TABLE 29.5: III Guttural Causative Verbs

	Simple Causative Action[1]	Intensive Causative Action
Perfect	አብጽሐ፡	አበጽሐ፡
Imperfect	ያበጽሕ፡	ያቤጽሕ፡
Subjunctive	ያብጽሕ፡	ያበጽሕ፡
Imperative	አብጽሕ፡	አበጽሕ፡
Infinitive	አብጺሐ፡	አበጺሐ፡

29.3   III Guttural Reflexive Verbs (ተበጽሐ፡ – "Arrive")

As mentioned previously, the reflexive verb in Gəʿəz functions much like the Hithpael verb in Hebrew; the subject(s) is performing the action to herself or the action can be reciprocal between two or more subjects. Note the prefixed ተ or ት on the simple reflexive along with the expected imperfect and subjunctive prefixes.

TABLE 29.6: III Guttural Reflexive Verbs (በጺሐ፡)

	Simple Reflexive Action	Intensive Reflexive Action
Perfect	ተበጽሐ፡	ተበጽሐ፡
Imperfect	ይትበጻሕ፡	ይትቤጻሕ፡
Subjunctive	ይትበጻሕ፡	ይትበጻሕ፡
Imperative	ተበጻሕ፡	ተበጻሕ፡
Infinitive	ተበጺሐ፡	ተበጺሐ፡

TABLE 29.7: III Guttural Reflexive Verbs (አስተበጽሐ፡)

	Simple Causative-Reflexive Action	Intensive Causative-Reflexive Action
Perfect	አስተብጽሐ፡	አስተበጽሐ፡
Imperfect	ይስተበጽሕ፡	ይስተቤጽሕ፡
Subjunctive	ይስተብጽሕ፡	ይስተበጽሕ፡
Imperative	አስተብጽሕ፡	አስተበጽሕ፡
Infinitive	አስተበጺሐ፡	አስተበጺሐ፡

29.4 III Guttural and Subject or Object Suffix

When a vowel appears as a subject verb ending or an object suffix is added to the subjunctive or imperative verb form, there is usually a stem vowel change from *ā* to *ə*:

TABLE 29.8: III Guttural Subjunctive and Imperative

III Guttural Subjunctive				III Guttural Imperative			
3ms	ይምጻእ፡	3mp	ይምጽኡ፡				
3fs	ትምጻእ	3fp	ይምጽአ፡				
2ms	ትምጻእ	2mp	ትምጽኡ፡	2ms	ምጻእ	2mp	ምጽኡ፡
2fs	ትምጽኢ፡	2fp	ትምጽአ፡	2fs	ምጽኢ፡	2fp	ምጽአ
1cs	እምጻእ	1cp	ንምጻእ፡				

Note the 2fs and 2fp forms both have an original *ə* due to the suffix vowel of ኢ on the 2fs and አ on the 2fp. Similarly, the 3mp and 2mp have the suffix vowel of ኡ, thus the short preceding ጽ.

3ms Subjunctive + Object Suffix

ይምጻእ፡ – "let him come"
ይምጽአኒ፡ +1cs suffix
ይምጻእከ፡ +2ms suffix
ይምጻእኪ፡ +2fs suffix
ይምጽኦ፡ +3ms suffix
ይምጽአ፡ +3fs suffix

Despite this normal vowel shift from *ā* to *ə*, this is not always the case, and there are occasions in which the *ā* is retained.

29.5 III Guttural Verbs Previously Introduced

መጽአ፡ – come
ነሥአ፡ – raise, lift up
መልአ፡ – fill, be full

ረትዐ፡ – be righteous
ረድአ፡ – help someone
ክልአ፡ – prevent

ገብአ፡ – return
መርሐ፡ – lead, guide
ፈርሀ፡ – be afraid
ጸንዐ፡ – be strong
ጠፍአ፡ – perish, vanish, go out like a flame
ፈትሐ፡ – untie, loosen

በጽሐ፡ – arrive
ስምዐ፡ – hear, obey
በዝኀ፡ – be many
ጸብአ፡ – fight, make war
ህድአ፡ – be quiet

29.6 III Guttural Verbal Adjectives[1]

Verbal adjectives are generally the equivalent of a passive participle, having both verbal and adjectival characteristics. Verbal adjectives can modify nouns, but they also can act as an adverb as will be seen in the examples below:

ምሉእ፡ – full, abundant
ስሙእ፡ – famous, notorious

ፍቱሕ፡ – open, forgiven person

29.7 III Guttural Agent Nouns[2]

መራሒ፡ – leader
ሰማዒ፡ (pl. ሰማዕት፡) – hearing, listening
ገባኢ፡ (pl. ገባእት፡) – mercenary, hired worker
ፈራሂ፡ – fearful, reverent

ፈታሒ፡ (pl. ፈታህት፡) – judge
ጸናዒ፡ (pl. ጸናዕት፡) – strong, fortified
ጸባኢ፡ (pl. ጸባእት፡) – warrior, soldier
ረዳኢ፡ – helper, assistant

29.8 III Guttural Verbal Nouns[3]

ምጽአት፡ – arrival, advent
መርሕ፡ (pl. አመርሕት፡) – leader
ምልእ፡ – what fills
ምልአ፡ እድ፡፡ – a handful
በምልኡ፡ – completely
ስምዕ፡ (pl. ስምዓት፡) – rumor, report; testimony; martyrdom
ብዝኀ፡ – multitude, large number
ግብአት፡ – return, conversion

ፍርሀት፡ (pl. ፍርሃት፡) – fear, dread, awe
ፍትሕ፡ – judgment
ርትዕ፡ – justice, what is true
ጽንዕ፡ / ጽንዕት፡) – hardness, strength
ጥፍአት፡ – extinction, destruction
ህድአት፡ – peace, tranquility
ረድኤት፡ – help, assistance, helper
ክልአት፡ – prohibition, prevention

29.9 Nouns with a Prefixed ም

There are several nouns from the III Guttural group that are formed with the prefixed ም. Those listed below occur frequently and should be put to memory:

---
1. See ch. 23.
2. See ch. 23.
3. See ch. 25.

ምምጻእ፡ – place of origin
ምግባእ፡ – refuge, place of return
ምጽናዕ፡ (pl. ምጽናዓት፡) – firmament (of heaven)
መብዝኅት፡ – majority, most of (something)

29.10 Vocabulary

1. ጸጋ፡ (pl. ጸጋት፡) – grace, favor, gift
2. ሀገር – town, city
3. ኀብአ፡ (subj. ይኀባእ፡) – hide or conceal; ተኀብአ፡ Gt – be hidden, or hide oneself
4. ኅቡእ፡ – hidden, concealed
5. በኅቡእ፡ – secretly
6. ምኅባእ፡ (pl. ምኅባኣት፡) – hiding place
7. ጸንሐ፡ (subj. ይጽናሕ፡) – wait, expect; አጽንሐ፡ CG – set traps or ensnare
8. ጽኑሕ፡ – waiting, expecting
9. ሠርዐ፡ (subj. ይሥራዕ፡) – put in order, arrange; ተሠርዐ፡ Gt – be arranged, be put in order
10. ሥሩዕ፡ – arranged, ordered
11. ሥርዐት፡ – order, arrangement, decree, law
12. ፈጸመ፡ D – complete, finish; ተፈጸመ፡ Dt – be completed, to be finished

29.11 Exercises

A. Translate the following:

1. ገበርከ፡ ኃጢአተከ፡ በኅቡእ፣ ወአነ፡ ባሕቱ፡ አቀሥፈከ፡ ከሡተ፡

2. አልቦ፡ ኅቡ፡ ነኀብእ፡ ወርቀነ፡

3. ሐነጸነ፡ ሀገሪተ፡ ንእስተ፡ ነኀድር፡ ባቲ፡ በሰላም፡

4. በእንተ፡ ምንት፡ ትክሕዱ፡ ሥርዐታትየ፡ ወትእዛዛትየ፡

5. ሐይወ፡ ኵሎ፡ ሐይወቶ፡ በጽድቅ፡ ወበርትዕ፡

6. እግዚአብሔር፡ ፈታሒከ፡ ውእቱ፡ ወረዳኢከ፡ በኵሉ፡ ግብሪከ፡

7. ይጸንሕ፡ ለክሙ፡ ኵልክሙ፡ ዕለተ፡ ምንዳቤ።

8. ወሶበ፡ ፈጸሙ፡ መልእክቶ፡ ኀደጎሙ፡ ወገብአ፡ ሰማየ።

9. አዘዘሙ፡ ለጸባእቲሁ፡ በእንተ፡ ሥርዐቶሙ፡ በጸብአ።

10. መኑ፡ ዘገብረ፡ ምጽናዐ፡ ሰማይ።

11. ንጸንሕ፡ ዝየ፡ እስከ፡ የዐርብ፡ ፀሓይ።

12. ኢትጽንሐኒ፡ እስመ፡ ኢይገብአ፡ ኀቤከ።

13. ጸሐፈ፡ ሎሙ፡ ሥርዐተ፡ ማኅበሮሙ፡ ዘበከማሃ፡ ይገብሩ፡ ኵሎ፡ ግብራቲሆሙ።

14. ሠናይ፡ ውእቱ፡ እስመ፡ መሀበነ፡ ረድኤተ።

15. ፈላስያን፡ ንሕነ፡ ወአልብነ፡ ምግባአ።

16. አጽንሐኒ፡ ከመ፡ ይአኅዙኒ፡ ወይቅትሉኒ።

17. አይቴ፡ ዘተኀባእከ፡ ሶበ፡ ኮኑ፡ የኀሥሡከ።

18. ሶበ፡ ሠርዐ፡ ጸባእቲሁ፡ ቅድሜከ፡ ፈራህከ፡ ወጐየይከ።

19. ለክሙ፡ ወለደቂቅክሙ፡ ተሠርዐ፡ ዝንቱ፡ ሕግ፡ ዘለዓለም።

20. እምነ፡ አይ፡ መካን፡ አንተ። ምንት፡ ውእቲ፡ ምምጻአከ።

21. በጸጋሁ፡ ለእግዚአብሔር፡ ዘበጻሕክሙ፡ ዘንተ፡ መካነ፡ ህዱአ፡ በሰላም።

22. ሰሚያሙ፡ ዘንተ፡ ጐዩ፡ ወተኀብኡ።

23. ሠርየሙ፡ ፍናዊሆሙ፡ ለፀሓይ፡ ወወርኅ።

24. ሠርዑ፡ እሎንቱ፡ ጠቢባን፡ ሥርዐተ፡ አውራኅ፡ ወሥርዐተ፡ ዓመታት።

B. Translate the following:

1. ፍትሐ፡ ዕልዋን፡ ወከሓድያን።

2. ጸባእያን፡ ጽኑዓነ፡ ልብ።

3. መብዝኅተ፡ ዝንቱ፡ ማኅበረ፡ መሃይምናን።

4. ውሉድ፡ ሰማዕያን።

5. ሰማዕት፡ ቅቱላን።

6. መብዝኅተ፡ ኍልቆሙ።

7. መራሒ፡ መሓሪ።

8. ዘአንበለ፡ ክልአት።

9. ፍርሀተ፡ ልብ።

10. እስከ፡ ምጽአቱ፡ ለወልድየ፡ ፍቁር።

11. ዐቃቤ፡ ሥራይ፡ ስሙዕ።

12. ሀገር፡ ጸናዒት።

13. በዕለተ፡ ፍትሕከሙ።

14. ጽንዐ፡ ኣዐዙ።

15. ወልድ፡ ንኡስ፡ ወፈራህ።

16. ብእሲ፡ ፈራሄ፡ እግዚአብሔር።

17. መርሕ፡ ጥቢብ፡ ወአማኒ።

18. ስምዕ፡ እኩይ።

19. ሞቅሕ፡ ፍቱሕ።

20. ኀጣውእ፡ ፍትሕት።

21. ጽንዐ፡ ሃይማኖትከ።

22. በቅድመ፡ ጸባኢተ፡ እግዚአብሔር።

23. ምጥማቅ፡ ምሉእ፡ ማየ።

G Verbs with III Guttural Roots

24. ብዝኁ፡ ጸሎታቲክሙ።

25. ብርሃን፡ ምሉእ፡ ሰማየ።

26. አምርሕት፡ አኩያን።

27. ህድአተ፡ ምዕራፎሙ።

28. በእንተ፡ ስምዐ፡ ቅዱስ፡ ማርቆስ።

C. 2 Peter 2:1–16. Translate the following:

¹ ወቦ፡ ባሕቱ፡ ሐሳውያን፡ ነቢያት፡ ማእከለ፡ ሕዝብ፡ ከም፡ እለ፡ ሀለዉ፡ ማእከሌክሙ፡ ወውስቴትክሙ፡ እለ፡ ሐሰተ፡ ይሜህሩ፡ ወእለ፡ ካሕደ፡ ያበውኡ፡ ዘሐርትምና፡ ወይክሕድዋ፡ ለእግዚአሙ፡ ዘተሣየጠሙ፡ ወያመጽእዎ፡ ላዕሌሆሙ፡ ፍጡነ፡ ለሙስና፡ ወለተሠርዎ።

² ወብዙኃን፡ ሰብእ፡ ይተልውዎሙ፡ ለእሉ፡ በእንተ፡ ዝሙቾሙ፡ ወይዘርፉ፡ ላዕለ፡ ፍኖተ፡ ጽድቅ።

³ ወይትከሐዱ፡ በቃል፡ ዘለሊሆሙ፡ ፈጠሩ፡ ወቦቱ፡ የሐውሩ፡ ወደይኖሙሰ፡ እምፍጥረት፡ ዘኢየዐርፍ፡ ወሕርትምናሆሙ፡ እንተ፡ ኢትዴቅስ።

⁴ ወእግዚአብሔርሰ፡ ለመላእክቲሁ፡ ጥቀ፡ አቢሶሙ፡ ኢመሐኮሙ፡ አላ፡ ወደዮሙ፡ ውስተ፡ ጽዕረ፡ ደይን፡ ዘርሱን፡ መጠዎሙ፡ ይትኩነኑ፡ ወይንበሩ፡ ውስተ፡ ጽዕረ፡ ደይን።

⁵ ወለዓለምስ፡ ቀዳምት፡ ኢመሐኮሙ፡ አላ፡ አትረፈ፡ ሰማኒተ፡ ነፍስ፡ ምስለ፡ ኖኅ፡ ዘወቀባ፡ ለጽድቅ፡ ከም፡ ይኩን፡ ዜናዊ፡ በጽድቅ፡ ወለባዕዳንስ፡ ሰብእ፡ ረሲዓን፡ ፈነወ፡ አይኀ፡ ላዕሌሆሙ።

⁶ ወለአህጉረ፡ ሶዶምኒ፡ ወገሞራ፡ አውዐዮን፡ ወገፍትዓን፡ ወከመዝ፡ ኮነሞሙ፡ ወአርአያ፡ ረሰዮሙ፡ ለደኃሪ፡ መዋዕለ፡ ኃጥኣን።

⁷ ወለጸድቅሰ፡ ሎጥ፡ ዘይትገፋዕ፡ እምእለ፡ ይኤብሱ፡ በምግባረ፡ ዝሙቶሙ፡ አድኅኖ።

⁸ወእንዘ፡ ይሬኢ፡ ወይሰምዕ፡ ጻድቅ፡ ወንዳር፡ ምስሌሆሙ፡ ወዕለተ፡ እምዕለት፡ ያጌዕርዋ፡ ለነፍሱ፡ ጻድቅት፡ በእከየ፡ ምግባሮሙ።

⁹ናሁኬ፡ አአምርን፡ ከመ፡ እግዚአብሔር፡ ይክል፡ አድኅኖቶሙ፡ እምነ፡ መንሱት፡ ለጻድቃን፡ ወለዓጥአንሰ፡ ዕለተ፡ ደይን፡ ትጸንሓሙ፡ ለተጽዕሮ።

¹⁰ወፈድፋደሰ፡ ለእለ፡ ይተልውዋ፡ ድኅሬሃ፡ ለፍትወቶሙ፡ ወያገምንዎ፡ ለሥጋሆሙ፡ ወያስተሕቅርዋ፡ ለፈጣሪሆሙ። ጽቡዓን፡ ወዝሉፋን፡ እለ፡ ኢይደነግፁ፡ ከመ፡ ይፅርፉ፡ ላዕለ፡ ስብሐቲሁ።

¹¹ዘውእቱ፡ ኅቤ፡ መላእክት፡ እለ፡ ልዑላን፡ እሙንቱ፡ እምኔሆሙ፡ በኃይል፡ ወበጽንዕ፡ ወኢይክሉ፡ ተዐግሦ፡ ከመ፡ ያብጽሑ፡ ላዕሌሆሙ፡ ደይነ፡ ጥፍአቶሙ።

¹²ውእቶሙኬ፡ ከመ፡ እንስሳ፡ ዘአልቦ፡ ቃል፡ ዘይትወለድ፡ ለሙስና፡ ወለተሰርጎ፡ እስመ፡ ይዘርፉ፡ ላዕለ፡ ዘኢያአምሩ፡ ለሕርትምናሆሙ፡ ወሎሙ፡ በሙስናሆሙ፡ ዕሴ፡ ዐመፃ።

¹³ወአስተሐወዝዎ፡ ለተደልዎ፡ ስታየ፡ ዕለቶሙ፡ ወይብልዑ፡ እንዘ፡ ሕብቁኃን፡ ወርኩሳን፡ እለ፡ ኢይጸግቡ፡ ወይትጐሐለዉ፡ በፍቅሮሙ፡ ወይትሜክሑ፡ ለቢጻሙ፡ ከመ፡ ዘሠናይ፡ ምግባሮሙ።

¹⁴ወምሉእ፡ ውስተ፡ አዕይንቲሆሙ፡ ዝሙት፡ ወንጢአት፡ እንተ፡ አልባቲ፡ ዘገበግሃ። ወይደነግፁ፡ ነፍሰ፡ ሰብእ፡ እለ፡ ስጡሕ፡ ልቦሙ፡ ወትዕግልት፡ ምግባሮሙ፡ ወየንድጉ፡ መርገም፡ ለውሉዶሙ።

¹⁵ወስሕትዋ፡ ለፍኖተ፡ ጽድቅ፡ ወተለውዋ፡ ለፍኖተ፡ በለዓም፡ ወልደ፡ ባዕር፡ ዘአፍቀራ፡ ለዕሴበ፡ ዐመፃ።

¹⁶ወተዛለፎ፡ ለበለዓም፡ በንጢአቱ፡ ዘኢይነብብ፡ አድግ፡ በቃለ፡ እጓለ፡ እመሕያው፡ ተናገረ፡ ወከልአ፡ ለነቢይ፡ አበዲሁ።

G Verbs with III Guttural Roots 211

Chapter 30

G I-ወ ROOT VERBS: THE REMAINING MOODS

30.1 I-ወ Root Verbs

In this chapter we will examine the remaining forms of the G I-ወ verbs, e.g., ወፈረ፡ – "be ashamed of." These forms include the imperfect, subjunctive, imperative, and infinitive. Due to the presence of the ወ in the first position, on occasion the subjunctive and imperative forms (and at times the verbal noun) can drop the I-ወ from the conjugated verb.[1] The I-ወ verbs for the imperfect follow this consonant/vowel pattern: ይ+C_1ăC_2əC_3, ይፈፍር፡ – "he will go to the country." The subjunctive follows two possible patterns ይ+C_1əC_2əC_3, ይውፍር፡, or ይ+C_2ăC_3, ይፈር፡ – "he may go to the country."[2] The imperative also follows two possible patterns C_1əC_2əC_3, ውፍር፡, or C_2ăC_3, ፈር፡ – "(you) go to the country!" The table below offers some examples of the I-ወ verbs:

TABLE 30.1: I-ወ Root Verbs

Perfect	Imperfect	Subjunctive	Imperative	Infinitive
ወረደ፡	ይወርድ፡	ይረድ፡	ረድ፡	ወሪድ፡
ወድቀ፡	ይወድቅ፡	ይደቅ፡	ደቅ፡	ወዲቅ፡
ወህበ፡	ይሁብ፡	የሀብ፡	ሀብ	ወሂብ፡
ወሰደ፡	ይወስድ፡	ይሰድ፡ / ይስድ፡ / ይውስድ፡	ሰድ፡ / ስድ፡	ወሲድ፡
ወለደ፡	ይወልድ፡	ይለድ፡	ለድ፡	ወሊድ፡
ወፅአ፡	ይወፅእ፡	ይፃእ፡	ፃእ፡	ወፂእ፡
ወገረ፡	ይመግር፡	ይገር፡ / ይውግር፡	ገር፡ / ግር፡ / ውግር፡	ወጊር፡
ወጠነ፡	ይወጥን፡	ይጠን፡ / ይውጥን፡	ውጥን፡	ወጢን፡
ውሕዘ፡	ይውሕዝ፡	የሐዝ፡ / ይውሕዝ፡	-	ወሒዝ፡

---

1. The presence of the Hebrew ו as the first consonant in a verb root is virtually nonexistent, but it has survived in Gəʿəz in the form of the ወ.
2. One should be aware that there are verbs that have three possible subjunctive forms, and also that there are verbs that have irregular imperfect forms that do not follow the patterns described above.

Students should notice that even in the perfect of the verbs the pattern varies from those presented in 30.1. In some cases, the verb has three *ă* vowels, while others shorten the II consonant vowel to a terminal *ə* vowel, for example, ወድቀ፡, ወፅአ፡, and still others may shorten both the I and II consonant vowels due to the gutturals, as in ውሕዘ፡. Unlike Hebrew, where the weak verbs are fairly standard in their inflections as far as vowel changes are concerned, in Gəʿəz weak verbs have some variations and these need to be recognized by the reader. One can also see similar vowel and consonant variations in the other verb moods.

TABLE 30.2: Perfect I-ወ Root Verb Paradigm (ወረደ፡ – "descend")

PGN	Perfect Forms	PGN	Perfect Forms
3ms	ወረደ፡	3mp	ወረዱ፡
3fs	ወረደት፡	3fp	ወረዳ፡
2ms	ወረድከ፡	2mp	ወረድከሙ፡
2fs	ወረድኪ፡	2fp	ወረድከን፡
1cs	ወረድኩ፡	1cp	ወረድነ፡

Note: The perfect I-ወ verbs conform to the regular declension pattern of the strong verb (for the most part). The variations come primarily in the other moods, which will be demonstrated in the tables to follow.

TABLE 30.2: Imperfect I-ወ Root Verb Paradigm

PGN	Imperfect Forms	PGN	Imperfect Forms
3ms	ይወርድ፡	3mp	ይወርዱ፡
3fs	ትወርድ፡	3fp	ይወርዳ፡
2ms	ትወርድ፡	2mp	ትወርዱ፡
2fs	ትወርዲ፡	2fp	ትወርዳ፡
1cs	እወርድ፡	1cp	ንወርድ፡

Note: The imperfect I-ወ verbs conform to the regular declension pattern of the strong verb.

TABLE 30.3: Subjunctive I-ወ Root Verb Paradigm

PGN	Subjunctive Forms Strong / Weak	PGN	Subjunctive Forms Strong / Weak
3ms	ይውግር፡ / ይግር፡	3mp	ይውግሩ፡ / ይግሩ፡
3fs	ትውግር፡ / ትግር፡	3fp	ይውግራ፡ / ይግራ፡
2ms	ትውግር፡ / ትግር፡	2mp	ትውግሩ፡ / ትግሩ፡
2fs	ትውግሪ፡ / ትግሪ፡	2fp	ትውግራ፡ / ትግራ፡
1cs	እውግር፡ / እግር፡	1cp	ንውግር፡ / ንግር፡

Note: as mentioned above the subjunctive has the most variations of the moods for I-ወ verbs. There is what is referred to as a strong pattern and a weak pattern in which the I-ወ drops out of the verb forms in the paradigm. Unfortunately, there is no obvious reason for a verb to form one way or the other, in fact, some verbs will form both ways (see e.g., ወገረ፡ – "throw, stone").

TABLE 30.4: Imperative I-ወ Root Verb Paradigm (ወረደ፡)

PGN	Imperative Forms	PGN	Imperative Forms
2ms	ሪድ፡	2mp	ሪዱ፡
2fs	ሪዲ፡	2fp	ሪዳ፡

a. Note with the imperative I-ወ verbs that the ወ is lost in the declension, but note there are exceptions to this feature with verbs such as ውፍር፡.[3]

b. The infinitive form of the paradigm verb ወረደ፡ appears as ወሪድ፡ (Note the *i* stem vowel following the second radical): – "to descend."

30.2 Causative I-ወ Root Verb (ወፈረ፡ – "Go into the Country")

Note the slight vowel changes on the I-ወ root in the perfect, imperfect, and subjunctive forms, while in the imperative and infinitive forms the causative አ drops off and the ው shifts to a ወ.

TABLE 30.5: Causative I-ወ Root Verb

	Simple Causative Action	Intensive Causative Action
Perfect	አውፈረ፡	አወፈረ፡
Imperfect	ያወፍር፡	ያዌፍር፡
Subjunctive	ያውፍር፡	ያወፍር፡
Imperative	አውፍር፡	ወፍር፡
Infinitive	አውፈር፡	ወፈር፡

30.3 Reflexive I-ወ Root Verb

Note the typical addition of the ይ to the I-ወ root in the imperfect and subjunctive forms, while in the perfect, imperative, and infinitive forms the reflexive ተ appears without the ይ. The other recognizable change is the vowel change on the I-ወ root that shifts from the ወ to a ዌ in the Dt imperfect form. Like its Hebrew counterpart, this voice can be reciprocal action between two subjects depending on the meaning of the verb.

TABLE 30.6: Reflexive I-ወ Root Verb

	Simple Reflexive Action	Intensive Reflexive Action
Perfect	ተወፍረ፡	ተወፈረ፡
Imperfect	ይትወፈር፡	ይትዌፈር፡
Subjunctive	ይትወፈር፡	ይትወፈር፡
Imperative	ተወፈር፡	ተወፈር፡
Infinitive	ተወፈር፡	ተወፈር፡

---

3. See Samuel A. B. Mercer, *Ethiopic Grammar with Chrestomathy and Glossary* (Oxford: Clarendon, 1920), 50.

30.4 Causative-Reflexive I-ω Root Verb

The causative-reflexive verb form appears peculiar to Ethiopic, but there may be some similarity to a stem in Arabic. However, it may be possible that it is related to the Hebrew Hishtaphel stem, which is related to the Hithpael stem, which is a reflexive stem. However, because the *Hishtaphel* occurs only with the verb חוה, it is difficult to make this determination. Note the typical addition of ይ to the I-ω root in the imperfect and subjunctive forms, while in the perfect, imperative, and infinitive forms the reflexive ተ appears with another prefix, አስ. The other recognizable change is the vowel change on the I-ω root that shifts from the ω to a ዌ in the Dt imperfect form.

TABLE 30.6: Causative-Reflexive I-ω Root Verb

	Simple Causative-Reflexive Action	Intensive Causative-Reflexive Action
Perfect	አስተውፈረ፡	አስተወረረ፡
Imperfect	ያስተወፍር፡	ያስተዌፍር፡
Subjunctive	ያስተውፍር፡	ያስተወፍር፡
Imperative	አስተውፍር፡	አስተወፍር፡
Infinitive	አስተውፈር፡	አስተወፈር፡

30.5 I-ω Root Verbal Adjectives in the ቅቱል፡ Pattern[4]

A verbal adjective is generally the equivalent of a passive participle. It has both verbal and adjectival characteristics. A verbal adjective can modify a noun, but it can also act as an adverb as will be seen in the examples below:

ውዱቅ፡ – fallen, lying fallen

ውሉድ፡ – sons, boys, plural of ወልድ፡

ውፁእ፡ – departing, emerging from, lacking in, alien to

30.6 I-ω Root Verbal Nouns[5]

The verbal noun, although derived from a verb, has no verbal characteristics. It functions as the present participle with the "-ing" added, such as "a liturgical *reading* of Scripture is held in the church every day." *Reading* is a noun acting like a verb. See the frequent verbal nouns below:

ርደት፡ – descent

ድቀት፡ – ruin, collapse

ልደት፡ – birth

ፀአት፡ – exit, departure

ሀብት፡ – gift

መግር፡ (pl. አውግር፡) – mound, hill

ውሒዝ፡ (pl. ውሒዛት፡, ውሒይዝት፡) – river, stream

ውሕዘት፡ – flow, flowing

---

4. See ch. 24.
5. See ch. 25.

30.7 I-ወ Root Agent Nouns from ቀታሊ፡[6]

ወላዲ፡ – parent
ወሃቢ፡ – donor or giver; adj. generous

30.8 I-ወ Root Nouns with Prefixed ም (with Various Vowels)

ሙራድ፡ (for ምውራድ፡) – place of descent
ሙላድ፡ – place of birth
ሙፃእ፡ – place of exit, source of
ሙጣዘ፡ ማይ፡፡ – aqueduct
ምገርት፡ – sling shot

30.9 Vocabulary

1. ትውልድ፡ (pl. ትውልዳት፡) – generation, offspring
2. ዐውድ፡ (pl. አዕዋድ፡) – neighborhood, vicinity
3. ዳቤላ፡ (pl. ዳቤላት፡) – male animal
4. ሐራ፡ – army, soldiers
5. ወረቀ፡ (subj. ይውርቅ፡) – spit
6. ምራቅ፡ – saliva, spit
7. አውተረ፡ CG – continue, persevere
8. ወትረ፡ adv. – continuously, always
9. ወረሰ፡ (subj. ይረስ፡) – inherit; አውረሰ፡ CG – make someone an heir; ተዋረሰ፡ Glt – gain possession of; ተወርሰ፡ Gt – gain by inheritance
10. ወራሲ፡ Gt heir
11. ርስት፡ Gt inheritance
12. ሰዐመ፡ (subj. ይስዐም፡) – kiss; ተስዕመ፡ Gt – be kissed; ተሳዐመ፡ Glt – kiss one another
13. ስዕመት፡ – a kiss
14. ረሰየ፡ D – put, set, or place; regard something

30.10 Exercises

A. Translate the following:

1. ዛቲ፡ ምድር፡ ምልእተ፡ አውግር፡ ይአቲ፡፡

---
6. See ch. 23.

2. ወደየ፡ ፍሮ፡ ወጎብስተ፡ ውስተ፡ ምጎባእ።

3. ኢይወርድ፡ ዝናም፡ በጊዜሁ።

4. ናሁ፡ አንቲ፡ ትወልዲ፡ ወልደ።

5. ሰአልናሁ፡ ከመ፡ የሀበነ፡ ማየ።

6. ተአዘዘ፡ ለወላድያሁ፡ ወነሥአ፡ ሎቱ፡ ብእሲተ።

7. ወገረ፡ እብነ፡ በሞገርቱ፡ ወቀተለ፡ እኅሁ።

8. ረከብዎ፡ ውስተ፡ ሙራደ፡ ደብር።

9. ይወድቅ፡ ዝንቱ፡ ቤት፡ ወኢየሐንጽዎ፡ ዳግመ።

10. እወግሮ፡ ውስተ፡ ምንዳድ።

11. መፍትው፡ ከመ፡ ንስዶ፡ ኃበ፡ መኮንን።

12. ጥቀ፡ እኩይ፡ ውእቱ፡ ዝንቱ፡ ትውልድ።

13. ኢኮኑሙ፡ ማኅደረ፡ እምድኅረ፡ ድቀተ፡ ቤቶሙ።

14. ሐነጹ፡ ሙሓዘ፡ ማይ፡ ነዋኀ፡ እምአድባር፡ እስከ፡ ሀገር።

15. እሁብክሙ፡ ወርቀ፡ ወብሩረ።

G I-ወ Root Verbs: The Remaining Moods 217

16. ትሁቡኒኒ፡ ኅብስተ።
    _____

17. ገሮ፡ ህየ፡ ወኢተሀቡ፡ ወኢምንተኒ፡ እምሲሳይ።
    _____

18. ሰድዎ፡ ኀቤየ፡ ከመ፡ እንግሮ።
    _____

19. መኑ፡ ወሀበከ፡ ዘከመዝ፡ ሀብተ፡ ክቡረ።
    _____

20. ትወስድ፡ ዘንተ፡ ዳቤላ፡ ኀበ፡ ዐጸድየ።
    _____

21. ኢትረድ፡ ኀበ፡ ሐይቅ።
    _____

22. ለንርከቦሙ፡ እምቅድም፡ ይውጥኑ፡ ይጽብኡ።
    _____

23. ነሀብከሙ፡ አልባሰ።
    _____

24. ረከብት፡ ምታ፡ ውዱቀ፡ ምዉተ፡ ውስተ፡ ፍኖት።
    _____

25. እወፅእ፡ እምሀገር፡ በጽባሕ።
    _____

26. ንበሪ፡ ዝየ፡ ከመ፡ ኢትደቁ።
    _____

27. ፈቀደት፡ ትግባእ፡ ቤታ፡ እምቅድም፡ ትለድ፡ ወልዳ።
    _____

B. Psalm 45:1–12. Translate the following.

ፍጻሜ፡ ዘደቂቀ፡ ቆሬ፡ በእንተ፡ ኀቡኣት፡ መዝሙር፡ ዘዳዊት።

[1]አምላክነ፡ ኀይልነ፡ ወጸወንነ፣ ወረዳኢነ፡ ውእቱ፡ በምንዳቤነ፡ ዘረከበነ፡ ፈድፋደ።

²በእንተዝ፡ ኢንፈርህ፡ ለእመ፡ አድለቅለቀት፡ ምድር። ወእመኒ፡ ፈለሱ፡ አድባር፡ ውስተ፡ ልበ፡ ባሕር።

³ደምፁ፡ ወተሐምጉ፡ ማያቲሆሙ፣ ወአድለቅለቁ፡ አድባር፡ እምኃይሉ።

⁴ፈለገ፡ ዘይዉሕዝ፡ ያስተፌሥሕ፡ ሀገረ፡ እግዚአብሔር፡ ቀደሰ፡ ማኀደሮ፡ ልዑል።

⁵እግዚአብሔር፡ ውስተ፡ ማእከላ፡ ኢትትሀወክ፤ ወይረድአ፡ እግዚአብሔር፡ ፍጽመ።

⁶ደንገፁ፡ አሕዛብ፡ ወተመይጡ፡ ነገሥት፣ ወወሀበ፡ ቃሎ፡ ልዑል፡ ወአድለቅለቀት፡ ምድር።

⁷እግዚአ፡ ኃያላን፡ ምስሌነ፣ ወምስካይነ፡ አምላኩ፡ ለያዕቆብ።

⁸ንዑ፡ ወትርአዩ፡ ገብሮ፡ ለእግዚአብሔር፣ ዘገብረ፡ መንክረ፡ በዲበ፡ ምድር።

⁹ይሰዕር፡ ፀብአ፡ እስከ፡ አጽናፈ፡ ምድር፣ ይሰብር፡ ቀስተ፡ ወይቀጠቅጥ፡ ወልታ፡ ወያውዒ፡ በእሳት፡ ንዋየ፡ ሓቅል።

¹⁰አስተርክቡ፡ ወአእምሩ፡ ከመ፡ አነ፡ ውእቱ፡ እግዚአብሔር፡ ተለዐልኩ፡ እምአሕዛብ፡ ወተለዐልኩ፡ እምድር።

¹¹እግዚአ፡ ኃያላን፡ ምስሌነ፣ ወምስካይነ፡ አምላኩ፡ ለያዕቆብ።

C. Psalm 1:1–6. Translate the following:

ፍከሬ፡ ዘጻድቃን፡ ወዘኃጣን፣ መዝሙር፡ ዘዳዊት፡ ሃሌሉያ።

¹ብፁዕ፡ ብእሲ፡ ዘኢሐረ፡ በምክረ፡ ረሲዓን፣ ወኢቆመ፡ ውስተ፡ ፍኖተ፡ ኃጥአን፣ ወዘኢነበረ፡ ውስተ፡ መንበረ፡ መስተሳልቃን።

²ዘዳእሙ፡ ሕገ፡ እግዚአብሔር፡ ሥምረቱ፣ ወዘሕገ፡ ያነብብ፡ መዓልተ፡ ወሌሊተ።

³ወየከውን፡ ከመ፡ ዕፅ፡ እንተ፡ ትክልት፡ ኀበ፡ ሙሓዘ፡ ማይ፣ እንተ፡ ትወህብ፡ ፍሬሃ፡ በጊዜሃ፣ ወቁጽላኒ፡ ኢይትነገፍ፣ ወኩሎ፡ ዘገብረ፡ ይፌጽም።

⁴አኮ፡ ከመዝ፡ ኃጥኣንሰ፡ አኮ፡ ከመዝ፡ ዳእሙ፡ ከመ፡ መሬት፡ ዘይሕፍዮ፡ ነፋስ፡ እምገጸ፡ ምድር።

⁵ወበእንተዝ፡ ኢይትነሥኡ፡ ረሲዓን፡ እምደይን፣ ወኢኃጥኣን፡ ውስተ፡ ምክረ፡ ጻድቃን።

⁶እስመ፡ ያአምር፡ እግዚአብሔር፡ ፍኖቶሙ፡ ለጻድቃን፣ ወፍኖቶሙ፡ ለኃጥኣን፡ ትጠፍእ።

Chapter 31

G II-ወ/የ ROOT VERBS: THE REMAINING MOODS

31.1 II-ወ/የ Root Verbs

In this chapter we will examine the remaining forms of the II-ወ/የ verbs, e.g., ቀወመ፡ / ቆመ፡ – "stand, rise up" and ሠየመ፡ / ሤመ፡ – "set, put in order."[1] These forms include the imperfect, subjunctive, imperative, and infinitive. You will notice below in the paradigm tables the middle ወ/የ will drop out in the perfect, subjunctive, and imperative; it remains in the imperfect and the infinitive forms. The consonant/vowel pattern for perfect verbs is as follows: $C_1oC_3ă$, ቆመ፡ – "he rose up"; the consonant/vowel pattern for the imperfect follows $ይ+C_1ăC_2əC_3$, ይቀውም፡ – "he will rise up." The consonant/vowel pattern for the subjunctive follows $ይ+C_1uC_3$, ይቁም፡ – "may he rise up." The consonant/vowel pattern for the imperative follows C_1uC_3, ቁም፡ – "(you) rise up!" Finally, the consonant/vowel pattern for the infinitive follows $C_1ăC_2iC_3$ (ቀዊም፡) – "to rise up." The II-የ roots behave similarly with the የ dropping out and the stem including the $ē$ vowel in the perfect. With the imperfect, the II-የ remains with the short $ə$ vowel. With the subjunctive and imperative, the II-የ drops out and the I consonant takes on an i vowel.

The table below offers some examples of the II-ወ/የ verbs:

TABLE 31.1: II-ወ/የ Root Verbs

PGN	Perfect ነወመ፡ / ሠየመ፡	Imperfect	Subjunctive	Imperative
3ms	ኖመ፡ / ሤመ፡	ይነውም፡ / ይሠይም፡	ይኑም፡ / ይሢም፡	—
3fs	ኖመት፡ / ሤመት፡	ትነውም፡ / ትሠይም፡	ትኑም፡ / ትሢም፡	—
2ms	ኖምከ፡ / ሠምከ፡	ትነውም፡ / ትሠይም፡	ትኑም፡ / ትሢም፡	ኑም፡ / ሢም፡
2fs	ኖምኪ፡ / ሤምኪ፡	ትነውሚ፡ / ትሠይሚ፡	ትኑሚ፡ / ትሢሚ፡	ኑሚ፡ / ሢሚ፡
1cs	ኖምኩ፡ / ሤምኩ	እነውም፡ / እሠይም፡	እኑም፡ / እሢም፡	—
3mp	ኖሙ፡ / ሤሙ፡	ይነውሙ፡ / ይሠይሙ፡	ይኑሙ፡ / ይሢሙ፡	—

---

1. Note: the inflection of these verbs is similar to Hebrew perfect verbs with middle ו and י.

PGN	Perfect ነወሙ፡ / ሠየሙ፡	Imperfect	Subjunctive	Imperative
3fp	ኖማ፡ / ሤማ፡	ይነውማ፡ / ይሠይማ፡	ይኑማ፡ / ይሢማ	—
2mp	ኖምክሙ፡ / ሤምክሙ፡	ትነውሙ፡ / ትሠይሙ፡	ትኑሙ፡ / ትሢሙ፡	ኑሙ፡ / ሢሙ፡
2fp	ሤማክን፡ / ሤምክን፡	ትነውማ፡ / ትሠይማ፡	ትኑማ፡ / ትሢማ፡	ኑማ፡ / ሢማ፡
1cp	ኖምነ፡ / ሤምነ፡	ንነውም፡ / ንሠይም፡	ንኑም፡ / ንሢም፡	—

a. In the perfect II-ω, the preceding vowel with the first consonant shifts from *ă* to *o*, while the preceding vowel in the II-የ verbs shifts from *ă* to *ē*.

b. In the imperfect II-ω/የ, note the II-ω and II-የ are retained but shift from the *ă* to the *ə* vowel.

c. In the subjunctive II-ω, the II-ω is dropped and the preceding first consonant vowel shifts from *ă* to *u*, while the preceding vowel in the II-የ verbs, which is also dropped, shifts from *ă* to *i*.

d. In the imperative forms, the vowel shift and loss of the ω/የ follow the subjunctive forms.

e. The infinitive form of the II-ω/የ root verbs ነወሙ፡ / ሠየሙ፡ appear as follows: ነዊም፡ / ሠዪም፡.

31.2 Alternate Forms for II-ω

There are a few verbs in Gəʿəz that appear with an *o* vowel rather than the *u* vowel in the subjunctive and imperative forms.

Perfect	Translation	Imperfect	Subjunctive	Imperative
ሐረ፡	"go, go forth"	የሐውር፡	ይሕር፡ / ይሑር፡	ሐር፡ / ሑር፡
ጾረ፡	"bear, carry"	ይጸውር፡	ይጽር፡ / ይጹር፡	ጾር፡ / ጹር፡

Two verbs at times retain the *ā* vowel in the subjunctive and imperative forms:

Perfect	Translation	Imperfect	Subjunctive	Imperative
ቦአ፡	"enter, penetrate"	ይበውእ፡	ይባእ፡	ባእ፡
ሞአ፡	"conquer"	ይመውእ	ይማእ፡ / ይሙእ፡	ማእ፡

Generally, the *ā* is present through the entire inflection rather than shifting to the *ə*: ይባእ፡ ትባእ፡ ትባእ፡ ትባኢ፡ እባእ፡ ይባኡ፡ ይባእ፡, etc.

A significant number of these II-ω/የ root type verbs exist in Gəʿəz and should be committed to memory: ሐረ፡ ቦአ፡ ሞአ፡ ሞተ፡ ሮጸ፡ ኮነ፡ ቆመ፡ ሠውዐ፡ (Subj. ይሡዕ፡) ኖኀ፡ ዖደ፡ ሤጠ፡ ሤመ፡ ሜጠ፡

31.3 II-ወ/የ Root Verbal Adjectives in ቅቱል:[2]

A verbal adjective is generally the equivalent of a passive participle. It has both verbal and adjectival characteristics. A verbal adjective can modify a noun, but it can also act as an adverb when it is in the accusative or when the adjective is prefixed with the preposition በ.

በፍጡን: = ፍጡነ: – quickly, swiftly, soon
በክሡት: = ክሡተ: – openly, publicly

31.4 II-ወ/የ Root Verbal Nouns[3]

The verbal noun, although derived from a verb, has no verbal characteristics. It functions as the present participle with the "-ing" added, such as "a liturgical *reading* of Scripture is held in the church every day." *Reading* is a noun acting like a verb. See the frequent verbal nouns below:

ሑረት: (pl. ሑረታት:) – going, manner of going
ሕዋር: (pl. ሕዋረት:) – ambulatory, porch
በአት: (pl. በአታት:) – entry, cave, den, cell
ሙዉት: – victory, defeat of others
ቆም: – height, stature
ቄመት: – nature, state, condition
ኑኅ: – length of time
ዑደት: – circle, orbit
ሤጥ: – price, value
ሢመት: (pl. ሢመታት:) – ordination, office, position
ሚጠት: – a turning to or from, change, mutation

31.5 II-ወ/የ Root Agent Nouns from ቀታሊ:[4]

You will see below that the norm for nouns from the II-ወ/የ root is to retain the ወ/የ rather than losing it as the case with most of the verb forms.

መዋኢ: – victorious
ረዋጺ: – running, swift
መዋኢቲ: – mortal
ቃዋሚ: – standing, stable, patron
ሠዋዒ: (pl. ሠዋዕት:) – sacrificer, priest

---

2. See ch. 24.
3. See ch. 25.
4. See ch. 23.

ዐዋዲ፡ – messenger, preacher

ሠያጢ፡ (pl. ሠየጥ፡) – seller, merchant

31.6 Other Nouns of Note

ቀዋም፡ – tall, erect

ማውታ፡ – corpse

እጓለ፡ ማውታ፡። – orphan

31.7 II-ወ/የ Root Nouns in the Pattern of ምቅታል፡

ምሕዋር፡ (pl. ምሕዋራት፡) – distance traveled in a given time

ምብዋእ፡ / ሙባእ፡ (pl. መባውእ፡ / ሙብዋእት፡) – place of entry, act of entering

ምርዋጽ፡ – distance run, race

ምቅዋም፡ / ምቋም፡ (pl. ምቅዋማት፡ / ምቋማት፡) – location where one stops or stands; ምቋመ፡ ማይ፡። – pool

ምሥያጥ፡ (pl. ምሥያጣት፡) – marketplace forum

ምሥዋዕ፡ – altar

31.8 Vocabulary

1. ኮከብ፡ (pl. ከዋክብት፡) – star
2. ኮከበ፡ ጽባሕ፡። – morning star
3. ፈረስ፡ (pl. አፍራስ፡) – horse
4. ጸመ፡ (subj. ይጹም፡) – fast (as in eating)
5. ጽዉም፡ adj. – fasting
6. ጾም፡ (pl. አጽዋም፡) – a fast, fasting
7. ኖመ፡ (subj. ይኑም፡) – sleep; አኖመ፡ / አነመ፡ CG – put to sleep
8. ንዋም፡ – sleep
9. ጾረ፡ (subj. ይጾር፡ / ይጹር፡) – carry or bear; አጸረ፡ / አጾረ፡ CG – make carry; ተጸውረ፡ Gt – be carried
10. ጽዉር፡ – bearing, burdened
11. ጾር፡ (pl. አጽዋር፡) – burden
12. ጸዋር፡ – carrier, porter
13. ጸዋሪ፡ (pl. ጸወርት፡) – one who carries or bears
14. ዓቀ፡ (subj. ይዕቅ፡) – take care for, be aware of; አዓቀ፡ CG – make known; ተዐውቀ፡ Gt – be noticed, perceived, revealed
15. ዕዉቅ፡ – familiar, well-known
16. አውሥአ፡ CG – respond, answer; ተዋጽአ፡ Glt – speak against, contradict
17. ሣእሣእ፡ – refined speech
18. ኵነነ፡ D – judge, punish; አኵነነ፡ CD – put someone in charge; ተኵነነ፡ Dt – be put in charge; Glt, ተካነነ፡ – become reconciled with

19. አፍአ፡ / አፍኣ፡ adv. – outside
20. ሶቤሃ፡ adv. – immediately, then

31.9 Exercises

A. Translate the following:

1. ዝንቱ፡ መካን፡ ጥቀ፡ ዕዉቅ፡ ውእቱ፡ በኩላ፡ ምድር።

   _____

2. ጸወርተ፡ ሕግ፡ ወዐቀብተ፡ ሃይማኖት፡ ርትዕት፡ ንሕነ።

   _____

3. ኢኪሁለ፡ ተኳንኖ፡ ምስለ፡ አንዊሁ፡ መላህቅት።

   _____

4. ተኵኒናሙ፡ ተወግሩ፡ ውስተ፡ ቤተ፡ ሞቅሕ።

   _____

5. ወሶበ፡ ተዐወቀ፡ ምክሩ፡ ተመየጥኩ፡ ላዕሌሁ፡ ወቀተልክዎ።

   _____

6. ወአምድኀረ፡ ንዋም፡ ነዋ፡ ተፈወሰ፡ እምሕማሙ።

   _____

7. ሰክብ፡ ወኑም፡ ከመ፡ ኢትኩን፡ ድኩም፡ በጽባሕ።

   _____

8. ረከብዎ፡ ለቅዱስ፡ ይነውም፡ ውስተ፡ በአቱ።

   _____

9. ዑቂ፡ ከመ፡ ኢትቅረቢ፡ ኀቤሁ፡ ዘእንበለ፡ ትእዛዙ።

   _____

10. አዘዘሙ፡ ለጸዋሪሁ፡ ይጹሩ፡ ንዋየ፡ ቤቱ፡ ወይገርዎ፡ አፍአ፡ እምሀገር።

    _____

11. ወአውሥአ፡ እንዘ፡ ይብል፡ አነ፡ ኢይክሥት፡ ለከሙ፡ ዘትፈቅዱ።

    _____

12. ዑቁ፡ ከመ፡ ኢይስምዑክሙ፡ እንዘ፡ ትነግሩ፡ ቃላተ፡ ዘከመዝ።

13. ሠምረት፡ በጥበቡ፡ ወበሃእሣአ፡ ንባቡ።

14. ነዋኅ፡ ቆም፡ ወሠናየ፡ ገጽ፡ ውእቱ።

15. ወሶበ፡ ኮነዎ፣ አውፅአዎ፡ አፍአ፡ እምሀገር፡ ወአመትዎ።

16. እሎንቱ፡ እሙንቱ፡ ጸባእት፡ እምሐራሁ፡ ለመኰንን፡ ዘአኮነኖ፡ ንጉሥ፡ ላዕሌነ።

17. ሶበ፡ አያቀነ፡ ምክሮ፣ ተነበነ፡ ምስሌሁ፡ ከመ፡ ንርድአ።

18. አኖም፡ እግዚአብሔር፡ ከመ፡ ይግበር፡ ብእሲተ፡ እምሥጋሁ።

19. ኢይክሉ፡ ጸዊማነሆሙ፡ ለአግልፎ፡ ዝንቱ፡ ኀሳር።

20. ለምንት፡ አጸርከኒ፡ ዘንተ፡ ዐቢየ፡ ጾረ፣ ወአነ፡ ንኡስ፡ ወድኩም።

21. ኢንክል፡ ሐይወ፡ በሰላም፡ እንዘ፡ ጸዋራነ፡ ኃጢአት።

22. ወረዱ፡ መላእክት፡ እምውስተ፡ ሰማይ፡ እንዘ፡ ይጸውሩ፡ እሳተ፡ በደዊሆሙ።

23. ጾር፡ ዘንተ፡ ወርቀ፡ በኀቡእ፡ ወዑቅ፡ ከመ፡ ኢይርከቡ፡ ወኢመኑሄ።

B. Isaiah 53:1–12. Translate the following:

¹እግዚኦ፡ መኑ፡ አምነነ፡ ቃለነ፣ ወለመኑ፡ ተከሥተ፡ መዝራዕቱ፡ ለእግዚአብሔር፤

²ወነገርነኒ፡ ከመ፡ ሕፀን፡ በቅድሜሁ፡ ወከመ፡ ሥርው፡ በውስተ፡ ምድር፡ ጽምእት፤ አልቦ፡ ራእዮ፡ ወኢትርሲተ፡ ርኣናሁ፡ አልቦ፡ ራእዮ፡ ወአልቦ፡ ላሕዩ።

³ወራእዮሂ፡ ምኑን፡ ወትሑት፡ እምኵሉ፡ ሰብእ፣ ብእሲ፡ ቅሡፍ፡ ውእቱ፡ ወሕሙም፣ እስመ፡ ሜጠ፡ ገጾ፡ ወአስተሐቀርዎ፡ ወኢሐሰብዎ።

⁴ወእቱስ፡ ነሥአ፡ ደዌነ፡ ወጾረ፡ ሕማመነ፡ ወበእንቲአነ፡ ሐመ፡ ወንሕነሂ፡ ርኢናሁ፡ ሕሙመ፡ ወቅሡፈ፡ በሕማም።

⁵ወእቱስ፡ ቈስለ፡ በእንተ፡ ኃጢአትነ፡ ወሐመ፡ በእንተ፡ ጌጋይነ፡ ትእምርተ፡ ሰላምነ፡ ወበቍስለ፡ ዚአሁ፡ ሐየውነ።

⁶ኵልነ፡ ከመ፡ አባግዕ፡ ተገደፍነ፣ ብእሲኒ፡ ዘዘዚአሁ፡ ሐረ፡ በፍኖቱ፡ ወስሕተ፡ ወመጠዎ፡ እግዚአብሔር፡ በእንተ፡ ኃጢአትነ።

⁷ወውእቱስ፡ ኢከሠተ፡ አፉሁ፡ በሕማሙ፡ ወመጽአ፡ ይጠባሕ፡ ከመ፡ በግዕ፤ ወከመ፡ በግዕ፡ ዘኢይነብብ፡ በቅድመ፡ ዘይቀርፆ፡ ከማሁ፡ ኢከሠተ፡ አፉሁ፡ በሕማሙ።

⁸እስመ፡ ይኔሥእዎ፡ ለፍትሑ፣ መኑ፡ ይነግር፡ ልደቶ፡ እስመ፡ ተአተተ፡ እምድር፡ ሕይወቱ፡ በኃጢአተ፡ ሕዝብየ፡ በጽሑ፡ ለሞት።

⁹ወእሁብ፡ እኩያነ፡ ህየንተ፡ ሞቱ፣ ወአብዕልተ፡ ህየንተ፡ መቅበርቱ፣ እስመ፡ ኢገብረ፡ ኃጢአተ፡ ወኢተረክበ፡ ሐሰት፡ ውስተ፡ አፉሁ።

¹⁰ወፈቀደ፡ እግዚአብሔር፡ ያንጽሖ፡ እምነ፡ መቅሠፍቱ፤ ወእመኒ፡ ወሀብክሙ፡ በእንተ፡ ኃጢአትክሙ፡ ትሬኢ፡ ነፍስክሙ፡ ዘርአ፡ ዘነዋኅ፡ የሐዩ።

¹¹ወይፈቅድ፡ ያእትት፡ ሕማመ፡ እምነፍሱ፡ ወያእዮ፡ ብርሃነ፡ ወይፍልጦ፡ በጥበቡ፡ ወያጸድቅ፡ ለጻድቅ፡ ለዘይትቀነዩ፡ ለጽድቅ፡ ወለሠናይ፡ ወለብዙኃን፡ ኃጢአቶሙ፡ ውእቱ፡ ይደመስሱ።

¹²ወበእንተዝ፡ ውእቱ፡ ይወርሳሙ፡ ለእስራኤል፡ ይመታርከሙ፡ ለጽኑዓን፡ እስመ፡ ተውህበት፡ ለሞት፡ ነፍሱ፣ ወተኍለቈ፡ ለብዙኃን፣ ወበእንተ፡ ኃጢአቶሙ፡ ተውህበ፡ ውእቱ።

Chapter 32

G VERBS FROM III-ወ/ይ ROOTS: THE REMAINING MOODS

32.1 III-ወ/ይ Root Verbs

In this chapter (review ch. 10 for perfect guttural verbs) we will examine the remaining forms of the III-ወ/ይ verbs (e.g., በከየ፡ – "weep" and አተወ፡ – "return home"). These forms include the imperfect, subjunctive, imperative, and infinitive. It should be noted the III-ይ verbs far outnumber the III-ወ verbs (see the list below). These verbs follow the consonant and vowel patterns found with the ይቀትል፡, ይ+C₁ăC₂əC₃[ə]; ይቅትል፡, ይ+C₁C₂əC₃[ə]; ይቅትል፡, ይ+C₁C₂ăC₃[ə]; ቅትል፡, C₁əC₂əC₃[ə]; ቅተል፡, C₁əC₂ăC₃[ə]. In the final syllable of the verb, the normal -əይ and -əዉ are normally displaced by the -i or -u when there is no ending added that begins with a vowel.

TABLE 32.1: III-ወ Root Verb Paradigm (See ch. 10 for G III Gutturals)

PGN	Perfect "follow"	Imperfect	Subjunctive	Imperative
3ms	ተለወ፡	ይትሉ፡	ይትሉ፡	—
3fs	ተለወት፡	ትትሉ፡	ትትሉ፡	—
2ms	ተለውከ፡ / ተሎከ፡	ትትሉ፡	ትትሉ፡	ትሉ፡
2fs	ተለውኪ፡ / ተሎኪ፡	ትትልዊ፡	ትትልዊ፡	ትልዊ፡
1cs	ተለውኩ፡ / ተሎኩ፡	እትሉ፡	እትሉ፡	—
3mp	ተለዉ፡	ይትልዉ፡	ይትልዉ፡	—
3fp	ተለዋ፡	ይትልዋ፡	ይትልዋ፡	—
2mp	ተለውክሙ፡ / ተሎክሙ፡	ትትልዉ፡	ትትልዉ፡	ትልዉ፡
2fp	ተለውክን፡ / ተሎክን፡	ትትልዋ፡	ትትልዋ፡	ትልዋ፡
1cp	ተለውነ፡ / ተሎነ፡	ንትሉ፡	ንትሉ፡	—

a. Note the two forms in the Perfect 1st and 2nd person (s/p) forms. With the second form, we see the loss of the III-ወ and the vowel in the preceding consonant shifts from ă to o with the relevant endings.

b. The first form of the 1st and 2nd person along with the 3rd person forms follow the vowel pattern of the perfect for the G strong verb.

c. Note the loss of the III-ω in the 3ms, 3fs, 2ms, 1cs, and 1cp imperfect forms when in the strong verb the final consonant has an ə vowel. In addition, we have the lengthening of the vowel on the preceding consonant to a *u* vowel.

d. The 2fs III-ω retains the *i* and the preceding vowel shortens to ə.

e. The 3mp retains the expected *u* vowel with the III-ω and the preceding vowel shortens to ə.

f. The 3fp and 2fp retain the expected *ā* vowel and the preceding vowel shortens to ə.

g. The subjunctive forms follow a similar pattern to the imperfect with the exception of the reduced vowel on the first consonant from ă to ə. The same vowel changes and loss of the III-ω occur.

h. The imperative form, like the imperfect loses the III-ω in 2ms and the III-ω follows the same imperfect vowel pattern for the 2fs, 2mp, and 2fp forms.

i. The infinitive form appears as ተሊዉ፡

TABLE 32.2: III-ፀ Root Verb Paradigm (See ch. 10 for G III Gutturals)

PGN	Perfect "dig"	Imperfect	Subjunctive	Imperative
3ms	ከረየ፡	ይከሪ፡	ይከሪ፡	—
3fs	ከረየት፡	ትከሪ፡	ትከሪ፡	—
2ms	ከረይከ፡	ትከሪ፡	ትከሪ፡	ከሪ፡
2fs	ከረይኪ፡	ትከርዪ፡	ትከርዪ፡	ከርዪ፡
1cs	ከረይኩ፡	እከሪ፡	እከሪ፡	—
3mp	ከረዩ፡	ይከርዩ፡	ይከርዩ፡	—
3fp	ከረያ፡	ይከርያ፡	ይከርያ፡	—
2mp	ከረይከሙ፡	ትከርዩ፡	ትከርዩ፡	ከርዩ፡
2fp	ከረይክን፡	ትከርያ፡	ትከርያ፡	ከርያ፡
1cp	ከረይነ፡	ንከሪ፡	ንከሪ፡	—

a. The III-ፀ verb follows some of the same patterns as the III-ω verb.

b. The perfect tense III-ፀ only has a single form unlike the III-ω perfect which has two forms in the 2ms, 2fs, 1cs, 2mp, 2fp, and 1cp. The vowel pattern and the endings are the same with the first form of the perfect III-ω verb.

c. The imperfect III-ዖ verb maintains the presence of the III-ዖ only in the 2fs, 3mp, 3fp, 2mp, and 2fp. In the remaining forms the ዖ assimilates into the middle consonant and the vowel of that consonant shifts from ă to i.

d. The pattern for the subjunctive form of the III-ዖ verb is identical to the imperfect except for the shortening of the first consonant vowel from an ă to a short ə.

e. The expected changes appear in the Imperative: the shortening of the first consonant vowel from an ă to a short ə and the assimilation of ዖ in the 2ms form and the ዖ with the same vowel endings as the Imperfect in the 2fs, 2mp, and 2fp, similar to what we see in the III-ω verb.

f. The infinitive form appears as ከሪይ፡.

TABLE 32.3: Most Common III-ω/ዖ Root Verbs

Root Type / Meaning	Perfect	Imperfect	Subjunctive	Imperative	Infinitive
III-ዖ / weep	በከዖ፡	ይበኪ፡	ይብኪ፡	ብኪ፡	በኪይ፡
name	ሰመዖ፡	ይሰሚ፡	ይስሚ፡	ስሚ፡	ሰሚይ፡
be old	በልዖ፡	ይበሊ፡	ይብሊ፡	—	በሊይ፡
be poor	ነድዖ፡	ይነዲ፡	ይንዲ፡	—	ነዲይ፡
be evil	አከዖ፡	የአኪ፡	ይአከይ፡	—	አኪይ፡
be great	ዐብይ፡	ይዐቢ፡	ይዕበይ፡	ዕበይ፡	ዐቢይ፡
refuse	አበዖ፡	የአቢ፡	ይአበይ፡	አበይ፡	አቢይ፡
see	ርእዖ፡	ይርኢ፡ / ይሬኢ፡	ይርአይ፡	ርኢ፡	ሬአይ፡
be burned up	ውዕዖ፡	ይውዒ፡	የዐይ፡	—	ወዒይ፡
place/set	ወደዖ፡	ይውዲ፡	ይደይ፡	ደይ፡	ወዲይ፡
flee	ጐዖ፡	ይጕዲ፡	ይጕየይ፡ / ይጕዲ፡	ጕየይ፡ / ጕየ	ጕዪ
be ill	ደወዖ፡	ይደዊ፡	ይድወይ፡	—	ደዋይ፡
III-ω / go home	አተወ፡	የአቱ፡	ይአት፡ ይአተው፡	አቱ፡ / አተው፡	አቲው፡
cross	ዐደወ፡	የዐዱ፡	ይዕዱ፡ / ይዕደው፡	ዕዱ፡ / ዕደው፡	ዐዲው፡

32.2 III-ω/ዖ Root Verbal Adjectives in the ቅቱል፡ Pattern[1]

A verbal adjective is generally the equivalent of a passive participle. It has both verbal and adjectival characteristics. A verbal adjective can modify a noun, but it can also act as an adverb, as will be seen in the two frequently appearing examples below:

---
1. See ch. 24.

ወዑይ፡ – hot, burning
ስሙይ፡ – named, called, famous

32.3 III-ወ/ይ Root Agent Nouns from ቀታሊ፡[2]

You will frequently find that the final *i* vowel is assimilated into the final ይ resulting in two possible spellings for the word በላይ፡, for example, በላዪ፡ or በላይ፡. See the frequent verbal nouns below:

በላዪ፡ – old, wearing out (adj.)
ጐያዪ፡(ዪ) – fugitive
ረአዪ፡ (pl. ረአያን፡ ረእያን፡ ረአይት፡) – observer, seer
ረአዪ፡ ኮከብ፡ – astrologer, star reader
ረአዪ፡ ጐቡኣት፡ – soothsayer

32.4 III-ወ/ይ Root Verbal Nouns

The verbal noun, although derived from a verb, has no verbal characteristics. It functions as the present participle with the "-ing" added, such as "the *feeding* of the five thousand was a miracle." *Feeding* is a noun acting like a verb.

ብካይ፡ – weeping, lamentation
ንዴት፡ / ንድየት፡ – poverty
አትወት፡ / አቶት፡ – return home, a return, crop yield
እኪይ፡ (pl. እኪያት፡) – evil, wickedness
ዕቢይ፡ (pl. ዕቢያት፡) – greatness, size, majesty
ጕያ፡ – flight
ራእይ፡ (pl. ርእያት፡) – vision, revelation
ርእየት፡ – appearance, aspect
ዋዕይ፡ – fire, heat, burning
ውዕየት፡ – burning, conflagration

32.5 III-ወ/ይ Nouns with Prefixed ም

ምእታው፡ – home, place of return, returning
ምጕያዪ፡ – refuge, asylum
ማዕዶት፡ – the opposite of something
ሙዳይ፡ (pl. ሙዳያት፡) – container, basket

---

2. See ch. 23.

32.6 Vocabulary

1. ዐዘቅት፡ – well, cistern
2. አረፍት፡ – wall, partition
3. ጥቅም፡ – wall, city wall
4. ሰፈየ፡ (subj. ይስፊ፡) – sew; ተሰፍየ፡ Gt – be sewn
5. ሰፋዪ፡ – sewer, tailor
6. መስፌ፡ – awl
7. ከረየ፡ (subj. ይክሪ፡) – dig; ተከርየ፡ Gt – be dug
8. ከራዪ፡ መቃብር፡ (pl. ከረይት፡) – grave digger in ከራዪ፡ መቃብር፡
9. ሐለየ፡ (subj. ይሕሊ፡) – sing, make music
10. ሐላዪ፡ (f. ሐላዪት፡, pl. ሐለይት፡) – singer
11. ማሕሌት፡ (pl. ማሕሌታት፡ መሐልይ፡) – song, singing, music
12. ጥዕየ፡ (subj. ይጥዐይ፡) – be healthy; አጥዐየ፡ CG – make healthy
13. ጥዑይ፡ (f. ትዒት፡) – a healthy person or place
14. ጥዒና፡ – good health
15. አብሐ፡ CG (root በወሐ) – allow, permit; ጥበውሐ፡ Gt – be permitted
16. ብዉሕ፡ – is permitted for someone + subj.
17. መባሕት፡ – power, permission, authority
18. አዝለፈ፡ CG – continue doing something, persevere in doing
19. ዝሉፈ፡ ለዝሉፉ፡ adv. – continuously
20. ዘልፈ፡ – always, frequently
21. ኢ . . . ዘልፈ፡ adv. – never (e.g., ኢገብረ፡ ዘልፈ፡ – "he will never do it")
22. ዘዘልፍ፡ adj. – perpetual

32.7 Exercises

A. Translate the following:

1. ስምዮ፡ ለወልድከ፡ ስመ፡ ዮሐንስ።

2. ዕቀብ፡ ንዋየከ፡ ወትረ፡ ከመ፡ ኢትንዲ።

3. ደዮ፡ ውስተ፡ ዐዘቅት፡ ወጐድጐ፡ ሆየ፡ እስከ፡ ይመውት።

4. አልቦ፡ ምሕረተ፡ ዘተዐቢ፡ እምሕርቱ።

5. አዘዘነ፡ ከመ፡ ንዳይ፡ ዘንተ፡ ዳቤላ፡ ውስተ፡ ዐጸዱ።

6. መኑ፡ ውእቱ፡ ዝንቱ፡ ብእሲ፡ ዘየዐቢ፡ በዊአ፡ ቤተነ።

7. መፍትው፡ ከመ፡ ንጉዴ፡ አምቅድመ፡ ይርአየነ።
   _____

8. ምንተ፡ ተሰምይዋ፡ ለዛቲ፡ ሀገር።
   _____

9. ውእተ፡ ጊዜ፡ ትሬአዩ፡ ተአምረ፡ ወመንክራተ።
   _____

10. ፈቀዱ፡ ይጉየዩ፡ ወባሕቱ፡ ኢክህሉ።
    _____

11. ኢትሑር፡ ውስተ፡ ፍኖት፡ ከመ፡ ኢይርአዩከ፡ ወይቅትሉከ።
    _____

12. እትዉ፡ ብሔረከሙ፡ ወኢትግብኡ፡ ዝየ።
    _____

13. ኢሠናይ፡ አልባስ፡ ዘይበሊ።
    _____

14. ኢተዐይ፡ መዕዐትከ፡ ላዕሌነ።
    _____

15. አበዩ፡ አርእዮቶ፡ መጻሕፍቲከሙ።
    _____

16. ሰከብ፡ ወኑም፡ ከመ፡ ኢትድወይ፡ ወትሙት።
    _____

17. ኢትእበይ፡ አዕብዮ፡ ስመ፡ ንጉሥከ።
    _____

18. እንዘ፡ ንቀርብ፡ ርኢነ፡ ሀገሮሙ፡ እንዘ፡ ትውዒ፡ በርሑቅ።
    _____

19. ይደዊ፡ ወልድየ፡ ወእፈርህ፡ ከመ፡ ኢይሙት።
    _____

20. አይቴኑ፡ ትፈቅድ፡ እደዎ፡ ለዝንቱ፡ ንዋይ።
    _____

21. መኑ፡ ዘይነዲ፡ በልቡ፡ እንዘ፡ የአምን፡ በእግዚአነ።

22. መኑ፡ ዘይገድፍ፡ ንዋዮ፡ አምቅድሙ፡ ይብሊ።

23. አዘዘነ፡ ከመ፡ ንዕደዉ፡ ዘንተ፡ ወሐዘ፡ ወነአገዝ፡ ዛተ፡ ምድረ።

24. ዕድዉ፡ ምድረ፡ መንገለ፡ ምዕራብ፡ እስከ፡ ትበጽሑ፡ ኀበ፡ ማኅደሮሙ።

25. አምጽአ፡ አሣእኑሁ፡ ኀበ፡ ሰፋዩ፡ ከመ፡ ይስፍዮሙ፡ በመስፈሁ።

B. Translate the following:

1. አብሐሙ፡ ይዕደዉ፡ ውስተ፡ ብሔሩ።

2. ሶበ፡ ሰምዖሙ፡ እንዘ፡ ይክርዮሙ፡ አረፍተ፡ ቤቱ፡ ቆመ፡ ወጎየ

3. ወሶበ፡ ተሰፈተል አሣእኒሁ፣ ወደዮሙ፡ ዲበ፡ እገሪሁ፡ ወነለፈ።

4. መፍትው፡ ከመ፡ እርክብ፡ ሰፋዩ፡ አልባስ፡ ከመ፡ ይሰፊ፡ ዐጽፍዮ።

5. ነቢዮሙ፡ ሀዮ፡ ክረዩ፡ ዐዘቃተ፡ ወሐነጹ፡ ጥቀሙ።

6. ሠጠቀ፡ አጻብዒሁ፡ እንዘ፡ ይሰፊ፡ በመስፌሁ።

7. መህረነ፡ መሐልየ፡ ሕዝብከ።

8. ኢትክሉ፡ እኒዘ፡ አህጉረ፡ ጥቅም፡ ዘሐነጹ፡ ሀዮ።

9. በውሕ፡ ለነ፡ ከመ፡ ነሀብክሙ፡ ዘንተ፡ መልአክተ።
   _____

10. አኮ፡ በሥራይ፡ ዘትጥዒ፡ አላ፡ በሃይማኖት።
    _____

11. ኢኪሀለ፡ ዐሪገ፡ እምዐዘቅት፡ ዘወድቀ፡ ውስቴቱ።
    _____

12. ኢብዉሕ፡ ለከሙ፡ ትባኡ፡ ዝየ።
    _____

13. መኑ፡ ዘወሀበከ፡ ዘከመዝ፡ መባሕተ።
    _____

14. ኮነ፡ ይመጽእ፡ ኀቤነ፡ ዘልፈ፡ ምስለ፡ ዜና፡ በእንተ፡ አዝማዲነ።
    _____

15. እንዘ፡ ነጎልፍ፡ እንተ፡ ኀበ፡ ቤተ፡ ክርስቲያን፡ ሰማዕነ፡ ቃለ፡ ካህን፡ ይሔሊ፡ ስብሐተ፡ እግዚእነ።
    _____

16. አቀሙ፡ ዲበ፡ ጥቅመ፡ ሀገር፡ ከመ፡ ይዕቀብዋ።
    _____

17. አዝለፉ፡ ገቢረ፡ እኪት፡ ወአበዩ፡ ሰሚዐ፡ ሊተ።
    _____

18. ኢትቁም፡ እምቅድመ፡ ትጥዐይ።
    _____

19. ረከብኩሁ፡ እንዘ፡ ይቀውም፡ ኀበ፡ አረፍተ፡ ቤቱ።
    _____

20. ወነዊም ሠሉስ፡ ጥዕየ፡ እምደዊሁ።
    _____

21. ንነብር፡ ዝየ፡ ለዝሉፉ፡ ወኢነግድገ፡ ዘልፈ።
    _____

22. ቀዳሚሁ፡ ኢከሀለ፡ ሐልየ፡ ወኢምንተኒ፤ አላ፡ እምድኀረ፡ ራእይ፡ ዘርእየ፡ በንዋም፡ ኮነ፡ ሐላዬ፡ ጠቢበ፡ ወሠናየ።
    _____

C. Daniel 7:9–28. Translate the following:

⁹ ወርኢኩ፡ እስከ፡ አንበሩ፡ መናብርተ፡ ወነበረ፡ ብሉየ፡ መዋዕል፡ ወልብሱ፡ ጻዕዳ፡ ከመ፡ በረድ፡ ወሥዕርተ፡ ርእሱ፡ ከመ፡ ፀምር፡ ወመንበሩሂ፡ እሳት፡ ዘይነድድ፡ ወሰረገላቲሁኒ፡ አፍሓም፡ ዘያንበለብል።

¹⁰ ወፈለገ፡ እሳት፡ ይውሕዝ፡ ቅድሜሁ፣ አእላፈ፡ አእላፍ፡ ይትለአክዎ፡ ወምእልፊት፡ አእላፍ፡ ይቀውሙ፡ ቅድሜሁ፣ ወነበረ፡ ዓውደ፡ ወከሠቱ፡ መጻሕፍተ።

¹¹ ወርኢኩ፡ ሰቤሃ፡ እምቃለ፡ ነገሩ፡ ዐቢይ፡ ዘይነብብ፡ ዝኩ፡ ቀርን፡ እስከ፡ ተአተተ፡ ዝኩ፡ አርዌ፡ ወጠፍአ፡ ወመህቡ፡ ሥጋሁ፡ ያውዕዩ፡ በእሳት።

¹² ወቆመ፡ ርእሶሙ፡ ለእልክቱ፡ አራዊት፡ ወተውህበ፡ ሎሙ፡ ነዋኀ፡ ሕይወት፡ እስከ፡ ዕድሜሆሙ።

¹³ ወርኢኩ፡ በራእየ፡ ሌሊት፡ ወናሁ፡ መጽአ፡ በደመና፡ ሰማይ፡ ከመ፡ ወልደ፡ እጓለ፡ እመሕያው፣ ወበጽሐ፡ ነበ፡ ብሉየ፡ መዋዕል።

¹⁴ ወተውህበ፡ ሎቱ፡ ምኩናን፡ ወክብር፡ ወመንግሥት፡ ወኮሎሙ፡ አሕዛብ፡ ወበሓውርት፡ ወነገድ፡ ተቀንዩ፡ ሎቱ፡ ወምኩናኑሂ፡ ምኩናን፡ ዘለዓለም፡ ዓለም፡ ዘኢያኀልቅ፡ ወመንግሥቱሂ፡ ዘኢይማስን።

¹⁵ ወርዕደኒ፡ መንፈስየ፡ አነ፡ ዳንኤል፡ ወደንገፀኒ፡ ልብየ፡ እምራእየ፡ ርእስየ።

¹⁶ ወሐርኩ፡ ወተጠየቅዎ፡ ለአሐዱ፡ እምእለ፡ ይቀውሙ፣ ወነገረኒ፡ ወአይድዐኒ፡ ፍካሬሁ፡ ጥየቃ፡ ኩሎ፡ ነገሮ።

¹⁷ እሉ፡ አርባዕቱ፡ አራዊት፡ ዓበይት፡ አርባዕቱ፡ ነገሥት፡ እሙንቱ፡ ይትነሥኡ፡ ዲበ፡ ምድር፡ ወየአትቱ።

¹⁸ ወይገብእ፡ መንግሥት፡ ለቅዱሳነ፡ ልዑል፡ ወይነብርዋ፡ ለዓለመ፡ ዓለም።

¹⁹ ወተጠየቁ፡ ካዕበ፡ በእንተ፡ ራብዕ፡ አርዌ፡ እስመ፡ ኪር፡ ውእቱ፡ እምኮሉ፡ አራዊት፡ ወግሩም፡ ውእቱ፡ ጥቀ፡ ወስነኑ፡ ዘኀጺን፡ ወጽፈሪሁኒ፡ ዘኆጺን፡ ወይበልዕሂ፡ ወየሐጽሂ፡ ወዘተርፈ፡ ይኪይድ፡ በእግሩ።

²⁰ ወበእንተ፡ እልክቱ፡ ዐሠርቱ፡ አቅርንቲሁ፡ ዘውስተ፡ ርእሱ፡ ወዝኩሂ፡ ካልእ፡ ዘበቈለ፡ ወመልጣሙ፡ ለዐርቱ፡ እለ፡ እምቅድሜሁ፡ አቅርንት፡ ዝኩ፡ ዘአዕይንት፡ ወአፉሁ፡ ይነብብ፡ ዐቢያተ፡ ወርእሱሂ፡ ዐቢይ፡ እምቢጹ።

²¹ ርኢክዎ፡ ለውእቱ፡ ቀርን፡ ይትቃተሎሙ፡ ለቅዱሳን፡ ወሞአሙ።

G Verbs from III-ወ/የ Roots: The Remaining Moods 235

²² እስከ፡ መጽአ፡ ብሉየ፡ መዋዕል፡ ወፈትሐ፡ ሎሙ፡ ለቅዱሳነ፡ ልዑል፡ ወበጽሐ፡ ዕድሜሁ፡ ወአጽንዑ፡ መንግሥቶሙ፡ ለቅዱሳን።

²³ ወይቤለኒ፡ አርዌ፡ ራብዕ፡ ራብዒት፡ መንግሥት፡ ይአቲ፡ ውስተ፡ ምድር፡ እንተ፡ ተዐቢ፡ እምኵሉ፡ እምኵሉ፡ መንግሥታት፡ ወትበልዕ፡ ኵሎ፡ መንግሥታተ፡ ምድር፡ ወይከይዳ፡ ወይቀጥቃጣ።

²⁴ ወዐሥርቱሂ፡ አቅርንት፡ ዐሠርቱ፡ መንግሥታት፡ ዘይትነሣእ፡ ዲበ፡ ምድር፡ ወእምድኅሬሙ፡ ይትነሣእ፡ ካልእ፡ ንጉሥ፡ ለእኩያን፡ አለ፡ ቅድሜሁ፡ ወያሰሮሙ፡ ለዐሠርቱ፡ ነገሥት።

²⁵ ወይነብብ፡ በነገረ፡ ልዑል፡ ወያስሕቶሙ፡ ለቅዱሳነ፡ ልዑል፡ ወይኔሊ፡ ይወልጥ፡ መዋዕለ፡ ወሕገ፡ ወይትወሀብ፡ ሎቱ፡ እስከ፡ ዕድሜሁ፡ ውስተ፡ እዴሁ፡ ወዓመት፡ ወመንፈቀ፡ ዓመት።

²⁶ ወነበረ፡ ዐውደ፡ ወይስዕሮ፡ ለመልአከ፡ ከመ፡ ያማስን፡ ለገሙራ።

²⁷ ወመንግሥተ፡ ወምኵናን፡ ወዐበየ፡ መንግሥት፡ ዘመትሕተ፡ ሰማይ፡ ወተውህበ፡ ለቅዱሳነ፡ ልዑል፡ ወመንግሥቱሂ፡ መንግሥት፡ ዘለዓለም፡ ዓለም፡ ወኵሉ፡ መኳንንት፡ ይትቀነዩ፡ ሎቱ፡ ወይትኤዘዙ፡ ሎቱ፡ እስከ፡ ዝየ፡ ወአሜሁ፡ ማኀለቅተ፡ ሕዝብ።

²⁸ ወእነ፡ ዳኔል፡ ዓሊናየ፡ ይትሀወከኒ፡ ጥቀ፡ በሕቁ፡ ወተወለጠኒ፡ ራእይ፡ ወዐቅብኩ፡ ነገሮ፡ ውስተ፡ ልብየ።

Chapter 33

GT AND GLT VERBS: THE REMAINING MOODS

33.1 Gt Imperfect, Subjunctive, and Imperative Forms

As mentioned previously, the Gt verbs are considered medio-passive verbs (see ch. 15) and are formed from the active G verb pattern with the addition of a ተ prefix (ተ+$C_1\breve{a}C_2C_3\bar{a}$): e.g., ቀተለ፡ – "he killed" and ተቀትለ፡ – "he was killed." Somewhat associated with the Gt, the Glt verb is designated as a reciprocal action verb. It has the same ተ prefix, but the $\breve{a}$ vowel on the first consonant lengthens to an $\bar{a}$ vowel (ተ+$C_1\bar{a}C_2\breve{a}C_3\bar{a}$) and reads ተቃተለ፡ – "kill one another": note the addition of the $\breve{a}$ with the second consonant that is not present in the Gt verb.

TABLE 33.1: Gt Imperfect, Subjunctive and Imperative

Verb Root Type	Perfect	Imperfect	Subjunctive	Imperative
Strong	ተቀትለ፡	ይትቀተል፡	ይትቀተል፡	ተቀተል፡
I Guttural	ተሐንጸ፡	ይትሐነጽ፡	ይትሐነጽ፡	ተሐነጽ፡
II Guttural	ተብህለ፡	ይትበሀል፡	ይትበሀል፡	ተበሀል፡
III Guttural	ተፈትሐ፡	ይትፈታሕ፡	ይትፈታሕ፡	ተፈታሕ፡
I-ወ	ተወልደ፡	ይትወለድ፡	ይትወለድ፡	ተወለድ፡
II-ወ	ተመውአ፡	ይትመዋእ፡	ይትመዋእ፡	ተመዋእ፡
III-ወ	ተርነወ፡	ይትረነው፡	ይትረነው፡	ተረነው፡
II-የ	ተመይጠ፡	ይትመየጥ፡	ይትመየጥ፡	ተመየጥ፡
III-የ	ተክርየ፡	ይትከረይ፡	ይትከረይ፡	ተከረይ፡

a. The forms of the Gt follow the rules that we have seen with the previous verb forms.

b. Note the imperfect and subjunctive forms look identical in the Gəʿəz script but differ only in the doubling of the middle consonant, which can be seen only in transliteration. So the imperfect is *yətqattal* and the subjunctive *yətqatal*. Therefore, close attention must be given to the context of these two verb moods.

c. In the imperfect and subjunctive forms, the inclusion of the ይ prefix results in the vowel reduction of the ተ Gt prefix to ə in the form of ት.

d. The middle consonant vowel in the perfect form lengthens from ə to ă.

e. This results in the vowel reduction in the final consonant in the imperfect and subjunctive from ă to ə.

f. The ተ Gt prefix vowel on the imperative form returns to ă, while the first and middle consonants include the ă and the final consonant appears in the short ə form with a silent vowel.

g. The III Guttural forms cause the vowel of the middle consonant to lengthen to an ā in the imperfect, subjunctive, and imperative.

h. The ወ and የ in the I, II, or III position result in no vowel changes in relation to the strong verb forms for the four moods.

i. On occasion the final ă+ወ of roots III-ወ may appear as *o* when there is no additional ending: e.g., for the verb ተርነወ፡ the forms may appear as ይትረኖ፡ (imperfect and subjunctive) and ተረኖ፡ (imperative).

j. If the first consonant is a dental or sibilant (ተ ጠ ፀ ደ ሰ ሠ ጸ ዘ) the ተ prefix is assimilated into the first consonant: e.g., in the verb ደለወ፡ the imperfect and subjunctive will appear as ይደለወ፡ with the ተ prefix assimilated into the first ደ. In the transliteration the ደ will be doubled, but this will not appear in the Gəʿəz script and will result in some difficulty for beginning readers.

k. As with Hebrew and other Semitic languages, the outward differences between a G and Gt is the shortening or lengthening of vowels.

33.2 Glt Reciprocal Verbs in the Imperfect, Subjunctive, and Imperative Forms

The Glt verb indicates a mutual interchange between two parties (see ch. 16). Like the Gt verbs above, these verbs are marked with a ተ prefix, but they also have a lengthening of the stem vowel from ă to ā between C_1 and C_2. The vocalization would look like this: ተ+C_1āC_2ăC_3ă. As mentioned previously, the Glt verbs can be divided into two categories: 1) verbs whose meanings are fairly predictable from the general idea of reciprocity; and 2) those verbs in which one must pay particular attention when it comes to ascertaining its meaning. In addition, Glt verbs should not be mistaken for Lt verbs, which they resemble, rather one must remember these verbs are linked to G or Gt verbs. The table below represents some of the common Glt verbs.

TABLE 33.2: Glt Imperfect, Subjunctive, and Imperative Forms

Verb Root Type	Perfect	Imperfect	Subjunctive	Imperative
Strong	ተቃረቢ፡	ይትቃረብ፡	ይትቃረብ፡	ተቃረቢ፡
I Guttural	ተኃለፊ፡	ይትኃለፍ፡	ይትኃላፍ፡	ተኃለፍ፡
II Guttural	ተካሐዲ፡	ይትካሐድ፡	ይትካሐድ፡	ተካሐዲ፡
III Guttural	ተጋብአ፡	ይትጋባእ፡	ይትጋባእ፡	ተጋብአ፡
I-ወ	ተዋለደ፡	ይትዋለድ	ይትዋለድ	ተዋለድ፡
II-ወ	ተቃወመ፡	ይትቃወም፡	ይትቃወም፡	ተቃወም፡
III-ወ	ተፋነወ፡	ይትፋነው፡	ይትፋነው፡	ተፋነው፡
II-የ	ተካየደ፡	ይትካየድ፡	ይትካየድ፡	ተካየድ፡
III-የ	ተራአየ፡	ይትራአይ፡	ይትራአይ፡	ተራአይ፡

a. Note the lengthening of the first consonant vowel from ă in the Gt to ā in the Glt. This long ā is retained in all three of the other moods: imperfect, subjunctive, and imperative.

b. Note in the III Guttural the middle consonant in the perfect has the ə vowel, while all the other weak forms maintain the ă vowel.

c. Note the vowel reduction of the ተ prefix in the perfect to the ት prefix in the imperfect and subjunctive, similar to the Gt verb above.

d. The imperative prefix returns to the ă vowel in the ተ prefix.

e. The final consonant in all the Glt imperfect, subjunctive, and imperative forms shortens to the ə vowel.

f. Like the Gt verbs above, if the first consonant is a dental or sibilant (ተ ጠ ፀ ደ ሰ ሠ ጸ ዘ) the ተ prefix is assimilated into the first consonant: e.g., in the verb ሠየጠ፡ with its reciprocal form ተሣየጠ the imperfect and subjunctive will appear as ይሣየጥ፡ with the ተ prefix assimilated into the first ሣ. In this case, the assimilation may lead to confusion with L verbs.

33.3 The Verb ሀለወ፡ – "Exist, Be" with the Subjunctive and Imperfect

The verb ሀለወ፡ with the object suffix followed by the subjunctive is used to show intention or obligation of the subject to perform the action of the subjunctive verb. For example, the phrase ሀለዎሙ፡ ይሐሩ፡ may be translated as "they intend to go" or "they should go." Another possible use, although less frequent, is ሀለወ inflected with a personal subject: e.g., ሀሎኩ፡ አሐር፡ may be translated as "I am (supposed) to go" or "I was to go."

In addition to its use with the subjunctive, ሀለወ፡ can be paired with an imperfect verb form. For example, ሀለወ፡ ይነብር፡ may be translated as past tense or as a continuous present – "he is or was sitting." It can also be read as something that will take place in the immediate future – "he is about to sit" or "he is going to sit." Context, of course, is the key to translating this verb properly.

33.4   Vocabulary

1. ኃጢአት፡ – sin
2. አብድ፡ – fool
3. እኅት፡ – sister
4. ሕዝብ፡ – people
5. ፈረስ፡ – horse
6. ሀገር፡ – country
7. ርእስ፡ – head
8. አንቀጽ፡ – door
9. ዘራዊ፡ – a prodigal
10. መስፍን፡ – prince
11. ቀሲስ፡ – priest
12. ዘቢዳ፡ – hair cloth, turban
13. ግምዔ፡ – pitcher, jar, vessel
14. ቀንዒል፡ – lamp
15. ሰይጣን፡ – demon, Satan, devil, adversary
16. አምላክ፡ – god (also means "Lord")
17. መትሕተ፡ – underneath
18. ዐውደ፡ – about, around
19. እንተ፡ – in the direction of
20. በእንተ፡ – with regard to, in direction of
21. ህየንተ፡ – instead of
22. እንበለ፡ – without, except
23. መቅድመ፡ – before, in preference to
24. ማዕዶተ፡ – beyond, along
25. ጠቃ፡ / ጥቃ፡ – close to
26. ቢጸ፡ – beside
27. ምእኃዘ፡ – beside, close to
28. ውእደ፡ / ወእደ፡ – along
29. ተክለ፡ – in place of
30. ተውላጠ፡ – for, in exchange for
31. መንጸረ፡ / እንጸረ፡ – over against
32. አምሳለ፡ / አርአየ፡ – like
33. መጠነ፡ – of the size of, as large as
34. ከዋላ፡ – behind, afterwards, in the rear
35. በዕብሬት፡ – for the sake of (with suffixes)
36. አመ፡ – at the time of

33.5   Exercises

A. Translate the following:

1. ይሰቅል፡ ሰላመ፡ ዓለም፡ በፈቃዱ፡ ለእግዚአብሔር፡

2. ማእዜ፡ ንትፈታሕ፡ እመአስሪነ፡

3. ዐቀብዎ፡ ለበድኑ፡ እንዘ፡ ይትገነዝ፡

4. ኢትትሐሠይ፡ አምቅድመ፡ ይትገበር፡ ግብርከ፡

5. ርኢኮ፡ ሰማያተ፡ እንዘ፡ ይትመልኡ፡ መላእክተ፡ ብርሃናዊያን።
   _____

6. ይእተ፡ ዕለተ፡ ኢትትመሐሩ፡ በነቢ፡ ፈታሕቲከሙ።
   _____

7. አንተ፡ ትትነሣእ፡ ውስተ፡ ሰማይ፡ እንዘ፡ ተሐዩ።
   _____

8. ወይሰብክ፡ ዝንቱ፡ ወንጌል፡ ኀበ፡ አጽናፈ፡ ምድር።
   _____

9. ይሁበከሙ፡ ዘይትፈቀድ።
   _____

10. ይትገደፉ፡ አብድንቲሆሙ፡ ለአራዊተ፡ ገዳም።
    _____

11. ሀለወነ፡ ኩሎነ፡ ንትሐተት፡ በኀበ፡ እግዚአብሔር።
    _____

12. ዝንቱ፡ ውእቱ፡ ስሙ፡ ለእግዚአብሔር፡ ዘኢይትነገር።
    _____

13. መጽኡ፡ ወነሥእዎ፡ ለብድኑ፡ ጽሚተ፡ እምቅድም፡ ይትቀበር።
    _____

14. እፈቅድ፡ እሰማዕ፡ እምቅድም፡ እሰድድ፡ እምድርየ።
    _____

15. ይትፈቀር፡ ክርስቶስ፡ እስመ፡ መሐሪ፡ ውእቱ፤ ይትፈራህ፡ እስመ፡ እግዚአ፡ ውእቱ።
    _____

16. ዝንቱ፡ ጾጋ፡ ይትፈቀድ፡ ፈድፋደ፡ እምኩሉ፡ ንዋይ፡ ምድራዊ።
    _____

17. በእንተ፡ ኀጢአትከ፡ ትትገደፍ፡ እማእከሌነ።
    _____

18. ትትሐተት፡ በእንተ፡ ኩሉ፡ ዘገበርከ።
    _____

19. ኢትትመዐዕ፡ ዳቤየ፡ እስም፡ አኮ፡ አነ፡ ዘገበርኩ፡ ዘንተ።

20. ዛቲ፡ ጸሎት፡ ትትነበብ፡ እምቅድም፡ ይትነበብ፡ ምንባበ፡ ወንጌል።

21. ሰበ፡ ርእየ፡ ኩሎሙ፡ ጸባእቲሁ፡ እንዘ፡ ይትቀተሉ፡ ፈርሀ፡ ወጐየ።

22. ምንተ፡ ይሰመይ፡ ስሙ፡ ለወልድከ።

23. በይእቲ፡ ዕለት፡ ይከውኑ፡ ኃጥኣን፡ ከመ፡ ዘኢይትፈጠር።

24. ዝንቱ፡ ውእቱ፡ አስማተ፡ በዓላት፡ ዘይትገበሩ፡ በማዕርክሙ።

25. ሰበ፡ ይትሐነጽ፡ ጥቅም፡ ሀገርክሙ፡ ኢይመውኡክሙ፡ ወኢመኑሄ።

26. ዝንቱ፡ ውእቱ፡ ግዕዞሙ፡ ለአበዊነ፡ ዘይደልወነ፡ ከመ፡ ንትመራሕ፡ በምግባራቲሆሙ።

27. ሰይፍ፡ ኢይትመየጥ፡ እምላዕሌክሙ፡ እስከ፡ ይመውቱ፡ ኩሎሙ፡ ኃጥኣን።

28. ተንሥኢ፡ ወሐሪ፡ ቤተኪ፡ ወአኒ፡ አሐውር፡ ምስሌኪ።

29. ይደልወክሙ፡ ከመ፡ ትትቀሥፉ፡ በእንተ፡ ዝንቱ፡ ግብር።

30. ይሰመይ፡ ዝንቱ፡ ወልድ፡ በስመ፡ አቡሁ።

31. ሀለው፡ እግዚአብሔር፡ ዘእንበለ፡ ይትፈጠር፡ ዓለም።

32. መፍትው፡ ንሑር፡ እምቅድም፡ ይትገበር፡ ሲሳየነ።

33. ሰማዕናሆሙ፡ እንዘ፡ ይትሐሠዩ፡ በእንተ፡ ሙአቶሙ።

_____

34. ለምንት፡ ንትመዋእ፡ በኀበ፡ ከሓድያን።

_____

35. ማእዜኑ፡ ትትመየጡ፡ አምነጢአትክሙ፡ ውስተ፡ ፍኖተ፡ ጽድቅ።

_____

36. ትትነሣእ፡ ወትጐዩ፡ ገብጸ፡ እስመ፡ የኀሥሡከ፡ ከመ፡ ይቅትሉከ።

_____

37. ውእተ፡ አሚረ፡ ትሰደዱ፡ ወትትቀተሉ፡ በእንቲአየ።

_____

38. አኀሥሥ፡ ሰፋዬ፡ ከመ፡ ይሰፈይ፡ ሣእንየ።

_____

39. ይትፈትሑ፡ አዕይንቲሆሙ፡ ወይርአዩ፡ ክብሮ፡ ለአምላክ።

_____

40. በዘንቱ፡ መካን፡ ይሰቀል፡ መድኀንነ፡ በመስቀለ፡ ዕፀ፡ እንዘ፡ ይሠዋዕ፡ በእንተ፡ እኁለ፡ እመሒያው።

_____

B. Ezekiel 28:1–19. Translate the following:

¹ ወነበቦኒ፡ እግዚአብሔር፡ ወይቤላኒ፤

² ወልደ፡ እጓለ፡ እመሒያው፡ በሎ፡ ለመልአከ፡ ጢሮስ፡ ከመዝ፡ ይቤ፡ እግዚአብሔር፡ እግዚእ፡ እስመ፡ ኖኅ፡ ልብከ፡ ወትቤ፤ አምላክ፡ አነ፡ ወመንበርተ፡ አምላክ፡ እነብር፡ በልበ፡ ባሕር፡ አንተ፡ ሰብእ፡ ወአኮ፡ አምላክ፡ ወረሰይከ፡ ልብከ፡ ከመ፡ ልበ፡ አምላክ።

³ ናሁ፡ አንተ፡ ትጠብብ፡ እምዳንኤል፡ ወኵሉ፡ ጠቢብ፡ ኢይትኀባእከ፡ ወጠቢባንሂ፡ ኢመሀሩከ፡ በጥበቢሆሙ።

⁴ በጥበብከ፡ ወበለባዊትከ፡ ገበርከ፡ ለከ፡ ኀይለ፡ ወአስተጋባእከ፡ ወርቀ፡ ወብሩረ፡ ውስተ፡ መዛግብቲከ።

⁵ በብዝኀ፡ ጥበብከ፡ ወበተግባርከ፡ አብዛኅከ፡ ኀይለከ፡ ወተዐበየ፡ ልብከ፡ በኀይልከ።

⁶ በእንተዝ፡ ከመዝ፡ ይቤ፡ አዶናይ፡ እግዚአብሔር፤ እስመ፡ ረሰይከ፡ ልብከ፡ ከመ፡ ልበ፡ አምላክ።

⁷ በእንተዝ፡ ናሁ፡ አመጽእ፡ ላዕሌከ፡ ነኪራነ፡ ኃያላነ፡ አሕዛብ፡ ወይመልጡ፡ ሰይፎሙ፡ ዲበ፡ ሥነ፡ ጥበብከ፡ ወየረኵሱ፡ ብርሃነከ።

⁸ ይደርብዩከ፡ ወይቀትሉከ፡ ወትመውት፡ በሐዊን፡ ወይዌርዉ፡ በድንከ፡ ውስተ፡ ልቡ፡ ባሕር።

⁹ እስከ፡ በሎሙ፡ ከመዝ፡ ለእለ፡ ይቀትሉከ፡ እስመ፡ ትቤ፡ እግዚአብሔር፡ አነ፤ እንዘ፡ አንተ፡ ሰብእ፡ ወኢኮንከ፡ እግዚአብሔር፡

¹⁰ ወብዙኃን፡ እለ፡ ይረግዙከ፡ ወሞተ፡ ቀላፋን፡ ትመውት፡ ወእለ፡ ይቀትሉከ፡ ቀላፋን፡ እሙንቱ፡ ወትመውት፡ በእደዊሆሙ፡ እስመ፡ አነ፡ ነበብኩ፡ ይቤ፡ አዶናይ፡ እግዚአብሔር፡ እግዚእ።

¹¹ ወነበበኒ፡ እግዚአብሔር፡ ወይቤለኒ፤

¹² ወልደ፡ እጓለ፡ እምሕያው፡ ንግሥ፡ ሰቆቃወ፡ ላዕለ፡ ንጉሠ፡ ጢሮስ፡ ወበሎ፤ ከመዝ፡ ይቤ፡ እግዚአብሔር፡ እግዚእ፤ አንተ፡ ማኅተም፡ ሥዕል፡ ምሉዐ፡ ጥበብ፡ ወፍጹም፡ ሥን።

¹³ በኤደን፡ ገነተ፡ አምላክ፡ ሀሎከ፡ ወኵሉ፡ እብን፡ ክቡር፡ ተድባብከ፡ ሰርድዮን፡ ወጳዝዮን፡ ወሥርድክስ፡ ተርሴስ፡ ወያክንት፡ ወኢያስፊድ፡ ሰንፔር፡ ወመረግደ፡ ወአሜቴስጦን፡ ወወርቅ፡ ግብረ፡ ከበሮከ፡ ወመዝሙርከ፡ ብከ፡ ወተደለዉ፡ በዕለተ፡ ፍጥረትከ።

¹⁴ አንተ፡ ኪሩብ፡ ቅቡዕ፡ ዘይጼልል፡ ወአቀምኩከ፡ ውስተ፡ ደብረ፡ አምላክ፡ ቅዱስ፡ ወሀሎከ፡ ማእከለ፡ አእባነ፡ እሳት፡ ታንሱ።

¹⁵ ንጹሕ፡ አንተ፡ በፍኖትከ፡ እምዕለተ፡ ፍጥረትከ፡ እስከ፡ አመ፡ ተረክበ፡ ጌጋይ፡ ላዕሌከ።

¹⁶ እብዝኅ፡ ተግባርከ፡ መልዐ፡ ወስቴትከ፡ ዐመፃ፡ ወጎጣእከ፡ ወአርኩሰከ፡ እምደብረ፡ አምላክ፡ ወአጠፍአከ፡ ኪሩብ፡ ዘተጼለለ፡ እማእከለ፡ አእባነ፡ እሳት።

¹⁷ ተለዓለ፡ ልብከ፡ በሥንከ፡ ወአማሰንከ፡ ጥበበከ፡ ምስለ፡ ክብርከ፡ ነጻሕኩከ፡ ዲበ፡ ምድር፡ በቅድመ፡ ነገሥት፡ ወወሀብኩከ፡ ይርአዩከ።

¹⁸ ወአርኰስከ፡ መቅደስከ፡ እምብዙኅ፡ ኃጢአትከ፡ ወኃጢአተ፡ ተግባርከ፡ ወአወፃእ፡ እሳተ፡ እማእከሌከ፡ ወይእቲ፡ ታበልዐከ፡ ወረሰይኩከ፡ መሬተ፡ ዲበ፡ ምድር፡ በቅድመ፡ ኵሎሙ፡ እለ፡ ይሬእዩከ።

¹⁹ ወያነክሩ፡ ላዕሌከ፡ ኵሎሙ፡ እለ፡ የአምሩከ፡ በውስተ፡ አሕዛብ፡ ኮንከ፡ ለድንጋጼ፡ ወኢሀለ፡ አንከ፡ ለዓለም።

Chapter 34

CG VERBS: THE REMAINING MOODS

34.1 CG Imperfect, Subjunctive, and Imperative Forms

The CG verbs can be used to indicate a causative type of action with the active voice (see ch. 18). The key words used in your translation will be "caused to" or "made to" do something. For example, the verb ነበረ፡ – "he sat" in its causative form አንበረ፡ is translated "he was made to sit." In Gəʿəz, the causative verbs can be derived from the base verbs G, D, L, and Q and are marked by a prefixed አ-. The $\bar{a}$ in the closed syllable of the prefix in the Imperfect and Subjunctive is unusual and may be due to the loss of the CG prefix አ.

CG verbs all display the same fundamental pattern of formation in the imperfect, subjunctive, and imperative moods except for the roots with II-ወ/የ. The causative forms follow a similar pattern to the corresponding G verbs except for the $\bar{a}$ of the prefix in the imperfect and subjunctive. The table below presents the simple causative verb declension of the imperfect, subjunctive, and imperative. This will be followed by a table covering the so-called weak verbs for comparison.

TABLE 34.1: Simple Causative Imperfect, Subjunctive, and Imperative

PGN	Perf.	Impf.	Subj.	Impv.	PGN	Perf.	Impf.	Subj.	Impv.
3ms	አቅተለ፡	ያቀትል፡	ያቅትል፡	—	3mp	አቅተሉ፡	ያቀትሉ፡	ያቅትሉ፡	—
3fs	አቅተለት፡	ታቀትል፡	ታቅትል፡	—	3fp	አቅተላ፡	ያቀትላ፡	ያቅትላ፡	—
2ms	አቅተልከ፡	ታቀትል፡	ታቅትል፡	አቅትል፡	2mp	አቅተልከሙ፡	ታቀትሉ፡	ታቅትሉ፡	አቅትሉ፡
2fs	አቅተልኪ፡	ታቀትሊ፡	ታቅትሊ፡	አቅትሊ፡	2fp	አቅተልከን፡	ታቀትላ፡	ታቅትላ፡	አቅትላ፡
1cs	አቅተልኩ፡	አቀትል፡	አቅትል፡	—	1cp	አቅተልነ፡	ናቀትል፡	ናቅትል፡	—

a. Note the infinitive form is አቅትሎ፡

b. Note the causative አ in the perfect and imperative forms. This is similar to the ה in the Hebrew Hiphil verbs and serves as a good key marker for the CG perfect verbs.

c. The causative imperfect and subjunctive prefix (ይ, ታ, ኣ, ን) appears with the *ā* vowel and results in the loss of the አ prefix found in the causative perfect.

d. Note in the imperfect pattern, the first consonant has the *ă* vowel lengthened from the short *ə*; the middle consonant shortens from the *ă* vowel in the perfect to the *ə* vowel.

e. The imperfect third consonant has the expected vowel variations identifying the PGN.

f. In the subjunctive forms, the first and second consonants have *ə* throughout and the third consonant has the expected vowel variations of the PGN endings.

TABLE 34.2 CG IMPERFECT, SUBJUNCTIVE AND IMPERATIVE

Verb Root Type	Perfect	Imperfect	Subjunctive	Imperative
Strong set in place	አንበረ፡	ያነብር፡	ያንብር፡	አንብር፡
I Guttural make sad	አሐዘነ፡	ያሐዝን፡	ያሐዝን፡	አሐዝን፡
II Guttural make rich	አብዐለ፡	ያበዕል፡	ያብዕል፡	አብዕል፡
III Guttural bring an offering	አምጽአ፡	ያመጽእ፡	ያምጽእ፡	አምጽእ፡
I-ወ send down	አውረደ፡	ያወርድ፡	ያውርድ፡	አውርድ፡
II-ወ establish	አቀመ፡ / አቀመ፡	ያቀውም፡	ያቅም፡ ያቅም፡	አቅም፡ / አቅም፡
III-ወ restore to life	አሕየወ፡	ያሐዩ፡	ያሕዩ፡	አሕዩ፡
II-የ thresh	አኬደ፡	ያከይድ፡	ያኪድ፡ / ያኪድ፡	አኪድ፡ / አኪድ፡
III-የ cause to weep	አብከየ፡	ያበኪ፡	ያብኪ፡	አብኪ፡

a. With the I Guttural verbs, there is no difference in the vowels of the strong imperfect, subjunctive, and imperative. It appears the imperfect and subjunctive have the ይ prefix, while the imperative has the አ prefix. However, what has actually occurred is the assimilation of the normal ይ prefix that precedes a guttural with the causative አ prefix, which results in the forming of the ይ prefix on the imperfect and subjunctive. A similar assimilation of the causative አ prefix occurs with all person prefixes in the imperfect including the ት and ን personal prefixes (see Rules of Contractions in ch. 2).

b. With the II Guttural verbs in the imperfect and subjunctive the three consonants of the root all have *ə*, which makes recognition easier. The imperative also follows this same short vowel pattern but with the አ prefix versus the ይ of the imperfect and subjunctive.

c. The III Guttural imperfect displays the ă vowel followed by the short ə vowels in the second and third consonants.

d. The III Guttural subjunctive and imperative forms have the short ə vowel on all three consonants and the ይ and አ prefixes as expected.

e. I-ወ imperfect, subjunctive, and imperative, as expected, all follow the same patterns as I Guttural.

f. With the II-ወ only the imperfect verb retains the II-ወ, while the first consonant in the perfect, subjunctive, and imperative all lengthen the vowel to an o or u. Note the two possible forms in each of the perfect, subjunctive, and imperative.

g. With the III-ወ subjunctive and imperative, all three consonants display the ə while the first consonant of the imperfect displays ă followed by ə on the second and third consonants. Note the perfect lengthens the vowel of the second consonant to ă.

h. Like the II-ወ, the II-ይ in the perfect, subjunctive, and imperative forms drops out, but is retained in the imperfect. Note the two possible forms in each of the subjunctive and imperative.

i. The III-ይ of the imperfect, subjunctive, and imperative forms follow the same vowel pattern as the III Guttural verbs. The exception is the perfect, which lengthens the second consonant vowel.

34.2 CG Verbal Nouns

CG verbs do not normally include verbal nouns except for the infinitive. On occasion a derived noun will be encountered that follows the አቅተላ፡ pattern, but this occurs rarely.

አርእይ፡ – (from the verb "to see," ርእየ፡) image, form, likeness, type
ዕረፍት፡ – rest, peace, quiet

34.3 CG Agent Nouns

There are numerous CG verbs that have an agent noun that follows the pattern of መቅትል፡ or መቅተሊ፡ and occur quite often. The following list offers some of the most frequent CG agent nouns:

ማእምር፡ – knowing, skilled, or a soothsayer (one who knows)
መብከይ፡ – professional mourner
መፍርህ፡ – dreadful, being in awe
ማሕምም፡ – grievous, afflicting with grief
ማሕይው፡ / ማሕየዊ፡ – life-giving, salvific
ማሕዝን፡ / ማሕዘኒ፡ – saddening or provoking sadness

መምክር፡ (pl. መማክርት፡) – counselor, advisor
መሥመሪ፡ / መሥመሪ፡ – pleasing to
መጥምቅ፡ – baptizer, as in John the Baptizer

34.4 Vocabulary

1. ሐስ፡ / ሐሰ፡ – sign of aversion
2. ሐዊሳ፡ / ሐዌሳ፡ – sign of joy
3. ሰይልየ፡ / ሴልየ፡ – woe is me!
4. ሶ፡ – please!
5. ባሕ፡ / ባሐ፡ / በሐ፡ – salutation
6. ነዓ፡ – come!
7. አ፡ / አሁ፡ – sign of sorrow
8. አ፡ – (marker of vocative) O!
9. አሌ፡ – alas!, unfortunately!
10. እንቋዕ፡ – joy!
11. ሂ – and, also; always suffixed
12. ህየንተ፡ suffixed with ዘ – instead of
13. እምዘ፡ – since
14. እምጣነ፡ በእምጣነ፡ – as long as
15. ሶበ፡ – when (temporal)
16. ቅድመ፡ እምቅድመ፡ – before that (with subjunctive)
17. ባሕቱ፡ – but, however, nevertheless
18. አላ፡ – but
19. አመ፡ – when, while
20. እመ፡ / እም፡ – if
21. ወእመሰ፡ – and if on the contrary
22. እስመ፡ – because
23. እስከ፡ – till that
24. እንበለ፡ – if not, except
25. እንከ፡ – then
26. እንዘ፡ – whilst
27. እንጋ፡ – perhaps
28. አው፡ – or
29. አንከረ፡ – wonder, be astonished, marvel
30. ድኅነ፡ – escape safely, be unharmed

34.5 Exercises

A. Translate the following:

1. ኢያወርድ፡ ዝናመ፡ በጊዜሁ፡

2. ፈነወ፡ አግብርቲሁ፡ ያብጽሐነ፡ ሀገረ፡

3. እግዚአብሔር፡ ያከሥለነ፡ በኩሉ፡ ዘንፈቅድ፡

4. ያኑኅ፡ እግዚአብሔር፡ መዋዕሊከሙ፡ ዲበ፡ ምድር፡

5. አጽንዑ፡ አልባቢከሙ፡ ወኢትፍርሁ፡

6. ሰበ፡ ይነግሩከ፣ አንተ፡ ኢታወሥእ።

7. ኢታስሕቶሙ፡ ለሕዝብየ፡ አምዕቀበተ፡ ሕግዮ።

8. አጥዕመን፡ ንስቲተ፡ ፍሬ።

9. ይእተ፡ አሚረ፡ ናዐውቀክ፡ ኪዳነ፡ ሐዲሰ።

10. ወበጊዜሃ፡ ያሐይያሙ፡ ለኵሎሙ፡ ምውታን፡ ኀቡረ።

11. ፈቀዱ፡ ከመ፡ ያንግሥዎ፡ ላዕሌሆሙ።

12. ታስሚ፡ ሀገርከ፡ ውስተ፡ ኵላ፡ ምድር።

13. ዝዩ፡ ትክሉ፡ ነቢረ፡ በሰላም፡ ወዳኅን።

14. መኑ፡ ዘያዕውነከ፡ ዘንተ፡ ገዳም።

15. ያፈጥኑ፡ ይገብሩ፡ ሰላመ፡ ምስሌነ።

16. ኢታንእሱ፡ ጥበበ፡ መጻሕፍተ፡ ቀደምት።

17. ኢታርሕቁ፡ ሕግየ፡ እምኀቤክሙ።

18. ኢታንድድ፡ እሳተ፡ እስከ፡ ይቄርር፡ ሌሊት።

19. ኢያተርፍ፡ ዝንቱ፡ ንጉሥ፡ እኩይ፡ አሐደ፡ እምሕዝብነ።

20. አዕርፊ፡ ዝየ፡ እስከ፡ ያገብአሙ፡ ለውሉዲኪ።

21. በእንተ፡ ምንት፡ ከመዝ፡ ታሐምማ፡ ለነፍስየ፡ እግዚኦ።

22. ታነድዮከ፡ ዛቲ፡ ሕይወት፡ ዘእንበለ፡ ክልአት።

23. ያርኒ፡ እግዚአብሔር፡ መሳኬው፡ ሰማይ፡ ወያወርድ፡ ዝናም።

24. ተናከርዖ፡ ለሕግነ፡ ወለግዕዝነ።

25. ጎበ፡ መኑ፡ ታዐቅብ፡ ንዋየከ።

26. ያጐጽ፡ ሰብአ፡ አፍራሲሆሙ፡ በፍርሀት፡ ዐቢይ።

27. አንትኑ፡ ታነብብ፡ ለነ፡ ዘንተ፡ መልእክተ።

28. ያረክበከሙ፡ ዝንቱ፡ መጽሐፍ፡ ብዕለ፡ መንፈሳዌ።

29. ለያሥምርከ፡ ምክርየ፡ ዘእንግረከ፡ ኦንጉሥ።

30. ኢታውዒ፡ ቤትየ።

31. ኢታብክየነ፡ በዜናከ፡ ሐዘን፡ አአረጋይ።

32. አሙተኒ፡ እስመ፡ ኢይፈቅድ፡ እሕየው።

33. ውእተ፡ ጊዜ፡ ታነጽሩ፡ መንገለ፡ ቤትየ፡ ወትበኪዩ።

34. ወታጽሕፎ፡ ዘንተ፡ ትእዛዘ፡ ዲበ፡ እብን፡ ዐቢይ።

35. ታወፅእዎ፡ አፍአ፡ እምቤቱ፡ ወትወግርዎ፡ በእብን።

36. ዝውእቱ፡ መጽሐፍ፡ በእንተ፡ መድኃኒተ፡ ዓለም።

37. ኢታዕርብ፡ ፀሐዮ፡ በዛቲ፡ ዕለት፡ እንዘ፡ ትጻውም።

38. ኣገብር፡ ለርእሰየ፡ መንበረ፡ ዘወርቅ።

39. አዘዘሙ፡ ከመ፡ ያንብሩ፡ ሥጋሁ፡ ህየ።

40. ለምንት፡ ታረኩሱ፡ ቤትየ፡ ቅዱሰ።

41. ለምንት፡ ተናክርክሙዋ፡ ለጥበበ፡ አበዊክሙ።

42. ታዐውዶ፡ ለዐዋዲከ፡ ውስተ፡ ኩሉ፡ በሓውርት።

43. ውስተ፡ ዝንቱ፡ መካን፡ ታሓንጽ፡ ሊተ፡ ቤተ፡ ሐዲሰ።

44. ወእምድኅረ፡ ዝንቱ፡ ምንዳቤ፡ አንተ፡ ታነፍስ፡ እምኅሳረ፡ ዓለም።

45. ናጹሮሙ፡ አጽዋሪከ።

46. አዕርግዎሙ፡ ውስተ፡ አረፍተ፡ ጥቅም፡ ዘሀገር።

47. ቆሙ፡ ውስተ፡ ሐመር፡ እንዘ፡ ያህድእ፡ ማዕበላተ፡ ባሕር፡ ቢቃሉ።

48. አርትዑ፡ ፍናዊከሙ፡ ወምግባሪከሙ፡ ከመ፡ ኢትሙቱ።
_____

49. ረከብዎ፡ እንዘ፡ ያጠምቆሙ፡ ለኵሎሙ፡ ሕዝብ።
_____

50. አብዕለነ፡ በንዋይ፡ መንፈሳዊ፡ አእግዚእነ።
_____

51. ኢታሕዝኖ፡ ለአቡከ፡ በሕይወቱ።
_____

52. ሶበ፡ ትወድቅ፡ አንተ፡ ናሁ፡ አነ፡ ኣነሥአከ።
_____

53. አብእዎሙ፡ ዝየ፡ ወአንብርዎሙ፡ ቅድሜየ።
_____

54. ያክሕዶ፡ ነገርከ፡ እምነ፡ ፈጣሪሁ።
_____

55. አላ፡ አቀድም፡ እምጽአ፡ ኀቤክሙ።
_____

56. ይቤሎሙ፡ ከመ፡ ያጽንሑ፡ ሎቱ፡ ሐመረ።
_____

57. ዘንተ፡ ኀሳረ፡ ያንልፍ፡ እምዲቤነ፡ ወነንድር፡ በሰላም፡ ለዝሉፉ።
_____

58. ኢታብልዩ፡ አሣእነክሙ፡ እስመ፡ ኢይከውነክሙ፡ ካልእነ።
_____

59. አክብር፡ አእመከ፡ ወእመከ፡ ኵሎ፡ መዋዕለ፡ ሕይወቶሙ።
_____

60. አነውሞ፡ ብዙኀ፡ ዓመተ፡ ከመ፡ ኢይርአይ፡ ድቀተ፡ ሀገር፡ ወፍልሰተ፡ ሕዝብ።
_____

61. ኣጸልም፡ ገጹ፡ ፀሐይ፡ ወይፈርህ፡ ኵሉ፡ ልብ።
_____

B. Acts 9:1–22. Translate the following:

¹ ወሳውልሰ፡ ዓዲሁ፡ ይትቄየም፡ አብያተ፡ ክርስቲያናት፡ ወይቀትሎሙ፡ ለአርዳእ፡ እግዚአነ፡ ወሐረ፡ ኀበ፡ ሊቀ፡ ካህናት።

² ወሰአለ፡ በኀቤሁ፡ መጽሐፈ፡ መባሕት፡ ለሀገረ፡ ደማስቆ፡ ወለመኳርብት፡ ለእመቦ፡ ዘይረክብ፡ በፍኖት፡ ዕደወ፡ ወአንስተ፡ ከመ፡ ያአትዎሙ፡ ኢየሩሳሌም፡ ሙቁሐኒሆሙ።

³ ወእንዘ፡ የሐውር፡ ሶበ፡ አልጸቀ፡ ለሀገረ፡ ደማስቆ፡ ግብተ፡ በረቀ፡ መብረቅ፡ እምሰማይ፡ ላዕሌሁ።

⁴ ወወደቀ፡ ውስተ፡ ምድር፡ ወሰምዐ፡ ቃለ፡ ዘይቤሎ፤ ሳውል፡ ሳውል፡ ለምንት፡ ትሰድደኒ፤

⁵ ወይቤሎ፥ መኑ፡ አንተ፡ እግዚእ፡ ወይቤሎ፡ አነ፡ ውእቱ፡ ኢያሱስ፡ ናዝራዊ፡ ዘአንተትሰድደኒ፡ ይብእሰከ፡ ረጊጽ፡ ውስተ፡ ቀኖት፡ በሊኀ።

⁶ ወእንዘ፡ ይርዕድ፡ አንከረ፡ ወይቤሎ፤ እግዚኦ፡ ምንተኑ፡ ትፈቅድ፡ እገብር፡ አነ፤ ወይቤሎ፡ እግዚእ፡ ተንሥእ፡ ወባእ፡ ሀገረ፡ ወበህየ፡ ይነግሩከ፡ ዘይደልወከ፡ ትግበር።

⁷ ወሰብእሰ፡ እለ፡ ምስሌሁ፡ ቆሙ፡ ያፀምኡ፡ ነገሮ፡ ወአልቦ፡ ዘይሬእዮ።

⁸ ወተንሥአ፡ ሳውል፡ እምድር፡ ወእንዘ፡ ክሡታት፡ አዕይንቲሁ፡ አልቦ፡ ዘይሬኢ፡ ወእንዘ፡ ይመርሕዎ፡ አብአዎ፡ ደማስቆ።

⁹ ወነበረ፡ ህየ፡ ሠሉስ፡ ዕለተ፡ እንዘ፡ ኢያሬኢ፡ ወኢይበልዕ፡ ወኢይሰቲ።

¹⁰ ወሀሎ፡ አሐዱ፡ ብእሲ፡ በሀገረ፡ ደማስቆ፡ ዘእምውስተ፡ አርድእት፡ ዘስሙ፡ ሐናንያ፡ ወአስተርአዮ፡ እግዚእነ፡ በራእይ፡ ወይቤሎ፥ ሐናንያ፡ ወይቤ፡ ነየ፡ እግዚኦ።

¹¹ ወይቤሎ፡ እግዚእነ፡ ተንሥእ፡ ወሐር፡ ሰኰተ፡ እንተ፡ ይብልዋ፡ ርትዕት፡ ወኀሥሥ፡ በቤተ፡ ይሁዳ፡ ዘስሙ፡ ሳውል፡ ዘሀገረ፡ ጠርሴስ፡ እስመ፡ ውእቱ፡ ናሁ፡ ይጼሊ።

¹² ወእንዘ፡ ይጸሊ፡ አስተርአዮ፡ ብእሲ፡ ዘስሙ፡ ሐናንያ፡ ቦአ፡ ኀቤሁ፡ ወወደየ፡ እዴሁ፡ ዲቤሁ፡ ከመ፡ ይርአይ።

¹³ ወአውሥአ፡ ሐናንያ፡ ወይቤ፡ እግዚኦ፡ ሰማዕኩ፡ በእንተ፡ ውእቱ፡ ብእሲ፡ በኀበ፡ ብዙኃን፡ ኵሎ፡ ዘይገብር፡ እኩየ፡ ዲበ፡ ቅዱሳኒከ፡ በኢየሩሳሌም።

¹⁴ ወዝየኒ፡ አስተበዋሐ፡ በኀበ፡ ሊቀ፡ ካህናት፡ መጽአ፡ ከመ፡ ይሞቅሐሙ፡ ለኵሎሙ፡ እለ፡ ይጼውዑ፡ ስመከ።

¹⁵ ወይቤሎ፡ አግዚአነ፥ ሑር፡ እስመ፡ ንዋየ፡ ኃሩየ፡ ረሰይክዎ፡ ሊተ፡ ከመ፡ ይጹር፡ ስምየ፡ በቅድመ፡ አሕዛብ፡ ወነገሥት፡ ወደቂቀ፡ እስራኤል።

¹⁶ ወእነ፡ አርእዮ፡ መጠነ፡ ህለዎ፡ ይሕምም፡ በእንተ፡ ስምየ።

¹⁷ ወሶቤሃ፡ ሐረ፡ ሐናንያ፡ ወበአ፡ ቤቶ፡ ወወደየ፡ እዴሁ፡ ዲቤሁ፡ ወይቤሎ፥ ሳውል፡ እኁየ፡ እግዚአነ፡ ኢየሱስ፡ ክርስቶስ፡ ፈነወኒ፡ ኃቤከ፡ ዘአስተርአየከ፡ በፍኖት፡ እንዘ፡ ትመጽእ፡ ከመ፡ ትርአይ፡ ወይምላእ፡ መንፈስ፡ ቅዱስ፡ ላዕሌከ።

¹⁸ ወሶቤሃ፡ ተሥዕዓ፡ እምአዕይንቲሁ፡ ከመ፡ ዘሳሬት፡ ወተከሥታ፡ አዕይንቲሁ፡ ወርእየ፡ ሶቤሃ፡ ወተንሥአ፡ ወተጠምቀ።

¹⁹ ወበልዐ፡ እክለ፡ ወጸንዐ፡ ወነበረ፡ ደማስቆ፡ ኀዳጠ፡ መዋዕለ፡ ምስለ፡ አርድእት።

²⁰ ወሰበከ፡ ቢዜሃ፡ በምኩራባት፡ ወመሀረ፡ በእንተ፡ ኢየሱስ፡ ክርስቶስ፡ እንዘ፡ ይብል፡ ውእቱ፡ ወልደ፡ እግዚአብሔር።

²¹ ወአንከሩ፡ ኩሎሙ፡ እለ፡ ሰምዑ፡ ወይቤሉ፥ አኮኑ፡ ዝንቱ፡ ዘከነ፡ ይፀብአሙ፡ ለእለ፡ ይጸውዑ፡ ዘንተ፡ ስመ፡ በኢየሩሳሌም፤ ወዝየኒ፡ በእንተዝ፡ መጽአ፡ ከመ፡ ይሞቅሓሙ፡ ወይስዶሙ፡ ኃበ፡ ሊቃነ፡ ካህናት።

²² ወሳውልሰ፡ ፈድፋደ፡ ይጸንዕሙ፡ ወይመውዖሙ፡ ለአይሁድ፡ እለ፡ ይነብሩ፡ ደማስቆ፡ ወያጽሕ፡ ሎሙ፡ ከመ፡ ውእቱ፡ ክርስቶስ።

Chapter 35

D, DT, CD VERBS: THE REMAINING MOODS

35.1 D Verbs: Imperfect, Subjunctive, and Imperative[1]

The D verb (similar to Heb. *piel*) is the three-letter root with the doubling of the second consonant (radical) in all forms following the stem vowel pattern $C_1 ăC_2 C_2 ăC_3 ă$[2] in the perfect, e.g., ነጸረ፡, *năṣṣără* – "he looked." However, the doubling does not appear in the Gəʿəz script nor do the verbs necessarily carry the intense definition as they do in Hebrew. The intensifying of the action of the verb can indicate frequent repetition or the force or completeness of the action. These intensive verbs tend to express the practices and usages that are in a series or group of individual acts and generally will continue for some time, e.g., ሐለወ፡ – "watch"; ሐለየ፡ – "meditate"; መረደ፡ – "hasten"; ሠገረ፡ – "take quick steps"; ኀየለ፡ – "exert strength." As you can see, these verbs generally show activity associated with carefulness or excitement.

The declension patterns of the imperfect, subjunctive, and imperative remain regular regardless of the root type, e.g., strong, I Guttural, III-ዐ, etc. The strong imperfect pattern includes the ይ prefix, ይ+$C_1 ēC_2 C_2 əC_3$(ə); the strong subjunctive also includes the ይ prefix, ይ+$C_1 ăC_2 C_2 əC_3$(ə); the strong imperative excludes the prefix like the perfect, $C_1 ăC_2 C_2 əC_3$(ə). The table below shows the patterns for the various root types for the D verb.

TABLE 35.1: D Imperfect, Subjunctive, and Imperative

Verb Root Type	Perfect	Imperfect	Subjunctive	Imperative
Strong complete	ፈጸመ፡	ይፌጽም፡	ይፈጽም፡	ፈጽም፡
I Guttural command	አዘዘ፡	ይኤዝዝ፡	የአዝዝ፡	አዝዝ፡
II Guttural teach	መህረ፡	ይሜህር፡	ይመህር፡ / ይምህር፡	መህር፡ / ምህር፡
III Guttural repent	ነስሐ፡	ይኔስሕ፡	ይነስሕ፡	ነስሕ፡

---
1. See ch. 7.
2. Keep in mind the doubling of the radical in Gəʿəz is not marked in any way, unlike the use of the *dagesh forte* in Hebrew.

Verb Root Type	Perfect	Imperfect	Subjunctive	Imperative
I-ወ add to	ወሰከ፡	ይዌስክ፡	ይወስክ፡	ወስክ፡
II-ወ heal	ፈወሰ፡	ይፌውስ፡	ይፈውስ፡	ፈውስ፡
III-ወ send	ፈነወ፡	ይፌንዉ፡	ይፈንዉ፡	ፈንዉ፡
II-የ examine	ጠየቀ፡	ይጤይቅ፡	ይጠይቅ፡	ጠይቅ፡
III-የ set	ረሰየ፡	ይሬስይ፡	ይረስይ፡	ረስይ፡

a. The infinitive strong form appears as ፈጽሞ፡ – to complete.

b. Note the perfect maintains the ă vowel throughout despite the weak consonants in the I, II, or III positions.

c. The imperfect, with the addition of the ይ prefix, results in the lengthening of the vowel with the first consonant to ē and the II and III consonants reduce to ə regardless of a weak consonant in the I, II, or III position.

d. The subjunctive varies from the imperfect in all categories: in the strong the vowel with the first consonant is ă, followed by ə on the II and III consonants.

e. The subjunctive weak verbs have significant variations. The ይ prefix in the I Guttural lengthens from ይ to ዩ, and the I Guttural has ă followed by the II and III Gutturals with ə.

f. The subjunctive II Guttural has two forms: one with ă on the I consonant, and the other with ə on the I consonant.

g. The remaining subjunctive weak verbs follow a similar vowel pattern: the ă vowel on the I consonant is followed by the II and III consonants with ə, regardless of the position of the weak consonant.

h. The imperative form maintains the ă vowel like the perfect form, but the II and III consonants have ə. The other weak forms follow a similar pattern except for the II Guttural verb, which has two forms: the first mirrors all the others, and the second variation has the reduced ə vowel on all three consonants.

35.2 Dt Verbs: Imperfect, Subjunctive, and Imperative Forms

As mentioned previously, the Dt verbs are considered medio-passive verbs (see ch. 15) and are formed from the active D verb pattern with the addition of a ተ prefix. The strong pattern is ተ+$C_1 ăC_2C_2 ăC_3 ă$; note the doubling of the middle consonant, but this does not appear in the Gəʿəz script, only in the transliteration. The verb maintains the force, intensity, or repetition but as a passive the action is directed toward the subject. The Dt verbs follow a similar pattern to the D verbs apart from the ă on the II consonant in the imperfect.

TABLE 35.2: Dt Imperfect, Subjunctive, and Imperative

Verb Root Type	Perfect	Imperfect	Subjunctive	Imperative
Strong	ተፈጸመ፡	ይትፌጸም፡	ይትፈጸም፡	ተፈጸም፡
I Guttural	ተአዘዘ፡	ይትኤዘዝ፡	ይትአዘዝ፡	ተአዘዝ፡
II Guttural	ተመህረ፡ / ተምህረ፡	ይትሜህር፡	ይትመህር፡	ተመህር፡
III Guttural	ተነስሐ፡	ይትኔሳሕ፡	ይትነሳሕ፡	ተነሳሕ፡
I-ወ	ተወስከ፡	ይትዌስከ፡	ይትወስከ፡	ተወስከ፡
II-ወ	ተፈወሰ፡	ይትፌወስ፡	ይትፈወስ፡	ተፈወስ፡
III-ወ	ተፈነወ፡	ይትፌነው፡	ይትፈነው፡	ተፈነው፡
II-የ	ተጠየቀ፡	ይጤየቅ፡	ይጠየቅ፡	ተጠየቅ፡
III-የ	ተረስየ፡	ይትፈሰይ፡	ይትረሰይ፡	ተረሰይ፡

a. The infinitive form appears as ተቀትሎ፡ – to make complete

b. Note the ተ prefix on the perfect and imperative forms. There are some vowel clues that will help distinguish between the two.

c. Note the ă on the last syllable of the perfect and the ə on the imperative. Note the II consonant on the imperative has the long ā with the III Guttural.

d. The perfect II Guttural has two forms: the first has the expected ă on all three root consonants and the second has the short ə vowel in the I and II consonants and the ă on the final consonant.

e. The imperfect form includes the expected ይ prefix and the ት prefix of the Dt verbs in all but the II-የ, in which the ት prefix appears to have assimilated into the first consonant due to the dental ጠ: note the vowel on the ት prefix has shortened from the perfect ă vowel to the ə vowel in the imperfect and subjunctive.

f. The imperfect I consonant now has the ē vowel in all root types. The II consonant has the ă vowel in all forms except the III Guttural which has the long ā vowel due to the III Guttural. This is the case in all but the perfect.

g. The imperfect III consonant has the short ə vowel in the strong, I, II, III Gutturals, and the II, III-ወ and the II, III-የ forms.

h. The subjunctive verb forms have the expected ይ prefix and the ት prefix of the Dt verbs in all but the III-ወ form in which the ት prefix appears to have assimilated into the first consonant due to the dental consonant ጠ.

i. The subjunctive I and II consonants have *ă* except for the III Guttural form where the II consonant takes *ā*. The III consonants are all marked with *ə*.

35.3   D Verbal Adjectives

The D verbal adjective (see ch. 24), as previously mentioned, is first an adjective derived from a verb that is used to describe a noun. It takes the appearance of the "-ing" verb in English such as "smiling eyes." D verbal adjectives generally appear in the ቅቱል፡ pattern but can be found in the ቀቲል፡, e.g., ሐዲስ፡, or ቀታል፡, e.g., ሠናይ፡ forms. The following is a list of common D verbal adjectives:

አዙዝ፡ – commanded, ordered
ዕቡይ፡ – arrogant, haughty; cf. ተዐበየ፡ Dt
ፍኑው፡ – sent
ፍሡሕ፡ – happy, joyous, rejoicing, ተፈሥሐ፡ Dt
ፍጹም፡ – completed, accomplished, fulfilled
ግሡጽ፡ – instructed, learned
ኩኑን፡ – judged, condemned
ምጡው፡ – handed over, delivered
ንሱሕ፡ – repentant
ርሱይ፡ – prepared, made ready
ስውር፡ – hidden, concealed
ስዑዕ፡ – summoned, invited
ሥኑይ፡ – adorned, lovely
ጥዩቅ፡ – perceptive, accurate
ጥዩቀ፡ (adv.) – accurately, carefully, precisely

35.4   D Agent Nouns

As mentioned previously (see ch. 23), the agent noun signifies someone or something that performs a habitual or professional action of the verb. Agent nouns in the D verb class fall into two categories: the less common ቀታሊ፡ and መቀትል፡. The following is a list of common D agent nouns:

መፈውስ፡ – physician
ነሳሒ፡ – a penitent one
መገሥጽ፡ – instructor, teacher
መሠንይ፡ – the best part (of)
መምህር፡ – teacher

መኰንን፡ – judge, administrator

መሣግር፡ – fisherman

35.5 D Verbal Nouns

The D verb has approximately nine different patterns which are used to form the verbal noun (see ch. 25). These roughly nine forms can be broken down into four subgroups that are determined by the verb stem. The verbal noun formed from the simple tri-radical stem simply doubles the II consonant, although this will not appear in the Gəʿəz script. Keep in mind the verbal noun can act as an adjective (e.g., ፈሪህ፡ – "one who is easily frightened"; ረዓድ፡ – "one who is anxious"; ተባዕ፡ – "masculine"; አዳም፡ – "something pleasant"). The following offers a breakdown of the four subgroups according to their spelling:

a. ቅትል፡ ቅትላ፡ ቅትላት፡ ቅተልና፡ (Note the ቅተልና፡ form doubles both the ት and the ና in transliteration, whereas the other three forms only double the middle consonant, the ት and ተ).

    ፍሥሓ፡ – joy, happiness

    ንስሓ፡ – repentance, regret

    ጽውዓ፡ / ጽዋዔ፡ – call, summons

    ቅድሳት፡ / ቅድስና፡ – holiness, sanctity–frequently used in construct chains–ሀገረ፡ ቅድሳት፡ – city of holiness (holy city)

    ሥን፡ – beauty

b. ቅታል፡ ቅታሌ፡ ቅተሌ፡ (Note the ቅተሌ፡ form shortens the long $\bar{a}$ in the second radical to the short $\breve{a}$).

    ፍና፡ (pl. ፍናው፡ ፍናዉ፡) – road or path

    ፍኖት፡ (from the D verb ፈነወ፡) – road or path

    ፍና፡ ሰርክ፡ – early evening (path to night)

    ፍጻሜ፡ – end, completion, perfection

    ሕዋጼ፡ – visit, visitation

    ንጸሬ፡ – a look, glance, ability to see

    ቅዳሴ፡ – sanctification, consecration, liturgy

    ኵነኔ፡ – judgment, condemnation

c. ቀተላ፡ (cf. the G verbal noun, which would not double the middle radical in transliteration: ኀሠሣ፡ – "the seeking"; ሐተታ፡ – "the investigation of, the examination of").

    አበሳ፡ – the committing of a crime or sin

    ደመና፡ – the clouding over

d. ቀትል፡ (represents the infinitive base without the final *o* vowel)

    ፈውስ፡ – cure, healing, medicine

The doubling of the middle consonant in the D, which is not present in the Gəʿəz script, makes determining the underlying verb, either G or D, difficult. In addition, Gəʿəz is less than consistent in this practice along with the possibility of a similar practice with G verbs and quadrilateral roots. See for example, the ending *-ennā* usually associated with D verbs can be used to derive nouns in G verbs: የውሀና፡ – "gentleness" (cf. G verb የውሀ፡ – be gentle); ርሥኣና፡ – "old age" (cf. G verb ረሥአ፡ – grow old); ልህቅና፡ – "old age" (cf. G verb ልህቀ፡ – grow old). A similar issue occurs with the ending *-ān*, which is associated with D verbs such as ሥልጣን፡ – "power or authority" (cf. D verb ሠለጠ፡ – exercise power). However, it is also used with G verbs such as ብዕዳን፡ – "change"; ብፅዓን፡ – "beatification"; ብርሃን፡ – "light"; ግዕዛን፡ – "manumission"; ርስዓን፡ – "forgetfulness"; ዕርቃን፡ – "nakedness"; ፍልጣን፡ – "splitting or dividing."

35.6 Dt Verbal Nouns

There are two verbal noun patterns (ትቅትልት፡ ተቃታል፡) that occur with some frequency in the Dt form. Note however, there are no verbal adjectives or agent nouns that are derived from Dt verbs. The following list offers those of somewhat high frequency:

ትእዛዝ፡ – command, law
ተፍጻሜት፡ – consummation, end, completion
ተግሣጽ፡ (pl. ተግሣጻት፡) – rebuke, instruction
ትርሲት፡ – equipment, clothing, furnishing
ተውሳከ፡ (pl. ተውሳካት፡) – an added part, supplement
ትምህርት፡ (pl. ትምህርታት፡) – doctrine, teaching, study
ትዕቢት፡ – arrogance, insolence
ትፍሥሕት፡ (pl. ትፍሥሕታት፡) – joy happiness
ተስፋ፡ – hope, expectation
ተግባር፡ – product, work, labor, creation

35.7 D Verb Nouns with Prefixed ም

These nouns from the D verb type seem to follow a similar pattern that we have previously seen in G verb derived nouns ምቅታል፡; however, the D version is read with the doubling of the middle consonant but, again, this does not appear in the Gəʿəz script, only in transliteration. A few of the more common nouns are listed below:

ምኩናን፡ – courtroom, place of judgment, province
ምስዋር፡ – hidden place, hiding place
ምጽላይ፡ – place to pray
ምሥናይ፡ – best part of (something)

35.8 CD Verbs

The causative of the D verbs follow the patterns of the D perfect, imperfect, subjunctive, and imperative verb forms. Note that there are no commonly occurring derived verbal nouns or adjectives from CD verbs. The table below highlights the regular pattern for the CD verbs.

TABLE 35.3: CD Imperfect, Subjunctive, and Imperative Forms

Verb Meaning	Perfect	Imperfect	Subjunctive	Imperative
Strong Verb put someone in charge	አኩነነ፡	ያኬንን፡	ያኩንን፡	አኩንን፡
III-ይ adorn, array	አሠነየ፡	ያሤንይ፡	ያሠንይ፡	አሠንይ፡
III-ው promise	አሰፈወ፡	ያሴፍው፡	ያሰፍው፡	አሰፍው፡

a. Note the prefix አ- in the perfect and imperative forms. The strong perfect verb form includes the ă vowel with all three consonants and the prefix, while the II consonant has a short ə vowel and the III consonant is terminal.

b. The III-ይ perfect verb form includes the ă vowel with all three consonants and the prefix, while the III-ይ imperative includes ă with the prefix and the I consonant, but the II and III consonants have ə.

c. The III-ው for the perfect and imperative follow similar vowel patterns as the III-ይ.

d. The imperfect includes the expected ይ prefix with the long ā vowel, followed by the long ē vowel on the I consonant on all three forms (strong, III-ይ, and III-ው), followed by the short ə vowel in the II and III consonants.

e. The subjunctive mood includes the expected ይ prefix with the short ă vowel on the I consonant on all three verb forms (strong, III-ይ, and III-ው), followed by the short ə vowel in the II and III consonants.

35.9   Vocabulary

1. አንከረ፡ CG – wonder, be astonished; ተነክረ፡ Gt – be admired; ተናከረ፡ Glt – be alien to, renounce
2. ድኀነ፡ (subj. ይድኀን፡) – escape safely, be safe; አድኀነ፡ CG – save, keep safe, rescue
3. ድኁን፡ – safe, unharmed
4. ዳኅን፡ (adj.) – safe, whole, sound
5. ዳኅን፡ / ዳኅነ፡ / ድኂና፡ – safety, well-being
6. መድኀን፡ / መድኀኒ፡ – savior, redeemer
7. መድኀኒት፡ – salvation, redemption
8. ጠየቀ፡ D – examine, observe closely; አጠየቀ፡ CD – inform someone of something; ተጠየቀ፡ Dt – seek certainty or clarity
9. ጸለየ፡ D – pray
10. በግዕ፡ (f. በግዕት፡; pl. አባግዕ፡) – sheep, lamb
11. ቀደሰ፡ D – sanctify or make holy; ተቀደሰ፡ Dt – be made holy
12. ሐደሰ፡ D – renew, renovate; ተሐደሰ፡ Dt – be made new, to be restored
13. ደመነ፡ D – become clouded
14. ድሙን፡ – clouded over
15. አበሰ፡ D – commit a crime or sin

16. አባሲ፡ / መአብሲ፡ – sinner, criminal
17. አበሳ፡ (pl. አበሳት፡) – sin, crime
18. ተረስየ፡ Dt – put on a garment, adorn oneself
19. ተገብረ፡ Dt – work, produce something

35.10 Exercises

A. Translate the following:

1. መገሥጽ፡ እኩይ።

2. ሥኑ፡ ገጹ።

3. እንዘ፡ ይኔስሑ፡ ቀርቡ፡ ወሰገዱ፡ ሎቱ።

4. አነ፡ እሄሉ፡ ምስሌክሙ፡ ለዝሉፉ።

5. እምነ፡ መኑ፡ ትትመሀሩ፡ ሣእሣአ።

6. ወሂበከ፡ ሊተ፡ ወርቀ፡ ሤጥ፣ እጌጥወከ፡ ዘተሣየጥከ።

7. መንበር፡ ርሱይ፡ ለክብሩ።

8. መሥንየ፡ ወራዙቲሆሙ።

9. መምህር፡ መሓሪ።

10. ነሳሒ፡ ፍቱሕ።

11. ኢመፍትውዑ፡ ከመ፡ ንመጥዋ፡ ለሀገር፡ ውስተ፡ እደዊሁ፡ ለዝንቱ፡ ከሓዲ።

12. ጸውዕ፡ ሊተ፡ ሰፋዬ፡ ተበትከ፡ ቅናትዮ፨

13. ረስዮ፡ መሥዋዕተ፡ ዲበ፡ መሥዋዕ፡ ወሑሩ፡ አፍአ፡ እምዝንቱ፡ መካን፨

14. ትጤይቁ፡ አልባቢክሙ፡ ወባሕቱ፡ ኢትረክቡ፡ ጽድቀ፨

15. መልእክት፡ ፍጹም፨

16. ምንፃብ፡ ስዉር፡ እምነላፍያን፨

17. ሀገሪት፡ ምጥው፡ ለመዋኢሃ፨

18. መራሒ፡ ግሡጽ፡ ወስሙይ፨

19. ትገብሩ፡ ኵሎ፡ ዘእኤዘዘክሙ፨

20. ሀሎ፡ ወትረ፡ ይሔውጾሙ፡ ለመሀይምናን፡ እለ፡ ቤተ፡ ክርስቲያን፨

21. እንዘ፡ ይጌሥጾነ፡ ይቤለነ፡ ብዙኅ፡ በእንተ፡ ቀደምቲነ፨

22. አንገዙ፡ እነስሑ፡ በእስሑ፡ በእንተ፡ ኀጢአትዮ፨

23. አርዳእ፡ ግሡጻን፨

24. ብእሲ፡ ሐሙም፡ ወነሳሒ፨

25. ብእሲት፡ ፍሥሕት፡ ወሥኔት፨

26. ሰማዒ፡ ፍጹም።

27. መኑ፡ ዘይኤምረነ፡ ፍኖተ።

28. ነጽር፡ ግዕዘ፡ ጻድቅ፡ ከመ፡ ታእምር፡ ጽድቀ።

29. ንበር፡ ዝየ፡ እስከ፡ ትፌጽም፡ ግብረከ።

30. አዘዞ፡ ከመ፡ ይፈንዎ፡ ለወልዱ፡ ውስተ፡ ገዳም።

31. ኃላፊ፡ ጽዉዕ፡ ለበዊእ።

32. መፈውስ፡ ጠቢብ፡ በምግባሩ።

33. ቤት፡ ርሱይ፡ ለንብረትክሙ።

34. መኑ፡ ይኬንን፡ መኳንንተ።

35. ጠይቁ፡ መጻሕፍተ፡ ጠቢባን፡ ቀደምት።

36. ንፌውሳ፡ ለነፍስከ፡ በእምነት፡ ወበፍቅር፡ ወአኮ፡ በሥራይ።

37. መኰንን፡ ዕቡይ።

38. መካን፡ ሥኑይ፡ ለዐቢይ፡ በዓል።

39. ላእከ፡ ፍንው፡ ውስተ፡ ሀገር።

40. ኀጥአን፡ ኮኑን፡ ወኢንሱሐን።

_____

41. ለመኑ፡ ንሬስዮ፡ ነጋሤ፡ ላዕሌነ።

_____

B. Exodus 4:18–31. Translate the following:

¹⁸ ወሐረ፡ ሙሴ፡ ወገብአ፡ ኀበ፡ ዮቶር፡ ሐሙሁ፡ ወይቤሎ፡ አሐውር፡ ወእግብእ፡ ኀበ፡ አኀዊየ፡ እለ፡ ውስተ፡ ብሔረ፡ ግብፅ፤ ወእርአይ፡ ለእመ፡ ዓዲሆሙ፡ ሕያዋን፤ ወይቤሎ፡ ዮቶር፡ ለሙሴ፥ ሑር፡ በዳኅን፡ ወእምድኅረ፡ ብዙኅ፡ መዋዕል፡ ሞተ፡ ንጉሠ፡ ግብጽ።

¹⁹ ወይቤሎ፡ እግዚአብሔር፡ ለሙሴ፡ በምድረ፡ ምድያም፥ ሖረ፡ ወሑር፡ ብሔረ፡ ግብፅ፡ እስመ፡ ሞቱ፡ ኩሎሙ፡ እለ፡ የኀሥሥዋ፡ ለነፍስከ።

²⁰ ወነሥአ፡ ሙሴ፡ ብእሲቶ፡ ወደቂቆ፡ ወጸዐኖሙ፡ ዲባ፡ አእዱግ፡ ወገብአ፡ ብሔረ፡ ግብፅ፡ ወነሥአ፡ ሙሴ፡ ለእንታክቲ፡ በትር፡ እንተ፡ እምኀበ፡ እግዚአብሔር፡ ውስተ፡ እዴሁ።

²¹ ወይቤሎ፡ እግዚአብሔር፡ ለሙሴ፥ እንዘ፡ ተሐውር፡ ወትገብእ፡ ብሔረ፡ ግብፅ፡ አእምር፡ ኩሎ፡ መድምምየ፡ ዘወሀብኩከ፡ ውስተ፡ እደዊከ፡ ከመ፡ ትግበሮ፡ ቅድሜሁ፡ ለፈርዖን፡ ወአነ፡ አጸንዕ፡ ልቦ፡ ወኢይፌንዎ፡ ለሕዝብ።

²² ወአንተሰ፡ ትብሎ፡ ለፈርዖን፥ ከመዝ፡ ይቤ፡ እግዚአብሔር፡ ወልድየ፡ ዘበኩርየ፡ ውእቱ፡ እስራኤል።

²³ ወእብለከ፡ ፈኑ፡ ሕዝብየ፡ ከመ፡ ይፀመዱኒ፡ ወአንተሰ፡ ኢፈቀድከ፡ ትፍንዎ፡ አእምኬ፡ እንከ፡ ከመ፡ እቀትሎ፡ አነ፡ ለወልድከ፡ ዘበኩርከ።

²⁴ ወኮነ፡ በፍኖት፡ በውስተ፡ ማኅደር፡ ተራከቦ፡ መልአከ፡ እግዚአብሔር፡ ወፈቀደ፡ ይቅትሉ።

²⁵ ወነሥአት፡ ሲፓራ፡ መላጼ፡ ወገዘረት፡ ከተማ፡ ነፍስቱ፡ ለወልዱ፡ ወወድቀት፡ ኀበ፡ እገሪሁ፡ ወትቤ፡ ለይኩን፡ ህየንቴሁ፡ ዝደም፡ ግዝሮሁ፡ ለወልድየ።

²⁶ ወሐረ፡ እንከ፡ እምኔሁ፡ እስመ፡ ትቤ፥ ለይኩን፡ ህየንቴሁ፡ ዝደም፡ ግዝሮሁ፡ ለወልድየ።

²⁷ ወይቤሎ፡ እግዚአብሔር፡ ለአሮን፥ ሑር፡ ተቀበሎ፡ ለሙሴ፡ ውስተ፡ ሐቅል፡ ወሖረ፡ ወተራከቦ፡ በደብረ፡ እግዚአብሔር፡ ወተአምኖ።

²⁸ ወአይድዖ፡ ሙሴ፡ ለአሮን፡ ኵሎ፡ ቃለ፡ እግዚአብሔር፡ ዘለአኮ፡ ወኵሎ፡ ተአምረ፡ ዘአዘዘ።

²⁹ ወሐሩ፡ ሙሴ፡ ወአሮን፡ አስተጋብኡ፡ ኵሎ፡ አእሩገሙ፡ ለደቂቀ፡ እስራኤል።

³⁰ ወነገርሙ፡ አሮን፡ ኵሎ፡ ቃለ፡ እንተ፡ ነገሮ፡ እግዚአብሔር፡ ለሙሴ፡ ወገብረ፡ ተአምረ፡ ቅድመ፡ ሕዝብ።

³¹ ወአምነ፡ ሕዝብ፡ ወተፈሥሑ፡ እስመ፡ ሐወጾሙ፡ እግዚአብሔር፡ ለደቂቀ፡ እስራኤል፡ ወእስመ፡ ርእየ፡ ሥቃዮሙ፡ ወአትሐተ፡ ሕዝብ፡ ርእሶ፡ ወሰገደ።

Chapter 36

L, CL, LT, CGT, CDT, CLT, CGLT VERBS: THE REMAINING MOODS

36.1 The L, CL, Lt Verbs: Imperfect, Subjunctive, and Imperative Forms

As mentioned previously (see ch. 7), the L verb class indicates the lengthening of the G verb *ă* vowel with the first consonant of the root to the long *ā*: $C_1āC_2ăC_3ă$, e.g., ባረከ፡, *bārăkă* – "he blessed." The CL verb indicates a causative action, and the Lt suggests a passive/reciprocal verb action. The following table offers the 3ms form of the perfect, imperfect, subjunctive, imperative of the verb "ruin or destroy."

TABLE 36.1: L, CL, Lt Verbs: Imperfect, Subjunctive, and Imperative

Verb Voice	Perfect	Imperfect	Subjunctive	Imperative
L ruin, destroy	ማሰነ፡	ይማስን፡	ይማስን፡	ማስን፡
CL	አማሰነ፡	ያማስን፡	ያማስን፡	አማስን፡
Lt	ተማሰነ፡	ይትማሰን፡	ይትማሰን፡	ተማሰን፡

a. Note in all moods of the L, CL, Lt verbs, the I consonant has the long *ā* vowel. The perfect II and III consonants have the short *ă* vowel.

b. The L imperfect and subjunctive forms include the expected ይ prefix, but the II and III consonant vowels have the short *ə* vowel.

c. The L imperative has the long *ā* vowel on I consonant and is followed by the II and III consonant vowels with the short *ə* vowel.

d. The causative CL perfect and imperative include the expected ሀ prefix and the long *ā* vowel on the I consonant.

e. The CL perfect II and III consonants have the short *ă* vowel and the imperative II and III consonants have the short *ə* vowel.

f. The CL imperfect and subjunctive combine the ይ prefix and the causative ሀ to ያ (and ታ, ና, etc.)

g. The Lt perfect and imperative moods include the passive/reciprocal ተ prefix and the long vowel on the I consonant.

h. The Lt perfect has the short *ă* vowel on the II and III consonants, while the imperfect, subjunctive, and imperative II and III consonants have *ə*.

i. The Lt imperfect and subjunctive have the expected ይ prefix. Note, however, the passive/reciprocal ተ prefix has shortened to *ə*.

j. These verbs will make similar vowel changes when the PGN markers are added to each form.

36.2 The L, CL, Lt Verbal Adjective, Agent Noun, and Verbal Noun

The verbal adjective for the L verb follows the ቀቱል፡ pattern: ሙሱን፡. The rare agent noun (see table below) usually follows the pattern ቃታሊ፡ as in the form ማሳኒ፡. There can be several verbal noun patterns for L verbs including ቀታሌ፡, ቀትላ፡, with the most common pattern ቃታል፡. The table below offers the L verbs that occur the most often in the texts.

TABLE 36.2: Frequently Attested L Verbs

Meaning	Perfect	Verbal Adj.	Verbal Noun	Agent Noun
Perish	ማስነ፡	ሙሱን፡	ሙስና፡	ማሳኒ፡
Mourn	ላሐወ፡	ሉሑው፡ / ልሑው፡	ላሕ፡	—
Rescue	ባልሐ፡	—	—	ባላሒ፡
Console	ናዘዘ፡	—	ኑዛዜ፡	ናዛዚ፡
Associate	ተሳተፈ፡	ሱቱፍ፡	ሱታፌ፡	—
Establish	ሣረረ፡	ሡሩር፡ / ሥሩር፡	ሡራሬ፡	ሣራሪ፡
Labor	ጸመወ፡	—	ጸማ፡	—
Bless	ባረከ፡	ቡሩክ፡	ቡራኬ፡	—
show mercy	ተሣህለ፡	—	ሣህል፡	—
Irritate	ሣቀየ፡	—	ሥቃይ፡	—

These verbal adjectives, verbal nouns, and the few agent nouns should be put to memory due to their frequency. In addition, there are several notable verbal nouns and adjectives that are considered G verbs but appear in verbal form as L types. The following serve as examples of these verbs:

በረከት፡ (pl. በረካታት፡) – blessing, success
ላሕ፡ – mourning, grieving
ሣህል፡ – mercy, clemency
መሥቄ፡ – goad, weaver's comb
መሠረት፡ – foundation

36.3 CGt, CDt, CLt, CGlt Imperfect, Subjunctive, and Imperative Forms

On each of the three verb types, G, D, and L,[1] a causative-reflexive stem appears with the following prefixes: አስት- in the perfect and imperative and ያስት- in the imperfect and subjunctive. There is much debate as to the origin of these verbs: they may be the causative of the reflexive verb, e.g., ተጋብአ፡ – "gather [intrans]" of አስተጋብአ፡ – "gather [trans.]"; probably from ገብአ፡ or the reflexive of the causative verb, e.g., አርአየ፡ – "show (something) of"; አስተርአየ፡ – "appear"; probably from ርአየ፡. These verbs must be memorized due to the origins of their base form. It is quite possible these were invented by a scribe to express an intended action or interpretation of an action.

TABLE 36.3: CGt, CDt, CLt, CGlt Verbs: Imperfect, Subjunctive, and Imperative

Verb Voice	Perfect	Imperfect	Subjunctive	Imperative
CGt	አስተ(ቀ)ቀተለ፡	ያስተቀትል፡	ያስተቅትል፡	አስተቅትል፡
CDt	አስተቀተለ፡	ያስተቄትል፡	ያስተቀትል፡	አስተቀትል፡
GLt/CGLt	አስተቃተለ፡	ያስተቃትል፡	ያስተቃትል፡	አስተቃትል፡

a. In the perfect CGt, the I consonant can appear with a short *ă* vowel or the less frequent short *ə* vowel.

b. The causative አ prefix appears in the perfect and the imperative, but as expected it is dropped in the imperfect and subjunctive.[2] The prefixed ስት appears in all four moods.

c. The I, II, and III consonants in the perfect and imperfect have the *ă* vowel, while the subjunctive and imperative I consonant have the short *ə* vowel. The imperfect, subjunctive, and imperative all have II and III consonants with the short *ə* vowel.

d. The perfect CDt verb follows the CGt except for the optional short *ə* vowel on the I consonant.

---
1. See "Rules of Contraction and Assimilation" in ch. 2.
2. See "Rules of Contraction and Assimilation" in ch. 2.

e. The imperfect changes the *ă* vowel in the I consonant to the long *ē* vowel but is followed by the II and III consonants with the short *ə* vowel.

f. The subjunctive has a short *ă* vowel on the I consonant and short *ə* vowels on II and III consonants.

g. The imperative root has the same vowel pattern as the root consonants as the subjunctive.

h. The GLt/CGLt imperfect and subjunctive verbs are identical: long *ā* vowel followed by two short *ə* vowels.

i. The perfect and imperative have the long *ā* vowel on the I consonant. The perfect has short *ă* vowels on the II and III consonants while the imperative has short *ə* vowels on the same.

j. These verbs will make similar vowel changes when the PGN markers are added to each form.

TABLE 36.4: CGt, CDt, CLt, CGlt Verbs: Imperfect, Subjunctive, and Imperative

Verb Voice	Infinitive	Perf. Act. Part. (P.A.P.)	Agent Noun	Verbal Noun
CGt	አስተቅትሎ(ት)፡	አስተቅቲል፡	መስተቅትል፡ / መስተቅትል፡	እስተቅታል፡
CDt	አስተቀትሎ(ት)፡	አስተቀቲል፡	መስተቀትል፡	—
GLt/CGLt	አስተቃትሎ(ት)፡	አስተቃቲል፡	መስተቃትል፡	እስተቁታል፡

a. The CGt, CDt, CLt, CGlt infinitive, P.A.P. and verbal noun all include the አስተ prefix, although the verbal noun has shortened the vowel on the አ and the ተ prefix.

b. The I consonant in the CGt infinitive has the short *ə* vowel; the CDt infinitive has the short *ă* vowel; and the GLt/CGLt infinitive has the long *ā* vowel. Each II consonant has the short *ə* vowel followed by the III consonant with an *o* vowel and a possible ተ attached on all three voices.

c. The P.A.P. has a similar I consonant vowel pattern as eh Infinitive for each voice but the II consonant has an *i* vowel on each occasion followed by a short *ə* vowel on the III consonant.

d. The agent noun is the most unusual as the አ prefix has changed to a መስተ prefix. The CGt form has to possibilities: one with a short *ă* or short *ə* vowel on the I consonant.

e. The CDt agent noun has the short *ă*, short *ə*, short *ə* vowel pattern for the root.

f. The GLt/CGLt agent noun has the long *ā*, short *ə*, short *ə* vowel pattern for the root.

36.4 Vocabulary

1. አስተብቍዐ፡ CGt – implore, beseech, intercede
2. አስተምሐረ፡ CGt – show mercy to, to seek mercy for self
3. አስተዋደየ፡ CGlt – accuse, bring charges against
4. አስተሐመመ፡ CGlt – study diligently, give close attention to
5. አስተዋሰበ፡ CGlt – marry off a child
6. አውሰበ፡ CG – marry
7. ሰብሳብ፡ – wedding, marriage
8. ብድብድ፡ – plague
9. ቀልቀል፡ – precipice
10. ፈድፋድ፡ – excess
11. ግልባብ፡ – veil
12. ምውልታው፡ – place of refuge
13. መለምልም፡ – new fruit
14. መንኩራኩር፡ – wheel
15. መንኮት፡ – axis, wheel, rotation
16. ነቀልቃል፡ – agitation
17. ልምላሜ፡ – verdure, tenderness
18. ልኅልኅና፡ – weakness

36.5 Exercises

A. Translate the following:

1. የህብከ፡ እግዚእነ፡ ሰላም፡ ወጥዒና፡ ከመ፡ ትብጻሕ፡ ውስተ፡ ፍጻሜ፡ ሕይወትከ፡ በፍሥሓ።

2. ኢያበውሓሙ፡ ለፍንዋን፡ ከመ፡ ይባኡ፡ ኀቤሁ።

3. ለይትቀተል፡ ዘይኤብስ፡ ላዕለ፡ ትእዛዘተ፡ እግዚአብሔር።

4. ኩነ፡ ፍጽምት፡ በኵሉ፡ ዘተገብሪ።

5. ወሰድዎሙ፡ ውስተ፡ ምኩናን፡ ወተረኪበሙ፡ መኣብሳነ፡ ተኰነኑ፡ ኩነኔ፡ ዐቢየ፡ ወዐጹብ።

6. አብሕዮ፡ ከመ፡ ይፈኑ፡ አጐሁ፡ ኀበ፡ መኰንን።
   _____

7. ከዊኖ፡ ግሡጸ፡ ወማእምረ፡ ሕግ፡ አጐዘ፡ ምህሮቶሙ፡ ለአሕዛበ፡ ሀገሩ።
   _____

8. በዝንቱ፡ ቃል፡ ወጠነ፡ ሰማይ፡ ደምኖ፡ ወንሰ፡ ብርሃነ፡ ፀሐይ።
   _____

9. ፈዲሞነ፡ ሕንጸተ፡ ቤተ፡ መቅደስ፡ ቀደስናሁ፡ በዐቢይ፡ ፍሥሓ።
   _____

10. እንዘ፡ ይሰብክ፡ ንስሓ፡ ወኀድገተ፡ ኀጢአት፡ ጸውዖሙ፡ ለሕዝብ።
    _____

11. ለምንት፡ ታዘልፉ፡ አብሶ፡ ላዕሌየ፡ ወተዐድዎ፡ እምሕገገረ።
    _____

12. ሐደሱ፡ ሀገሮሙ፡ ወሐነጹ፡ ጥቀመ፡ ጽኑዐ፡ ዐውዳ።
    _____

13. ኩን፡ ንሱሐ፡ ወኢትኩን፡ ኮነኔ።
    _____

14. አልቦ፡ ምስዋር፡ ዘይሴውር፡ ርእሶ፡ ቦ።
    _____

15. ትሔድሱ፡ በዓላተ፡ ዘንደግሙ፣ ወትደግሙ፡ አንብቦ፡ መጻሕፍተ፡ ቅድሳት፡ ኩሎ፡ አሚረ።
    _____

B. Genesis 18:1–15. Translate the following:

¹ ወአስተርአዮ፡ እግዚአብሔር፡ ለአብርሃም፡ በኀበ፡ ዕፀ፡ ምንባሬ፡ እንዘ፡ ይነብር፡ ኀበ፡ ጾተ፡ ሐይመት፡ ቀትረ።

² ወሰብ፡ አልዐለ፡ አዕይንቲሁ፡ ወነጸረ፡ ወናሁ፡ ሠለስቱ፡ ዕደው፡ ይቀውሙ፡ መልዕልቴሁ፡ ወርአዮ፡ ወሮጸ፡ ለተቀብሎቶም፡

እምኖናተ፡ ሐይመት፡ ወሰገደ፡ ውስተ፡ ምድር።

³ ወይቤሎሙ፡ አጋእስትየ፡ እመ፡ ረከብኩ፡ ሞገሰ፡ በቅድሜ፡ አዕይንቲከሙ፣

⁴ ናምጽእ፡ ማየ፡ ወንኀብ፡ እገሪክሙ፡ ወታጽሉ፡ ታሕተ፡ ዕፅ።

⁵ ወናምጽእ፡ ጎብስተ፡ ወትብልዑ፡ ወእምዝ፡ ትሐሩ፡ ኀበ፡ ሐለይክሙ፡ አምከሙ፡ ግሕሥክሙ፡ ኀበ፡ ግብርክሙ፤ ወይቤልዎ፡ ግበር፡ ከማሁ፡ በከመ፡ ትቤ፡፡

⁶ ወሮጸ፡ አብርሃም፡ ኀበ፡ ሳራ፡ ብእሲቱ፡ ውስተ፡ ሐይመታ፡ ወይቤላ፡ አፍጥኒ፡ ወአብሕኢ፡ ሠለስተ፡ መሣልሰ፡ ስንዳሌ፡ ወግበሪ፡ ደፍንተ፡፡

⁷ ወሮጸ፡ አብርሃም፡ ኀበ፡ አልህምት፡ ወነሥአ፡ አሐደ፡ ላህመ፡ ንኡሰ፡ ወሠናየ፡ ወወሀበ፡ ለቀኃልዔሁ፡ ወአፍጠነ፡ ገቢሮቶ፡፡

⁸ ወአምጽአ፡ ዕቋነ፡ ወመዓረ፡ ወውእተ፡ ላህመ፡ ዘገብረ፡ ወአቅረበ፡ ሎሙ፡ ወበልዑ፡ ወውእቱሰ፡ ይቀውም፡ ኀበ፡ ዕፅ፡ ወይማጥቃሙ፡፡

⁹ ወይቤልዎ፡ አይቴ፡ ሳራ፡ ብእሲትከ፤ ወይቤሎሙ፡ ነያ፡ ውስተ፡ ሐይመት፡፡

¹⁰ ወይቤሎ፡ ሶበ፡ ገበእኩ፡ እመጽእ፡ ኀቤከ፡ ዓመ፡ ከመ፡ ዮም፡ ትረክብ፡ ሳራ፡ ውሉደ፡ ወሰምዐት፡ ሳራ፡ እንዘ፡ ትቀውም፡ ኀበ፡ ኆኅት፡ እንዘ፡ ህለወት፡ ድኅሬሁ፡፡

¹¹ ወአብርሃምሰ፡ ወሳራ፡ ልህቁ፡ ጥቀ፡ ወኀለፈ፡ መዋዕሊሆሙ፡ ወንድጋ፡ ለሳራሂ፡ ትከቶ፡ አንስት፡፡

¹² ወሠሐቀት፡ ሳራ፡ በባሕቲታ፡ እስመ፡ ትቤ፡ በልባ፡ ዓዲዩኑ፡ እስከ፡ ይእዜ፡ ወእግዚእየኒ፡ ልህቀ፡፡

¹³ ወይቤሎ፡ እግዚአብሔር፡ ለአብርሃም፡ ምንት፡ አሥሐቃ፡ ለሳራ፡ በባሕቲታ፡ እስመ፡ ትቤ፡ ዓዲዩኑ፡ እስከ፡ ይእዜ፣ ወእግዚእየኒ፡ ልህቀ፣ ወአማንኑ፡ እወልድ፡ ወናሁ፡ ረሣእኩ፡ አንሰ፡፡

¹⁴ ቦኑ፡ ነገር፡ ዘይሰአኖ፡ ለእግዚአብሔር፡ በዝንቱ፡ ጊዜ፡ ሶበ፡ ገበእኩ፡ ኀቤከ፡ ትረክብ፡ ሳራ፡ ውሉደ፡፡

¹⁵ ወከሀደት፡ ሳራ፡ እንዘ፡ ትብል፡ ኢሠሐቁ፡ እስመ፡ ፈርሀት፡ ወይቤላ፡ አልቦ፡ ሠሐቁ፡፡

Chapter 37

MULTILITERAL VERB ROOTS

37.1 Quadriliteral Verb Roots

Thus far, our focus has been on Gəʿəz verbs with three consonants or consonant vowels that made up the root of the verb. From these roots the derived forms emerged that appear in Gəʿəz. In this final chapter on verbs, we will examine the Q verb roots that are made up of more than three consonants, usually four (and sometimes five or even six). The same derived stems occur with these multiliteral verbs: the simple stem Q, the causative stem CQ, the reflexive-passive stem Qt, and the causative-reflexive stem Qlt.[1] All the stems conjugate as expected; there is, however, an additional form in the simple, reflexive-passive, and the causative-reflexive. Each stem forms in the perfect, imperfect, subjunctive, and imperative, along with the infinitive (and gerund). The table below presents the four stems in the four primary moods.

TABLE 37.1: Quadriliteral Verbs: The Perfect, Imperfect, Subjunctive, and Imperative

Stem	Perfect	Imperfect	Subjunctive	Imperative
Q be astonished	ደንገፀ፡	ይዴነግፅ፡	ይደንግፅ፡	ደንግፅ፡
Qt be afflicted	ተመንደበ፡	ይትመነድብ፡	ይትመንደብ፡	ተመንደብ፡
CQ cause affliction	አመንደበ፡	ያመነድብ፡	ያመንድብ፡	አመንድብ፡
Qlt afflict oneself or one another	ተመናደበ፡	ይትመናደብ፡	ይትመናደብ፡	ተመናደብ፡

a. Note the similarity in prefixes in each of the forms compared to the three consonant roots. The ተ prefix in the Qt and Qlt perfect and imperative, the አ prefix in the CQ perfect and imperative, the ይ prefix in the Q imperfect and subjunctive, ይት prefix in the Qt and Qlt imperfect and subjunctive, and the ያ prefix in the CQ imperfect and subjunctive.

---

1. Two other derived verbs can occasionally appear–the CQt, አስተመንደበ , and the CQlt, አስተመናደበ

b. Note that in the Q moods, the I and II consonants have the same vowels while the perfect has the ă vowel in the III and IV consonants, and the imperfect, subjunctive, and imperative have the shortened ə vowel on these two consonants.

c. A similar vowel pattern to the Q perfect can be seen in the Qt perfect.

d. The Qt imperfect also has the ă vowel on the I and II consonants followed by the short ə vowel on III and IV.

e. The Qt subjunctive begins with the ă vowel on the I consonant followed by the short ə vowel on II, the ă vowel on the III and the short ə vowel on IV. The imperative follows a similar vowel pattern as the subjunctive in the Qt.

f. The CQ perfect follows the Q perfect vowel pattern, the CQ imperfect follows the Qt vowel pattern, and the CQ subjunctive and imperative follow the Q subjunctive vowel pattern.

g. The Qlt has the ă vowel on the I consonant followed by the long ā vowel on the II consonant and the ă vowel on III and IV. The Qlt imperfect, subjunctive, and imperative follow a similar pattern apart from the short ə vowel on IV.

The following table presents the paradigm for the simple verb with four consonants. Be careful not to mistake the first መ in the perfect for the agent noun in the CGt, CDt, CLt, CGlt verbs.

TABLE 37.2: Quadriliteral Simple Verb Paradigm

PGN	Perfect	Imperfect	Subjunctive	Imperative
3ms	መንደበ፡	ይመነድብ፡	ይመንድብ፡	
3fs	መንደበት፡	ትመነድብ፡	ትመንድብ፡	
2ms	መንደብከ፡	ትመነድብ፡	ትመንድብ፡	መንድብ፡
2fs	መንደብኪ፡	ትመነድቢ፡	ትመንድቢ፡	መንድቢ፡
1cs	መንደብኩ፡	እመነድብ፡	እመንድብ፡	
3mp	መንደቡ፡	ይመነድቡ፡	ይመንድቡ፡	
3fp	መንደባ፡	ይመነድባ፡	ይመንድባ፡	
2mp	መንደብክሙ፡	ትመነድቡ፡	ትመንድቡ፡	መንድቡ፡
2fp	መንደብክን፡	ትመነድባ፡	ትመንድባ፡	መንድባ፡
1cp	መንደብነ፡	ንመነድብ፡	ንመንድብ፡	

a. The infinitive form, መንድቦ፡, has the ă vowel with the I consonant followed by the short ə in the II and III consonants and the IV consonant ends with the o vowel.

b. Note the same PGN endings for each of the verb moods. See the vowel pattern notes from table 37.1.

c. Note the vowel shifts in the perfect (except 3fs due to the short ት ending) when the PGN ending (2ms, 2fs,1cs, 2mp, 2fp, 1cp) is added but not when the vowel is added to the IV consonant to signify the PGN of the verb (3mp, 3fp).

d. The imperfect and subjunctive follow the expected PGN prefix pattern (ይ: 3ms, 3mp, 3fp; ት: 3fs, 2ms, 2fs, 2mp, 2fp; አ: 1cs; ን: 1cp). Vowel suffixes are added to the IV consonant where expected (2fs, 3mp, 3fp, 2mp, 2fp).

e. Note in the imperfect 1cs the III consonant has lengthened from the short ə vowel to the short ă vowel for reasons that are unclear. Possibly due to the አ prefix, but this does not occur in the subjunctive; however, the I consonant shifts from the short ă vowel to the short ə vowel, again for reasons that are unclear.

f. The imperative forms follow the subjunctive except for the subjunctive prefixes.

37.2 Quadriliteral Verbs with II-ወ/የ

There are several quadriliteral verbs that have a middle weak II-ወ/የ that have a contraction that results in them appearing as L verbs. The -ă+የ contracts to the long ē vowel and the ă+ወ contracts to the o vowel. The following table offers two examples:

TABLE 37.3: Quadriliteral Verbs with II-የ

Verb Voice	Perfect	Imperfect	Subjunctive	Imperative
Simple action pursue	ዴገነ፡	ይዴግን፡	ይዴግን፡	ዴግን፡
Causative	አዴገነ፡	ያዴግን፡	ያዴግን፡	አዴግን፡
Passive/Reciprocal	ተዴገነ፡	ይዴግን፡	ይዴግን፡	ተዴግን፡

a. As you can see, these quadriliteral verbs differ from the three radical root L verbs due to the loss or contraction of the fourth radical.

b. With the II-የ verbs, rather than the I consonant vowel lengthening to the ā vowel as in the L verbs, the vowel is the ē vowel in all moods.

c. The perfect II and III consonants both have the ă vowel and the causative has the expected አ prefix and the passive has the expected ተ prefix except with the imperfect and subjunctive in which the ተ prefix has dropped out because of the dental I consonant in this example.

d. The imperative simple and causative action forms follow the perfect except for the short ə vowel on the II and III consonants. The passive form includes the ă vowel in the II consonant and the short ə vowel on the III consonant.

e. The imperfect and subjunctive mirror each other in all voices. The passive forms, like the imperative, include the ă vowel on the II consonant and the short ə vowel on the III consonant.

f. These verbs will make similar vowel changes when the PGN markers are added to each form.

TABLE 37.4: Quadriliteral Verbs with II-ው

Verb Voice	Perfect	Imperfect	Subjunctive	Imperative
Simple action To lock in chains	ሞቅሐ፡	ይሞቅሕ፡	ይሞቅሕ፡	ሞቅሕ፡
Causative	አሞቅሐ፡	ያሞቅሕ፡	ያሞቅሕ፡	አሞቅሕ፡
Passive/Reciprocal	ተሞቅሐ፡	ይትሞቃሕ፡	ይትሞቃሕ	ተሞቃሕ፡

a. With the II-ው verbs, rather than the I consonant vowel lengthening to the ā vowel as in the L verbs, the vowel is the o vowel in all moods.

b. The vowel on the II consonant in all forms except the imperfect, subjunctive, and imperative passive is the short ə vowel. The imperfect, subjunctive, and imperative passive forms have the long ā vowel on the II consonant.

c. Unlike the II-ይ verbs, all four passive/reciprocal forms contain the ተ prefix, although the vowel shortens to the ə vowel in the imperfect and subjunctive.

d. These verbs will make similar vowel changes when the PGN markers are added to each form.

The verbal nouns and adjectives for these quadriliteral verbs with II-ው/ይ follow the pattern of the L and Q verbs.

TABLE 37.5: Quadriliteral Verbal Adjectives, Verbal Nouns, and Agent Nouns with II-ው/ይ

Meaning	Perfect	Verbal Adj.	Verbal Noun	Agent Noun
err	ጌገየ፡	ጊጉይ፡	ጌጋይ፡	—
pursue	ዴገነ፡	—	—	ዴጋኒ፡
tell	ዜነወ፡	—	ዜና፡	ዜናዊ፡ / መዜንው
nourish	ሴሰየ፡	—	ሲሳይ፡ / ሲሲት፡	መሴሲ፡
take captive	ፄወወ፡	ፄውው፡ / ፄውው፡	ፄዋ(ዌ፡)	—
imprison	ሞቅሐ፡	ሙቁሕ፡	ሙቃሔ፡	—
shepherd	ተኖለወ፡	—	—	ኖላዊ፡

37.3 Quadriliteral Verbs of Special Note

Most verbs in Gəʿəz are of the three-consonant root, but the four consonant verb roots occur somewhat frequently. There is one type that needs special note. This verbal root follows the pattern of $C_1C_2C_1C_2$, in other words, a reduplication of the I and II consonants in the III and IV positions. For the most part, the vowels for these verbs are short *ă* on the I, III, and IV consonants and the short *ə* vowel on the II consonant; however, there are exceptions as will be seen below*:

ለምለመ፡ – grow green, blossom
ቀጥቀጠ፡ – crush or grind
በድበደ፡ – die of disease
ፈድፈደ፡ – be numerous
ጐድጐደ፡ – knock

a. Two somewhat similar verbs may fall into this category but in this case only the I consonant is doubled, and the vowel is lengthened to the long *ē*.
*ጌገየ፡ – err, go astray, sin
*ሴሰየ፡ – nourish, sustain

b. Another quadriliteral verb is the result of turning a three-consonant noun into a four-consonant verb. In many of these cases, the noun fell out of use and is only recognizable through the verbal form.
ሞቅሐ፡ (from ሞቅሕ፡ – fetter) – put in prison
አማጎበረ፡ – (from ማጎበር፡ – council) – convene a council
ተአምለከ፡ Qt (from አምላክ፡ – God) – become divine
ተመሀተ፡ Qt (from ምህት፡ – phantom, ghost) – become a ghost
አመስጠረ፡ CQ (from ምስጢር፡ – mystery) – deal in mysteries
መንኮሰ፡ Q (from መነኮስ፡ – monk, nun) – become a monk
አሰንበተ፡ CQ (from ሰንበት፡ – Sabbath) – observe the Sabbath
መጽወተ፡ Q (from ምጽዋት፡ – charity) – practice charity

37.4 Nouns and Adjectives

There are also some quadriliteral nouns that do not have associated verbs.

ተከላ፡ (from ተከላው፡) – wolf
ኮከብ፡ (from ከውከብ፡) – star
ድንግል፡ – virgin

The verbal adjective follows the pattern of the word $C_1 \partial C_2 C_3 u C_4$ (ድኑፅ፡ – "astonished").
The verbal noun has three possible patterns: $C_1 \partial C_2 C_3 \bar{a} C_4 \bar{e}$, ድንጋፄ፡; $C_1 \partial C_2 C_3 \partial C_4 \bar{a}$, ድንግፃ፡; $C_1 \partial C_2 C_3 \partial C_4 \bar{a}$, ድንግፃ፡.

37.5 Quinquiliteral Verb Roots

The five consonant root verb is very rare in Gəʿəz and generally is the result of root reduplication. The perfect mood looks similar to the causative verbs with an አ prefix. The imperfect and subjunctive have the expected ይ prefix, while the imperative also has the አ prefix like the perfect. The following table offers an example of these verbs:

TABLE 37.6: Quinquiliteral Verb Example: (Q)–shake, tremble

Perfect	Imperfect	Subjunctive	Imperative	Infinitive
አድለቀለቀ፡	ያድለቀልቅ፡	ያድለቅልቅ፡	አድለቅልቅ፡	አድለቅልቆ፡(ት)

37.6 The N Quinquiliteral Verb

The final verb we will discuss is identified as the N Verb. It consists of an ን prefix attached to a quadrilateral root of the $C_1C_2C_1C_2$ type. They appear in the simple N and the reflexive N forms. The table below offers a sample of each type:

TABLE 37.7: The N and Nt Quinquiliteral Verb

Type	Perfect	Imperfect	Subjunctive	Imperative
N move, shake continuously	አንቀልቀለ፡	ያንቀለቅል፡	ያንቀልቅል፡	አንቀልቅል፡
Nt move oneself continually	ተንቀልቀለ፡	ይንቀለቀል፡	ይንቀልቀል፡	ተንቀልቀል፡

a. The distinguishing marker for this verb of the ን is present in the I consonant position followed by the doubling of the II and III consonants in the IV and V positions in all moods of the five-consonant root.

b. The N perfect and imperative also display an አ prefix in the first position and the imperfect and subjunctive include a ይ prefix.

c. The N perfect follows the vowel pattern አ+$C_1C_2ăC_3C_4ăC_5ă$, while the imperative follows a slightly modified pattern: አ+$C_1C_2ăC_3C_4əC_5$ with the III, IV, and V consonants all having a short ə vowel.

d. The N imperfect follows the vowel pattern ይ+$C_1C_2ăC_3C_4ăC_5$, while the subjunctive has slight modifications: ይ+$C_1C_2ăC_3C_4əC_5$ with the III, IV, and V consonants all having a short ə vowel.

e. The Nt perfect follows the same vowel pattern as the N verb with the ተ prefix replacing the አ prefix.

f. The Nt imperfect (rare) reduces the vowel on the prefix to a short ə vowel – ይ and lengthens the IV consonant vowel to a short ă from a short ə vowel.

g. The Nt subjunctive (rare) has the same short vowel prefix ይ and lengthens the vowel on the IV consonant from a short ə to a short ă vowel.

h. The Nt imperative follows the same vowel pattern as the N imperative with the exception of the lengthened IV consonant vowel from a short ə to a short ă vowel.

i. The verbal noun in this verb class follows the pattern of ነቀልቃል፡ – motion, shaking.

37.7 Vocabulary

1. አስቆቀወ፡ (impf., ያስቆቁ፡) – mourn, lament
2. ሰቆቃው፡ (verbal noun) – mourning, lamenting
3. አድለቅለቀ፡ – shake or tremble
4. ድልቅልቅ፡ (verbal noun) – shaking, trembling
5. አቅያሕይሐ፡ – grow reddish
6. ቀይሕ፡ – red
7. ጐድጐደ፡ Q – knock on a door
8. አንጐድጐደ፡ N – thunder
9. አንጸፍጸፈ፡ N – ooze
10. ጸፍጸፍ፡ – juice
11. አንገርገረ፡ N – roll or spin
12. ነገርጋር፡ (verbal noun) – rolling, spinning, possession by a spirit (related to epileptic seizures)
13. አንጐርጐረ፡ N – be angry
14. አንቀልቀለ፡ N – move or quake
15. ነቀልቃል፡ (verbal noun) – moving or quaking
16. አንሰሰወ፡ (impf. ያንሱ፡) – walk about, go for a stroll
17. አንበልበለ፡ N – flame or blaze
18. ነበልባል፡ (verbal noun) – flaming, blazing
19. ጸዐድዒድ፡ (adj.) – whitish
20. ጸዐዳ፡ – white
21. መዓርጊር፡ (adj.) – sweet
22. መዓር፡ – honey
23. ደመንማኒ፡ – cloudy, gloomy
24. ደመና፡ – cloud

37.8 Exercises

A. Proverbs 8:1–36. Translate the following:

¹ ናሁ፡ አንተሰ፡ ጥበበ፡ ጽብክ፡ ወአእምሮ፡ ጡብ፡ ቃል፤

² እስመ፡ ውስተ፡ ጽንፈ፡ ነዋኃት፡ ይእቲ፡ ወማእከለ፡ ቤታ፡ ይእቲ፡ ቆመት።

³ ወውስተ፡ አናቅጾሙ፡ ለኃያላን፡ ትጸንሕ፡ ወበውስተ፡ ፍናው፡ ትትፌሳሕ።

⁴ ኪያክሙኬ፡ ሰብእ፡ አስተበቍዕ፤ ወአነግር፡ ቃለ፡ ዚአየ፡ ለውሉደ፡ ሰብእ።

⁵ አእምሩ፡ ጥበበ፡ የቃሃን፡ ወዓብዳም፡ አጥርጡ፡ ልበ።

⁶ ስምዑኒ፡ እስመ፡ መፍትው፡ አየድዕ፤ ወአወፅእ፡ እምከናፍርየ፡ ርቱዐ፡

⁷ እስመ፡ ጽድቃ፡ ይነብብ፡ ጉርዔየ፡ ርኩስ፡ በቅድሜየ፡ ከናፍረ፡ ዐመፃ።

⁸ ወጽድቅ፡ ኮሉ፡ ቃለ፡ አፋየ፡ ወአልቦ፡ እምውስቴቶሙ፡ ጠዋይ፡ ወመዐቅፍ።

⁹ ኮሉ፡ ርቱዕ፡ በቅድሜሆሙ፡ ለእለ፡ የአምሩ፡ ወርቱዕ፡ ለእለ፡ ይረክቡ፡ ልቡና።

¹⁰ ንሥኡ፡ ትምህርተ፡ ወኢኮ፡ ብሩር፡ ወአእምሮ፡ እምወርቅ፡ ፍቱን፡ ወተወከፉ፡ ተአውቆትየ፡ እምወርቅ፡ ጽሩይ።

¹¹ እስመ፡ ትኄይስ፡ ጥበብ፡ እምዕንቈ፡ ዘብዙን፡ ሤጡ፤ ወኮሉ፡ ክቡር፡ ኢመጠና፡ ላቲ።

¹² አነ፡ ጥበብ፡ አሕደርኩ፡ ምክረ፡ ወአእምሮ፡ ወሕሊና፡ አነ፡ ጸዋዕኩ።

¹³ ፈራሂ፡ እግዚአብሔር፡ ይጸልእ፡ ዐመፃ፤ ጽልአ፡ ወትዕቢተ፡ ወፍናወ፡ እኩያተ፡ ጸላእኩ፡ ወዓዲ፡ ጸላእኩ፡ ጠዋይተ፡ ፍናወ፡ እኩያን።

¹⁴ ሊተ፡ ምክር፡ ወሊተ፡ እዘዝ፡ ሊተ፡ አእምሮ፡ ወሊተ፡ ጽንዕ።

¹⁵ ብየ፡ ነገሥት፡ ይነግሡ፡ ወኃያላን፡ የአምሩ፡ ወይጽሕፉ፡ ጽድቀ።

¹⁶ ብየ፡ ዓቢያን፡ ይከብሩ፤ ወምውኳንንት፡ ብየ፡ ይአኀዙ፡ ምድረ።

¹⁷ አነ፡ ለእለ፡ ያፈቅሩኒ፡ አፈቅር፡ ወእለ፡ የኃሥሡ፡ ኪያየ፡ ይረክቡ፡ ሞገሰ።

¹⁸ ክብር፡ ወብዕል፡ ኀቤየ፡ ሀሎ፡ ወጥሪት፡ ብዙኅ፡ ወጽድቅ፡ ኀብይብ፡ ሀሎ፤

¹⁹ ወፍሬ፡ ዚአየ፡ ይትኃራይ፡ እምወርቅ፡ ወእምዕንቈ፡ ወማእረርየ፡ ይኂስ፡ እምብሩር፡ ጽሩይ።

²⁰ ወውስተ፡ ፍናወ፡ ጽድቅ፡ አንሶሱ፡ ወማእከለ፡ አሠረ፡ ጽድቅ፡ እትመያየጥ።

²¹ ከመ፡ እከፍሎሙ፡ ጥሪተ፡ ለእለ፡ የአምሩኒ፤ ወመዛግብቲሆሙ፡ እምላእ፡ ተድላ።

²² እግዚአብሔር፡ ወለደኒ፡ ቀዳሜ፡ ኮሉ፡ ለተግባር፤

²³ ወፈጠረኒ፡ እምቅድመ፡ ይሣርር፡ ይሣርር፡ ዓለም፡ ወዘእንበለ፡ ይግበር፡ ምድረ።

²⁴ ወዘንበለ፡ ይግንር፡ ቀላያተ፡ ወዘእንበለ፡ ይፁኡ፡ ውንቅዐተ፡ ማያት።

²⁵ ወዘእንበለ፡ አድባር፡ ይተከሉ፡ ወእምቅድመ፡ ኮሉ፡ አውግር፡ ወለደኒ።

²⁶ ወእምቅድመ፡ ይግበር፡ በሐውርተ፤ ወዓለም፡ ዘይትነደር፡ እምሰማይ።

²⁷ አሙ፡ ያስተዳሉ፡ ሰማያተ፡ ሀሎኩ፡ ወአሙ፡ ያጸንዕ፡ መንበረ፡ ዚአሁ፡ ላዕለ፡ ነፋላት፡ ሀሎኩ፤

²⁸ ወአሙ፡ ጽኑዕ፡ ይገብር፡ በመልዕልተ፡ ደመናት፡ ወደሙ፡ ያፀንዕ፡ አንብሮ፡ አንቅዕተ፡ መያት፤

²⁹ ወአሙ፡ ያነብር፡ ወሰነ፡ ለባሕር፡ ወመያይ፡ ኢይወፅኡ፡ እምፉ፡ ዚአሁ፡ ወአሙ፡ ጽኑዕ፡ ይገብር፡ መሠረታተ፡ ምድር፤

³¹ ሀሎኩ፡ ምስሌሁ፡ እንዘ፡ አስተዋድድ፡ አነ፡ ይእቲ፡ እንተ፡ እትፌሣሕ፡ እንተ፡ ፀብሐት፡ በኰሉ፡ ጊዜ፡ ወእትፌሣሕ፡ እምኔሁ፤

³² ወአሙ፡ ይትፌሣሕ፡ ዓለም፡ ፈጺሞ፡ ኮንኩ፡ አነ፡ እትፌሣሕ፡ እጓለ፡ እመሕያው።

³³ ወይእዜኒ፡ ወልድየ፡ ስምዑኒ፡ ብፁዓን፡ እለ፡ የዐቡ፡ ፍኖትየ።

³⁴ ደቂቅየ፡ ስምዑኒ፡ ጥበበ፡ ወዒትፈጽሙ፡ አፈክሙ፤

³⁵ ብፁዕ፡ ብእሲ፡ ዘይሰምዓኒ፡ ቃለየ፡ ወብፁዕ፡ ዘየዓቅብ፡ ፍኖትየ፡ ወዘይተግህ፡ ውስተ፡ አናቅጸ፡ ዚአየ፡ እንተ፡ ጸብሐት፡ መዘየዓቅብ፡ ራዛተ፡ መባእየ።

³⁶ እስመ፡ ፍናውየ፡ ግናው፡ ሕይወት፡ ዘረከበኒ፡ ረከበ፡ ሕይወተ፡ ወይዴለው፡ ፈቃዱ፡ በኀበ፡ እግዚአብሔር።

Chapter 38

SYNTAX

38.1 Sentence Structure

Syntax in any language speaks of the main parts of a sentence and the order in which they are presented. The basic syntax in English is subject, verb, and object (if present). In Gəʿəz, like other Semitic languages, the basic syntax is verb, subject, object (if present), e.g., ויצו יהוה אלהים על האדם – "and the Lord God commanded the man"; ወአዘዘ፡ እግዚአብሔር፡ ለአዳም፡ – "and God commanded to Adam" (Gen 2:16). (In the Gəʿəz here, the presence of the ለ indicates a command to someone, much like על in the Hebrew construction.) However, in Gəʿəz these syntactical structures are not hard and fast rules, and the normal order of verb, subject, object (VSO) may vary (as it does in Hebrew), either for the purpose of emphasis or due to certain syntactical restraints. As stated previously, on most occasions the subject agrees in gender and number with the verb, but not always. The following examples demonstrate some variation in this pattern:

ባረከ፡ እግዚአብሔር፡ ለሰንበት፡፡ (VSO) – "blessed God, the Sabbath"
ሰንበት፡ ባረከ፡ እግዚአብሔር፡፡ (OVS) – "the Sabbath, (was) blessed (by) God"
እግዚአብሔር፡ ለሰንበት፡ ባረከ፡፡ (SOV) – "God, the Sabbath, blessed"
ባረከ፡ ሰንበት፡ እግዚአብሔር፡፡ (VOS) – "blessed the Sabbath, God"

As in Hebrew, the author generally changes word order as a point of emphasis of a particular component of the sentence; Gəʿəz is no different.

38.2 Other Components of Syntax and Interpretation

Please note well that the following list is not exhaustive.

38.2.1 Conditional Parts of a Sentence

The first component that we will examine is conditional parts of a sentence. In Gəʿəz, a conditional sentence is introduced with the term እም፡ or ለእም፡. Occasionally the apodosis is marked with ወ-. For the most part, the protasis of the conditional sentence occurs in the perfect, and the apodosis is in the imperfect and suggests an action occurring in the present or future: እም፡ ነበርከ፡ ዝየ፡ ወይረቡቱከ፡፡ – "if you remain here, they will find you."[1] For the sentence to describe a past action, both the protasis and apodosis will be in the perfect: እመ፡ ርኅብኩ፡ ወሀቡኒ፡ ኅብስተ። "if I was hungry, they gave me bread." If the author is attempting to suggest a future event, then the protasis will also be an imperfect verb. If this is the case, you may find an imperative or subjunctive in the apodosis if the context requires: እመ፡ ረከብከ፡ ብእሴ፡ ርኁበ፡ ሀቡ፡ አብልዖ። – "if you find a hungry man, give him bread."

38.2.2 Definiteness of the Noun

a. There is no article in Gəʿəz. You must determine by context or what suggestions follow below.

b. Words that are the only representative in their class are definite, e.g., death.

c. Proper names are definite.

d. Several words can express definiteness: ውእቱ፡ (m.s. pronoun); ዝክቱ፡ ዝኩ፡ (sing. adj./pronoun); ዘ (rel. prn.); ዝንቱ፡ (adj./prn.)

e. A suffix pronoun on a noun may also indicate definiteness.

38.2.3 Indefiniteness of the Noun

a. Simple nouns are generally indefinite; e.g., ነቢይ፡ – "prophet"; መሠግር፡ – "fisherman."

b. The following words may indicate indefiniteness (one or anyone): ብእሲ፡ ሰብእ፡ ብእሲት፡ አሐዱ፡ አሐቲ፡.

c. Indefiniteness can be indicated by the use of the preposition እምነ፡ – "from, out of."

d. Indefiniteness can be indicated by the use of ቦ- – "there is," in periphrasis.

38.2.4 Relationship between Nouns

a. The construct state indicates the genitive relationship.

b. The following words when used periphrastically indicate the genitive relationship: ዘ-, እንተ፡, እለ፡.

c. The preposition ለ can function like a genitive marker or referential marker, as in the phrase እግዚአ፡ ለኩሉ፡ – "lord of all."

d. Infinitives and certain descriptive words can govern the accusative; e.g., ስእኑ፡ ሐዊአ፡ – "they could not go"; ፈርሀ፡ ነቢረ፡ ህየ፡ – "he was afraid to remain there."

e. Prepositions generally indicate a relationship between nouns.

---

1. The *protasis* is the clause that expresses the condition in a conditional sentence (*if you wanted me*, I would volunteer). The *apodosis* is the consequential clause of a conditional sentence (if you wanted me, *I would volunteer*).

f. Nouns occur in apposition: e.g., ብእሲ፡ ነጋዲት፡ – lit. "a man of strangeness" = "a stranger."

38.2.5 Verbs Governing the Noun in the Accusative

What follows are some sample possibilities.

a. Adverbial accusative: e.g., በከየ፡ መሪረ፡ – "he wept bitterly."

b. Accusative of purpose: e.g., ተፈሥሐ፡ ፍሥሐ፡ ዐቢየ፡ – "he rejoiced with great joy."

c. Accusative with verbs of saying: e.g., ይቤሉኒ፡ – "they said to me."

d. Accusative used after reflexive verbs or passive verbs governing two accusatives: e.g., ድልወ፡ ዘተረክበ፡ – "he was found worthy."

38.2.6 Verbs Subordinated to Other Verbs

a. The second verb will show the manner, circumstances, or time of the action of the first verb.

b. Two verbs may be set side by side without the conjunction ወ, e.g., ደገመ፡ ፈነወ፡ – "again, he sent out."

c. On occasion the primary verb may be subordinated to an infinitive: e.g., ቀደምኩ፡ ነጊሮተክሙ፡ – "I had expected to tell you."

d. The second verb may be in the imperfect with the conjunction ወ: e.g., ነበሩ፡ ወየዐቅብዎ፡ "they sat down watching him."

e. Verbs indicating beginning or ending are generally connected by እንዘ፡

f. The second verb may indicate purpose or consequence.

38.2.7 Simple Sentences

a. All complete sentences contain a subject.

b. Sentence predicate is usually a verb or an adjective.

c. The personal pronoun may be used as a copula.

d. The words ሀለወ፡ (to exist) and ኮነ፡ (to be) can be used as copulas.

e. Predicate will agree in gender and number with the subject.

f. The three particles ኢ፡, አኮ፡, and አልቦ፡ are used for negation.

38.2.8 Interrogative Sentences

a. No special word or sign – context reveals the interrogative.

b. Can be introduced by በ፡ as in በ፡ ሁ፡ – "is that the case."

c. Most common interrogative is the enclitic ሁ or the term ቡሁ፡.

d. The negative interrogative is expressed as ኢ . . . ሁ፡ ኢያንበብሙሁ፡ – "have you not read?"

e. A dependent interrogative is introduced by እመ፡,ለእመ፡, or እም፡.

38.2.9 Copulative Clauses

a. The particle ወ, enclitic ዜ, emphatic ኒ, ወ—ሰ, are used when contrasting, ወእምዝ፡ – "and then," አው፡ – "or," ወእሙዜ፡ – "or even."

b. Casual expressions are generally introduced by እስመ፡ – "because"; the resulting clause or concluding clause is usually indicated by ኪ፡ – "thus," or እንከ፡ – "then, therefore."

38.2.10 Attributive Relative Clauses

a. The attributive relative clause is usually identified with a relative pronoun or relative particle such as ኀበ፡ – "where," or አመ፡ – "when."

b. When an antecedent is present, the relative pronoun at times will not agree in gender and number: e.g., አንስትያ፡ ዘኀረዩ፡፡ – "wives with whom they might choose."

c. If the relative pronoun is referring to a suffixed pronoun, the relative pronoun will include ሉ-.

d. The relative construction is used often to express participial or adjectival ideas: e.g., ዘኢያአመረ፡ – "unwitting," ዘሀሎ፡ – "present," ዘይልህቅ፡ – "the elder," ዘለዓለም፡ – "everlasting."

e. In conjunctional relative clauses, the declarative clause is introduced by ዘ.

f. Supplementary object clauses following verbs that indicate seeing, saying, among others, are introduced by ከመ፡, እስመ፡, ዘከመ፡, በከመ፡, እፎ፡.

g. Final clauses are introduced by ከመ፡, ዘ-, ለ-.

h. Consecutive clauses are introduced by እስከ፡, ከመ፡, እንዘ፡.

i. Comparative clauses are introduced by ከመ፡, ዘከመ፡, በከመ፡, እምነ፡.

38.2.11 Optative Expressions

a. Wish or desire may be indicated by the perfect or the subjunctive.

b. Usually introduced by እመ፡, እም፡, ሶበ፡, e.g., ሶበ፡ ሞትነ፡፡ – "should that we had died."

38.2.12 Adjective Issues

In Gəʿəz, adjectives normally follow the noun they are modifying but this is not a firm rule. As with the noun, the author can place emphasis on the adjective by the position it takes in the sentence; in most cases if the adjective precedes the noun, then it is for emphatic purposes. The following is an example of a preceding adjective in two cases from Ps 68:15 (16, Heb.): ደብር፡ እግዚአብሔር፡ ደብር፡ ጥሉል፡ – "a/the mountain of God [is like] a/the mountain of Bashan," here the author appears to be placing his emphasis on the mountain.

38.2.13 Adverb Issues

In Gəʿəz, an adverb can either precede or follow the verb it is modifying. Those that precede the verb are generally negative while all others follow the verb.

38.2.14 Contrary-to-Fact Conditions

In these instances, the protasis will be introduced with the term ሶበ፡ and the verb(s) in the apodosis that follows is marked with እም. For example, ሶበ፡ ረከብክዎ፡ አምአኃዝክዎ፡ ወእምቀተልክዎ፡፡ – "If I had found him, I would have seized him and killed him." In these situations, the apodosis verb needs to be a Perfect for the past and Imperfect for the present.

38.2.15 The "If . . . How Much More . . ." Construction

These constructions are found in the teachings of Jesus. Matthew 7:11 offers the most familiar example.

ዘአንትሙ፡ እንከ፡ እንዘ፡ አኩያን፡ አንትሙ፡ ተአምሩ፡ ሠናየ፡ ሀብተ፡ ውኂበ፡ ለውሉዲክሙ፡ እፎ፡ ፈድፋደ፡ አቡክሙ፡ ዘበሰማያት፡ ይሁብ፡ ሠናየ፡ ለእለ፡ ይሰአልዎ፡፡

"If you, being evil, know how to give a good gift to your children, how much more so will your Father in heaven give good things to those who ask him?"

In this construction, the እፎ፡ is usually followed by ፈድፋደ፡ or እንከ፡ ፈድፋደ፡.

38.2.16 Repeated Prepositions በበ፡ ለለ፡ ዘዘ፡

You will often find these repeated prepositions that reflect a distributive notion (see e.g., Matt 4:24; 18:22; 20:2; 20:10; 21:41). Two of these phrases deserve special note: በበ፡ ንስቲት፡ – "little by little," and በበ፡ አብሬቶሙ፡ – "each in his own turn."

38.2.17 Third-Person Singular Pronominal Suffixes: Special Purpose – *-ሁ, -u, -ሃ, -ā*

These third-person suffixes can at times denote the force of a definite article or a demonstrative pronoun. If the context requires or permits it, then it may be necessary to translate such words as ብእሲሁ፡

– "that man" or "that particular man" rather than "his man." These occurrences often appear in relation to periods of time: e.g., በዕለቱ፡ – "on that day."

38.2.18 Other Issue of Special Note

The third-person plural of an active verb with a direct object can function like a passive verb: ይሰድዱከ፡ – "you will be persecuted" (lit., "they will persecute you"). The lack of a clear subject in a certain context is a marker for this usage.

LEXICON

Please note that this lexicon serves only as a supplement to the grammar. Students should obtain Wolf Leslau, *Comparative Dictionary of Ge'ez* (Wiesbaden: Harrassowitz, 2006) or Wolf Leslau, *Concise Dictionary of Ge'ez* (Wiesbaden: Harrassowitz, 1989) for a more complete vocabulary of Gəʿəz.

ሀ

ሃ – possessive suffix 3fs pronoun – her, its; marker of accusative with proper nouns
ሀለወ፡ (ሀሎ፡) – exist or to be
ሃይማኖት፡ – faith
ህድአ፡ – quiet down; CG አህድአ፡ – to pacify, make tranquil; ህዱአ፡ – (adj. quiet, tranquil)
ሀገር፡ ንስቲት፡ – a small village, town
ሀገር፡ – country
ሀገሪት፡ – town, city
ህየ፡ በህየ፡ – there, in that place
ህየንተ፡ suffixed with ሀ- – instead of
ሂ – also, and, even
ሁ possessive suffix 3ms pronoun – his, its; interrogative particle

ለ

ለ- – to, for
ላህም፡ (pl. አልህምት፡) – bull, cow
ልህቀ፡ – grow older (mature), grow in size
ልህቃት፡ – old age
ልሂቅ፡ (f. ልህቅት፡) – adult, grownup, old
ሌሊት፡ – night
ለምለመ፡ – grow green, blossom
ሊቅ፡ (pl. ሊቃን፡) – elder, chief

ለአከ፡ – send

ላእከ፡ (pl. ላእካን፡) – servant

ላዕለ፡ – on, upon, down onto, over, above, about, concerning

ልምላሜ፡ – freshness, moisture, softness

ልሳን፡ (pl. ልሳናት፡) – tongue or language; ልሳን፡ ዮናናዊያን፡ – Greek; ልሳን፡ ዕብራይስጥ፡ – Hebrew

ልብ፡ (pl. አልባብ፡) – heart, mind, intellect

ልብስ፡ (pl. አልባስ፡) – clothing, garment

ልኅልኅና፡ – weakness

ልኡከ፡ – sent (one), apostle, messenger

ሐ

ሐለየ፡ (subj. ይሕሊ፡) – sing, make music

ሐላዪ፡ (f. ት፡) (pl. ሐለይት፡) – singer

ሐመ፡ / ሐመመ፡ (ይሐምም፡ ይሕምም፡) – "be ill, suffer illness or pain"; CG, አሕማም፡ – "afflict with illness"

ሐመር፡ (f./m.; pl. አሕማር) – boat or ship

ሐራ፡ – army, soldiers

ሐሰ፡ / ሓሰ፡ – sign of aversion

ሐብል፡ (pl. አሕባል፡) – rope, cord

ሐብለ፡ አነዳ፡ – thong

ሐተተ፡ – to investigate; Gt ተሐተተ፡ – to be investigated

ሐተታ፡ – investigation, interrogation

ሕኑጽ፡ – built, constructed

ሕንጽ፡ / ሕንጻት፡ / ሕንጻ፡ – building, construction

ሐዊሳ፡ / ሐዌሳ፡ – sign of joy

ሐዋርያ፡ (pl. ሐዋርያት፡) – apostle

ሕዋጼ፡ – visit, visitation

ሐወጸ፡ (D) – inspect, look at, visit

ሐይቅ፡ (pl. ሐይቃት፡) – seashore

ሐደሰ፡ (D) – renew, renovate; Dt, ተሐደሰ፡ – be made new, to be restored

ሐዲስ፡ (f. ሐዳስ፡ pl. ሐደስት፡) – new (ሐግ፡ ሐዲስ፡ – New Testament)

ሐዕም፡ – a taste, flavor (e.g., vanilla)

ሕዝብ፡ – people

ሐዘነ፡ – be/become sad

ሕዙን፡ – sad

ሐዘን፡ – sadness, grief

ሕይወት፡ – life, lifetime

ሕያው፡ (f. ሕያውት፡) – alive, living

ሕግ፡ (pl. ሕገግ፡) – law; በሕግ፡ – legally or lawfully

መ

መህረ፡ G – teach
ማሃይምን፡ (f. ማሃይምንት፡) – faithful (one), believer
መልአ፡ (trans.) – fill with something
መልአክ፡ (pl. መላአክት፡) – angel, messenger
ማሕሌት፡ (pl. ማሕሌታት፡ መሓልይ፡) – song, singing, music
መሓሪ፡ – one who is merciful
መምህር፡ – teacher
መሠንይ፡ – the best part (of)
መሠግር፡ – fisherman (pl. መሠገራን፡)
መርሐ፡ – lead, guide
መሰምልም፡ – new fruit
መስኮት፡ (pl. መሳከው፡) – window
መስቀል፡ (pl. መሳቅል፡) – cross
ማሰነ፡ ማሰነ፡ – be ruined, destroyed; perish; become corrupt, rotten; CL, አማሰነ፡ – corrupt, destroy, wipe out; Lt, ተማሰነ፡ – passive of CL
መስፌ፡ – awl
መስፍን፡ – prince
ሞቅሐ፡ (from ሞቅሕ፡ – fetter) – put in chains/imprison; Qt, ተሞቅሐ፡ – be bound in chains; CQ, አሞቅሐ፡ – have someone put in prison
ሞቅሕ፡ (pl. መዋቅሕት፡) – bonds, chains
መቅድመ፡ – before, in preference to
መቅደስ፡ – temple, sanctuary
መባሕት፡ – power, permission, authority
ሙብረቅ፡ መባርቅት፡ – narrow path (usually in mountains)
ሞት፡ – death
ሞተ፡ – die
መትሕተ፡ – underneath
ማኅበር፡ – council
መንገለ፡ – to, toward, in the direction of
መንጸረ፡ / አንጸረ፡ – over against
መንፈስ፡ (pl. መንፈሳት፡ / መናፍስት፡) – spirit of various kinds
መንፈስ፡ ቅዱስ፡ – Holy Spirit
መንፈሳዊ፡ (f. መንፈሳዊት፡) – of the spirit, spiritual
መንኮሰ፡ (Q) (from መነኮስ፡ – monk, nun) – become a monk
መንክር፡ (pl. ምንክራት፡) – miracle, marvel, wonder
መንኮት፡ – ax
መንኩራኩር፡ – wheel
ማእስ፡ / ማዕስ፡ (pl. አምእስት፡ / አምዕስት፡) – skin, hide, leather

Lexicon 291

ማእከለ፡ – among, in the midst of

መከረ፡ – plan, propose, decide on; (subj. ይምክር፡); CG, አምከረ፡ advise, give counsel to; Glt, ተማከረ፡ take counsel together (used with ምስለ፡) – deliberate and decide to + subj.

መካሪ፡ – counselor, advisor

መካን፡ (pl. መካናት፡) – place, locale

መኰንን፡ – judge, administrator

መዋዕል፡ – days

መዓር፡ – honey

መዕበል፡ / ማዕብል፡ (pl. ማዕብላት፡) – wave, flood

ማዕዶተ፡ – beyond, along

መዓልት፡ (m./f.) – day

መዓልተ፡ – during the day

መዓርጊር፡ (adj.) – sweet

ማይ፡ (ማያት፡) – water

ምድር፡ – land, earth, ground

መድኃን፡ (pl. መድኃናን፡) – savior, redeemer

መገሥጽ፡ – instructor, teacher

መጠነ፡ – of the size of, as large as

መጠወ፡ – surrender, to hand over

መተረ፡ – cut, cut off; Gt, ተመትረ፡ – be cut, to be cut off

መጽሐፍ፡ (pl. መጻሕፍት፡) – book, document, writing, inscription

መጽአ፡ – come

መጽወተ፡ (Q) (from ምጽዋት፡ – charity) – practice charity

መፈውስ፡ – physician

ምሁር፡ – learned (person), expert

ምሕረት፡ – mercy, pity

ምሕረ፡ / መሐረ፡ (subj. ይምሐር፡) – have mercy upon; CG, አምሐረ፡ – cause to have mercy; Gt, ተምሕረ፡ – be shown mercy

ምራቅ፡ – saliva, spit

ምስለ፡ – with, in the company of

ምስል፡ (pl. ምስል፡ ምስላት፡ አምሳል፡) – likeness, form, image

ምስጢር፡ (ምስጢራት፡) – mystery (emphasis on Eucharist)

ምቅሥፍት፡ (pl. ምቅሠፋት፡) – punishment, beating, divine punishment

ምት፡ (pl. አምታት፡) – husband

ምጋባእ፡ (pl. ምጋባአት፡) – hiding place

ምንዳቤ፡ – affliction, torment

ምእኃዘ፡ – beside, close to

ምውልታው፡ – place of refuge

ምዉት፡ (pl. ምዉታን፡) – dead

ምዕራፍ፡ (pl. ምዕራፋት፡) – quiet place, resting place, chapter of a book

ምድር፡ ጽባሕ፡ – eastern region

ምድራዊ፡ (f. ምድራዊት፡) – of the world, worldly

ምጡው፡ – handed over, delivered

ሜጠ፡ Gt, ተመይጠ፡ – turn away, divert, be converted

ሠ

ሠምረ፡ (subj. ይሥመር፡) – take delight, be please with; CG, አሥመረ፡ – please, delight + obj. suffix

ሥሙር፡ – pleasing, nice, pleasant (with ለ, በነበ)

ሠርዐ፡ (subj. ይሥርዕ፡) – put in order, arrange; Gt, ተሠርዐ፡ – be arranged, be put in order

ሠናይ፡ (f. ሠናይት፡) – beautiful, fine, good

ሠነየ፡ – be beautiful, good

ሠጠቀ፡ (subj. ይሥጥቅ፡) – cut, split; Gt, ተሠጥቀ፡ – be cut or split; ሥጡቅ፡ – cut, split; ሥጥቀት፡ – cutting, splitting

ሥራይ፡ (pl. ሥራያት፡) – medicine, herbs, incantations, spells, magic

ሥርዐት፡ – order, arrangement, decree, law

ሥሩዕ፡ – arranged, ordered

ሥን፡ – beauty

ሥኑይ፡ – adorned, lovely

ሣእሣእ፡ – refined speech

ሣእን፡ (pl. አሥአን፡ አሥኣን፡ አሣእን፡) – shoe, sandal

ሥጋ፡ (pl. ሥጋት፡) – body, flesh, esp. of the flesh as opposed to the spirit

ሥጋዊ፡ – fleshly (not spiritual)

ረ

ረሰየ፡ (D) – put, set, or place; regard something

ረትዐ፡ – be righteous

ራትዕ፡ (f. ራትዕት፡) – just, righteous

ራእይ፡ – vision, revelation

ረአዪ፡ (pl. ረአያን፡ ረኣያን፡ ረአይት፡) – observer, seer

ረአዪ፡ ከካብ፡ – astrologer, star reader

ረአዪ፡ ጎቡኣት፡ – soothsayer

ረኵሰ፡ – be unclean, impure; CG, አርኰሰ፡ – pollute, contaminate, defile

ረድአ፡ – help someone; Gt, ተረድአ፡ – be helped; Glt, ተራድአ፡ – help one another

ረድእ፡ (pl. አርዳእ፡ አርድእት፡) – helper, disciple

ርሕቀ፡ (subj. ይርሐቅ፡) – be distant, remote (spatial or temporal); CG, አርሐቀ፡ – remove, to delay; Glt, ተራሐቀ፡ – separate mutually (from)

ርሑቅ፡ – far away, remote

ርሕቀት፡ – a period of time or a measure space

ርስት፡ – inheritance

ርሱይ፡ – prepared, made ready

ርጉው፡ – open (adj.)

ርእስ፡ – head

ርእስ፡ (pl. አርእስት፡) – head, summit, chief (can occur with suffix as a reflexive or intensive pronoun: ቀተለ፡ ርእሶ፡ – he killed himself

ርእየት፡ – appearance, aspect

ርኩስ፡ (f. ርክስት፡) – unclean

ሮሜ፡ – Rome

ሮጸ፡ – run

ሰ

ሰላም፡ – safety

ሰሐበ፡ – pull, drag, draw, attract; Gt, ተስሕበ፡ – be pulled

ሰምዐ፡ – hear, hear of, obey

ሰመየ፡ – name (something, someone)

ሰማይ፡ (m./f.) heaven (pl. ሰማያት፡)

ሰማያዊ፡ (f. ሰማያዊት፡) – heavenly, divine

ሰቀለ፡ (subj. ይስቅል፡) – suspend, hang up, crucify; Gt, ተስቅለ፡ – be crucified; ስቅለት፡ – crucifixion; መስቀል፡ (pl. መሳቅል፡) – cross

ስቆቃው፡ (verbal noun) – mourning, lamenting

ሰብሳብ፡ – wedding, marriage

ሰበከ፡ – preach

ሰባኪ፡ – preacher

ሰብአ፡ ሥራይ፡ – wizards, witches, dealers in spells

ሰኔት፡ (ዕለት፡) – the next day; ሳኔታ፡ – the next day; በሳኔታ፡ – on the next day

ሰአለ፡ – ask for

ሰከበ፡ – lay, lay down

ሰወረ፡ (D) – hide, conceal; Dt, ተሰወረ፡ – be hidden

ሰዐመ፡ (subj. ይስዐም፡) – kiss; Gt, ተስዕመ፡ – be kissed; Glt, ተሳዐመ፡ – kiss one another

ሰይልየ፡ / ሴልየ፡ – woe is me!

ሰይፍ፡ (pl. አስያፍ፡ አስይፍት፡) – sword

ሰዳዲ፡ – persecutor, exorcist

ሰገደ፡ – bow down

ሰፈየ፡ (subj. ይስፊ፡) – sew; Gt, ተሰፍየ፡ – be sewn

ሰፋዪ፡ – sewer, tailor

ስሕተ፡ – err, stray (from path or doctrine)

ስሑት፡ – led into error

ስሕተት፡ – error, sin

ስም፡ (pl. አስማት፡) – name, fame, reputation

ስብሐት፡ (pl. ስብሐታት፡) – praise, hymn of praise
ስብአዊ፡ – man, humankind
ስእለት፡ – request, prayer
ስእነ፡ – be unable; Gt, ተስእነ፡ – be impossible (+ inf.); can take the personal objective suffix in the dative:
    ተስእነኒ፡ ሐዊረ፡ – it was impossible for me to go
ስኡን፡ – impotent, powerless
ስዉር፡ – hidden, concealed
ስዉዕ፡ – summoned, invited
ስዕመት፡ – a kiss
ሰይጠን፡ – demon, Satan, adversary
ስዱድ፡ – expelled, exiled
ስጉድ፡ – prostrate in worship
ሲሳይ፡ – food, sustenance
ሱ፡ – please!
ሶም፡ (pl. አጽዋም፡) – a fast, fasting
ሶር፡ (pl. አስዋር፡) – burden
ሶበ፡ – when (temporal)
ሶቤሃ፡ – (adv.) immediately, then
ሱታፌ፡ / ሱታፍ፡ – companion, associate

ቀ

ቃል፡ (pl. ቃላት፡) – voice, word, sound
ቀልቀል፡ – precipice
ቀርበ፡ to draw near, approach (ኀበ፡ ውስተ፡ ለ-)
ቀሲስ፡ – priest
ቀሠፈ፡ (subj. ይቅሥፍ፡) – beat or whip; Gt, ተቀሥፈ፡ – be beaten; ቅሡፍ፡ – beaten, afflicted
ቀበረ፡ – bury, inter
ቀንዲል፡ – lamp
ቀደመ፡ – go before, precede; CG, አቅደመ፡ – put or place first, to happen or exist; Gt, ተቀድመ፡ – occur, take place first; Glt, ተቃደመ፡ go/come out to meet
ቀዲሙ፡ – (adv.) – first, at first, previously; እምቀዲሙ፡ – before this, from the beginning
ቀደሰ፡ (D) – sanctify or make holy; Dt, ተሐደሰ፡ – be made holy
ቀይሕ፡ – red
ቀጥቀጠ፡ – crush or grind
ቅሥፈት፡ – punishment, affliction
ቄረ፡ / ቄረረ፡ – be cold, cool; to cool off (anger); CG, አቈረረ፡ – cause to be cold or angry
ቄሪር፡ (f. ቄራር፡) – cold, cool
ቅሩብ፡ – near, nearby, adjacent (with ለ, ኀበ); at hand
ቅቡር፡ – buried

Lexicon 295

ቀታሊ፡ (pl. ቀተልት፡) – murderer, killer, one who kills
ቅቱል፡ – slain
ቅናት፡ (pl. ቅናታት፡ ቅናውት፡) – belt
ቅድመ፡ before (spatial); in the presence of – በቅድመ፡ (adverb: previously, beforehand)
ቅድመ፡ እምቅድመ፡ – before that (with subjunctive)
ቅዳሴ፡ – sanctification, consecration, liturgy
ቅድሳት፡ / ቅድስና፡ – holiness, sanctity; frequently used in construct chains – ሀገረ፡ ቅድሳት፡ – city of holiness (holy city)
ቄጸል፡ (m./f.) – leaf or foliage (pl. አቍጽል፡)

በ

በ- – in, into, by, with
በላዪ፡ – old, wearing out (adj.)
ባሕ፡ / ባሑ፡ / በሐ፡ – salutation
ባሕር፡ (አብሕርት፡) – sea, ocean
ባሕቱ፡ – but, however, nevertheless
በሕግ፡ – legally, lawfully
በረቀ፡ (subj. ይብርቅ፡) – flash as lightning; CG, አብረቀ፡ – cause lightning
በርናበስ፡ – Barnabas
ባረከ፡ – bless
በረድ፡ (m.) – hail
በሰላም፡ – safely, in peace
በበይናቲ፡ (prep.) – among, between; used with Glt verbs of reciprocal action
ቤተ፡ ሞቅሕ፡ – prison
በተከ፡ (G) – break; Gt, ተበትከ፡ – break (intrans)
በትእዛዘ፡ – at the command of
በኅቡእ፡ – secretly
በአምሳለ፡ – in the likeness of
በእንተ፡ ዘ- – because
በከመ፡ (prep.) – according to, in accordance with
በከየ፡ – weep, mourn
በድን፡ (pl. አብድንት፡) – corpse
ባዕድ፡ (f. ባዕድ፡ pl. በእዳን፡) – other, different, alien
ባዕል፡ (f. ባዕልት፡) – rich, wealthy
ቢድበደ፡ – die of disease
በጽሐ፡ – arrive
በጽሚት፡ – in private
በዕሡብ፡ – with difficulty
በዕብሬት፡ – for the sake of (with suffixes)

በግዕ፡ (f. በግዕት፡ pl. አባግዕ፡) – sheep, lamb
ቤተ፡ ንጉሥ፡ house of the king, palace
ቤተ፡ ልሔም፡ – Bethlehem
ቤተ፡ መቅደስ፡ – Jerusalem Temple
ቤዘወ፡ (Q/L) – redeem (with: በ-; from: እም-); Qt, ተቤዘወ፡ – be redeemed; redeem oneself
ብሉይ፡ – old, worn out
ብሔረ፡ አግዓዚ፡ – Ethiopia
ብሔር፡ (pl. ቢሓውርት፡) – region, province, district, earth
ብርሃን፡ (ብርሃናት፡) – light
ብርሃናዊ፡ (f. ብርሃናዊት፡) – of or pertaining to light, radiant
ብሩር፡ (pl. ብሩራት፡) – silver
ብርት፡ – copper
ብቱክ፡ – broken
ብእሲ፡ – man, husband (pl. ሰብእ፡)
ብእሲት፡ – woman, wife (pl. አንስት፡)
ብእንተ፡ – in regard to, in the direction of
ብካይ፡ – weeping, lamentation
ብዉሕ፡ – is permitted for someone
ብዕለ፡ – be rich
ብዑል፡ – rich, wealthy
ብዙኅ፡ – many, much
ብድብድ፡ – plague
ቢጸ፡ – beside
ቦአ፡ – enter

ተ

ተሐሠየ፡ / ተሐሥየ፡ (Gt) – rejoice
ታሕተ፡ – under, below
ተመሀተ፡ (Qt; from ምሁት፡ – phantom, ghost) – become a ghost
ተምሕረ፡ – be shown mercy
ተማከረ፡ – take counsel together (used with ምስለ፡) – deliberate and decide to + subj.
ተምዕዐ፡ / ተምዐ፡ (at: ላዕለ፡ ዲበ፡ በእንተ፡) – Gt, become angry
ተረስየ፡ (Dt) – put on a garment
ተርጐመ፡ – translate
ትርጓሜ፡ (pl. ትርጓማት፡) – translation, interpretation
ተርፈ፡ / ተረፈ፡ (G) – remain, survive; CG, አትረፈ፡ – leave behind
ተራፊ፡ – survivor
ትሩፍ፡ (f. ትርፍት፡ pl. ትሩፍት፡) – excellent, outstanding; can be used as virtue, excellence
ተሳተፈ፡ (Lt) – associate with; share something

ተስናእው፡ (Qlt) – come to an agreement

ተቀድመ፡ – occur, take place first; Glt, ተቃደመ፡ – go/come out to meet

ተነበየ፡ (Dt) – prophesy (to: ለ; against: ላዕለ፡)

ተአምላከ፡ (Qt; from አምላክ፡ – God) – become divine

ተከለ፡ – in place of

ተካየደ፡ – make a treaty, pact, or covenant

ተውላጠ፡ – for, in exchange for

ትውልድ፡ (pl. ትውልዳት፡) – generation, offspring

ተዝካር፡ – memorial, feast, commemoration

ተገብረ፡ (Dt) – work, produce something

ተጠየቀ፡ – seek certainty or clarity

ተፈሥሐ፡ (Dt) – rejoice (in: በ-, በእንተ፡, ላዕለ፡, ዲበ፡)

ተፋለሰ፡ – wander as exiles

ተፋትሐ፡ – engage in a legal case with

ትእምርት፡ – miracle

ትእዛዝ፡ (pl. ትእዛዛት፡) – order, command, edict

ትኩል፡ – planted, implanted

ቶታን፡ (pl. ቶታናት፡) – shoelace

ጎ

ኃለፈ፡ – pass by

ኃሠሣ፡ (pl. ኃሠሣት፡) – wish, desire

ኃሠሠ፡ (G) – seek, look for; Gt, ተኃሠ፡ – seek for oneself; Glt, ተኃሠሠ፡ – discuss with one another

ኃሳር፡ (pl. ኃሳራት፡) – poverty, wretchedness

ኃበ፡ – by, with, at, or near

ኃበረ፡ / ኀበረ፡ – connected to or associated with; CG, አኃበረ፡ – associate; Gt, ተኃበረ፡ – associate with someone

ኃብአ፡ (subj. ይኃባእ፡) – hide or conceal; Gt, ተኃብአ፡ – be hidden, or hide oneself

ኃደረ፡ – reside, dwell, inhabit; ኃደረ፡ ላዕለ፡ – reside in, possess as in demons; CG, አኃደረ፡ – cause to dwell; Gt, ተኃድረ፡ – be inhabited; Glt, ተኃደረ፡ – live together

ኃደገ፡ (G) – leave, divorce, abandon; Gt, ተኃድገ፡ – be left, be divorced; Glt, ተኃደገ፡ – divorce someone

ኃጥእ፡ (f. ኃጥእት፡) – sinful, wicked; noun – sinner

ኃጢአት፡ (ኃጣውእ፡ ኃጣይእ፡) sin (m., f.)

ኃጺን፡ (pl. ኃጸውንት፡) – iron, sword, weapon

ኃፈረ፡ / ኀፍረ፡ (subj. ይኃፍር፡) – be ashamed; Gt, ተኃፈረ፡ – be put to shame

ኃፍረት፡ (pl. ኃፍረታት፡) – shame, impropriety

ኃፀበ፡ (subj. ይኃፅብ፡) – wash; Gt, ተኃፀበ፡ – wash oneself; ኃፁብ፡ – washed; ኃፀብት፡ – washing, ablution; ምንፃብ፡ – bath, place for bathing

ኄር፡ (f. ኄርት፡) – good, excellent

ኅሉፍ፡ – crossing, passing

ኅብስት፡ (ኅባውዝ፡) – bread
ኅብረት፡ – union, association, accord
ኅቡር፡ – joined, associated; ኅቡረ፡ – (adverb) together, jointly
ኅቡእ፡ – hidden, concealed
ኀዳር፡ – residing, dwelling
ኀድረት፡ – residing, dwelling
ኅድገት፡ – remission (of debts)
ኅድጋት፡ / ኅዳጋት፡ – divorce
ኅዱግ፡ – abandoned, divorced
ኀጢአት፡ – sin
ኍልቍ፡ / ኍልቈ፡ (pl. ኍለቍ፡) – number, amount
ኆኅት፡ (pl. ኆኃታት፡ ኃዋኀው፡) – door, doorway

ነ

ናሁ፡ – behold
ነሥአ፡ – raise, lift up
ነቀልቃል፡ – agitation; (verbal noun) – moving or quaking
ነሳሒ፡ – a penitent one
ነስሐ፡ – repent of
ነበበ፡ – speak to, to tell
ነባሪ፡ – household servant
ነቢይ፡ (pl. ነቢያት፡) – prophet
ነብልባል፡ (verbal noun) – flaming, blazing
ነአስ፡ – young girl; ንእስ፡ – childhood
ነኪር፡ (f. ነካር፡ pl. ነከርት፡) – strange, alien, foreign, wonderful
ነዊኅ፡ (f. ነዋኅ፡ pl. ነዋኅት፡) – high, tall, distant
ነዋኅ፡ – tall
ነዓ፡ – come!
ነደ፡ – burn; CG, አንደደ፡ – set fire; Glt, ተናደደ፡ – burn with mutual passion
ነድ፡ – flame
ነዳይ፡ (f. ነዳይት፡) – poor, destitute
ነግሠ፡ – become ruler, king; CG, አንገሠ፡ – cause someone to rule
ንጉሥ፡ (pl. ነገሥት፡) – king, ruler, one who rules
ንግሥት፡ – queen (pl. ንግሥታት፡)
ነገረ፡ – say, tell
ነገር፡ (pl. ነገራት፡) – speech, account, thing
ነገርጋር፡ (verbal noun) – rolling, spinning, possession by a spirit (related to epileptic seizures)
ነጸረ፡ – look, look at
ነፋስ፡ (pl. ነፋሳት፡) – wind

ነፍሰ፡ – blow (as in the wind); CG, አንፈሰ፡ – breathe something out (like fire)

ነፍስ፡ (pl. ነፍሳት፡) – soul, spirit, breath

ንስሓ፡ – repentance, regret

ንሱሕ፡ – repentant

ንስቲት፡ – small or little amount; found in construct chain, ንስቲተ፡ ኅብስት፡ – a little bread; as an adjective, ሀገር፡ ንስቲት፡ – a small village, town

ንቡር፡ – sitting, seated, residing

ንእሰ፡ (subj. ይንአስ፡) – be small, young; CG, አንአሰ፡ – make small

ንኡስ፡ (f. ንእስት፡) – small, little; young

ንዋም፡ – sleep

ንዋይ፡ (pl. ንዋያት፡) – vessel, instrument

ንዐ፡ impv. – come!; forms: 2ms, ነዐ፡; 2fs, ነዒ፡; 2mp, ነዑ፡; 2fp ነዓ

ንዴት፡ / ንድየት፡ – poverty

ንዱድ፡ – burning

ንፃሬ፡ – a look, glance, ability to see

ኖመ፡ (subj. ይኑም፡) – sleep; CG, አኖመ፡ / አነመ፡ – put to sleep

ኖኅ፡ – be high

አ

አ፡ /አሀ፡ – sign of sorrow

አላ፡ – but

አሌ፡ – alas!, unfortunately!

አልቦ፡ ኍልቁ፡ – there is no limit, innumerable

አሕነጸ፡ – have built

አሕዘነ፡ – make sad

አሕየወ፡ – restore to life, heal, cure

አመ፡ – when, while, at the time of

አምሳለ፡ – like

አምላክ፡ – Lord, god

እማእከለ፡ – from among

አመስጠረ፡ (CQ; from ምስጢር፡ – mystery) – deal in mysteries

አመረ፡ – tell, show, indicate, make known

አሚር፡ (m./f.) – day; used only in certain fixed expressions ወእቱ፡/ይእተ፡ አሚረ፡ (on that day)

አማኅበረ፡ (from ማኅበር፡ – council) – convene a council

አምነ፡ – be true, to believe; Gt, ተአመነ፡ / ተአምነ፡ – to be believed, have faith in, confess sins

አመንደበ፡ (CQ) – afflict, oppress; Qt, ተመንደበ፡ – be oppressed, afflicted

አሞአ፡ / አምአ፡ – make someone victorious

አረሚ፡ (adj. አረማዊ፡) – pagans, heathens, non-Christians

አርትዐ፡ – make right, correct

አርኀወ፡ (CG) – open; Gt, ተርኀወ፡ – be opened

አርአየ፡ – show someone something, to reveal

አርከበ፡ – cause someone to find something

አርዌ፡ (m./f.; pl. አራዊት፡) – animal, wild beast

አረጋዊ፡ (f. አረጋዊት፡; pl. አረጋውያን፡) – old person

አረጋይ፡ / አረጋይ፡ (f. አረጊት፡; pl. አእሩግ፡) – old person

አረፍት፡ – wall, partition

አስሐትያ፡ – ice, hail, snow, frost

አስምዐ፡ – announce, summon as a witness

አስመየ፡ – be well known, famous

አሰረ፡ – tie up, bind; Gt, ተአሰረ፡ – be tied up, bound

እሱር፡ – bound, tied, captive

እስረት፡ – binding, tying

አስቆቀወ፡ (impf. ያስቆቁ፡) – mourn, lament

አስተሓመመ፡ (CGlt) – study diligently, give close attention to

አስተምሐረ፡ (CGt) – show mercy to, to seek mercy for self

አስተብቍዐ፡ (CGt) – implore, beseech, intercede

አስተዋሰበ፡ (CGlt) – marry off a child

አስተዋደየ፡ (CGlt) – accuse, bring charges against

አሰንበተ፡ (CQ; from ሰንበት፡ – Sabbath) – observe the Sabbath

አሰፈወ፡ (CD) – promise; Dt, ተሰፈወ፡ – hope for, expect, look forward to

አቅበረ፡ – cause, allow, order someone to bury someone

አቅተለ፡ – cause or order someone to kill someone

አቅያሕይሐ፡ – grow reddish

አብ፡ (pl. አበው፡) – father

አብለየ፡ – age, make old

አብሐ፡ (CG) – allow, permit; Gt, ተበውሐ፡ – be permitted

አበሳ፡ (pl. አበሳት፡) – sin, crime

አበሰ፡ (D) – commit a crime or sin

አባሲ፡ / መአበሲ፡ – sinner, criminal

አባት፡ – father

አብዐለ፡ – make rich

አብዝኀ፡ – multiply, make numerous

አብድ፡ – fool

አተወ፡ – go home, depart from home

አኀዘ፡ – seize, grasp, hold; Gt, ተአኀዘ፡ – be seized, grasped; CG, አአኀዘ፡ – order someone held; Glt, ተአኀዘ፡ – be involved in battle with

አነዳ፡ – skin, hide, leather

አንሥአ፡ – raised, cause to rise

አንሶሰወ፡ (impf. ያንሶሱ፡) – walk about, go for a stroll

አንቀልቀለ፡ (N) – move or quake

አንቀጽ፡ (pl. አናቅጽ፡) – gate, door
አንቋዕ፡ – joy!
አንበልበለ፡ (N) – flame or blaze
አንበበ፡ – read, recite
አንተ፡ – in the direction of
አንከረ፡ (G) – wonder, be astonished; Gt, ተነከረ፡ – be admired; Glt, ተናከረ፡ – be alien to, renounce
አንደየ፡ – reduce to poverty
አንገርገረ፡ (N) – roll or spin
አንጐርጐረ፡ (N) – be angry
አንጐድጐደ፡ (N) – thunder
አንጸረ፡ – cause to look
አንጸፍጸፈ፡ (N) – ooze
አኖኀ፡ / አነኀ፡ – extend, put forth
አእመረ፡ (CG) – know, understand, comprehend; Gt, ተአምረ፡ – be known, be understood
አእመነ፡ – convert
አአከየ፡ – make something bad (toward: ላዕለ፡ ዲበ፡)
አከሐደ፡ – contradict, not believe
አው፡ – or
አውለደ፡ – cause someone to bear a child
አውሥአ፡ (CG) – respond, answer; Glt, ተዋሥአ፡ – speak against, contradict
አውሰበ፡ (CG) – marry
አውተረ፡ (CG) – continue, persevere
አዕረፈ፡ (CG) intrans. – rest, find rest; trans. – give rest
አዕቀበ፡ – hand someone something
አዕበየ፡ – make great, increase
አዕደወ፡ – lead or take across
አዝለፈ፡ (CG) – continue doing something
አዝሉፈ፡ / ለዝሉፉ፡ – (adv.) continuously
አይኅ፡ – the flood
አድለቅለቀ፡ – shake or tremble
አድወየ፡ – make ill; አድለቅለቀ፡ – shake or tremble
አግበረ፡ – make or order someone to do or make something
አጥመቀ፡ (CG) – baptize; Gt, ተጠምቀ፡ – be baptized
አጥበበ፡ – make wise
አጽሐፈ፡ – cause someone to write
አጽበረ፡ ጽቡረ፡ (CG) – work clay
አጽባዕት፡ (pl. አጻብዕ፡) – finger, toe
አጽንዐ፡ – make firm, grasp strongly; በልቡ፡ – learn by heart
አጽደቀ፡ – make righteous, just
አፍቀረ፡ (CG) – love; Gt, ተፈቅረ፡ – be loved; Glt, ተፋቀረ፡ – love one another
አፍርሀ፡ – frighten

አፍርንጅ፡ – the Romans
አፍአ፡ / አፍኣ፡ (adv.) – outside
እመ፡ / እም፡ – if
እም፡ (pl. እማት፡) – mother
እምህየ፡ – from there, from that place
እምባነ፡ / በእምባነ፡ – as long as
እምማእከለ፡ – from among
እሙነ፡ (adv.) – truly
እማነ፡ – truth; (adj.) እማነ፡ – true, faithful; (adv.) በእማነ፡ – truly, in truth
እሙን፡ – faithful, trustworthy
እምነት፡ – faith, belief
እምዘ፡ – since
እምዝ፡ – then, next, thereupon
እምዝየ፡ – from here, from this place
እስመ፡ – because, for, since
እሳት፡ – fire
እስረት፡ – binding, tying
እሱር፡ – bound, tied, captive
እስራኤል፡ – Israel
እስከ፡ – until, up to, as far as
እስክንድርያ፡ – Alexandria
እብን፡ (እበን፡ አእባን፡) – stone
እትወት፡ / እቶት፡ – return home, a return, crop yield
እኅት፡ (pl. አኃት፡) – sister
እኃዝ፡ / አኃዝ፡ – fist
እጓዚ፡ – owner, master, lord
እኁዝ፡ – captive, held, possessed
እኁዘ፡ አጋንንት፡ – possessed by a demon
አኅደረ፡ – be made to dwell; Gt, ተኃድረ፡ – be inhabited; Glt, ተኃደረ፡ – live together
እኁ፡ (pl. አኃው፡) – brother
እንበለ፡ / ዘእንበለ፡ – without, except for
እንበለ፡ – if not, except
እንከ፡ – then
እንዘ፡ – whilst
እንጋ፡ – perhaps
አንፈሰ፡ – breathe
እኪይ፡ (pl. እኪያት፡) – evil, wickedness
እኩይ፡ – evil, wicked
እዝን፡ (pl. እዘን፡ አእዛን፡) – ear
እዘዘ፡ – commanded, ordered
እድ፡ (እደው፡) – hand

አድወየ፡ – make ill

እግር፡ (pl. እገር፡ አእጋር፡) – foot

አግበረ፡ – make or order someone to do or make something

እግዚእ፡ (f. እጋዝእት፡; pl. እጋእስት፡) – lord, master, leader, chief

እግዚአብሔር፡ – Lord, God

እንሰ፡ እመሕያው፡ – humankind; lit., child of the mother of the living (Eve)

እንል፡ (እንላት፡) – young animal

ኢ- – negative prefix to verbs

ኢየሱስ፡ ክርስቶስ፡ – Jesus Christ

ኦ (vocative particle) – O!; ኦንጉሥ፡ – O king!; እግዚኦ፡ – O Lord!

ከ

ከሃሊ፡ – powerful, capable; ከሃሊ፡ ኩሉ፡ – omnipotent (strong in all things); ከሃሊ፡ + infinitive – capable of

ከልአ፡ – prevent, withhold; Gt, ተከልአ፡ – abstain (from)

ካልእ፡ (f. ካልእት፡) – other, another, associate

ከሓዲ፡ – infidel, non-believer

ክሕድ፡ – lack of faith, heresy, rebellion

ከመ፡ (prep.) – like, as; (conj.) that

ከመ፡ ይመስለኒ፡ ከመ፡ ወርኅ፡ – it looks like the moon to me

ከሠተ፡ – reveal, uncover; Gt, ተከሥተ፡ – be revealed, be uncovered

ከረየ፡ (subj. ይክሪ፡) – dig; Gt, ተከርየ፡ – be dug

ከብረ፡ – be glorious, magnificent; CG, አክበረ፡ – make glorious

ኮከብ፡ (pl. ከዋክብት፡) – star

ኮከበ፡ ጽባሕ፡ – morning star

ከወላ፡ – behind

ከራዪ፡ (pl. ከረይት፡) – grave digger

ኪዳን፡ (pl. ኪዳናት፡) – pact, treaty, covenant

ኪዳን፡ ሐዲስ – New Testament

ኪዳን፡ ብሊት፡ – Old Testament

ኰነነ፡ (D) – judge, punish; CD, አኰነነ፡ – put someone in charge; Dt, ተኰነነ፡ – be put in charge; Glt, ተካነነ፡ – become reconciled with

ኩሎ፡ ዕልተ፡ (f./m.) – every day, all day

ኩሎ፡ ጊዜ፡ – always

ኲነኔ፡ – judgment, condemnation

ኩኑን፡ – judged, condemned

ክህለ፡ / ከህለ፡ – be able, to prevail against (+ obj. suff.); Gt, ተክህለ፡ – be possible (+ inf.); CG, አክህለ፡ – enable, to make able; can take the personal objective suffix in the dative

ከሕደ፡ – deny, repudiate

ክሕይት፡ – denial, apostasy

ክሡት፡ – uncovered, bare, open eyes
ክሳድ፡ / ክሃድ፡ (pl. ክላዳት፡ / ክላውድ፡ / ክላውድ፡) – neck
ክብር፡ (f. ክብርት፡) – glorious
ክርስቲያናዊ፡ – Christian

ወ

ወ – and, but
ወሀበ፡ – give
ወለት፡ (pl. አዋልድ፡) – daughter, girl
ወለደ፡ (Gt) ወለደ፡ – bear a child; Gt, ተወልደ፡ – be born
ወልድ፡ (pl. ውሉድ፡) – son, child, boy
ወረሰ፡ (subj. ይረስ፡) – inherit; CG, አውተረ፡ – make someone an heir; Gt, ተወርሰ፡ – gain by inheritance; Glt, ተዋረሰ፡ – gain possession of
ወራሲ፡ – heir
ወርቅ፡ – gold, money
ወሬዛ (pl. ወራዙት፡) – youth, young man
ወርኅ፡ (አውራኅ፡) – moon
ወትረ፡ (adv.) – continuously, always
ወሰከ፡ (D) – add (to: ዲበ፡ ላዕለ፡), increase, augment; Dt, ተወሰከ፡ – be added to
ወሰደ፡ – lead, bring, take
ወንጌል፡ – gospel
ወንጌላዊ፡ (f. ወንጌላዊት፡) – gospel (adj.); evangelist (noun)
ወእመሰ፡ – and if, on the contrary
ውእይ፡ – along
ወኮነ፡ ሶበ፡ – and when, and while (used with imperfect)
ዋዕይ፡ – fire, heat, burning
ወድቀ፡ – fall down
ወገረ፡ (G) – throw, stone someone; Gt, ተወገረ፡ = Dt ተወገረ፡ – be stoned; Glt, ተዋገረ፡ – throw stones at one another
ወደየ፡ – put, place, set
ወፅአ፡ – go, come forth, emerge
ውሕዘ፡ – flow
ውዕየ፡ – be burned up, consumed by fire
ውዕየት፡ – burning, conflagration

ዐ

ዐርበ፡ / ዕርበ፡ (subj. ይዕረብ፡ ይዕርብ፡) – set as in the sun; CG, አዕረበ፡ – cause to set
ዐረብ፡ – west (direction)

ዐርብ፡ – Friday (ዕለተ፡ ዐርብ፡ / ዐርብ፡ ዕለት፡)

ዐርቢ፡ / ዐረባዊ፡ – western, Arabian; ምዕራብ፡ / ምዕራቢ፡ ፀሓይ፡ – the west

ዐቀበ፡ – guard, keep watch on, take care of, observe or keep (the law)

ዐቢይ፡ (f. ዐባይ፡; pl. ዐበይት፡) – big, large, important, great

ዐውደ፡ – about, around

ዐውድ፡ (pl. አዕዋድ፡) – neighborhood, vicinity

ዐዘቅት፡ – well, cistern

ዐይን፡ (pl. አዕይንት፡) – eye; ሰብአ፡ ዐይን፡ – spies

ዐደወ፡ – cross (a goal)

ዐጽቅ፡ (pl. አዕጹቅ፡ / አዕጹቃት፡) – branch, palm branch

ዐጸበ፡ / ዐጽበ፡ (subj. ይዕጽብ፡ / ይዕጸብ፡) – be hard, difficult; ዐጹብ፡ – harsh, difficult

ዕጽብ፡ / ዐጽብ፡ – harshness, difficulty

ዐጹብ፡ – harsh, difficult

ዐጽፍ፡ (pl. ዐጽፋት፡ / አዕጽፍት፡) – tunic, cloak, mantle

ዕለት፡ – day

ዕልው፡ – evil

ዕርገት፡ – ascent, assumption into heaven

ዕቅበት፡ – guarding, keeping vigil

ዕቁብ፡ – under guard, reserved

ዕቅብት፡ (f.; pl. ዕቁባት፡) – concubine

ዕብራዊያን፡ – the Hebrews

ዕቢይ፡ (pl. ዕቢያት፡) – greatness, size, majesty

ዕቡይ፡ – arrogant, haughty (Dt, ተዐበየ፡)

ዕዉቅ፡ – familiar, well-known

ዕድ፡ (pl. ዕደው፡) – community of men

ዕፅ፡ (m./f.) tree (pl. ዕፀው፡)

ዓለም፡ (pl. ዓለማት፡) – world, eternity

ዓለማዊ፡ – worldly

ዓመት፡ ዓም፡ (pl. ዓመታት፡) – year

ዓብየ፡ – be great

ዓዲ፡ (adv.) – still, yet, again

ያቀ፡ (subj. ይዑቅ፡) – take care for, be aware of; CG, አያቀ፡ – make known; Gt, ተዐውቀ፡ – be noticed, perceived, revealed

ያደ፡ – go around, surround

H

ዘ- – that, the fact that

ዛ፡ ዛቲ፡ ዝንቱ፡ – this

ዘልፈ፡ – always, frequently

ዘመድ፡ (አዝማድ፡) – family, relatives, tribe

ዘብዳ፡ – goat hair cloth

ዘበጠ፡ (subj. ይዝብጥ፡) – beat, whip; Gt, ተዘበጠ፡ – be whipped, or beaten; Glt, ተዛበጠ፡ – beat one another; ዘባጢ፡ – fighter

ዘከረ፡ – remember, mention; Dt, ተዘከረ፡ – be remembered

ዝሉፈ፡ ለዝሉፉ፡ (adv.) – continuously

ዝቡጥ፡ – beaten

ዝናም፡ (m./f.; pl. ዝናማት፡) – rain

ዜና፡ (pl. ዜናት፡) – report, story, account

ዝየ፡ በዝየ፡ – here, in this place

የ

ዮሐንስ፡ – John

ዮናናዊያን፡ – the Greeks

ደ

ደለወ፡ – weigh, be useful, suitable; Gt, ተደለወ፡ / ተደልወ – be weighed

ደመነ፡ (D) – become clouded

ደመና፡ (pl. ደመናት፡) – cloud

ደመንማኒን፡ – cloudy, gloomy

ደም፡ (ደማት፡) – blood

ደቂቅ፡ – children, offspring

ዳቤላ፡ (pl. ዳቤላት፡) – male animal

ዳኅን፡ (adj.) – safe, whole, sound; ዳኅን፡ / ድኅና፡ / በዳኅን፡ – safely, peacefully

ደዌ፡ (pl. ደዌያት፡) – sickness, illness, disease

ደገመ፡ – do something again (+inf.)

ድልቅልቅ፡ (verbal noun) – shaking, trembling

ድሙን፡ – clouded over

ድርሀም፡ (pl. ድርሀማት፡ ደራሀም፡) – drachma, denarius

ድኅረ፡ behind, in back of

ድኅነ፡ (subj. ይድኀን፡) – escape safely, be safe; CG, አድኅነ፡ – save, keep safe, rescue

ድኁን፡ – safe, unharmed

ድንግል፡ (pl. ደናግል፡) – virgin, celibate monk

ዴገነ፡ – pursue or to chase

ዲበ፡ – on, upon, onto

ገ

ገመል፡ (pl. ገመላት፡ አግማል፡) – camel
ገሠጸ፡ – rebuke, reproach
ገባሪ፡ (pl. ገባርት፡) – maker, craftsman
ገባር፡ (as a collective) – workers, laborers; follows the pattern $C_1ăC_2āC_3$, ቀታል፡ (*qatāl*)
ገብአ፡ – return or go back
ገነዘ፡ (G) – prepare for burial; Gt, ተገንዘ፡ – be prepared for burial; CG, አግነዘ፡ – cause someone to be buried
ጋኔን፡ (pl. አጋንንት፡) – evil spirit, demon; ዘጋኔን፡ (pl. አለ አጋንንት፡) – one possessed by an evil spirit
ገነት፡ (pl. ገነታት፡) – garden, Eden
ገዳም፡ (m.; pl. ገዳማት፡) – wilderness
ገደፈ፡ (subj. ይግድፍ፡) – throw, cast, discard; Gt, ተገድፈ፡ – be thrown away, be discarded
ገጽ፡ (pl. ገጻት፡) – face, appearance
ግልባብ፡ – veil
ግምዔ፡ – pitcher, vessel, flask
ግሡጽ፡ – instructed, learned
ግብር፡ (pl. ግብራት፡ ግበር፡) – deed, act, work, liturgy
ግቡር፡ – worked, made, finished
ግኑዝ፡ – prepared for burial
ግዕዝ፡ (pl. ግዕዛት፡) – mode of life, manner; nature, quality, essential nature (of persons and things)
ግዕዝ፡ አግዓዚ፡ – the Ethiopians
ግዱፍ፡ – thrown, cast, rejected
ጊዜ፡ (pl. ጊዜያት፡) – time
ጐንደየ፡ – last, remain; delay, tarry; CG, አጐንደየ፡ – put off, delay, defer; Qlt, ተጐናደየ፡ – delay in doing
ጐየ፡ – flee
ጕያ፡ – flight
ጐያይ፡(ዪ) – fugitive
ጐድጐደ፡ – knock on a door

ጠ

ጠቃ፡ / ጥቃ፡ – close to
ጠበ፡ – be wise
ጠቢብ፡ (f. ጠባብ፡ pl. ጠቢባት፡) – wise, prudent, skilled
ጠየቀ፡ (D) – examine, observe closely; CD, አጠየቀ፡ – inform someone of something; DT, ተጠየቀ፡ – seek certainty or clarity
ጠፍአ፡ – go out (a light, fire); CG, አጥፍአ፡ – extinguish, destroy, annihilate
ጥሙቅ፡ – baptized (CG verb አጥመቀ፡)
ጥራዝ፡ (pl. ጥራዛት፡) – fragment of a book
ጥቀ፡ – very, extremely

ጥቅም፡ – wall, city wall

ጥንት፡ – beginning

ጥዑም፡ – tasty, delicious

ጥዑይ፡ (f. ትዒት፡) – a healthy person or place

ጥዕመ፡ / ጠዐመ፡ (subj. ይጥዐም፡ / ይጥዕም፡) – taste, experience; CG, አጥዐመ፡ – give to someone to taste or experience

ጥዕየ፡ (subj. ይጥዐይ፡) – be healthy; CG, አጥዐየ፡ – make healthy

ጥዒና፡ – good health

ጥዮቀ፡ (adv.) – accurately, carefully, precisely

ጥዮቅ፡ – perceptive, accurate

ጴ

ጴጥሮስ፡ – Peter

ጸ

ጸልመ፡ / ጸለመ፡ (subj. ይጽለም፡ ይጽልም፡) – grow dark, grow blind; ጸልመ፡ ገጹ፡ – he became angry; CG, አጸለመ፡ – make blind, make dark; ጽሉም፡ – dark, obscured; ጸሊም፡ (f. ጸላም፡); ጽልመት፡ – darkness; መዋዕለ፡ ጽልመት፡ – days of wane; አመ፡ X-u ለጽልመተ፡ Y – "pm the X-day of the month of Y"

ጸሎት፡ (pl. ጸሎታት፡) – prayer(s)

ጸለየ፡ (D) – pray

ጸሐፈ፡ – write

ጸሐፊ፡ – scribe

ጸማ፡ ፃማ፡ (pl. ጸማት፡ ፃማት፡) – labor, toil, work

ጸብአ፡ – fight; Glt, ተጸብአ፡ – fight one another

ጸብእ፡ (pl. አጽባእ፡ ጸብአት፡) – war, battle

ጸንሐ፡ (subj. ይጽናሕ፡) – wait, expect; CG, አጸንሐ፡ – set traps or ensnare

ጸዋር፡ – carrier, porter

ጸዐዳዊድ፡ (adj.) – whitish

ጸዐዳ፡ – white

ጸድቀ፡ – be righteous, faithful, true

ጸድቅ፡ (f. ጸድቅት፡; pl. ጸድቃን፡) – righteous, just, true, faithful

ጸጋ፡ (pl. ጸጋት፡) – grace, favor, gift

ጸጉር፡ – hair, fur, feathers

ጸፍጸፍ፡ – juice

ጸመ፡ (subj. ይጹም፡) – fast (as in eating)

ጸረ፡ (subj. ይጸር፡ / ይጹር፡) – carry or bear; CG, አጸረ፡ / አጸረ፡ – make carry; Gt, ተጸወረ፡ – be carried

ጽሑፍ፡ – written

ጽሕፈት፡ – act of writing

ጽመ፡ – secretly

ጽሚተ፡ – in secret; በጽሚተ፡ – in private

ጽነፈ፡ አጽናፍ፡ – ends of the earth; outer edges

ጽንፍ፡ – edge, margin, hem, shore

ጽኑሕ፡ – waiting, expecting

ጽኑዕ፡ (f. ጽንዕት፡) – strong, powerful, harsh, severe, lasting

ጸዋሪ፡ (pl. ጸወርት፡) – one who carries or bears

ጽውም፡ (adj.) – fasting

ጽውዓ፡ / ጽዋዔ፡ – call, summons

ጽዉር፡ – bearing, burdened

ጸጕር፡ – hair, fur, feathers

ፀ

ፀሐይ፡ (ፀሐይ፡ ፀሐያት፡) – sun

ፀምር፡ – wool

ፀንሰ፡ (subj. ይፀንስ፡ ይፀስ፡) – become pregnant by (እም-); Gt, ተፀንሰ፡ – be conceived

ፀረፈ፡ / ፀረፈ፡ (subj. ይፀርፍ፡) – blaspheme (ላዕለ, ለ, against)

ፀራፊ፡ (adj.) – blasphemous, wicked, impious (noun ፀራፊ፡; pl. ፀራፍያን፡ – blasphemer)

ፅንስት፡ – pregnant

ፄወወ፡ (Q/L) – take captive, exile; Qt, ተፄወወ፡ – be taken captive

ፈ

ፈለሰ፡ – separate, go away, depart, emigrate; CG, አፍለሰ፡ – send away, deport, exile; Glt, ተፋለሰ፡ – wander as exiles

ፈረሰ፡ (pl. አፍራስ፡) – horse

ፈርሀ፡ – be afraid

ፈቀደ፡ – (subj. ይፍቅድ፡) want, wish, desire; Gt, ተፈቅደ፡ – be wanted, be desired

ፈቃዲ፡ (pl. ፈቀድት፡) – one actively seeking something, necromancer

ፈትሐ፡ – untie, loosen; Gt, ተፈትሐ፡ – be loosened; CG, አፍትሐ፡ – bring judgment to; Glt, ተፋትሐ፡ – engage in a legal case with

ፈነወ፡ – send

ፈወሰ፡ – cure, heal; Dt, ተፈወሰ፡ – be healed, cured

ፈድፋደ፡ – exceedingly, very much, greatly

ፈድፈደ፡ – be numerous

ፈድፈድ፡ – excess

ፈጣሪ፡ – Creator (always refers to God)

ፈጠረ፡ – create, fabricate; Gt, ተፈጥረ፡ – be created

ፈጠነ፡ – be swift, quick; CG, አፍጠነ፡ – hurry or hasten (+ inf.)

ፈጸመ፡ (D) – complete, finish; Dt, ተፈጸመ፡ – be completed, be finished

ፍሉስ፡ – exiled, in exile

ፍሥሓ፡ – joy, happiness

ፍሡሕ፡ – happy, joyous, rejoicing (Dt, ተፈሥሐ፡)

ፍሬ፡ – fruit

ፍቁር፡ – beloved (C verb አፍቀረ፡)

ፍና፡ (pl. ፍናው፡ ፍናዌ፡) – road or path

ፍና፡ ሰርክ፡ – early evening (path to night)

ፍኑው፡ – sent

ፍኖት፡ (pl. ፍናው፡) (from the D verb ፈነወ፡) – road or path

ፍጡር፡ – created

ፍጡን፡ – swift, quick

ፍጻሜ፡ – end, completion, perfection

ፍጹም፡ – completed, accomplished, fulfilled

MANUSCRIPT IMAGES

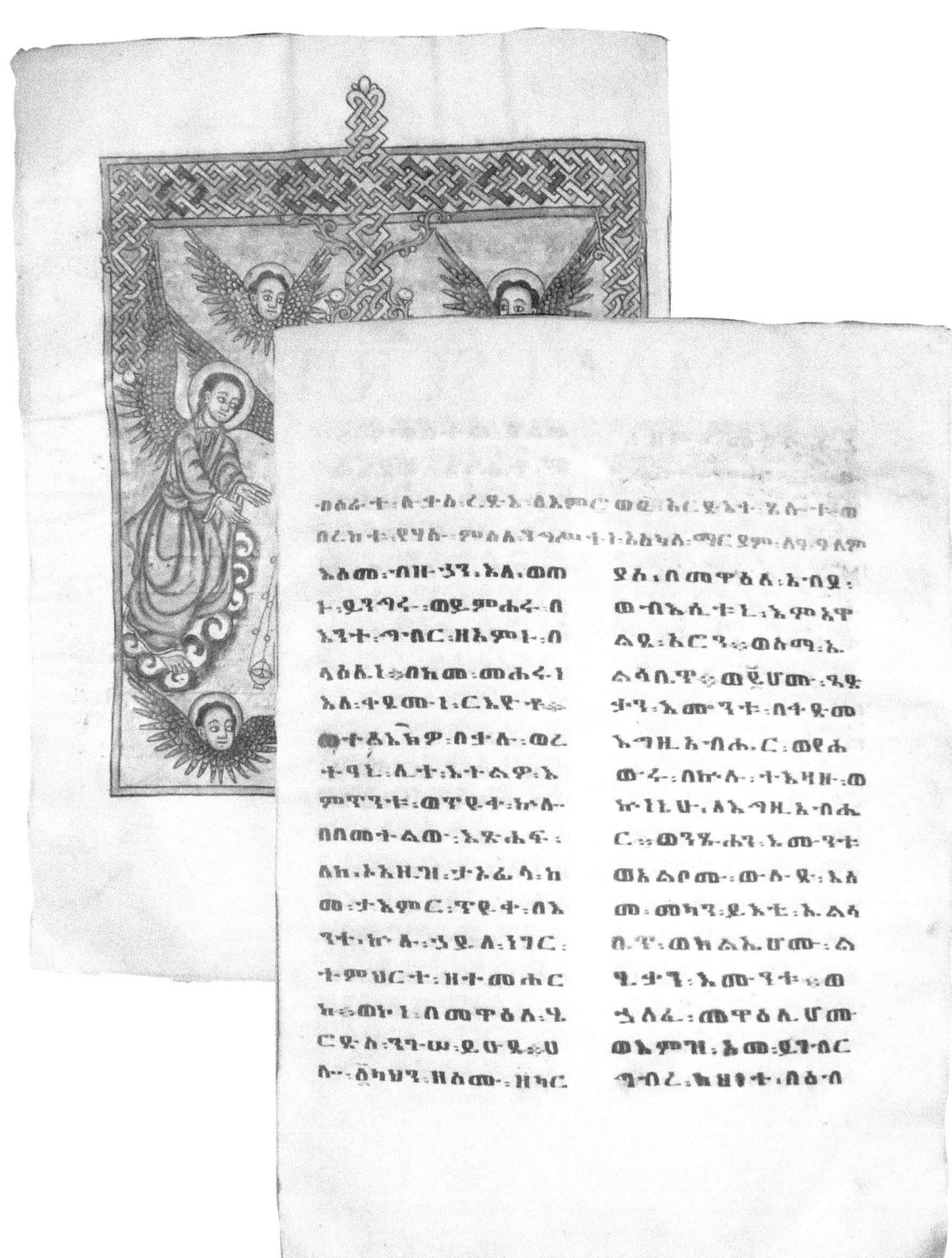

EMIP 339, Weiner Codex 149. Four Gospels of Empress Zäwditu. The book contains the Gospel of Matthew (f. 1r), Gospel of Mark (f. 52r), Gospel of Luke (f. 85r), and Gospel of John (f. 149r). A note of ownership on f. 148r and a closing record on f. 201r identifies the book as belonging to "Queen of Queens, Zäwditu, baptismal name Askalä Maryam." Haila Selassie is also mentioned. In the closing record (f. 201r), the book is dated 1918 EC (= 1926/7 CE), during the administration of Abuna Matewos (1889–1926) and in the time of Echage Gäbra Mänfäs Qeddus, Abbot of Dabra Libanos monastery and holder of the office of Echage in the Ethiopian Orthodox hierarchy. The scribe's name, Gäbrä Maryam, is also listed. The book measures 140 x 92 x 45 mm and contains i + 201 folios. The text was laid out in two columns, each with 19–20 lines. The book was bound with two wooden boards covered with tooled leather. There are four illuminations, one each located before the four Gospels: 1) the nativity (f. i v); 2) the institution of the Last Supper (f. 51v); 3) the angel of the Lord speaking with the priest Zechariah; and 4) John writing before the glorified Christ (f. 148v). The book was owned by Mr. Gerald Weiner, financier and philanthropist from Highland Park, Illinois. When the importance of the manuscript became clear, Mr. Weiner agreed to return it to Ethiopia, where Professor Steve Delamarter delivered it to Abuna Pawlos.

ዘንሁነፃር፡ኩፉሊ፡መዋዕላቴሕ
ዓ፡ወስዑዕ፡ለግብር፡ዳወታትቀ
ስተሰብእቶሙ፡ሊፉየዓሰተሆ

ወኩነፀዳዊ፡ዘቱ፡ዘፀዋሁ፡ኣዠ
ቲቁአስፉኤል፡እምነግብጂ፡በዘ
ርሳአከብሉዕስፉ፡ፍክዕስፉኣ
ወኡቱ፡ወርዓተናገር፡እግዚአ
ሔር፡ስሙ፡ሴ፡እንዘይብዘሕ፡ዕርዓኝ
ቢየዘወከተደብረ፡ዘኣያወብዝ፡ከመ
ክስእሊ፡ጀስተኣብነ፡ዘአግዐወተ
እግዝ፡ዘመወነ፡ጸሐፍከ፡ታስብዮ
ሙቀወሆር፡ገሙ፡ወከተደብር
እግእ፡ኣብሐር፡ወጎደረሕብሐተ
እግእ፡እብሔረውከተደብረሲኣ
ወጸለሙ፡ደመፍስዲ፡ስዕለተወ
ወኝሊሙ፡በዕለተ፡ሳበዕተ፡በ
ማእከለዴ፡ወናዘወር፡እኒየ፡ከብከፈለ
እግእ፡ኣብሔርስከሙ፡አስተዘ፤
ይድውስተርእስዴ፡ብርቀወሱሎ
ሙ፡ሴ፡ውከተዴመሲ፡ኣርብካዕለ
ተወኣርብኳ፡ሊተወለመከርቶ፡
ወእመርእግዚኣብሐር፡ዘፉ
ሚ፡ወዘኛድምጻ፡ነገርኩፉሊ፡
ኩሉ፡መወዕለ፡ሕዋ፡ወበእግ፡ወስ
ምዕቀወዘ፡ኣንበርብ፡ልከውበ
ትኮሎ፡ነገር፡ዘእግበክከበሐ
ነደ፡ብር፡ወጸፈር፡ውተኣመጸ
ሐፉክከሙ፡ደርእየትውሊዶሙ
ከሙ፡ዓደግስሙ፡በእንተከሱስ
ኩደ፡ዘነግብሩ፡ለስክስተ፡ስርዓት
ዘእኣወርዕ፡ማእክሊየወማእከ

ሙ፡ወስተ፡ተስሱ፡ዓመተታ፡ስማ
በከሙ፡ተናገር፡ስሙ፡ሴ፡ብሔር
ሲናኣወሀር፡ግኝማ፡እጀኛተ፡

ሴኮዮም፡ለትውሕደሙ፡ዘብጀ
ሕ፡ናዘከሙ፡ናዘዘኒ፡ክሙን
አሙ፡ዘመነኝ፡እዝከወዘነገር፡ስበዒ
ሆሙ፡በከተሱ፡ትከሙ፡ወበዛ
ሕ፡ሆምባያሮ፡ወያእምፉ፡ከመ
ተኢ፡ጀሐፍ፡ስከሶ፡ዘተስ፡ዘኔ
እይዴከኢየም፡እስሙ፡እኒኣም
ር፡ምረቸሙ፡ወከሰሙ፡ይውከ
ዘንበለ፡አእመሙ፡ውስተየኸድ
እንተ፡መሐፈሌ፡ለአብርሃም፡ወሊ
ከሐወያዕቆብ፡እንዘ፡ኣብሊከ
ዘርከሙ፡ኣው፡ብ፡ምድር፡እን ተ፡
ትውኣ፡ሐሊበ፡ወመዓረቀወደ
ልሁ፡ወይደዋግ፡ወይትመየጡንስ
እምስተነ፡ር፡ዘበእስ፡ኢየዳዓ
ዶሙ፡ኣእምኔ፡ኑ፡ነቢሆሙ
ወትሰማዕ፡ተ፡ከማዕ፡ለክምዕ፡ት
ሙ፡እሰው፡ደይከሥ፡ትእኘዝከዘ
ሉ፡እኒ፡እዝመ፡ወየሐውዕዮ
ዓረ፡አሕዛብ፡ወይዓር፡ኮቶሙ
ወደዓር፡ሳማሙዶተተነዮለ
ኣማልከቲሆሙ፡ወደኸንምኛ
ዕቱረ፡ስምንጅቢ፡ወለዓዕር፡ወስሙ
ስርዓት፡ወደትጠፑሉ፡ብዙኝ፡
ወደትሳዙ፡ወደወጅቁ፡ውክተኣ
ደዐር፡እምከዓደትሠርዓትየ

እብኝ፡ሕዓፀወትዘዘብዘስሊኝ
ዚ፡አብሔር፡በከሙ፡ይብሉዕሮ
ዓው፡ከተር፡እሱ፡ደብር፡ፀ፡፡

ተእዛዝወብታትየካደነከወስ፡
በተትውቅሣትዮ፡ዘቀደከከ
ሲ፡ዘወአእመውወብተረነካ
መቅደሆ፡ዘወዳስከሊ፡ተበኣከ
ሕምሂር፡ከመ፡እዋደም፡ደምየስዕ
ሌሁ፡ወደሳድቅወነግብራሙ
ፍሐሐት፡ወእስወማልፍር፡ወስ
ነገ፡ዘዝአያሙ፡ለስሐትወዘደ
ብሐው፡ከድ፡ሙ፡ለአጋነንት፡ወለ
ሁሱ፡ከዳ፡ተተአሕተረ፡በርቀወል
ፌነ፡ናቢሙ፡ሰማዓት፡ከመለስ
ማዕሐሙ፡ወኢያነም፡ወአሐ
ዕቱኒ፡ይተትሹቀወስእሃ፡ረአሙ
ሙ፡ሕጌቀተ፡ጻሎሙ፡ወደረዝስ
ዕሙ፡ወሆ፡እጀርሁ፡ደሆዊ
ኑ፡ስገዘረ፡አኩደ፡በቀቶሙ፡አዕይ
ንት፡ወእሆንብ፡ዝዕየ፡እምነገረ
ወ፡እሚጥዖሙ፡ወከተእደሐል
ዘብ፡ለሃዊ፡ወሐብለው፡ስተ
ልያቀወለስከልሱ፡እማአከም
ጅር፡ወአዘርዓሙ፡ማዕክለለኣሐዛ
ወደረከወቱሉ፡ሕግየወሆለቱ
እዘዝህ፡ወሁሱ፡ዎቾትከ፡ወድረለ
ሕግሆ፡ወደስተ፡ሰርተወስፅ
ተ፡ወበዓለ፡ወእ፡የርዕወለሥ፡ርከ
ወእምዝ፡ደትመየው፡ናቢየኝ
እክሉ፡እሕዘብ፡በከሱ፡ልዕበፐሙ፡
በከሱ፡ነፍስሙ፡ወበሶሱ፡ደልሙ፡

EMIP 743, Čeläqot Selassie 2, Ministry of Tourism number C4-IV-154 (f. 1r), late 17th century. The book contains the book of Enoch (f. 1r), Genesis (f. 24r), Exodus (f. 46v), Leviticus (f. 68v), Numbers (f. 84r), Deuteronomy (f. 105v), Joshua (f. 125r), Judges (f. 139r), Ruth (f. 153r), Jubilees (f. 155r), and Job (f. 187r). The book measures 175 x 145 mm and has ii + 198 folios. The text is laid out in three columns each with about 32 lines. Quires are numbered in the upper left of the first folio of each quire. The book is bound between two boards covered in tooled leather, and the book quarter-bound again. Chapter headings are numbered with rubrication. Names of the biblical books are listed in the top margin of the text. There is occasional evidence of scribal intervention to erase or strike out words and even lines of text. Intermarginal notes offer mnemonic keys for commentary on the text. A note of secondary ownership, written in blue ink, is written in the upper margin of folios 41r and 118v: "Belonging to [the church of] Däbrä Mahrät Čeläqot Selassie." A loose folio, stitched lightly to the back of folio 67, contains a diagram of the temple complex. This manuscript was digitized in Ethiopia at the church of Čeläqot Selassie in Tigray, by the EMIP project (Haile Maryam, photographer). On the final folio of the book is a full color illumination depicting a kneeling saint (a woman) and a standing child. The inside covers of the book are covered with red fabric, visible between the turndowns.

EMIP 1035, Mihur Gedam 60, 15th/16th century. Gospel of John, ወንጌል፡ ዘዮሐንስ፡ 350 x 250 x 30 mm. The codex has been disbound, and most of the folios are loose. Many of the folios have dark stains; some have been nibbled by rodents. An elaborate *harag* (an intricate piece of artwork) stands at the head of the Gospel of John. There are many *crux ansata* symbols and intercolumnar symbols on every page. A subscription at the conclusion of the Gospel (digitized as f. 7r) indicates that the number of strophes in the book are 2006 (literally 20 hundred and 6). This manuscript was digitized in Ethiopia at the monastery of Mihur Gedam in Tigray, by the EMIP project (Haile Maryam, photographer).

መእነነዝ፡ ይንብብ፡ቀልዪ   ዕል፡ጦተ፡ንጉሠ፡ግብጽ፡ወ
ክጸሃፉ፡ወላእጋእ፡ልሳን፡ኋ   ይቢሉ፡እግዚአ፡ብሔር፡ሳ
ኍ፡ወይቢሉ፡እግዚአ፡ብሔር፡   ሴ፡ብምይምይ፡ደ፡ያም፡ኋ
ለሙሴ፡መኑ፡ወሀቦ፡አፈ፡ለእ   ሐር፡ብሔረ፡ግብጽ፡እስ
ኔ፡ለእማሕያው፡ወመነ፡ፈጠ   ወቱ፡ቱሎሙ፡እለ፡የነሥአ፡ሙ
ረ፡ከነሀሎ፡ወጸሙመ፡ወዘይሬ   ዊ፡ለንፉስክ፡ወእንሥአ፡ሙ
እ፡ወዕዉረ፡አኮሁ፡እነ፡ውእ   ሴ፡እንታክቱ፡ብትር፡እንተ፡
ቱ፡እግዚእ፡እግዚአ፡ብሔር፡   እምነብ፡እግዚአ፡ብሔር፡
ወይእዜኒ፡ሐር፡ወአነ፡እፌ   ውስተ፡እዴሁ።
ትሕ፡አፉከ፡ወአሴብወክ፡   ወይቢሉ፡እግዚአ፡ብሔር፡ለ
ዘሀለወክ፡ትንብብ፡ወይቢ   ሙሴ፡እንዘ፡ተሐውር፡ወት
አስተበቍዕክ፡ነሥሥ፡ለክ   ገብእ፡ብሔረ፡ግብጽ፡አእ
በዕደ፡ዘይአል፡ተልእኮ፡   ምር፡መሂ፡ምየ፡ቱሎ፡ዘወ
ወትምዕዕ፡እግዚአ፡ብሔር፡   ሀብኩክ፡ውስተ፡እደዊክ፡
መተ፡ለዕለ፡ሙሴ፡ወይቢሉ   ከሙ፡ትግበሮ፡በቅድሚሁ
እኑ፡ውእቱ፡እግዚአ፡ብሔር፡   ለፈርዖን፡ወኢይፌንዎ፡
ወኖቱ፡አሮን፡እኍከ፡ሌዋዊ   ለሕዝብዩ፡ወአንተስ፡ትብ
ወእእምር፡ከሙ፡ናብይ፡እንብ   ሉ፡ለፈርዖን፡አመዝ፡ይቤ፡እ
ብ፡ለከ፡ናሁ፡ውእቱ፡ይወፅ   ግዚአ፡ብሔር፡ወለየ፡ዘበ
እ፡ይትቀበልክ፡ወየርእይ   ቸርዩ፡ውእቱ፡እስራኢል፡
ክ፡ወይትፌሣሕ፡ወትነግር   ወእብላክ፡ፈኑ፡ሕዝብየ፡ክ
ወትወዴ፡ቃልየ፡ውስተ፡አፉ   ሙ፡ይጸምዱኒ፡ወለእመ፡
ሁ፡ወሐሙሴ፡ወጋብእ፡ኃ   አንተ፡ኢፈቀደክ፡ከፈንዎቶ
ኩ፡የቶር፡ንሙሁ፡ወይቢሉ   ሙ፡እነምርኬ፡አውአኑተ፡
እሐውር፡ወእንገብእ፡ኃብ፡እ   ትሎ፡ወልደክ፡ዘበኲርከ፡
ጋዊየ፡ኔለ፡ውስተ፡ብሔረ፡   ወኮን፡በፈናት፡በውስተ፡ማ
ግብጽ፡ወእርአይ፡ለእመ፡   ኃደር፡ተራከቦ፡መልአክ፡እግ
ናዲሆሙ፡ሕያዋን፡ወይቢሉ   ዚአ፡ብሔር፡ወፈተደ፡ይቅት
የቶር፡ለሙሴሐር፡በደኃን   ሎ፡ወነሥአት፡ሲታራ፡ማ
ወእምዩ፡ፍሬ፡ብዙኁ፡ነዋ   ዊ፡ወገዘረች፡ክተማእንፉስቱ
                    ለወልዳ፡ወወድቀት፡ኃብ፡እ

EMIP 1038, Mihur Gedam 63, 15th century, fragment of an Octateuch (Orit). At the time of its digitization, this manuscript was a stack of loose and disbound folios. At some point the folios that made up the original codex were divided into two stacks. These were digitized as EMIP 1037 and EMIP 1038. The originals are still in Ethiopia. At some point a reconstruction of the original codex could be made with the digitized images. But to this point we can only describe imprecisely the contents of the two stacks of folios. Among the stack of folios designated EMIP 1038, we can find the beginning folios for the books of Genesis (1r), Numbers (10r), Leviticus (20v), Joshua (73r), Exodus (130r), and Deuteronomy (165r). The book measures 450 x 340 x 170 mm. This manuscript was digitized in Ethiopia at the monastery of Mihur Gedam in Tigray by the EMIP project (Haile Maryam, photographer). The *harags* in the manuscript are splendid, ornate, and full color and extend half and three quarters of the way down the folios, between columns and in both side margins (see folios 1r, 10r, 20v, 73r, 130r, 165r). Marginal lines indicate the smaller divisions of the books. There are no indications of strophe counts at the conclusion of the books.

ዘልደት

EMIP 1048, Addis Alem 6, Ministry of Tourism number AI-IV-85. Orit and the Story of the Death of Moses of Nebura 'Ed Kefle Marafiya. A short text on folio 201v mentions that the book was produced in the forty-fourth year of the reign of Emperor Menilek the second, dated December 29, 1909 (in the Ethiopian month of Taḫśaś). The owner is also mentioned, Däjazmač Abba Tabor, whose baptismal name was Wäldä Mädḫǝn, and the scribe is also mentioned, Zäläqä, baptismal name Wäldä Tǝnś'i. It contains vi + 205 folios. The text is laid out in two columns of 30 lines. The book was digitized in Ethiopia at the Addis Alem Church, a short drive west of Addis Ababa, by the EMIP project (Haile Maryam, photographer). This location was a second seat of Emperor Menilek's government after Ankobar and before Addis Ababa. Many books labeled as belonging to Emperor Menilek are there. This codex has been previously microfilmed by the Ethiopian Manuscript Microfilm Library (EMML) as project number 5592. On almost every page, the codex shows substantial scribal intervention, with many lines erased and written over, or with other lines written interlineally. The book has been foliated, probably as part of the EMML project. The more recent owner of the book, Kefle Marafiya, held the high title of Nebura 'Ed, used only in reference to the priest of Saint Mary's Church in Axum and the priest of the church in Addis Alem.

ሰለውኩ፡ህየ፡ወመጽእሉ፡ወይቤሎ፡   አየ፡ሐወ፡በሕባግው፡መሐምዮ፡ሰራሳ
እጋዜእብሐር፡ለዕይጣንቱ፡ኪኢስ   ኩ፡ወዓመውኩ፡ስክንቴሁወእንተኒ፡
ቀሊዓየ፡ኢዮብ፡አከመ፡እልቦ፡ክመ   ትንብርውከተ፡መግለወዐዊያት፡ወ
ኩ፡በጸ፡በሆሀ፡ድር፡ብእሲየዋሕወ   ከሰሊ፡ሊተ፡ታንዖርቃወእንሂእ
ጽቁ፡ወንጹሕ፡ወፈራሄ፡እግዚአብ   ውድ፡ወእትሀል፡ወአሐውርንም
ሐር፡ወይትጋሰ፡እምኑተሉ፡ሕሱም   ሐ፡ርብሐሪ፡ወእምቱ፡ቤተ፡ወእጽ
ወዲየ፡ዋሐ፡ወእንከ፡ትቢታሐ   ገስ፡እንዝ፡እብልነ፡አዘ፡የዐብሐ
ሉናዎኮ፡በከንቴ፡ወተሠጥም፡ስ   ይ፡ከመ፡ዕዕርፍ፡እስምፀፀዕ፡ወእ
ጣን፡ለእግዚአብሐር፡ወይቢላ፡ዕ   ምዮ፡ዘሰላሲየ፡ክዚ፡ወካከቲ፡
ክብ፡ዘግብስክ፡እለሉ፡ዘአጥዖ፡ይ   ሃለሳየ፡እግዚአብሐር፡ወሙተው
ብ፡ቤ፡ዘንፍ፡ሐወገልቱ፡ፈኑ፡እዴከ፡   ንጽራ፡ወቤላ፡ወአለሕቲ፡እንእብደ፡
ወከስ፡ዐጽምቲሁ፡ወሠጋሁአ   አነተ፡ተናገርከ፡ዘውናየ፡ቃነአን
መውስተ፡ገጽከ፡ኢአሪክእከክ፡በ   እምነእግዚአብሐር፡ወከከሐ፡ኢ
ሎ፡እግዚአብሐር፡ለዕይጣንቱ፡ነሁ፡መ   ንትጌሠኔ፡ወበዕሉም፡ዘከነ፡
መውክሉሁ፡እለውሕፎ፡ክነዐቅብየ   ዘአበስ፡ኢዮብቱ፡ዮመ፡እግዚእብሐር
ወቃለዐይጣን፡እምዳንበ፡እግዚአብሐር፡
ወእዳዘለኤዮብልገስ፡እኩይ፡እ   ኮ፡ሎ፡እኩየ፡ዘገከቡ፡ለእዮብ፡ሠ
ምእግራክከ፡ርእሁ፡ወነዛእነጋልው፡   ኩቶ፡ሰውላ፡ቤሁ፡እምብሐር
ወእሐዘይሐክክታ፡ክሎ፡ወውክተሱ   እልፈዝቲጌናዊ፡ዓስውወበዐፅ
ክንብር፡በሐምድ፡ወከፈረእ፡እንሞ   ዩከ፡እውኒናፅ፡ወክፈንዱ፡ወሰር፡
ሀግሐወና፡ቢዐረብዙነዳወዓስል   እጌናዊ፡ግልወመጫኩ፡ሳበ፡ከን
ቴሎ፡ብእተሁ፡አከ፡ሰመግእነኒ፡   ቤሁስመው፡የሐውኮ፡ዋ፡ወደሪንዝወ፡
ተትዴግሱኩት፡ብልቱ፡አፀሐ፡ዳነበ፡   ወርከይው፡አምርሑተ፡ወኢያ፡ምር
መውዕሰዳዲ፡ገርኩ፡ሰአሕጋእብለ፡   ወእውየው፡ስዊ፡ይቃልዔ፡ረሐቢ
ርቱ፡ትሑ፡መስነነዝ፡ክርከ፡አም   ከደ፡ወሰ፡ብው፡አልካሔ፡መወሰ
ልደኒ፡በርሠዚ   ይ፡ሐመደ፡አስተፅስከመ፡ወበየፈ፡

EMIP 1924, Capuchin Franciscan Retreat and Research Center 91, 18th century. The book is bound between two boards and then quarter-bound in leather. The book contains books of the Ethiopic Old Testament. The first book (5r–47v) is the book of Psalms laid out in a very rare format, namely, in two columns with justified margins (i.e., not written as strophes) each with 29 to 30 lines. The text is densely written with 19 to 29 letters per column. The remaining contents of the book include Proverbs I (f. 49r) and Proverbs II (f. 58v), Ecclesiastes (f. 61v), Wisdom of Solomon (f. 65v), Job (f. 76r), Isaiah (f. 99r), and Ezra (f. 126v). The book is made of 150 folios. A brief note at the end of folio 138v gives the name of the owner, Aläqa Wäldä Hana, along with his father and mother.

Appendix

AN ADVANCED READING: THE CONFESSION OF FAITH OF EMPEROR GELAWDEWOS[1]

በስመ፡ አብ፡ ወወልድ፡ ወመንፈስ፡ ቅዱስ፡ ፩ አምላክ።

ዝንቱ፡ ውእቱ፡ ሃይማኖትየ፡ ወሃይማኖተ፡ አበውየ፡ ነገሥተ፡ እስራኤላዊያን፡ ወሃይማኖተ፡ መርዔትየ፡ እለ፡ ሀለዉ፡ በዐጸደ፡ መንግሥትየ።

ንሕነ፡ ነአምን፡ በ፩፡ አምላክ ወበ ወልዱ፡ ዋሕድ፡ ኢየሱስ ክርስቶስ፡ ውእቱ፡ ቃሉ፡ ወውእቱ፡ ኃይሉ። ውእቱ፡ ምክሩ፡ ወውእቱ፡ ጥበቡ። ዘሀለወ፡ ምስሌሁ፡ እምቅድመ፡ ይትፈጠር፡ ዓለም። ወበደኃሪ፡ መዋዕል፡ መጽአ፡ ኃቤነ፡ እንዘ፡ ኢየዐርቅ፡ እመንበረ፡ መለኮቱ። ወተሰብአ፡ እመንፈስ፡ ቅዱስ፡ ወእማርያም፡ አምቅድስት፡ ድንግል። ወተጠምቀ፡ በዮርዳኖስ፡ በ፴፡ ክረምት፡ ወኮነ፡ ብእሴ፡ ፍጹመ። ወተሰቅለ፡ ዲበ፡ ዕፀ፡ መስቀል፡ በመዋዕለ፡ ጲላጦስ፡ ጶንጤናዊ። ሐመ፡ ወሞተ፡ ወተቀብረ፡ ወተንሥአ፡ በሣልስት፡ ዕለት። ወእምዝ፡ በ፵ዕለት፡ ዓርገ፡ በስብሐት፡ ውስተ፡ ሰማያት፡ ወነበረ፡ በየማነ፡ አቡሁ። ወካዕበ፡ ይመጽእ፡ በስብሐት፡ ይኰንን፡ ሕያዋነ፡ ወሙታነ፡ ወአልበ፡ ማኅለቅተ፡ ለመንግሥቱ።

In the name of the Father and of the Son and of the Holy Spirit, one God.

This is my faith and the faith of my fathers, the kings of Israel, and the faith of my flock who live within the fold of my dominion.

We believe in one God and in his only Son Jesus Christ who is His word and is His power; He is His counsel and His wisdom; who was with Him before the world was created. In the last days he came to us while not abandoning his divine throne. He was incarnated from the Holy Spirit and from the holy virgin Mary. He was baptized in the Jordan in the thirtieth year and became a perfect man, and he was crucified on the wood of the cross in the days of Pontius Pilate. He suffered, died, was buried, and rose on the third day. After this, on the fortieth day, he ascended in glory into the heavens and sat at the right of his Father. He will come again in glory, and will judge the living and the dead, and there is no end to his kingdom.

And we believe in the Holy Spirit, life-giving Lord, who proceeds from the Father.

---

1. The following text is from Hiob Ludolf, *Commentarius ad suam historiam aethiopicam* (Frankfurt, 1691), 237–41, and is public domain. Translation is by Ralph Lee.

ወነአምን፡ በመንፈስ፡ ቅዱስ፡ እግ
ዚእ፡ ማሕያዊ፡ ዘሥረፀ፡ እምአብ።
ወነአምን፡ በአሐቲ፡ ጥምቀት፡ ለ
ሥርየተ፡ ኃጢአት፡ ወንሴፎ፡ ትንሣ
ኤ፡ ሙታን፡ ለሕይወት፡ ዘይመጽእ፡
ለዓለም፡ አሜን።
ንሕሰ፡ ነሐውር፡ በፍኖተ፡ ንጉሥ፡
ጽዮሕ፡ አማናዊ፡ ወኢንጸን፡ ኢለየ
ማን፡ ወኢለፀጋም፡ እምትምህርተ፡
አበዊነ፡ ፲ወ፪ሐዋርያት፡ ወጳው
ሎስ፡ ፈልፈለ፡ ጥበብ፡ ወወ፸ወ፪
ርድእት፡ ወ፫፻፲ወ፰ርቱዓን፡ ሃይማ
ኖት፡ ዘተጋብኡ፡ በኒቅያ፡ ወ፻፶ወ
በቆስጥንጥያ፡ ወ፪፻ በኤፌሶን።
ከመዝ፡ እሰብከ፡ ወከመዝ፡ አሜ
ህር፡ አነ፡ ግለውዴዎስ፡ ንጉሥ፡ ዘኢት
ዮጵያ፡ ወስመ፡ መንግሥትየ፡ አጽና
ፍ፡ ሰገድ፡ ወልደ፡ ወናግ፡ ሰገድ፡ ወ
ልደ፡ ናእድ።
ወበእንተ፡ ምክንያተ፡ አክብሮትነ፡
ዕለተ፡ ቀዳሚት፡ ሰንበት፡ አኮ፡ ዘ
ናከብራ፡ ከመ፡ አይሁድ፡ እለ፡ ሰቀ
ልዎ፡ ለክርስቶስ፡ እንዘ፡ ይብሉ፡ ደ
ሙ፡ ላዕሌነ፡ ወላዕለ፡ ውሉደነ።
እስመ፡ እምንቱሰ፡ አይሁድ፡ ኢይቀ
ድሑ፡ ማየ፡ ወኢያነድዱ፡ እሳተ፡ ወ
ኢያበስሉ፡ ጸብሐ፡ ወኢይሐብዙ፡
ኅብስተ፡ ወኢይትፈለሱ፡ እምቤት፡
ውስተ፡ ቤት።

ወባሕቱ፡ ንሕነሰ፡ ናከብራ፡ እ
ንዘ፡ ናዓርግ፡ ባቲ፡ ቍርባነ፡ ወንገብር፡
ባቲ፡ ምሳሐ፡ በከመ፡ አዘዙነ፡ አበ
ዊነ፡ ሐዋርያት፡ በዲድስቅልያ።
አኮ፡ ዘናከብራ፡ ከመ፡ ሰንበተ፡ እ
ሑድ፡ እንተ፡ ይእቲ፡ ዕለተ፡ ሐዲስ፡
ዘይቤ፡ ዳዊት፡ በእንቲአሃ፡ ዛቲ፡ ዕለ
ት፡ እንተ፡ ገብረ፡ እግዚአብሔር፡ ን
ትፈሣሕ፡ ወንትኃሣይ፡ ባቲ። እስ
መ፡ ባቲ፡ ተንሥአ፡ እግዚእነ፡ ኢየሱ
ስ፡ ክርስቶስ፡ ወባቲ፡ ወረደ፡ መንፈ

We believe in one baptism for the forgiveness of sins; and we hope for the resurrection of the dead for life that will come, forever. Amen.

And we follow the level and true path of the king, and we do not deviate, neither to the right nor to the left, from our fathers' doctrine, the Twelve Apostles, and of Paul, the fountain of wisdom, and of the 72 disciples, and of the 318 Orthodox in faith who assembled in Nicaea, and of the 150 in Constantinople, and of the 200 in Ephesus. I, Claudius, King of Ethiopia, preach and teach in this way. My regnal name is ʾAsənāf Săgăd, son of Wănāg Săgăd, son of Nāʾod.

Concerning the reason for our honoring Saturday (the first Sabbath), we do not honor it like the Jews who crucified Christ saying, "his blood is on us and on our children." For those Jews do not draw water, light fires, cook stew, or bake bread and do not roam from house to house.

Rather we honor it when we offer up the Eucharist on it, and prepare the love-feast as our fathers, the Apostles, commanded us in the *Didascalia*. We do not honor it like Sunday which is the new day of which David said, "This is the day which God has made, let us rejoice and be glad in it" (Ps 118:24). Because on it our Lord Jesus Christ was raised, and on it the Holy Spirit came down on the Apostles in the upper room (Acts 1:13) of Zion. And on it he was incarnated in the womb of Saint Mary, always a virgin. And on it he will come again as a reward for the righteous and for the recompense of the sinners.

Regarding the ritual of circumcision,

ስ፡ ቅዱስ፡ ላዕለ፡ ሐዋርያት፡ በጽር
ሐ፡ ጽዮን። ወባቲ፡ ተሰብአ፡ ውስተ፡
ከርሠ፡ ቅድስት፡ ማርያም፡ ድንግል፡
በኩሉ፡ ጊዜ፡፡ ወባቲ፡ ይመጽአ፡ ደ
ግመ፡ ለዕሴተ፡ ጻድቃን፡ ወለፍደ፡
ኃጥአን።

ወበእንተ፡ ሥርዐተ፡ ግዝረትኒ፡ አ
ኮ፡ ዘንትገዘር፡ ከመ፡ አይሁድ፡ እ
ስመ፡ ንሕነ፡ ናአምር፡ ቃለ፡ ምህሮሁ፡
ለጳውሎስ፡ ፈልፈለ፡ ጥበብ፡ ዘይቤ፡
ተገዝሮሂ፡ ኢይበቍዕ፡ ወኢተገዝሮ
ሂ፡ ኢያኀልጥ፡ ዘእንበለ፡ ዳእሙ፡
ሐዲስ፡ ፍጥረት፡ ዝውእቱ፡ አሚን፡
በእግዚእነ፡ ኢየሱስ፡ ክርስቶስ።

ወካዕበ፡ ይቤ፡ ለሰብአ፡ ቆሮንቶስ፡ ዘ
ሂ፡ ነሥአ፡ ግዝረተ፡ ኢይንሣእ፡ ቍል
ፈተ፡ ኵሉ፡ መጻሕፍተ፡ ትምህርቱ፡
ለጳውሎስ፡ ሀለው፡ ኅቤነ፡ ወይሜህ
ረነ፡ በእንተ፡ ግዝረት፡ ወበእንተ፡
ቍልፈት፡፡ ወባሕቱ፡ ግዝረትሰ፡ ዘኮ
ነ፡ በኀቤነ፡ በልማደ፡ ሀገር፡ ከመ፡ ብ
ጥነተ፡ ገጽ፡ ዘኢትዮጵያ፡ ወኑባ።
ወከመ፡ ስቍረተ፡ እዝን፡ ዘሰብአ፡ ሀ
ንድ፡ ዘንተሰ፤ ዘንገብር፡ አኮ፡ በዐቂ
በ፡ ሕገገ፡ ኦሪት፡ ዳእሙ፡ በልማደ፡ ሰ
ብእ።

ወበእንተ፡ በሊዐ፡ ሐራውያኒ፡ አ
ኮ፡ ዘንትከላእ፡ በዐቂበ፡ ሕገገ፡ ኦ
ሪት፡ ከመ፡ አይሁድ፡ ለዘኒ፡ በልዐ፡
ኢናስቈርር፡ ወኢናረኵሶ፡ ወለዘኒ፡
ኢበልዐ፡ ከመ፡ ይብላዕ፡ ኢናገብሮ።
በከመ፡ ጸሐፈ፡ አቡነ፡ ጳውሎስ፡ ለ
ብሔረ፡ ሮሜ፡ እንዘ፡ ይብል፡ ዘኒ፡ በል
ዐ፡ ኢይመንኖ፡ ለዘኢይበልዐ፡ ወለኵ
ሎሙ፡ እግዚአብሔር፡ ተወክፎ
ሙ፡ መንግሥተ፡ እግዚአብሔር፡
ኢኮነት፡ በምብልዕ፡ ወበመስቴ፡ ኵ
ሉ፡ ንጹሕ፡ ለንጹሐን፡ ወእኩይሰ፡ ለ
ሰብእ፡ በሊዐ፡ ምስለ፡ ዕፍረት።
ወማቴዎስ፡ ወንጌላዊ፡ ይቤ፡ አልቦ፡ ዘ

we are not circumcised like the Jews, because we know the word of the teaching of Paul, fountain of wisdom, which says (1 Cor 7:19; Gal 5:6), "circumcision is of no benefit nor uncircumcision, nothing will empower except the new creation which is believing in our Lord Jesus Christ."

Furthermore, he says to the Corinthians (1 Cor 7:18), "he who receives circumcision let him not remove the foreskin." All the books of Paul's teaching are available to us, and they instruct us about circumcision and about the foreskin. But the circumcision which we have is according to the custom of the country — like the scarification of the face of Ethiopia and Nubia; and like the piercing of the ears of the Indians. What we do is not because of the observance of the laws of the Old Testament, but rather because of people's custom.

And concerning the eating of pork, we do not refrain because of observing the laws of the Old Testament, like the Jews. We do not loathe the one who eats [pork], nor do we consider them unclean; and we do not force to eat it the one who does not eat it. As our father Paul wrote to the province of Rome, saying, "those who eat must not despise those who do not eat, but God has accepted all of them" (Romans 14:3). "The Kingdom of God did not come into being through eating or drinking; everything is pure for the pure, but it is evil for man to eat with offensiveness" (Romans 14:17 and 20). And Matthew the evangelist says (Matt 15:11, 17), "Nothing can defile man - except that which comes out from his mouth. But that which enters the

ይክል፡ አርኩሶቶ፡ ለሰብእ፡ ዘእንበ
ለ፡ ዘይወፅእ፡ እምአፉሁ፡ ወዘሰ፡
ውስተ፡ ከርሥ፡ ይበውእ፡ ወይትገም
ር፡ ጽም፡ ወይትገደፉ፡ ወይትከውሉ፡
ወያነጽሕ፡ ኩሎ፡ መባልዕተ፡ ወበ
ብሂለ፡ ዝንቱ፡ ቃሉ፡ ነስተ፡ ኩሎ፡
ሕንጸ፡ ስሕተቶሙ፡ ለአይሁድ፡ እለ፡
ተምህሩ፡ እመጽሐፈ፡ ኦሪት።
ሊተሰ፡ ሃይማኖትየ፡ ወሃይማኖተ።
ካህናት፡ ማአምራን፡ እለ፡ ይሜህሩ፡
በትእዛዝየ፡ በዐፀደ፡ መንግሥትየ፡
ወኢይትገሑሡ፡ እምፍኖተ፡ ወንጌል፡
ወእምትምህርተ፡ አቡነ፡ ጳውሎስ፡
ኢለየማን፡ ወኢለፀጋም። ወበመጽ
ሐፈ፡ ታሪከ፡ ጽሑፍ፡ ሀሎ፡ በመ
ጽሐፈ፡ ዚአነ፡ አስመ፡ ቆስጠንጢ
ኖስ፡ ንጉሥ፡ አዘዘ፡ በመዋዕለ፡ መን
ግሥቱ፡ ለኩሎሙ፡ እለ፡ ተጠምቁ።
አይሁድ፡ ከመ" ያብልዕዎሙ፡ ሥ
ጋ፡ ሐራውያ፡ በዕለተ፡ ትንሣኤሁ፡
ለእግዚእነ፡ ኢየሱስ፡ ክርስቶስ።
ወባሕቱ፡ በከም፡ አዳም፡ ልቡ፡ ለሰብ
እ፡ ይትኔረም፡ እምበላዐ፡ ሥጋ፡
እንስሳ፡ በዘያፈቅር፡ ሥጋ፡ ዓሣ፡
ወቦ፡ ዘያፈቅር፡ በሊዐ፡ ሥጋ፡ ደር
ሆ። ወቦ፡ ዘይትኔረም፡ እምበላዐ፡
ሥጋ፡ በግዕ፡ ወኩሉ፡ ዘከመ፡ አዳም፡
ልቡ፡ ይትሉ፡ ከመዝ፡ ውእቱ፡ ሥ
ምረቱ፡ ወፈቃዱ፡ ለሰብእ። በአንተ፡
መብልዐ፡ ሥጋ፡ እንስሳስ፡ አልቦ፡ ሕ
ገ፡ ወአልቦ፡ ቀኖና፡ ውስተ፡ መጽሐ
ፈ፡ ሐደስ፡ ኩሉ፡ ንጹሕ፡ ለንጹሐን፡
ወጳውሎስ፡ ዘሰ፡ የአምን፡ ኩሎ፡ ለ
ይብላዕ።

ዘንተ፡ ኩሎ፡ ዘጽሐፉ፡ ለጽሐፍ፡
ከመ፡ ታአምር፡ ጽድቀ፡ ሃይማኖት
የ፡ ተጽሕፈ፡ በ፲፻ወ፭፻ወ፶፻ወ፭
ዐመት፡ እምልደተ፡ እግዚእነ፡ ኢየ
ሱስ፡ ክርስቶስ፡ አመ፡ ፳ወ፫ለሰኔ፡
በሀገረ፡ ዳሞት።

stomach finishes up in the latrine and is thrown out and poured away but all food purifies."

And by saying these words he has demolished the structure of the Jews' errors which they had learned from the Old Testament.

For me, my faith and the faith of the learned priests who teach at my command within the territory of my kingdom does not deviate from the path of the Gospel or from the teaching of our father Paul – neither to the right or the left. In the book of history it is written, in our book, that Emperor Constantine commanded, in the days of his reign, all the baptized Jews as if to give them the flesh of pigs on the day of the resurrection of our Lord Jesus Christ. However, just as it delights the heart of people to abstain from eating the flesh of animals, there are those who love fish meat and those who love to eat chicken meat; or those who abstain from eating mutton – let everyone follow what delights their heart; thus are the inclination and desire of people. Regarding the eating of the flesh of animals, there is no law and no canon in the Book of the New Testament; to the pure everything is pure; and Paul says, "whoever believes may eat everything."

All this that I wanted to write, is so that you comprehend the truth of my religion.

Written in the year 1555 from the birth of our Lord Jesus Christ, on the 23rd of Sane (= June) in the region of Damot.

BIBLIOGRAPHY

Butts, Aaron M. "Gəʽəz (Classical Ethiopic)." Pages 117–44 in *The Semitic Languages*. Edited by J. Huehnergard and N. Pat-El. 2nd ed. Routledge Language Family Series. New York: Routledge, 2019.

Charles, R. H. *The Ethiopic Version of the Book of Enoch*. Oxford: Clarendon, 1906.

———. *The Ethiopic Version of the Hebrew Book of Jubilees*. Oxford: Clarendon, 1895.

Dillman, August. *Biblia Veteris Testamenti Aethiopica*. Leipzig: Weigel, 1853–1894.

———. *Ethiopic Grammar*. 2nd ed. Rev. by Carl Bezold. Eugene, OR: Wipf & Stock, 2005.

———. *Lexicon linguae aethiopicae*. Leipzig: Weigel, 1865.

Knibb, Michael A., and Edward Ullendorff. *The Ethiopic Book of Enoch*. Vol. 1: Text and Apparatus. Oxford: Clarendon, 1978.

Lambdin, Thomas O. *Introduction to Classical Ethiopic (Geʽez)*. Harvard Semitic Studies 24. Atlanta: Scholars Press, 1978.

Leslau, Wolf. *Comparative Dictionary of Geʽez (Classical Ethiopic): Geʽez-English / English- Geʽez with an Index of Semitic Roots*. Wiesbaden: Harrassowitz, 2006.

———. *Concise Dictionary of Geʽez*. Wiesbaden: Harrassowitz, 1989.

Mercer, Samuel A. B. *Ethiopic Grammar with Chrestomathy and Glossary*. Oxford: Clarendon, 1920.

Mittwoch, Eugen. *Die tradtionelle Aussprache des Äthiopischen*. Berlin: de Gruyter, 1926.

Nickelsburg, George W. E., and James C. VanderKam. *1 Enoch: A New Translation*. Minneapolis: Fortress, 2004.

Procházka, Stephan. *Altäthiopische Studiengrammtik*. Orbis Biblicus et Orientalis 2. Fribourg: Academic Press; Göttingen: Vandenhoeck & Ruprecht, 2004.

Raineri, Osvaldo. *Introduzione Alla Lingua Geʽez (ethiopico classico)*. Roma: Orientalia Christiana, 2002.

Tesfasilassie, Leuel, and Abiy Yigzaw. "The Focus of Teaching Geʽez Consonant Sounds in Google Newspaper." *International Journal of Law, Humanities, and Social Science* 1.3 (July 2017): 42–52.

Tesfasilassie, Leuel, Abiy Yigzaw, and Muluken Andualem. "The Focus of Teaching Geʽez Noun and Pronoun Words in Google Newspaper." *International Journal of Law, Humanities, and Social Science* 1.3 (July 2017): 1–29.

Ullendorf, Edward. *The Ethiopians: An Introduction to Country and People*. 3rd ed. Oxford: Oxford University Press, 1973.

———. *The Semitic Languages of Ethiopia: A Comparative Phonology*. London: Taylor's Press, 1955.

VanderKam, James C. *The Book of Jubilees*. Scriptores Aethiopici Tomus 88. Louvain: Peeters, 1989.

Weninger, Stefan. *Geʽez (Classical Ethiopic)*. Münich: Lincom Europa, 1993.